Kate Binder

Sams **Teach Yourself**

Adobe®
Photoshop® CS4

in **24** Hours

SAMS 800 East 96th Street, Indianapolis, Indiana, 46240 USA

Sams Teach Yourself Adobe Photoshop CS4 in 24 Hours

Copyright © 2009 by Sams Publishing

All rights reserved. No part of this book shall be reproduced, stored in a retrieval system, or transmitted by any means, electronic, mechanical, photocopying, recording, or otherwise, without written permission from the publisher. No patent liability is assumed with respect to the use of the information contained herein. Although every precaution has been taken in the preparation of this book, the publisher and author assume no responsibility for errors or omissions. Nor is any liability assumed for damages resulting from the use of the information contained herein.

ISBN-13: 978-0-672-33042-1

ISBN-10: 0-672-33042-3

Library of Congress Cataloging-in-Publication data is on file.

Printed in the United States of America

First Printing October 2008

Trademarks

All terms mentioned in this book that are known to be trademarks or service marks have been appropriately capitalized. Sams Publishing cannot attest to the accuracy of this information. Use of a term in this book should not be regarded as affecting the validity of any trademark or service mark.

Warning and Disclaimer

Every effort has been made to make this book as complete and as accurate as possible, but no warranty or fitness is implied. The information provided is on an "as is" basis. The author and the publisher shall have neither liability nor responsibility to any person or entity with respect to any loss or damages arising from the information contained in this book or from the use of the CD or programs accompanying it.

Bulk Sales

Sams Publishing offers excellent discounts on this book when ordered in quantity for bulk purchases or special sales. For more information, please contact

> **U.S. Corporate and Government Sales**
> **1-800-382-3419**
> **corpsales@pearsontechgroup.com**

For sales outside of the U.S., please contact

> **International Sales**
> **international@pearson.com**

Acquisitions Editor
Mark Taber

Development Editor
Songlin Qiu

Managing Editor
Patrick Kanouse

Project Editor
Seth Kerney

Copy Editor
Krista Hansing Editorial Services, Inc.

Indexer
Tim Wright

Proofreader
Linda Seifert

Technical Editor
Doug Nelson

Publishing Coordinator
Vanessa Evans

Book Designer
Gary Adair

Composition
TnT Design, Inc.

Contents

About the Author

Kate Binder is a graphics expert who works from her home in New Hampshire, doing design and production for books, magazines, e-books, and websites. She is the author of several books, including *iMac Portable Genius* (Wiley, 2008), *Sams Teach Yourself Adobe Photoshop Elements 6 in 24 Hours* (Sams, 2008), *Easy Mac OS X Leopard* (Que, 2007), and *The Complete Idiot's Guide to Mac OS X* (Alpha, 2001). She is the coauthor of several more books, including *Microsoft Office: Mac v.X Inside Out* (Microsoft Press, 2002), *SVG for Designers* (McGraw-Hill/Osborne Media, 2002), and *Get Creative: The Digital Photo Idea Book* (McGraw-Hill/Osborne Media, 2003). To those interested in a successful career as a designer, photographer, or computer book writer, Kate recommends acquiring several retired racing greyhounds (find out more at www.adopt-a-greyhound.org)—she finds her own pack of greyhounds extraordinarily inspirational. Kate can be reached via her website at www.prospecthillpub.com.

Dedication

This one's still for the dogs—both the thousands of greyhounds who've found a loving home and the thousands who never will.

Acknowledgments

Thanks most of all to Carla Rose, who laid the strong foundation on which this book is built. I also owe a great deal to my friends at Sams and to the pros at Adobe for letting me play with their new toys.

We Want to Hear from You!

As the reader of this book, *you* are our most important critic and commentator. We value your opinion and want to know what we're doing right, what we could do better, what areas you'd like to see us publish in, and any other words of wisdom you're willing to pass our way.

You can email or write me directly to let me know what you did or didn't like about this book— as well as what we can do to make our books stronger.

Please note that I cannot help you with technical problems related to the topic of this book, and that due to the high volume of mail I receive, I might not be able to reply to every message.

When you write, please be sure to include this book's title and author as well as your name and phone or email address. I will carefully review your comments and share them with the author and editors who worked on the book.

Email: graphics@samspublishing.com

Mail: Mark Taber
           Associate Publisher
           Sams Publishing
           800 East 96th Street
           Indianapolis, IN 46240 USA

Reader Services

Visit our website and register this book at informit.com/register for convenient access to any updates, downloads, or errata that might be available for this book.

Introduction

Photoshop CS4 is the latest and greatest version of a program that has set the standard for image manipulation since 1987. Photoshop CS4 comes in two versions: Standard and Extended. Photoshop CS4 Standard is the image-editing powerhouse photographers and artists have always loved, with new features such as previews that show how your images will look to people who are color-blind, auto-alignment and auto-blending of image content on separate layers, a new Masks panel that puts sophisticated controls for both pixel and vector masks in a single location, an Adjustments panel for applying and managing editable image corrections, and more. Meanwhile, for users in specialized industries such as research science, Photoshop CS4 Extended has complex features that most people don't need, including 3D image creation, video layers, tools for image analysis, measurement and counting abilities, rotoscoping (painting on film or video), 32-bit painting, and database connectivity. If you're interested in learning more about the powerful capabilities in Photoshop CS4 Extended, turn to Appendix B, "A Quick Walk on the Extended Side," for a rundown on its features.

In this book, we look primarily at what Photoshop CS4 Standard has to offer. If you've used an earlier version of Photoshop, you'll be amazed by the new features you'll find in this version. On the other hand, if this is your first experience with Photoshop, you'll be amazed to find that it's really not as difficult to work with as it looks. The Photoshop interface will be immediately familiar if you've used other Adobe software.

This book was written using beta versions of the software, so some of the figures might be slightly different from what you see on your screen when you're using the final release version of Photoshop CS4. We've done our best to keep the book as accurate as possible, and my editors and I hope that any differences you do run across will be minor.

If this is your first foray into working with digital images, I recommend that you work on the hours of this book one at a time, without skipping the activities or exercises. There's really no way to become an overnight expert, in Photoshop or in anything else, but *Sams Teach Yourself Adobe Photoshop CS4 in 24 Hours* will definitely get you up and running in 24 hours or less. The book is divided into 24 one-hour lessons, rather than chapters, and each lesson should take you about an hour to complete. Some lessons might take more time, some less. Just don't try to work through all 24 lessons in one 24-hour day, even if you can manage to stay awake that long. The best way to retain what you've learned is to take a little time between the lesson sessions to try things out. Be sure to spend time simply messing around in Photoshop, learning what's on the menus and what happens when you click here and there.

Here's one for you to start with: At the far right end of Photoshop CS4's new Application bar, you'll see a pop-up menu of workspaces—different combinations of visible panels, keyboard shortcuts, and selected menu commands designed for working in particular ways. From the pop-up menu, choose What's New in CS4, and then click Yes in the resulting dialog. Now each menu command that's new or modified in Photoshop CS4 appears highlighted in blue so you can pick it out. Take some time to check out what's new before you switch back to the Essentials workspace, where you started. Now you're ready to get started—let's go!

Downloading the Book's Source Images

I've provided a few of the source images for the book's exercises on the publisher's website. To download the images, go to http://informit.com/register.

Please be aware that all images are protected by copyright and cannot be used for any purpose other than to work on the exercises.

Conventions Used in This Book

This book uses the following conventions:

- ▶ Menu choices are shown with the name of the menu followed by a comma and then the name of the submenu: File, New.

- ▶ Shortcut key combinations are shown like this:

    For Mac OS, hold down the Command key and press the indicated letter: Command-X.

    For Windows, hold down the Control key and press the indicated letter: Ctrl+X.

- ▶ Text that you should type is shown in bold monospaced type: `myfilename`.

- ▶ Filenames and URLS are shown in monospaced type: `mypicture.jpg`.

This book also presents information in the following sidebars:

NOTE	TIP	CAUTION
Notes offer interesting information related to the current topic.	Tips offer advice or show you an easier way to perform a task.	Cautions alert you to a possible problem and suggest ways to avoid it.

PART I
Getting Started

HOUR 1
Exploring Photoshop Basics

Photoshop is big and powerful, and you can spend years mastering it. All that is true—yet Photoshop is still quite accessible to beginners. Think of the program as being like a swimming pool: You don't have to start with the deep end; you can step gently into the shallow end and move forward at your own pace. While you're doing that, you should expect to have a lot of fun. Whether it's giving your boss the pointy hairdo he really should have or bringing a faded picture of your grandparents back to life, many of the things you do in Photoshop will put a smile on your face.

Finding Your Way Around

When you first open Photoshop, you'll see its Tools panel on the left side of the screen, the Application Bar and the Tool Options bar just under the menus at the top of the screen, several sets of panels docked on the right side of the screen, and a Welcome box in the middle with links to some introductory Help topics. You won't see a work area because Photoshop, unlike many other programs, doesn't automatically create a new document for you. This actually makes sense because most of your work in Photoshop will be done on pictures that you have brought in from some other source. Maybe you'll be using images from your digital camera or scanner. Possibly you'll work on files you've downloaded from the Internet or on photos from a CD-ROM. In Hour 2, "Opening and Saving Files," you will learn all about opening these pictures. Right now, let's take a quick tour of Photoshop's interface so you'll know what you're seeing in the hours to come.

WHAT YOU'LL LEARN IN THIS HOUR:

▶ Finding Your Way Around
▶ What's on the Menus?
▶ Setting Preferences

The Workspace

Each version of Photoshop brings new and more powerful ways to work with digital images. While many of Adobe's engineers are working away to create these new tools and techniques, another group of engineers is tweaking and streamlining Photoshop's interface to make it work better for you. Photoshop CS4 introduces a few new ideas that we take a look at now.

The Application Frame and Application Bar

New to Photoshop CS4 are the Application Frame and the Application Bar, designed to minimize screen clutter and distraction.

The Application Frame packs the entire Photoshop interface into a single window with a neutral gray background that you can resize, minimize, or maximize (see Figure 1.1). Of course, this all sounds very familiar to Windows users because it's the way all Windows applications work. Now Mac users have the option of using Photoshop this way, or turning off the Application Frame (choose Window, Application Bar) and sticking to the Mac's standard application interface, which allows the desktop and other applications to show behind Photoshop windows. Each open document has its own window within the frame, and you can either dock document windows to the top of the Application Frame or pull them free of the Application Frame to float within the frame.

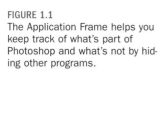

FIGURE 1.1
The Application Frame helps you keep track of what's part of Photoshop and what's not by hiding other programs.

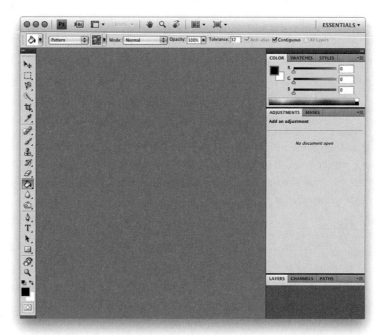

The Application Bar automatically turns on whenever the Application Frame is on; when the Application Frame is off, you can choose to show or hide the Application Bar (choose Window, Application Bar). The Application Bar contains the following (see Figure 1.2):

FIGURE 1.2
Buttons on the Application Bar perform functions that you might need at any time, no matter what you're doing or what kind of image you're editing. Windows users will find them on the menu bar.

► Standard window buttons for closing, minimizing, and maximizing the entire Photoshop application. These appear only when the Application Frame is active.

► A Photoshop icon to let you know you're in Photoshop instead of any other Creative Suite application.

► A Launch Bridge button, for easy access to your image collection.

► A Show Guides/Grid/Rulers menu.

► A Zoom-level entry field, with a small pop-up menu containing four choices: 25%, 50%, 100%, and 200%.

► Buttons for the Hand tool, the Zoom tool, and the new Rotate View tool (turn to "Viewing Tools," later in this hour, to learn more about that).

► An incredibly useful new Arrange Documents menu, with various options for arranging multiple document windows on the screen. You'll also find many of these commands in the Arrange submenu of the Window menu, but you can access their functions much more easily here.

► A Screen Mode menu that offers quick access to Photoshop's three different screen modes: Standard Screen Mode, Full Screen Mode, and Full Screen Mode with Menu Bar. The Tools panel previously contained buttons for these, but now you'll find them here and in a Screen Mode submenu of the View menu.

► A Workspace menu that enables you to change window, menu, and panel configurations to suit the particular task you're tackling. You can use the workspaces Adobe has created, and you can set up and save your own. As with the Arrange commands, these commands are located in a submenu at the top of the View menu.

TIP

What's New, Doc?

While you're getting used to Photoshop CS4, it's a good idea to switch to the What's New in CS4 workspace for a few days. Any command that's new or that has substantially changed from Photoshop CS3 is highlighted in blue, making it easier for you to spot modifications.

Tabbed Windows

When image windows are docked to the Application Frame, they're tabbed. You see only one window, with tabs across the top giving the names of all the other open images (see Figure 1.3). Click a tab to switch to viewing that document.

FIGURE 1.3
Tabbed windows save a lot of screen space.

You can control tabbed windows by Ctrl-clicking or right-clicking their tabs to bring up a contextual menu that enables you to close the current image, close all open images, dock all floating windows into the Application Frame along with the one on which you're clicking (Mac users only), or move a docked image to a new floating window. At the bottom of this contextual menu are the New Document and Open Document commands, which work just like the New and Open commands in the File menu.

Workspace Presets

Given the number of panels (formerly called palettes) that Photoshop offers, along with the various ways you can store and combine those panels, you have thousands of different ways to configure your workspace. Of course, we all have our favorite combinations, and most of us have preferred setups for particular jobs. That's why Photoshop's workspaces feature exists—to enable you to arrange panels the way you like them once and then return to that arrangement at any time with a simple menu command.

The program starts with several logical arrangements, including one for color correction (Color and Tone), one for web design (Web), and one that's good for pretty much anything, called Essentials. These are all found both in the Workspace submenu of the Window menu, as well as in their own menu at the right end of the Application Bar. Switching to one is a simple matter of choosing it from the menu. If you develop your own favorite configuration, choose the Save Workspace command from either of these menus. Give the new workspace a logical name and click Save. Your own workspace then appears in the menus next to Adobe's workspaces.

The Save Workspace dialog (see Figure 1.4) also gives you the option of including modified keyboard shortcuts and menus in your saved work-spaces. You can change keyboard shortcuts and choose which commands appear in any menu (and which ones don't) using the Keyboard Shortcuts and Menus command at the bottom of the Edit menu. For example, I use the Trim command a lot to trim off excess whitespace (or transparent space) around an image. The first thing I do when installing a new copy of Photoshop is choose Edit, Keyboard Shortcuts, and assign Shift+Ctrl+T to that command, which is located in the Image menu (see Figure 1.5).

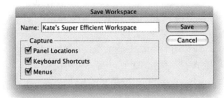

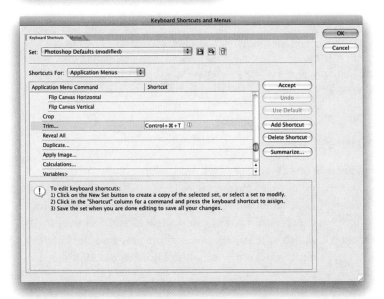

FIGURE 1.4
Be sure to give your workspace preset a name that will make sense to you when you see it in the menu.

FIGURE 1.5
Photoshop lets you customize menus and keyboard shortcuts to your heart's content.

Let Me Count the Ways

Panels, schmanels, you're thinking—what's the big deal? How many things can you really do to panels, anyway? Well, here's a little list to get you started:

▶ You can drag floating panels into a dock by dragging them to the left or right side of the screen, and you can drag docked panels out of a dock so that they float.

▶ You can drag floating panels to any place on the screen, and you can reorder docked panels by dragging so that the ones you use most are at the top of the dock.

▶ You can show and hide both the docks and each individual panel. To hide a dock, drag it by the top so that it's floating instead of attached to the side of the screen; then click the round Close button in the upper-left corner. You can show it again by using the Window menu to show any of the panels it contains, and you can redock it by dragging it back to the side of the screen.

▶ The panel groups you start out with aren't set in stone; you can drag panels out of their groups and leave them by themselves or drag them into other groups. To move a panel to a different group, drag its title bar over the title bars in the new group so that a blue outline appears around the entire new group; then release the mouse button.

▶ You can stack floating panels together so that you can move them as one. Just drag one floating panel by its title bar to the bottom of another panel. When you see a blue highlight across the bottom of the upper panel, release the mouse button.

▶ Of course, you can resize panels or even minimize them by double-clicking their title bars so that they're normal width but minimal height.

▶ You can collapse an entire dock's worth of panels to icons, to save space. Then you can click an icon to restore the panel to full size, and you can drag the icons up and down within the dock to reorder them.

If you tend to just leave panels where they are and work with what Photoshop gives you, take this opportunity to try reconfiguring your workspace. Move a few panels around; hide the ones you don't use. Find the arrangement that works for you, and then save it as your very own workspace preset so you can return to it any time you like.

The Tools Panel

The Tools panel, like an artist's paint box, holds all the tools you'll use to draw, paint, erase, and otherwise work on your picture. If you've used a previous version of Photoshop, you might be in for a few surprises. Some of the tools have changed locations and gained new capabilities over the years. Photoshop CS4 also offers one extremely cool new one: the Rotate View tool. You'll find four categories of tools in Photoshop's Tools panel:

- ▶ Selection tools
- ▶ Painting tools
- ▶ Path, Type, and Pen tools
- ▶ Viewing tools

We talk about all of these tools in detail later, but let's take a quick look at them now. Figure 1.6 shows the Tools panel with all the tools labeled. Note that you can switch the Tools panel from one column to two columns and back again by clicking the bar at its top.

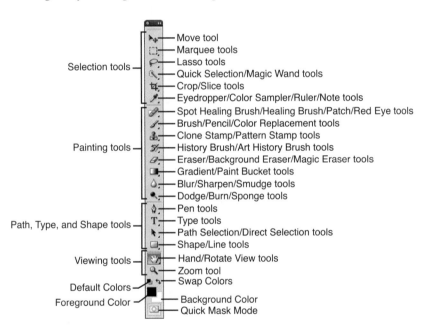

Selection tools
- Move tool
- Marquee tools
- Lasso tools
- Quick Selection/Magic Wand tools
- Crop/Slice tools
- Eyedropper/Color Sampler/Ruler/Note tools

Painting tools
- Spot Healing Brush/Healing Brush/Patch/Red Eye tools
- Brush/Pencil/Color Replacement tools
- Clone Stamp/Pattern Stamp tools
- History Brush/Art History Brush tools
- Eraser/Background Eraser/Magic Eraser tools
- Gradient/Paint Bucket tools
- Blur/Sharpen/Smudge tools
- Dodge/Burn/Sponge tools

Path, Type, and Shape tools
- Pen tools
- Type tools
- Path Selection/Direct Selection tools
- Shape/Line tools

Viewing tools
- Hand/Rotate View tools
- Zoom tool
- Swap Colors

Default Colors
Foreground Color
- Background Color
- Quick Mask Mode

FIGURE 1.6
Photoshop's tools are grouped within the Tools panel by function.

NOTE

What's That Thing?

Because Photoshop has so many tools, some of them have to share slots in the Tools panel. Any time you see a tiny black triangle in the lower-right corner of a tool icon in the Tools panel, other tools are hiding behind the one you can see Click on any tool that has a triangle and hold down the mouse button (or right-click) to see what other tools are available.

Selection Tools

The first group of tools in the Tools panel are called **Selection tools** because you use them to select all or part of a picture or to select a color. Three basic kinds of Selection tool exist: the Marquees, the Lassos, and the Quick Selection and Magic Wand tools. A selected area is indicated by a blinking dashed border called a **marquee,** after old-fashioned flashing movie theater marquee lights. To make a selection, you click and drag the Marquee and Lasso tools over and around the part of an image you want to select. Figure 1.7 shows the pop-up menus for the Marquee and Lasso Selection tools.

The Quick Selection tool selects by color. It's similar to (but cooler than!) the old Magic Wand tool, which is now hidden in the Quick Selection tool's pop-up menu (and which you'll find, in future hours, is a better choice in some situations). You can just click and drag to "paint" over an area you want to select, and the Quick Selection tool extends the selection to include all the nearby areas that have similar colors.

Now we come to some tools that aren't used for making selections, but that are related to the Selection tools we've looked at so far. First, next to the Marquee tools is the Move tool. After you've made a selection, you can click and drag with the Move tool to move the selected part of the image to a different location.

The remaining oddball tools in the Selection area are the Crop tool, the Slice tools, and the Eyedropper/Color Sampler/Ruler/Note tools. You can use the Crop tool to change the size of the picture's canvas, deleting everything outside the area you select. The Slice tools are designed specifically for creating web images; with it, you can divide an image into multiple areas, each of which loads separately on a web page and can link to a different web location. You'll learn more about slicing in Hour 24, "Going Online with Photoshop."

The Eyedropper tool picks up a sample of any color you click on, making it the active color so that you can paint with it. The Color Sampler tool places a reference point on the screen wherever you click and displays all of the color information about that spot in the Info panel. You can keep track of the information for as many as four samples at a time. You use the Ruler tool to measure dimensions and angles in the picture. Click and drag a line to measure a distance between two points and see it displayed in the Info panel. To measure an angle, first create a measured line. Then place your cursor on one of its two endpoints. Hold down the Option (Mac) or Alt (Windows) key while clicking and dragging from the endpoint of the first line in the direction of the angle. Again, the angle's measurement is displayed in the Info panel.

Finally, the Note tool works like the yellow stickies it resembles. Use it to place notes on your documents while you're working on them. The note icon can go either on the canvas or in the area adjacent to it within the document window, and its text is visible in the Notes panel. The notes don't appear on printouts of the image.

NOTE

Which Selection Tool, When

To learn more about the most effective ways of making selections for different purposes, turn to Hour 3, "Making Selections."

NOTE

The More Things Change

Longtime users of Photoshop are probably wondering just what's different from previous versions. In Photoshop CS4, the Slice tools have been moved into the same slot as the Crop tool, and the Eyedropper tool, with its companions (the Color Sampler, Ruler, and Note tools), has been moved up into the Selection tools section for the first time. It used to reside in the Viewing tools section.

Painting Tools

The Painting tools haven't changed from the previous version of
Photoshop; the set still contains 22 tools in 8 slots. Among these are a
Brush, a Pencil, and a Clone Stamp (which works like a rubber stamp).
These all apply "paint" to the canvas in some way, just like the real-life
tools they emulate. You can change the tip width and angle of most of
these tools. The Pencil tool and Brush tool share a space in the Tools panel
with the Color Replacement tool, which does just what its name implies as
you paint with it. A button on the Tool Options bar turns the regular Brush
into an airbrush, and you can adjust the paint flow, just like a real airbrush,
with a slider. The Clone Stamp tool picks up and copies a brush-shaped
piece of the background and "stamps" it wherever you click, once or multiple times (see Figure 1.8). You'll also find various erasers that, as you
might expect, take away part of the picture. You can use a plain square
"block" eraser or you can erase with any of the Brush shapes. Two special-
purpose erasers, the Background and Magic Erasers, can automatically
erase a background or a selected color.

FIGURE 1.8
Here I've used the Clone Stamp to
give this bowling-ball-loving dog a
twin.

Four special retouching tools are part of the Painting set as well: the
Healing Brush (whose icon looks like a Band-Aid), the Spot Healing Brush
(a Band-Aid overlapping a round selection), the Patch (which looks as if it
belongs on the knee of someone's jeans), and the Red Eye tool (a single-
function tool introduced in Photoshop CS1).

The Spot Healing Brush and regular Healing Brush tools are even better than the Clone Stamp for retouching small areas within a picture because they work only on the spot, wrinkle, or scar you want to remove, without affecting the surrounding area. The Patch, on the other hand, covers a larger area, and Photoshop automatically blends the patched area evenly into the background. It's great for covering up large, intrusive objects in the middle of your photos. The Red Eye tool is essential for fixing eye color in flash photos.

The History Brush, combined with the History panel, enables you to selectively undo and redo as many of your changes or individual brush strokes as you want, throughout the image or in specific areas. The Art History Brush imitates different painting styles, adding brushstroke textures as you paint.

With the Gradient tool, you can create backgrounds that shade from one color to another or even run all the way through the rainbow. The Paint Bucket, which shares space with the Gradient tool, pours paint (the Foreground color) into any selected area.

Finally, this section contains tools that move, blur, and change the intensity of the image. These are the Blur/Sharpen/Smudge tools and the Dodge/Burn/Sponge tools. The second and third tools of each set are found on pop-up menus. We'll look at these tools in detail in Hour 6, "Choosing and Blending Colors," and Hour 8, "Different Ways to Paint."

Path, Type, and Shape Tools

The Path, Type, and Shape tools do a variety of useful things, all of which make use of **vector paths** to create elements in a picture. The icon of a letter *T* represents the Type tool, which puts scalable type on your picture. The Path tools, represented by a fountain pen icon, draw reshapable paths, which can form lines or shapes. After you have drawn a line or shape, you can use the Path tools to select a portion of your path and reshape it. Path tools can be used as both Selection tools and Painting tools. In Hour 13, "Using Paths," you'll learn how to work with all of the Path tools.

The Shape tools are Pen tools that can draw both filled and unfilled shapes, including rectangles, ellipses, polygons, and more complex shapes. The Line tool is also part of this set. It draws straight lines that, when you hold down the Shift key, can be constrained to 45° or 90° angles, just as if you had used an architect's T-square and triangle. Figure 1.9 shows the Shape tools and some of the shapes that you can use with them.

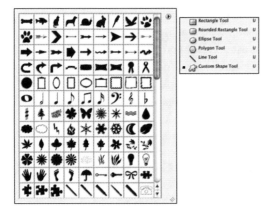

FIGURE 1.9
You can create your own custom shapes, too.

Viewing Tools

Three Viewing tools are available: the Hand tool, the Rotate View tool, and the Zoom tool. The Zoom tool is shaped like an old-fashioned magnifying glass, and the Hand tool, not surprisingly, is shaped like a hand. The Rotate View tool's icon is a bit harder to figure out—it's a hand rotating a piece of paper. With the Zoom tool, you can zoom in by clicking the tool on the canvas to see a magnified view of your picture, or zoom out by pressing Option (Mac) or Alt (Windows) as you click the image. You can also click and drag the Zoom tool to enlarge a specific part of the image. When you zoom in, the picture is usually too big to see all at once, so you can use the Hand tool to move the image around within the window. Use the Hand tool, shown in Figure 1.10, to slide the part of the picture you want to see or work on into a convenient spot. Press the spacebar while using any other tool to temporarily switch to the Hand tool.

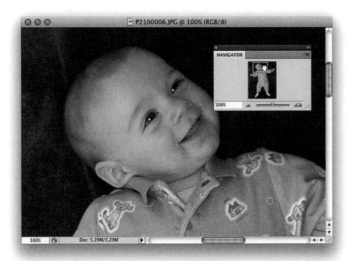

FIGURE 1.10
The Hand tool moves an image within its window. You can use it either in the image window or, as seen here, in the Navigator panel.

New in Photoshop CS4 is the Rotate View tool, which you can use to turn the image's canvas within its window to match your preferred angle for drawing. This feature will be most useful if you use a graphics tablet for painting, because you can match the image window to the angle at which you hold the tablet. To use the Rotate View tool, just click and drag; press Shift to constrain the rotation to 45° increments. You'll see a compass rose in the image window as you rotate the canvas (see Figure 1.11), so you can see how much rotation you're applying as you drag.

FIGURE 1.11
Rotating the image enables me to more easily edit the picture with a graphics table.

NOTE

Sorry, Charlie

If the graphics card in your computer doesn't support OpenGL, you won't be able to use the Rotate View tool (and a few other new features in Photoshop CS4). Time to upgrade!

Tool Shortcuts

Every one of these tools can be selected by clicking its icon in the Tools panel, but Photoshop gives you another, even easier way to access the tools. Instead of clicking the tools you want to use, you can type a single-letter shortcut to select each tool. To toggle through the available tools where there are pop-up menus, press Shift plus the shortcut letter until you reach the tool you want. Table 1.1 lists the tools with their shortcuts. Dog-ear this page so that you can refer to the table until you have memorized the shortcuts.

TABLE 1.1   Tools and Their Shortcuts

Tool	Shortcut
Move	V
Marquee	M
Lasso	L
Quick Selection/Magic Wand	W
Crop/Slice	C
Eyedropper/Color Sampler/Ruler/Note	I
Spot Healing Brush/Healing Brush/Patch/Red Eye	J
Brush/Pencil/Color Replacement	B
Clone Stamp/Pattern Stamp	S
History Brush/Art History Brush	Y
Erasers	E
Gradient/Paint Bucket	G
Dodge/Burn/Sponge	O
Pen	P
Type	T
Path Selection	A
Shape	U
Hand	H
Rotate View	R
Zoom	Z
Switch Background/Foreground Colors	X
Default Colors	D
Quick Mask Mode	Q

The Tool Options Bar

In early versions of Photoshop, tool options were set on a panel just like the Layers or History panel. With version 6, users learned to reach for the Tool Options bar instead (see Figure 1.12). As you change tools, the controls available on the Options bar change according to whatever options are available for that tool. If the Options bar isn't visible, choose Window, Options, or simply double-click any tool to display the Options bar, set to the controls for that tool.

NOTE

Give and Take

The Blur, Sharpen, and Smudge tools no longer have a keyboard shortcut in Photoshop CS4; they had to relinquish R to the new Rotate View tool. Of course, you can remap *your* tool shortcuts to any keys you like by choosing Edit, Keyboard Shortcuts. Choose Tools from the Shortcuts For pop-up menu and go to town!

FIGURE 1.12
Any toolbar component with a triangle next to it has a pop-up menu.

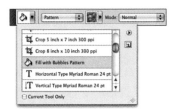

FIGURE 1.13
The tool presets that come with Photoshop include some that you'll probably *never* use, but they do give you the idea.

Tool Presets

As with workspace presets, you can save combinations of tool settings as tool presets, and Photoshop comes with a collection of built-in presets to get you started. The Tool Presets menu is located at the far-left end of the Options bar (see Figure 1.13). You can use tool presets to save specific option sets for tools you use often, such as a big soft-edged brush shape for painting clouds or a small hard-edged eraser for touching up tiny details.

To make your own preset, all you have to do is switch to the tool you want to use and set its options on the Options bar. Then click the arrow to display the Tool Presets menu and click the Create New Tool Preset button at the right side of the menu. Enter a name for the tool preset and click OK.

What's on the Menus?

Photoshop's menus contain hundreds of commands, some special to Photoshop and others standard across programs, that enable you to open and manipulate files. Whenever you see an arrow or an ellipsis to the right of a menu command, it indicates that there is either a submenu, in the case of the arrow, or a dialog box, in the case of the ellipsis. In this section, we take a few minutes to flip through the menus and get a general idea of what's in each one; you'll get an up-close view of Photoshop's menu commands in later hours.

The File and Edit Menus

Many of the commands in Photoshop's File and Edit menus will be familiar to anyone who has used other Mac or Windows programs. The File menu lets you work with files: opening, closing, saving, importing and exporting, printing, and, of course, quitting the program. The File menu is also home to several time-saving automation features that you'll learn about in Hour 19, "Taking Advantage of a Few Useful Tricks."

The File Browser, first introduced in Photoshop 7, was renamed Bridge in Photoshop CS2, and it's come a long way since then. Choose File, Browse in Bridge to check it out. Naturally, you can see all the data about your photo or scanned image while you preview it, and you can add your own keywords to help Bridge locate and open your files. In addition, you can save groups of images that you want to open at the same time. When you open Bridge, you can search the folders on your hard drive by selecting them, then sort and filter the contents by file type, keywords, date, or other criteria. After you've found the folder you want, all its pictures appear in a separate Bridge pane as if they were slides on a light table (see Figure 1.14). To open a picture, just double-click its thumbnail. You'll also see all the information available about the picture, including its size, its color mode, the date and time it was shot, the make and model of camera used, and a lot more data than you'll ever need to know.

FIGURE 1.14
The Bridge displays thumbnails of all the images in a folder.

NOTE

Mac Users Take Note

As of Photoshop CS, the Preferences command moved to the far-left Photoshop menu in Mac OS X; in Windows, it's still under the Edit menu.

The Edit menu includes all the editing commands you're familiar with from other programs: Cut, Copy, Paste, Clear, and the most important one—Undo. It also contains the Transform commands, to scale, skew, distort, and rotate images, and the Stroke and Fill commands, for applying paint to selections.

The menus that you might not be as familiar with (unless you've spent a lot of time working in other graphics programs) are as follows:

- Image
- Layer
- Select
- Filter
- View
- Window

The Image Menu

The Image menu, shown in Figure 1.15, contains several submenus. The first of these, Mode, enables you to select a color mode for your image. Most of the time, it makes sense to work in RGB mode because that's what your monitor displays. Hour 4, "Specifying Color Modes and Color Models," discusses color modes in detail. The second submenu, Adjustments, you'll probably visit every time you work on a photo. It's home to all kinds of color adjustment commands, from automatic level and color corrections to sliders that let you tweak contrast, change red roses to blue ones, and so on. You will learn how to use the tools on the Adjustments submenu in Hour 5, "Adjusting Brightness and Color."

FIGURE 1.15
The Adjustments submenu is chock-full of the commands you need to turn average photos into great ones.

The Image menu also has commands to enlarge an image or the canvas it's on, plus additional ones to invert colors, posterize, and even correct color and saturation by example.

The Layer Menu

Many users consider the ability to work on different layers to be Photoshop's most powerful feature. This enables you to combine images, create collages, and make corrections without having to worry about damaging the original picture. Think of it as similar to working on sheets of transparent plastic. Each layer is completely separate from the others. You can paint on a layer, change its opacity, or modify it in any other way without disturbing the background or parts of the picture that are located on other layers.

You can use the commands in the Layer menu to create new layers, to merge multiple layers into one, and to apply layer effects, styles, and color adjustments. Figure 1.16 shows what's on the Layer menu. Hour 5, "Adjusting Brightness and Color," and Hour 11, "Creating Layered Images," teach you how to work with all kinds of layers.

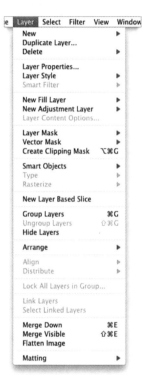

FIGURE 1.16
The Layer menu is Photoshop's longest menu.

The Select Menu

You have Selection tools, so why do you need a Select menu? The commands in the Select menu enable you to create selections based on color alone, with no tool, as well as modify areas you have selected with the Selection tools. You can enlarge or reduce a selected area by a specific number of pixels, or feather its edges so that when you cut and paste the selection, it appears to fade into the background on which you have pasted it. In Hour 3, you'll learn all the tricks for selecting parts of a picture and manipulating selections.

NOTE

Filter Fact

In the previous paragraph, I said
that your Filter menu contains "at
least" 13 categories of filters.
The number could be more if you
install third-party filters, such as
Alien Skin's Eye Candy or the
Andromeda filters. These filters
appear at the bottom of the Filter
menu in their own submenus.

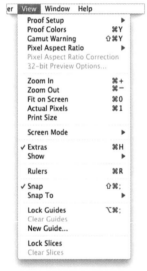

FIGURE 1.17
The View menu controls how your
picture looks onscreen.

NOTE

Which Units to Choose

When creating image for the
Web, you'll probably want to set
your rulers to pixels. Print
designers, on the other hand,
might prefer to use inches, centimeters, or picas, depending
on the standard their publica-
tions use.

The Filter Menu

Some filters are useful; others are pretty frivolous. But working with filters
is some of the most fun you'll have in Photoshop. In the Filter menu, you'll
find at least 13 different categories of filters: Blur, Artistic, and Stylize, for
example. You can use these commands to modify and enhance your
images in hundreds of ways. In fact, you can do so much with filters that
we spend all of Hour 14, "Getting Started with Filters"; Hour 15,
"Applying Filters to Improve Your Picture"; Hour 16, "Applying Artistic
Filters to Turn Your Picture into Art"; and Hour 17, "Applying Funky
Filters," applying them to your pictures.

The View Menu

As with the Zoom tool, the View menu's commands enable you to zoom
into and out of the picture. As you can see in Figure 1.17, the View menu
also contains commands governing rulers, guides, and grids that enable
you to place objects precisely within an image. The Show command's a
submenu gives you access to grids, guides, notes, layer or selection edges,
slices, and more.

You can set the rulers to measure in pixels, inches, centimeters, millimeters,
points, or picas, or by percentage—whichever you're most familiar with.
You can set this in the Preferences dialog (choose Photoshop, Preferences,
Units & Rulers for Mac OS X, or Edit, Preferences, Units & Rulers for
Windows). Or, if you prefer, you can right-click or Ctrl-click on either ruler
to choose a unit of measure from a pop-up menu. Whichever method you
use, the unit you choose also determines the unit of measure for the New
dialog box.

Guides, which you can show, hide, and delete in the View menu, are lines
that you drag into your picture to help you position type or some other
element that you want to add to the picture. They don't show up in printouts or web images.

To place guides, follow these steps:

1. If you don't see the rulers at the side and top of the image window, choose View, Rulers to make them visible.

2. To place a horizontal guide, click on the ruler at the top of the window and drag downward. You'll see a horizontal line following your cursor down the canvas as you drag. The guide's position is shown in the ruler on the left.

3. To add a vertical guide to the image, click on the ruler at the left side of the window and drag across the image. A vertical line moves across the canvas under your cursor. The top ruler shows you the position of the line. See Figure 1.18 for an example of a vertical guide.

4. To switch the orientation of a guide while you're dragging it out from a ruler, press the Option (Mac) or Alt (Windows) key.

TRY IT YOURSELF ▼

Place a Guide

FIGURE 1.18
Guides let you place objects precisely.

You can place a guide while any tool is active, but after you've placed a guide, you must use the Move tool to reposition it. You can hide it by choosing View, Show, Guides to remove the check mark. To get rid of the guides entirely, choose View, Clear Guides. To lock guides in place, press Option-Command-; (semicolon) (Mac) or Alt+Ctrl+; (Windows).

TIP

Moving Guides in a Hurry

When almost any tool other than the Move tool is active, you can temporarily switch to the Move tool by pressing Command (Mac) or Ctrl (Windows). As soon as you release the modifier key, the tool reverts to the original. This trick doesn't work with any of the Path or Shape tools or the Hand tool.

The Show Grid command (choose View, Show, Grid) places an entire grid of guidelike lines over your image, like a layer of transparent graph paper. With both guides and the grid, you can choose View, Snap to make objects stick to a guide or gridline as they near it. Choose options from the View, Snap To submenu to determine what your selections will snap to and what they won't.

If you like guides, you'll love smart guides. Choose View, Show, Smart Guides to turn on this feature. Now, whenever you drag a layer around within the image window, you'll see magenta guides appear as it nears the edges of objects on other layers, so you can align it with other image elements automatically. Smart guides show up only when they're needed; the rest of the time, they won't get in your way.

The Window Menu

You can access most of Photoshop's commands in several ways. The easiest way, generally, is to use the panels. Photoshop's panels give you information about your picture, and character and paragraph controls for the Type tool. The panels contain options for many of the tools in the Tools panel, a choice of brush sizes and shapes, and colors; you also get access to layers, paths, and channels. In addition, you'll find Actions and History panels to help you work more efficiently, and to see what you've done and back up when necessary. The Window menu enables you to show and hide each of these panels, as needed. If you're not ready to use some panels, such as Actions, close them, minimize them, or collapse them to icons so your screen remains as uncluttered as possible.

For CS4, Adobe has redesigned Photoshop's panels yet again. You can store them all in collapsible docks at the sides of the screen so that they're out of the way when you need to see what you're doing, yet easily accessible with a single click. The docks are translucent gray areas that expand as needed to hold the number of panels you store there.

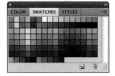

FIGURE 1.19
Click the title bar on a grouped panel to bring it forward.

To use the panel docks, follow these steps:

TRY IT YOURSELF ▼

Dock and Undock Panels

1. Click at the top of the dock on the right side of the screen to collapse the panels it contains into icons—pictures representing each panel's function.

2. Click a panel icon to pop that panel out from the dock; click the same icon again to slide the panel back into the dock.

3. Drag an icon out of the dock to set the panel free so that you can place it anywhere you want on the screen.

4. To expand the panels, click the dock again in the same place.

5. Click the dock area above the Tools panel (also known as the Tools panel). Instead of collapsing and expanding, the panel switches between a tall, single-column configuration and a shorter double-column layout. You can also drag the Tools panel out of the dock so that it floats on your screen.

The Help Menu

The final menu is the Help menu, which gives you access to Photoshop's comprehensive help database, which is essentially the entire manual, with a good search function. Other commands in this menu let you check for updates to Photoshop, manage your Adobe product registration, and visit Adobe's website.

Setting Preferences

As you become more familiar with Photoshop, you might want to change how it handles certain tasks. You might want to use the System Color Picker instead of the Adobe Color Picker, for example. Or you might need to measure in inches for one project and centimeters for another. You might want to change the color of the guides because they're too similar to the background color in your photo. You can make all these changes and many more in the Preferences dialog box, which is accessible under the Photoshop menu in the Mac OS X version of Photoshop and in the Edit menu in Windows. Figure 1.20 shows the General tab of the Preferences dialog box.

TIP

Did You Lose a Panel?

If you "lose" a panel and can't get it back, you can always return to the panel configuration Photoshop started with by choosing Window, Workspace, Essentials.

FIGURE 1.20
Set your personal preferences
here.

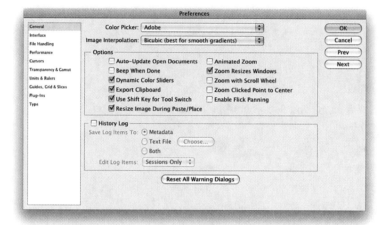

Click the Next button to scroll through the Preferences dialog boxes. You
might encounter some preferences that you don't understand. For now,
leave these at their default settings. As you learn more about Photoshop,
you can come back and change preferences as necessary. We talk about
many of these preference settings in the hours to come.

Summary

You are starting to learn your way around the Photoshop interface. You
learned how to move the interface's elements to suit your own needs during this hour. You looked at the Tools panel and at Photoshop's menus,
and you learned about guides, grids, and rulers. Finally, you learned about
setting preferences.

Q&A

Q. What are the Foreground and Background colors?

A. The Foreground color is the uppermost of the two colored squares near the bottom of the Tools panel. When you paint, the brush applies the Foreground color. The Background color is the lower square of the two, and it's the color you see when you erase "paint" from the canvas.

Q. Why are there trash cans at the bottom of some of the panels, such as the History and Layers panels?

A. Clicking the trash can button at the bottom of the Layers panel deletes the selected layer or layers. Similarly, clicking the trash button on the History panel deletes a selected history state. You'll learn more about these specific panels when we look at undoing in Hour 2 and layers in Hour 11, and you'll learn about the trash buttons on the Channels, Paths, and Swatches panel later in the book as well.

Q. What are the symbols next to many of the commands in Photoshop's menus?

A. Those are keyboard shortcuts, and they're the key (no pun intended!) to harnessing Photoshop's power efficiently. The more keyboard shortcuts you know, the faster you can move in Photoshop. I recommend that you work on learning them by going to the appropriate menu for each command, taking note of the keyboard shortcut, closing the menu without choosing the command, and then using the keyboard shortcut. After a few days of this routine (which you can use with any program, not just Photoshop), you'll find yourself working much more quickly.

Workshop

Quiz

1. Which tools are part of the Painting group?

    A. Pen

    B. Healing Brush

    C. Magic Wand

    D. Gradient

2. True or false: Guides show up in image printouts as faint gray lines.

3. The docks at the sides of the screen provide a home for

    A. Tool presets

    B. Open documents

    C. Panels

    D. Preference settings

Answers

1. **B and D.** The Pen tool is part of the Path, Type, and Shape group, and the Magic Wand is a Selection tool.

2. **False.** Guides show only onscreen, and only in Photoshop, not in other programs.

3. **C.** You can dock panels to either side of the screen; the left side starts with just the Tools panel, but you can put any panels you like over there.

Exercises

1. Open a digital photo in Photoshop and try some of the tools you learned about in this hour. Use the Brush to paint some squiggles and lines. Then click one of the Eraser tools and erase part of the image. Try dragging the Smudge tool across the picture. Select a piece of the picture with one of the Selection tools, switch to the Move tool, and move the selected area to another part of the page. Have fun, and don't worry—you won't break anything.

2. If you have an Internet connection, choose Help, Photoshop Online to visit Adobe's website and see what's there.

HOUR 2
Opening and Saving Files

As a Photoshop user, you'll work with existing image files, create new ones, and save your changes to the files you work on. Along the way, you'll need to make some decisions about those files. That means you need to learn about the characteristics of a Photoshop file, including the various formats Photoshop can read and write, the color modes you can use for different kinds of images, how to determine an image's size and resolution, and how to create and use metadata to keep better track of your files. Of course, you'll also need to know how to get images from your camera or scanner into Photoshop. In this hour, you'll learn all this and more.

Working with Files

Photoshop can open and save images in many file formats, which are different ways of organizing the information in a file so that it can be used by other applications, printed, or placed on a web page. Each file format is like a different language. Every program that uses image files can speak one or more languages, but not all programs speak the same set of languages. So the format in which you save each image file depends on what programs will need to open or display that image. For example, web browsers can usually open JPEG, GIF, and PNG files, so a web image should be saved in one of those formats. Page-layout programs, on the other hand, are more likely to understand TIFF and EPS files, so those formats are the ones you should use when you're saving a picture to be used in a newsletter or other document.

File formats are usually indicated by three-letter filename extensions, such as `.doc` for a word processing document and `.bmp` for a bitmapped graphic. Because you can hide the filename extensions in both Windows and Mac OS X, you might not see extensions. But rest assured, they're there.

WHAT YOU'LL LEARN IN THIS HOUR:

▶ Working with Files
▶ Saving Your Work
▶ Undoing and Redoing
▶ Using Version Cue

Most file formats can accommodate some, but not all, of Photoshop's special features. For example, if your image uses layers (we talk more about layers in Hour 11, "Creating Layered Images"), saving it in JPEG or EPS format flattens the layers so that you can no longer edit them separately. To preserve layers, you need to save in a format that can accommodate them. Your best choice is Photoshop's **native** format, which can accommodate all of the program's special features. The filename extension for Photoshop format is .psd, which stands for "Photoshop document." Because other programs in which you want to use your pictures might not be capable of reading Photoshop native format, you need to save a copy of a completed image in a compatible format when you're ready to use the picture outside Photoshop.

A second native file format, called Large Document Format (.psb), was introduced in Photoshop CS. It's meant to handle very large files—more than 2GB in size; think of it as Photoshop Big. This format was developed to let you work with and save multiple layers in a very large document. Anything you save as a .psb file can be opened only in Photoshop CS or later. You can make the format available by choosing Preferences, File Handling and turning on PSB support in the dialog box. If you share files with users of versions of Photoshop prior to Photoshop CS, leave it off.

Photoshop can read and write dozens of graphics formats; here's a rundown on the most commonly used formats in that group.

- ▶ **Bitmap (.bmp)**—This is a standard graphics file format for Windows.

- ▶ **Camera Raw**—This is the native format of high-end digital cameras. Essentially, when Photoshop opens a camera raw file, it uses the "raw," or unmodified, camera data to produce, in effect, a digital "negative." You can assign color corrections, sharpen the focus, compensate for spherical lens aberrations, and make other corrections picture by picture as they are copied to your computer. Don't worry if your camera doesn't produce camera raw files, however—this format is mostly useful only to professional photographers. And Photoshop can't save to raw format; it's a read-only format.

- ▶ **GIF (.gif)—Graphics Interchange Format** is one of the three common graphics formats you can use for web publishing. All of these formats incorporate **compression** so that they yield smaller files that take less time to download.

- ▶ **JPEG (.jpg)—Joint Photographic Experts Group** is another popular format for web publishing.

▶ **PDF** (.pdf)—Adobe Acrobat's **Portable Document Format** is a system for creating documents that look the same and print correctly no matter what kind of computer you use to open them—Windows, Mac OS, or Linux.

▶ **PNG** (.png)—**Portable Network Graphic** is a newer and, theoretically, better format for web graphics than either GIF or JPEG, combining GIF's efficient compression with JPEG's unlimited color palette. However, some older or less popular browsers don't support it completely. (We discuss these formats and their use in web publishing in Hour 24, "Going Online with Photoshop.")

▶ **TIFF** (.tif)—**Tagged Image File Format** files can be saved for use on either Mac OS or Windows machines. This is one of the preferred formats for desktop publishing programs, such as InDesign and QuarkXPress. When you save an image in TIFF format, you can choose whether to include layers. If you do include layers in a TIFF file, the file might not be compatible with all desktop publishing programs; in this case, you'd need to open the file in Photoshop again and resave it without layers. You can also choose to use LZW compression or leave the file at its normal size; unless you encounter printing problems with LZW TIFFs, there's no reason not to use this useful feature.

▶ **EPS** (.eps)—**Encapsulated PostScript** is another format often used for desktop publishing. It uses the PostScript page description language, and both Mac OS and PC can use it.

▶ **Raw (usually** .raw)—This format saves image information in the most flexible format for transferring files between applications, devices (such as digital cameras), and computer platforms. Don't confuse this format with Camera Raw—although it's another format that you're unlikely to encounter except in special circumstances.

These file formats, and some less common ones, such as Targa and Scitex CT, are available in the Save dialog box—choose File, Save, or File, Save As. Just look for the Format pop-up menu. Figure 2.1 shows the Save As dialog box with the formats available.

If you work on a Mac and need to share files with non-Mac users—or if you just like to stay on the safe side—choose Preferences, File Handling. In the dialog box, click the check boxes to make sure that Photoshop automatically adds a filename extension to each file you save and to keep it in lower case (as required by some older software).

FIGURE 2.1
Photoshop CS4 can save your
work in any of these formats.

NOTE

Windows Users Take Note

In Windows, double-clicking an
image file opens Photoshop only
if the file's extension (.bmp, for
instance) is associated with
Photoshop. Sometimes installing
new applications associates
extensions with those other programs. GIFs and JPEGs are noto-
riously remapped to Microsoft
Internet Explorer, for example,
whereas Paint usually grabs
BMP. If double-clicking doesn't
open an image in Photoshop,
double-check the extension settings in the File Types tab of the
Folder Options dialog box in the
Control Panel. Or, if you're using
Windows Vista, open the Control
Panel and click Programs; then
click Make a File Type Always
Open in a Specific Program. In
Vista's Classic View, open
Default Programs and click
Associate a File Type or Protocol
with a Program.

Opening Files

Opening a file in Photoshop is as easy as it is in any other application. You
can open as many images as your computer's memory (RAM) can hold,
which is just one reason you can never have too much RAM. If a file is of
the proper type (a file format that Photoshop recognizes), all you have to
do is double-click it to open it and launch Photoshop as well, if it's not
already running. (If Photoshop is already open, you can either double-click
an image file's icon or choose File, Open in Photoshop.) You can also drag
and drop a compatible file onto the Photoshop CS4 icon to open that file.

When you open files using the Open command, Photoshop's Open dialog
(see Figure 2.2) displays all the files that have formats it can open. As you
can see, Photoshop also displays a thumbnail of the selected image. To
make sure that previews are included in the image files you create, choose
Preferences, File Handling, and then choose Always Save from the Image
Previews pop-up menu in the dialog.

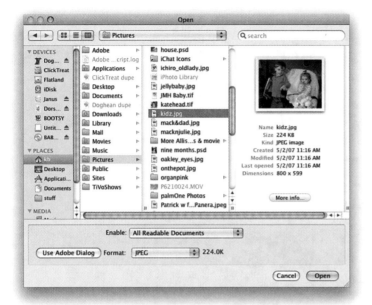

A **thumbnail** or **thumbnail sketch** is an artist's term for a small version of a picture, so called because it's often no bigger than a thumbnail. A thumbnail version of an image can be stored in a file along with the full-size image so that some programs, including the Mac OS and Windows, can see the image file's contents without having to open it.

As you've seen, Photoshop supports most graphics formats. You must have some image files somewhere on your hard drive, so let's find one and open it.

1. Choose File, Open or press Command-O (Mac) or Ctrl+O (Windows) to display the Open dialog box.

2. Use the dialog box to locate the file you want to work on. Try looking in the Pictures or My Pictures folder within your Documents folder.

3. Double-click the file's name, or click it once and then click the Open button.

Browsing for Images

If you have only a few graphics files, and if you're really good at keeping things organized, finding the document you're looking for isn't difficult. However, if you're like me, your files are all over the place, and they're often named with the apparently random numbers the camera assigns.

That's why Photoshop's Bridge (see Figure 2.3) remains one of the program's most useful features. It helps you preview all your images, sort them, search them, and even read their **metadata**—information about the files themselves. You can scroll through the information in Bridge's Metadata tab to determine what lens and shutter settings the camera used, whether the exposure required a flash, and the precise minute and second the picture was taken—virtually everything you need to know except where it was shot. Actually, some special-purpose digital cameras with GPS connections *can* tell you where each picture was taken, and, of course, many camera phones include built-in GPS capabilities.

FIGURE 2.3
You can drag the dividers to change the size of any of the frames that make up the Bridge window.

Navigate Within Bridge

To open Bridge, choose File, Browse in Bridge, and then follow these steps to take it for a spin:

1. Click a tab at the upper-left (Favorites or Folders) and navigate through the folder hierarchy to locate the folder you want. Whenever you select a folder containing image files, you'll see all its images displayed in the Content tab, as if on a slide viewer. If this is the first time that you've viewed this folder's contents in Bridge, it might take few minutes to display all the thumbnails, but don't let that put you off; the display will be lightning-fast the next time you look at this folder in Bridge.

2. If folders are nested inside the one you originally opened, you'll see them as folder icons in the Content tab. Double-click a nested folder to see the images it contains.

3. Scroll through the folders and the images within them until you find the one you want. Double-click the thumbnail image in the Content tab or the preview in the Preview tab to open the image file in Photoshop. The Folders tab, in the upper-left corner of the Bridge window, shows the location of the file you're opening.

4. If the folder you're looking at contains a lot of files, you can hide the ones that don't match using the Filter tab. Click next to the criteria you want to use—such as JPEG File and a creation date—to hide all files that don't meet those criteria. Then you can choose the file you're looking for from a much smaller number of images.

5. To keep track of groups of related photos, you can create collections in the Collections tab. Click New Collection to add a collection, and assign it a name. Drag pictures over the new collection to include them; then click the collection to view only the photos it contains. You can also create smart collections that add new images automatically based on metadata and keywords; we look at using these in the next section.

TRY IT YOURSELF ▼

Navigate Within Bridge

continued

You can configure Bridge's setup to suit your needs. Bridge comes with several predesigned arrangements, including Metadata, for viewing very small thumbnails alongside lots of file info, and Output, for previewing how images will look when output in various ways. Click an option at the top of the Bridge window to choose a different view (see Figure 2.4).

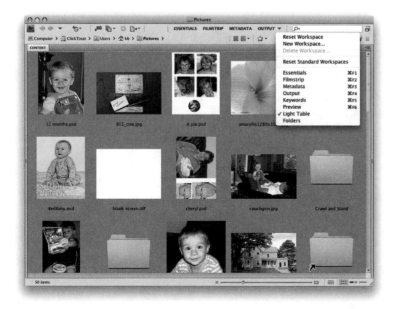

FIGURE 2.4
Bridge is highly customizable; you can set it to display just the information that interests you.

Creating and Using Metadata

As I mentioned earlier in this hour, metadata is information about an image that's included in the file along with the actual picture. To get an idea of what sort of data can show up in a file's metadata, open Bridge and take a look at the Metadata tab (see Figure 2.5). Bridge divides metadata into several categories:

FIGURE 2.5
Metadata is automatically stored with each image, and you can add more data to it, if you want.

▶ **File Properties**—These bits of info qualify as an image's vital statistics, and they're not editable in Bridge. They include the file's color mode, size, resolution, name, creation date, and modification date, for starters.

▶ **IPTC Core**—Established by the International Press Telecommunications Council (IPTC), this data set includes all kinds of things that press organizations might need to know about an image, such as who created it, its subject, where it was taken, and what usage rights apply. You can edit any of these fields.

▶ **Camera Data (EXIF)**—The Exchangeable Image File Format is a standard for storing information within image files, especially JPEG files. Most digital cameras use EXIF to store metadata about the images they generate. This includes the camera's focal length and aperture value, as well as whether a flash was used. This data, if it's available, can't be edited in Bridge.

▶ **Audio**—You can add any of several types of data in the Audio category, mostly applicable to music, such as artist, genre, and instrument. Of course, you're unlikely to apply any of this information to a Photoshop file, but Bridge functions as a media organizer for all the programs in Adobe's Creative Suite, including Flash and Premiere.

▶ **Video**—Fields in this category include Scene and DateShot, which are the sort of information you'd want to keep track of for snippets of video footage.

▶ **DICOM**—The Digital Imaging and Communications in Medicine standard enables medical professionals to track metadata in medical images. It includes fields such as Patient Name, Patient Sex, Referring Physician, and Study Description.

▶ **Mobile SWF**—This kind of information is stored in Flash (SWF) files; again, Photoshop users are unlikely to use this metadata, but it's great for Flash designers. Fields include Content Type and Forward Lock (which specifies whether the file can be transferred to another device).

To add your own metadata to an image, just click in a text field and enter the text you want to include. Pencil icons indicate the fields you can modify.

Smart collections can be based on any combination of metadata values, both data you've inserted yourself and data that was already part of the file (such as its name). For example, you could make a collection that includes all JPEG files created in Italy during 2008 using a flash, to keep track of your vacation photos. You can also create smart collections based on keywords, which you can think of as your own custom metadata. Bridge's Keywords tab, located alongside its Metadata tab (see Figure 2.6), enables you to create keywords (click New Keyword at the bottom of the tab) and assign them to a selected image or group of images by checking the box next to each keyword.

Importing a File

Photoshop's Import command (choose File, Import) lets you open files that
have been saved in unusual formats or that aren't on your hard drive.
Typically, these include images created with your scanner or digital camera, and special image types such as individual frames of video.

Importing from Digital Cameras

Photoshop can import pictures directly from most digital cameras. The easiest way to do this is to use Bridge; after you've plugged in your camera,
open Bridge and choose File, Get Photos from Camera, or click the Get
Photos from Camera button in the toolbar. In the resulting Photo
Downloader dialog box (see Figure 2.7), you can choose your camera and a
location for the photos; then click Get Photos. Photoshop copies the photos
into a new folder on your computer's hard drive. If you want to change
the default folder name or filenames for the imported photos, choose new
options in the Import Settings section of the dialog.

Bridge can recognize most cameras, but if it doesn't see yours, don't worry.
Most cameras come with a Photoshop plug-in that you can drop into the
Plug-ins folder. After you've quit Photoshop and restarted the program, a
new command appears in the Import submenu, named to match your camera. When you choose this command, you'll see whatever interface the
camera designer has created for importing photos. To work on the camera's pictures in Photoshop, you must import them using this plug-in and
then open them from within Photoshop. Check your camera's instruction
manual to learn how to use the particular plug-in for your camera.

FIGURE 2.7
The Photo Downloader is primarily used to specify where you want your photos stored and how you want them named.

Scanning Pictures

Digital cameras generate most digital photos these days. But there are still plenty of times when you'll need to scan artwork for use in Photoshop, whether it's because you have only a print of the photo in question or because the art isn't a photo—perhaps it's a drawing or some other flat object you need to reproduce. Photoshop doesn't offer a universal scanning interface analogous to the Photo Downloader, so scanning is handled either by your operating system or via a plug-in supplied by your scanner manufacturer.

This means that what you see when you bring up your scanner interface probably won't look exactly like Figure 2.8. But the principles are the same:

1. You do a preview scan (sometimes called an overview scan).

2. Then you select the area of the scanner bed that you want to include in the scan. Some scanner software is smart enough to guess at the area you want to scan, but you can usually override the selection if the program guesses wrong.

FIGURE 2.8
This is the Home version of Epson's Mac scanning software; the plug-in also has Automatic and Professional modes.

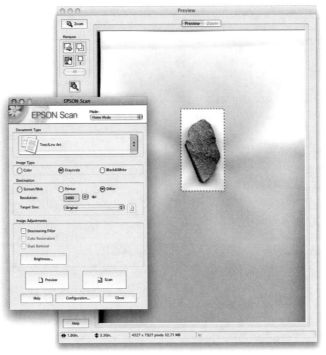

FIGURE 2.9
Scanning an object is much quicker than photographing it and transferring the picture to your computer, and it often results in a better image.

3. You choose the kind of image you're scanning—color, grayscale, or black and white. Remember, a black-and-white photo is actually a grayscale image that contains hundreds of shades of gray. You'll most likely use the black-and-white setting when you're scanning text or a line drawing, such as a floor plan.

4. You choose an image resolution for the scan, which could involve specifying an actual number or telling your scanner software what you plan to do with the image—print it or just display it on the Web.

5. You can choose a few image adjustments, such as sharpening, to be performed as the scan is made. I prefer to work on the raw image data in Photoshop, but if you're in a hurry to get some photos up on your website, letting the scanner do the work is a time-saving option.

6. Finally, you click Scan and wait for the new image to open in Photoshop (see Figure 2.9). When it does, you need to save it, choosing a name, location, and format in the Save dialog.

Importing Video Images

You can also turn video frames into layers within a Photoshop image. Choose File, Import, Video Frames to Layers, and navigate to the video file you want to open. In the Import Video to Layers dialog box, use the slider to choose the range of frames to import; then click OK. Photoshop turns each frame into a separate layer that you can view, hide, and edit individually. Turn to Hour 11 to learn how to manipulate layers.

Starting a New Image

When you don't want to start with an existing image, you can have Photoshop create a blank canvas in any size, ready for your artwork. To get started, choose File, New (the first command in Photoshop's File menu). In the New dialog box (see Figure 2.10), you can enter a name for your new file or leave it untitled for now. Other choices have to be made now, however. The following sections show you how to set up a new file.

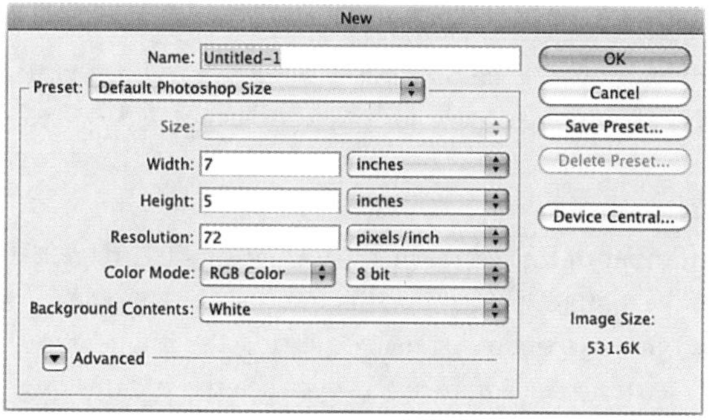

FIGURE 2.10
The New dialog box enables you to create a blank document to your individual specifications.

Image Size

The simple way to specify an image size is to use the Preset and Size pop-up menus. The Preset pop-up lists several categories: Clipboard, Default Photoshop Size, U.S. Paper, International Paper, Photo, Web, Mobile & Devices, Film & Video, and Custom. After you choose a Preset option, the Size menu becomes available so that you can choose among the sizes in that category. For example, when you choose U.S. Paper from the Preset menu, your Size choices are Letter, Legal, and Tabloid. Photoshop CS4 also includes a wide selection of TV and video formats, including PAL and

NOTE

Scanning Outside Photoshop

Your scanner might have come with a scanning program that you like, or you might be a Mac user and prefer to do all your scans using the Image Capture program that comes with Mac OS. Either way, if you're saving scanned files and then bringing them into Photoshop, be sure to use a format such as TIFF that doesn't have **lossy compression**, as JPEG does. Lossy compression removes image data, causing a loss of quality every time you save. Never save files in a lossy format until you're sure you're done working with them. You can learn more about compression, both lossy and **lossless**, in "Making Your Files Smaller," later in this hour.

NOTE

If Video Really Moves You

Photoshop CS4 Extended adds the capability to work with full-motion video right within Photoshop. If that sounds like something you need to look into, turn to Appendix B, "A Quick Walk on the Extended Side," to learn more.

HDTV screen sizes, as well as sizes customarily used with phones, hand-held organizers, and other devices. Of course, you can also specify a custom size for your image—width and height—in pixels, inches, centimeters, points, picas, or columns across. All of these settings are available in pop-up menus (see Figure 2.11).

FIGURE 2.11
Photoshop offers you standard image sizes for print and electronic images, as well as the option of entering a custom size.

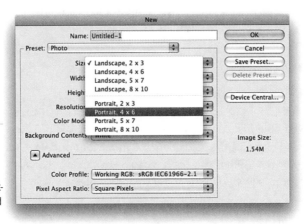

The Default Photoshop Size option in the Size pop-up menu provides you with a 7×5-inch work area, a convenient size for most projects.

Resolution

Resolution refers to the number of pixels per inch (ppi) within an image, which determines the image's quality. Each pixel is a square of a single color. When we look at an image from a distance or shrink the image to make the pixels smaller, we don't see squares; our eyes see the picture. As you might imagine, a higher resolution gives you a sharper, more detailed image but results in a larger file that takes longer to open and to transfer online. Most images that you see in print have a resolution ranging from 150 ppi to 300 ppi. Your computer's monitor, on the other hand, probably displays 72 ppi, which is substantially fewer than 300. Therefore, you always set the resolution for an image depending on how you plan to output the picture—will you print it or will it be only displayed onscreen?

Color Mode and Background Contents

The New dialog also offers you a choice of color modes for the image file you're creating. We talk a lot more about color modes in Hour 5, "Adjusting Brightness and Color." For now, stick with RGB (based on primary colors of red, green, and blue)—it offers you the widest range of

---

It's Magic!

If you've copied an image to the Clipboard when you create a new document, the dialog box automatically shows the size of the copied image. If you switch to another size option and then change your mind, choose Clipboard from the Preset pop-up menu to reset the dialog to the size of the image on the Clipboard.

Plan Ahead...

If you intend to publish your images on the Web, ignore resolution completely. Instead of thinking of an image as "so-many-inches by so-many-inches at 72 ppi," think of the image as being "this-many-pixels by this-many-pixels." Consider how much of the web page the image will cover. If, on the other hand, you are printing to a high-quality color inkjet or laser printer, set the resolution to 200 ppi. Use 300 ppi only if you need to create high-quality color prints.

available colors and is optimal for printing on inkjet printers and displaying onscreen. You also need to decide what color you want the Background
layer to be; think of this as the canvas or paper color. You can choose black,
white, or any other color, or you can choose to start with a transparent
layer and skip the Background layer entirely, which is akin to painting or
drawing on a transparency sheet.

The New File

After you click OK in the New dialog box, a new, empty window or tab
opens. This is the **active window**, and the **canvas** is the large white square
within it. You can have more than one window open within Photoshop at
the same time, but only one can be the active window. The active window
is always in the foreground. This is where you create and edit images. If
Open Documents as Tabs is checked in the Interface preferences, multiple
windows are grouped together; you switch documents by clicking the
appropriate tab.

You can enlarge the window itself by clicking and dragging its lower-right
corner. This doesn't change the size of your image's canvas, however; it's
just a way to see more of the canvas at one time when you're zoomed in at
a high magnification. If you do want to change the size of the canvas, you
can do so by choosing Image, Canvas Size. In the Canvas Size dialog, you
can specify a new height and width for the canvas, as shown in Figure
2.12. Click any of the nine squares in the Anchor section to specify the
point from which the canvas expands or shrinks.

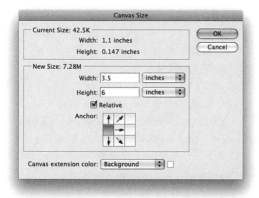

FIGURE 2.12
Click a square in the Anchor proxy
to position the existing contents of
the canvas in the corresponding
area of the enlarged canvas.

If you want to enlarge or shrink the canvas by a specific amount of space,
you'll find the Relative check box very useful. Check the Relative box to
add or subtract the specified amount to the size of the existing canvas.

Enter a positive value to make the canvas larger and a negative value to make it smaller. Remember, if you want to add a specific measurement on all four sides of your image, you need to double that amount in the Width and Height fields so that the correct amount is added all the way around.

Saving Your Work

The most important thing to know about saving your work is this: Do it often! Computers can shut down unexpectedly, and software can crash. Occasionally pressing Command-S (Mac) or Ctrl+S (Windows) to save as you go along takes only a couple seconds, and it can prevent the nightmare scenario of having to do your work all over again if disaster strikes.

The first time you save a picture, you'll see the Save As dialog, shown in Figure 2.13. Give the file a name and choose an appropriate format to save it in from the pop-up menu (check out the "Choosing a Format" section later in this hour for help). Navigate to the folder where you want to save the file, and click Save to save the file.

FIGURE 2.13
Saving a file in Photoshop

CAUTION

Cross-Platform Concept

For Mac OS users only: If you have to work cross-platform—that is, on both a Mac and a PC—always choose to include file extensions with your files. This option is found in the File Handling section of the Preferences dialog. Also, always check Use Lower Case to be sure that your file is compatible with both Windows and UNIX.

You can find the option to save a copy of your current image in the Save As dialog box—check As a Copy to use it. As with Save As, the As a Copy option lets you save the file with a new name and in a new location. The difference is that, after you use Save As, you're working in the new file. But if you use As a Copy, you save a copy of the file as it is at that moment, but you're still working on the original file, not the copy. Saving with As a Copy checked is especially useful for making a backup copy before you try a drastic change, such as reducing color depth or increasing

JPEG lossiness, or for saving the file in a different format. Suppose that you create a logo for your business and want to use it in print and on the Web. You'd save it as a TIFF or EPS file to print from, and you'd save a copy as a JPEG or PNG file for your web page. The word copy is automatically added to the filename, but you can delete it if you're saving the copy in a different format, because the new file's filename extension will be different from the original's.

The final Save option, located in the File menu, is Save for Web & Devices. It brings up a gigantic dialog box that contains the settings you need to optimize an image for use on websites or on the small screens of cell phones and handheld organizers. For example, you can see the effects of varying amounts of JPEG compression, so you can choose a setting that balances file size and image quality. You'll learn about these options in detail in Hour 24.

Choosing a Format

With so many possible formats, how can you decide which one to use? It's really not so difficult. As long as you are working on an image, keep saving it as a Photoshop document (.psd). This makes sense, especially after you learn to work in layers, because Photoshop's native format can save the layers, whereas most other formats require that you merge the layers into one. After you have flattened the layers, you can't split them apart again. Type is another feature that most other formats don't support; type in a JPEG file, for example, turns into part of the background image, meaning that you can't edit it. So as long as you think you'll want to go back to a picture and modify it, save a copy as a Photoshop document.

When you finish working on the picture and are ready to place it into another document for printing, save a copy as an EPS file if it's going to a PostScript-compatible printer. If you aren't sure how the image will be printed, save it as a TIFF, because TIFF is compatible with most printers and page-layout programs. If you're going to place your picture on a web page, choose GIF or PNG-8 if the picture is line art, has large areas of solid color, or uses a limited color palette. Choose JPEG or PNG-24 if the picture is a photograph or continuous tone art (lots of colors). If you want to import the picture into some other graphics program for additional work, choose Photoshop format if the other program supports it, and TIFF if the other program doesn't recognize Photoshop files.

Making Your Files Smaller

Some file formats have built-in compression, which automatically shrinks the file as small as possible when it saves. In the case of TIFF, Photoshop does this by a means called lossless compression, so there's no image degradation or blotchy color. LZW compression (named for its inventors, Lempel, Ziv, and Welch) is also used by GIF and PDF formats.

Other formats, such as JPEG, use lossy compression. *Lossy* means, as you might guess from the name, that some of the data making up the image is lost in the compression process. Instead of 20 shades of blue in the sky in a TIFF file, the same image in a JPEG file might have only 5 shades of blue. And, yes, you *can* see the difference. Unfortunately, compression is necessary when you are displaying images on the Web, in a multimedia presentation, or in another situation where upload time or storage space is limited. JPEG saves files in the least possible amount of disk space. But remember that if you save a JPEG image a second time as a JPEG, it is compressed again and loses more information. If you work on a JPEG file a lot, you can end up with an unreadable picture. If you're going to work on a picture, save it as a Photoshop file; don't make it a JPEG until you're done with it and ready to post it on your web page. If you have to change the image, trash the JPEG file and go back to the Photoshop version; make the change and save a new JPEG.

Backup Strategies

I'm sure you already have a comprehensive backup plan in place for your entire computer system, with multiple backups and off-site storage. After all, it's well known that there are only two kinds of computer users: those who have experienced a hard drive crash, and those who will experience one in the future. Anyway, whether or not you've kept up current backups, if you do extensive work in Photoshop, you'll want to protect your time investment by backing up the images you've so painstakingly created. Here are a few guidelines for doing that:

▸ Save a version of each image in layered Photoshop format, even if you think you'll never want to edit the file again. Better safe than sorry!

▸ When you're no longer actively working with an image, burn those native Photoshop backup files, which tend to be quite large, to CD or DVD so that they're not filling up your hard drive.

▶ Give your image files meaningful names so that searching for a file doesn't become a guessing game, and consider using metadata, as described earlier in this hour in "Creating and Using Metadata." The more information *about* a file that's saved *with* the file, the easier it will be to find when you need it.

▶ Don't forget to back up the fonts you used in an image along with the image file. If you need to change the text, you'll need to have the appropriate fonts installed.

▶ If you create custom Actions, brushes, and color palettes, don't forget to save those, too. You might not *need* them to work on a particular file, but you'll undoubtedly find them useful for future projects, and it's a shame to lose all the time you put into creating them. You can save any of these things using the Save command in the appropriate palette menu.

Undoing and Redoing

Photoshop's History panel and History Brush tool are designed for those of us who don't get everything right the first time—in other words, pretty much everyone. The History panel keeps a list of every tool you've used and every change you've made, up to a predetermined number you can set in the History Options panel menu. You can also take "snapshots" of the work in progress and use these as saved stages to which you can revert. Figure 2.14 shows the History panel for a picture that's had a lot of changes made to it.

FIGURE 2.14
The History palette logs each change made to the current picture.

You can click any previous step to revert to it if a change to an image doesn't work out the way you anticipated. The History panel is more useful in some ways than simply being able to choose the Undo command multiple times, because the History panel lets you undo and redo selectively by choosing the step you want to revert to. More important, it enables you to save your work as you do it and still go back and undo. In early versions of Photoshop, and in some other programs, after you save your work, Undo isn't available. We discuss the uses of the History panel and the History Brush (which lets you undo as much or as little of a change as you want) in greater detail in Hour 8, "Different Ways to Paint."

Of course, you can always use Command-Z (Mac) or Ctrl+Z (Windows) to toggle the Undo and Redo commands in a single step. For multiple undos, press Command-Option-Z (Mac) or Ctrl+Alt+Z (Windows) repeatedly.

Using Version Cue

If you're using Photoshop as part of Adobe Creative Suite, you have access to a great utility called Version Cue that's integrated into the Open and Save dialog boxes of all the Creative Suite programs. It keeps track of previous versions of files and of alternate versions created during the design process, so you can always locate the version you, or your client, need. Version Cue also enables you to share files with other people in a workgroup, keeping track of who's working on which file at any given time, and it groups related files so that you have easy access to all the parts of a project.

To turn on Version Cue within Photoshop, go to the File Handling section of the Preferences dialog and check the box labeled Enable Version Cue.

Version Cue organizes files into projects. You assign each file to a project the first time you save it. To be able to do this, Mac users need to make sure they're using the Adobe Open and Save dialogs. If not, you'll see a Use Adobe Dialog button in the Open and Save dialogs; click it to see the Adobe dialog, which includes a Favorites area on the left. Click Version Cue in the Favorites column to see your projects, if you have any (see Figure 2.15).

FIGURE 2.15
With Version Cue, you must assign each file to a project.

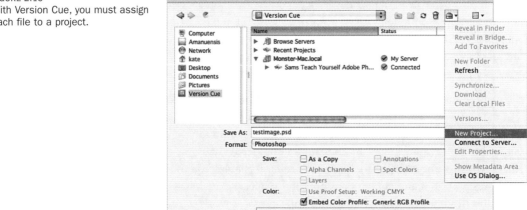

When Version Cue is active, you can save different versions of a file by choosing File, Check In as you work. Each time, you're asked to enter comments about the new version. If you want to return to a previous version at any time, you can do so from the Open dialog box—choose Versions from the Tools pop-up menu in the upper-right corner of the dialog, and you'll see a list of the versions you've saved for that image (see Figure 2.16).

FIGURE 2.16
The comments entered with each new version enable you to remind yourself or co-workers of what changed with that version.

Summary

Photoshop can work with many kinds of image files from many sources. You can open most files by either double-clicking the file or using the Open dialog box, and you can import others using plug-in filters. If you have a digital camera or scanner, it probably came with a Photoshop plug-in that enables you to import pictures directly into Photoshop. Check your owner's manual or the company's website.

Logically enough, Photoshop can also save documents in all the formats it can open (except Raw). Different formats have different purposes, and they yield different file sizes. Some are specifically intended for web use, others for printing. Choose a format based on the intended use of the image.

The History palette shows a step-by-step list of everything you've done to an open image. You can travel backward or forward through the History list by clicking any step and easily undo or redo your changes, even if you have already saved the document. For an even more powerful "time travel" effect, you can use Version Cue to keep track of multiple versions of each file you work on.

Q&A

Q. If higher-resolution images are sharper and more detailed, can I restore detail in a blurry picture by increasing its resolution?

A. In a word, no. If the details you're missing don't exist in the picture, you won't magically get them back by increasing the image's resolution. What you will get is a bunch of added pixels that represent Photoshop's best guess of what the missing detail looks like, based on the pixels surrounding each new pixel.

Q. When should I use Save a Copy, as opposed to Save As?

A. Use Save a Copy when you want to make a copy of the picture you are working on and then continue to work on the original instead of the copy. Suppose that you have a picture called Roses that you have worked on and saved. If you save a copy as Roses copy and then keep working, you will still be working on the original Roses, and Roses copy will be a closed file on your hard drive that looks just like the original Roses at the point when you saved the copy.

Q. Can you clarify the difference between lossy compression and lossless compression?

A. The difference is easy to understand, even though it might be hard to remember because the two terms are so similar. Lossy compression removes image data to make an image more uniform (fewer colors and flatter areas with less detail) and, thus, smaller in file size. Lossless compression simply uses more efficient methods of encoding image data without removing any so that you still have all the pixels you started with.

Workshop

Quiz

1. JPEG, GIF, and PNG have something in common. What is it?

    A. They're all color modes that Photoshop can use.

    B. They're all web formats, recognized by web browsers.

    C. They're country codes for places where you can buy Photoshop at a steep discount.

2. The filename extension for Photoshop's native file format is

   A. PHP

   B. PHO

   C. PSD

3. The Default Photoshop Size preset gives you a file that's

   A. 3×5 inches

   B. 4×6 inches

   C. 7×5 inches

4. Which of the following is not a common metadata field that Bridge recognizes?

   A. Dominant Color

   B. Resolution

   C. Format

Answers

1. **B.** JPEG is also most likely the format in which your digital camera saves the images it creates.

2. **C.** But don't forget, if you really go crazy with an image and make it huge, you can save it in the PSB format, which supports extremely large images and very high numbers of layers.

3. **C.** The other two sizes, however, are common photo print sizes.

4. **A.** But you can use any metadata field to contain any information you want. So you could put each image's dominant color in a field that you're not using, such as one of the IPTC Core fields.

Exercises

1. Open one of your own digital photos or art files and save it in different formats. See how the format affects the file size.

2. Create a new, blank image file and try some tools, as you did after the last hour. Now look at the History palette and see what you've done. Click an entry and watch the image revert to what it looked like after you applied that tool or command. Click again on the last entry in the list to restore all your changes to the image.

HOUR 3
Making Selections

Now that you've learned how to bring images in and out of Photoshop, it's time to move on to doing some fun stuff with those pictures. The first step is to learn how to isolate the part of the picture you want to work on. That's where selections come in; when part of the image is selected, the changes you make affect only that area, leaving the rest of the image alone. In this hour, you'll learn several methods of making selections and how to know which method to use for a given situation.

The Selection Tools

Photoshop offers several tools designed for selecting part of a picture. The Selection tools include the Marquee tools, the Lasso tools, the Quick Selection tool, and the Magic Wand. Each of these tools enables you to make selections in a particular way, such as punching a shape out of an image or selecting all of the sky. Using these tools, individually or in combination, you have the power to select the whole picture or just a single pixel. To refresh your memory, Figure 3.1 shows the Selection tools. (The pop-up menus are shown alongside the Tools panel so that you can see what's on each of them.) The Crop tool is grouped with the Selection tools because you use it to select the portion of an image that you want to keep; we talk about how to use it later in this hour. In the lower-right corner, you can also see the Slice tool, which you use to divide web images into segments. You'll learn all about it in Hour 24, "Going Online with Photoshop."

Rectangular and Elliptical Marquees

All of the Marquee tools—the Rectangular, Elliptical, Single Column, and
Single Row Marquee tools—occupy a single slot in the upper-left corner of
the Tools panel. To select whichever of the tools is currently "on top," just
click it or press M on your keyboard. To switch from that tool to any other
Marquee tool, click and hold the Marquee tool in the Tools panel to bring up
the pop-up menu, then choose the tool you want from the menu. If you press
Shift+M while any Marquee tool is active, you switch to the Rectangular
Marquee; press the same keys again to switch to the Elliptical Marquee.

Now that you know how to access the Elliptical and Rectangular Marquee
tools, let's talk about what you can do with them. To select part of your
image with the Rectangular Marquee, click at one of the area's corners and
drag to form a rectangular area. When you release the mouse button, the
selection is complete. The Elliptical Marquee tool works the same way as the
Rectangular Marquee tool, except that it selects an oval area instead of a rectangular area. No matter which tool you use to create a selection, the area is
bounded by a moving dashed line, often referred to as "marching ants."

To experiment with the Marquee tool's many uses, first create a new file
(go back to Hour 2, "Opening and Saving Files," if you can't remember
how). Give yourself some room to work; the Photoshop Default Size preset
should work well. Then follow these steps:

1. Click the Marquee tool in the Tools panel.

    As you move the tool over the canvas, the cursor appears as a
    crosshair.

2. While the cursor is over the canvas, click and hold the mouse button,
    and then drag out a rectangular selection.

    Experiment with dragging out an elliptical selection. Try dragging
    from different directions.

3. Switch to the Brush tool and drag it across the entire canvas. You'll
    see that the tool can paint only within the selected area.

You can move a selection around the canvas by clicking and dragging it with any of the selection tools active. If you click outside the selection area, that selection disappears; then you can drag to create a new selection. If you want to add more area to an existing selection, press and hold the Shift key before you start dragging. Keep holding the Shift key as you make additional selections. (You'll see a plus sign beneath the crosshair whenever the Shift key is held down.) Where the selected areas overlap, they merge to form one larger selected shape. Figure 3.2 shows both single marquee shapes and a combination of shapes making a selection that somewhat resembles a city skyline.

To select a perfectly square or round area, choose Fixed Ratio from the Style pop-up menu on the Tool Options bar and enter 1 in both the Width and Height fields, or just press the Shift key after you start dragging the shape. Use Fixed Size to make multiple selections that are the same size.

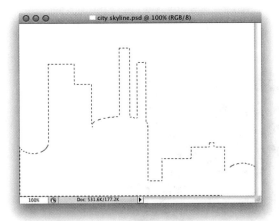

FIGURE 3.2
You can combine square and round selections to make larger, more complex selections.

TIP

Pushing Your Buttons

If your memory for keyboard shortcuts is already overloaded, you'll be relieved to know that you can also combine selections using the four buttons at the left end of the Tool Options bar: New Selection, Add to Selection, Subtract from Selection, and Intersect with Selection. That last button enables you to select the area that the original selection and your new selection have in common.

To deselect an area inside another area (making what graphic artists call a **knockout**), press Option (Mac) or Alt (Windows) as you drag the inner shape. (You'll see a minus sign appear beneath the crosshair.) For instance, if you have a circle selected and you drag another smaller circle inside it while pressing Option (Mac) or Alt (Windows), the selected shape is a torus (better known as a doughnut).

The thin, horizontal (Single Row) and vertical (Single Column) Marquee tools select a single row of pixels across the entire width or height of the image, either horizontally or vertically. You might find them useful for cleaning up the edges of an object.

NOTE
Layer Pitfalls

If you copy or paste something onto your canvas and then try to work with a selection in a different area of the picture, you might see an error dialog saying "Could not complete your request because the selected area is empty." This is Photoshop's way of reminding you that you have added another layer to your picture by pasting into it, and the part of the picture that you want to work with isn't on that new layer. Look at the Layers palette and click the layer on which you want to work, to make it the active layer. You'll learn all about working with layers in Hour 11, "Creating Layered Images."

FIGURE 3.3
Selecting an object with the Lasso requires a significant amount of patience if you want the selection to be precise.

TIP
L Is for Lasso

You can switch to the currently active Lasso tool from any other tool by pressing L. And you can press Shift+L to cycle through the three different Lasso tools: Lasso, Polygonal Lasso, and Magnetic Lasso. You'll find that you can use keyboard shortcuts such as these to access almost all the tools that Photoshop's Tools panel contains. To learn the shortcut for a particular tool, place your mouse over the tool for a second or two, without clicking, and check out the ToolTip that appears.

Whenever there's an active selection, you can edit only the area within the confines of the marquee as long as a selection is active. Thus, after you make a selection, you can perform whatever action you want, but before you move on to work on another part of the image, you must turn off, or **deselect**, the selection by clicking outside the selected area with one of the Marquee tools or by pressing Command-D (Mac) or Ctrl+D (Windows). Until you do this, you can edit only within the selection's boundaries. You can use a selection to restrict changes such as color shifts to a single area of an image, or even to erase a piece of the picture. When a selection is active, you can remove the active selected piece by pressing the Backspace/Delete key.

The Lasso Tool

As useful as the Marquee tools are, even when you use them to combine multiple selections, sometime you have to select irregular shapes that the Marquee tools just can't accommodate. Perhaps you might need to select a single flower from a bunch or, as in Figure 3.3, remove the "Basil" tag from the flower bed.

That's when you should haul out the Lasso tool. You can use it to select an area by drawing along the edges of the space with the tip of the "rope" in the tool's cursor. Using the Lasso tool to select an object in this way requires a steady hand and good hand-eye coordination, as well as a clean mouse or trackball. As with the Marquee tools, you can add to your Lasso selection by holding the Shift key and dragging to select other parts of the image.

TRY IT YOURSELF ▼

Make a Selection with the Lasso Tool

To create a selection with the Lasso tool, follow these steps:

1. Choose the Lasso tool from the Tools panel or press L to switch to it.

2. Click on an edge of the object you want to select and carefully drag the Lasso tool around it. You will see a solid line trailing behind the cursor as you drag. Remember, the active part of the Lasso cursor is the very bottom tip of the "rope."

3. When you're close to completely enclosing the selection, you can release the mouse button. Photoshop automatically completes the selection with a straight line between the point where you started dragging and the point where you left off. If you release the mouse button before you have traced all the way around, the ends of the lasso line will still connect, even if it means drawing a line through the center of the object. If that happens, press and hold the Shift key and use the Lasso tool again to finish selecting the object.

The Polygonal Lasso Tool

The Polygonal Lasso tool works much the same way as the regular Lasso tool. As its name implies, however, the Polygonal Lasso tool makes irregular **straight-edged** selections instead of curved ones. It's actually easier to use than the main Lasso tool when you need to make detailed selections, because you can control it much more easily. Instead of simply dragging to create a selection line, as you do with the regular Lasso, you click the Polygonal Lasso to place points, and Photoshop connects the points with straight lines. You can place as many points as you need, as close together or as far apart as necessary. Figure 3.4 shows the tool in use.

FIGURE 3.4
The Polygonal Lasso tool works great for selecting this "boat," which has straight sides and few curves.

▼ TRY IT YOURSELF

Create a Selection Using the Polygonal Lasso Tool

To select an area with the Polygonal Lasso tool, follow these steps:

1. Click the Lasso tool and hold until you see the pop-up menu, then choose the Polygonal Lasso tool. Or just press Shift+L until the Polygonal Lasso tool is active.

2. Click once in the canvas. Now move your mouse. Notice that a line follows your Polygonal Lasso wherever you move it. (Try to resist the temptation to simulate Tarzan swinging through the trees on a vine.)

3. Click again. This completes the first line segment in the selection and sets another point from which you can drag. Move the mouse to the next corner point you want to create and click again.

   With two sides set, you have a choice. Either you can continue to select the image or you can double-click to close off the selection with a straight line between the first point you created and the last one.

   When the cursor nears your starting point, Photoshop adds a small circle to the normal Polygonal Lasso cursor. This lets you know that, if you click, the selection will be completed.

4. Click to finish your selection.

The Magnetic Lasso Tool

The Magnetic Lasso is really fun to use. As you drag it around any shape with a reasonably well-defined edge, the selection snaps right to that edge. Select it and use it just as you did the Polygonal Lasso. Because it finds edges by looking for differences in contrast, the Magnetic Lasso is most effective when you're selecting irregular objects that stand out from their backgrounds. You can use the Tool Options bar to set several parameters. Width refers to how close to the edge the Magnetic Lasso must be to recognize it (see Figure 3.5). Contrast determines how different the pixels must be in brightness value for the Lasso to recognize them. Frequency determines how often the Lasso sets its anchor points. (Anchor points are the points indicated by boxes on a line. Drag them to adjust the shape of the selection.)

TIP

You Always Have Options

Many of Photoshop's tools, including the Selection tools, have additional options. Controls that enable you to change these settings are located on the Tool Options bar. Whenever you select a new tool, be sure to check out its options.

FIGURE 3.5
Set the Contrast value according to the amount of contrast between the object you're trying to select and what surrounds it. Here, there's a decent amount of contrast between the dark chair and the green leaf, so the selection forms easily.

The Quick Selection Tool

One of the coolest features in Photoshop CS4 is the Quick Selection Tool, guaranteed to make your image-editing life easier. Together with the Magic Wand, this is a different kind of Selection tool than the ones we've looked at so far. The Marquee and Lasso tools select pixels based on their positions in the image—you draw a shape, and everything inside that shape is selected. The Quick Selection Tool, on the other hand, selects pixels based on color values. This is often the easiest way of all to select objects that contrast strongly with the areas around them, and it's also a good way to make sure you're selecting all of an object so that you can edit it—change its color, blur it, whatever you have in mind.

With the Quick Selection tool, you "paint" a selection by clicking and dragging across an object you want to select. As you drag the cursor across the object, Photoshop selects the pixels you drag across, along with other, nearby pixels of similar colors. Each time you release the mouse button, Photoshop "cleans up" the edges of your selection. You can also click the Refine Edges button to make your own tweaks to the selection.

▼ TRY IT YOURSELF

Make a Quick Selection

To use the Quick Selection tool, follow these steps:

1. Choose the Quick Selection tool from the Tools panel, or press W.

2. Choose a brush diameter in the Tool Options bar to set the size of the Quick Selection tool. If your Cursor preferences are set to Normal Brush Tip, the circular cursor shows you the size of the tool with respect to your image.

3. Paint across an object that stands out from its background. The selection grows as you drag the cursor.

4. Press Option (Mac) or Alt (Windows) and paint over areas you want to remove from the selection.

5. Click the Refine Edge button on the Options bar to clean up your selection. Making sure the Preview box is checked, experiment with the settings until the selection is the way you want it; then click OK.

Cursor size is important when you're working with the Quick Selection tool. The larger the cursor, the more different-colored pixels it sweeps over as you click and drag, and the more colors are included in the selection. You can change the cursor size as you work; it's usually best to start with a large-ish cursor to select the bulk of the object you're targeting, and then switch to a smaller cursor to add bits around the edges (see Figure 3.6).

Magic Wand

If you like what the Quick Selection tool does, but you want more control over the selection process, the Magic Wand is for you. Using the Magic Wand tool, you can build a color-based selection one click at a time. The big difference is that you can decide how similar colors must be to be included in the selection, using the Tolerance setting in the Tool Options bar. The lower the Tolerance setting, the less tolerance the Magic Wand has for color differences. Thus, for example, if you set the Tolerance higher (it ranges from 0 to 255), it selects all variations of the color that you initially select. At lower Tolerance settings, the Magic Wand declines to select pixels that aren't very close to the original color on which you clicked.

As with the previously described tools, the Magic Wand can make and merge selections if you press the Shift key as you click the areas to select.

Settings on the Tool Options bar enable you to specify whether the Magic Wand should select everything in the picture that matches the specified color or select only matching pixels that touch each other. For example, if you have a picture with several yellow flowers and your Tolerance setting is high, clicking with the Magic Wand selects as much and as many of the flowers as the Tolerance setting allows (see Figure 3.7). If you check Contiguous in the Tools Options bar, however, that same click selects only the parts of the flower you click on that are within the tolerance *and* are right next to each other.

FIGURE 3.7
Allowing the Magic Wand to select discontiguous pixels can save you a lot of time. Here, I've selected all the pink parts of the purse with a single click.

The Magic Wand is most useful for selecting objects that are primarily one color, such as a flower or a brightly colored T-shirt. It's ideal when you need to select the sky in a landscape. In a few minutes, you'll see exactly how to do this, but first, you've got some other selection tricks to learn.

The Select Menu

You've probably noticed that, in addition to the Selection tools you've just learned about, Photoshop features a Select menu, shown in Figure 3.8. In my opinion, this menu's most useful commands are the first four. All creates a selection marquee around the entire canvas. Deselect removes the selection marquee from the image, regardless of its shape or position, and no matter which method you used to create that selection. Reselect replaces the marquee if you accidentally deselect it before you're done using it. Inverse switches the selection so that everything that wasn't selected before is selected now, and everything was selected before is *not* selected now. For instance, if I had a photo of an apple on a plate, I could select the apple and then choose Inverse to select the plate and the background. Inverting is extremely useful— you'll find yourself using this command quite a bit.

FIGURE 3.8
The Select menu and Modify submenu offer several ways to create and adjust selections.

Modifying Selections

The commands in the Select, Modify submenu enable you to change your selections in several ways. For example, Border takes the value you specify and creates a selection that many pixels wide around the edges of the previous selection. Smooth is helpful when you've made a Lasso selection with a shaky hand or when you're trying to clean up a Magic Wand selection. This command smoothes out bumps in the Marquee line by as many pixels as you specify. Expand and Contract, as their names suggest, force your selection to grow or shrink by the number of pixels you specify in the dialog box.

The most frequently used command in the Modify submenu, however, is Feather, which enables you to make selections with fuzzy, **feathered** edges instead of hard ones. It's helpful when you want to select an object from one picture and paste it into another, because it blurs the edges of the selection slightly so that they blend in better with the selection's new background. You determine how much feathering is applied to a selection by entering a number of pixels in the Feather Selection dialog box, shown in Figure 3.9. Experiment with feathering selections to find out what works best in different situations. For one thing, you'll find that a setting that works perfect on an object in a low-resolution image will be way too low for the same object in a high-resolution version of the same image.

FIGURE 3.9
You determine the amount of feathering applied to a selection in the Feather Selection dialog box.

▼ TRY IT YOURSELF

Make a Feathered Selection

To make a feathered selection, follow these steps:

1. Open any picture you like, or shoot a new one and transfer it to your computer.

2. Choose any of the Selection tools and use it to select, as precisely as possible, a section of the picture.

3. Choose Select, Feather, or press Shift+F6 to open the Feather Selection dialog box.

4. Enter an amount in the Feather Radius field. Start with 5, then click OK. If the selection looks right to you, go to the next step; otherwise, undo and repeat step 3 with a different value.

5. Copy the selection and paste it into a new file so you can see the effect of the feathering. Remember, Photoshop inserts the size of the copied selection into the New dialog, so all you need to do to make a file the right size is press Command-N (Mac) or Ctrl+N (Windows) and click OK.

Refining Selections

Having made a selection, you can clean it up with an incredible degree of control and accuracy, using the controls in the Refine Edge dialog box (see Figure 3.10). First, create a selection using any tool or method you prefer. Then either choose Select, Refine Edge or click the Refine Edge button on the Tool Options bar to enter the clean-up phase.

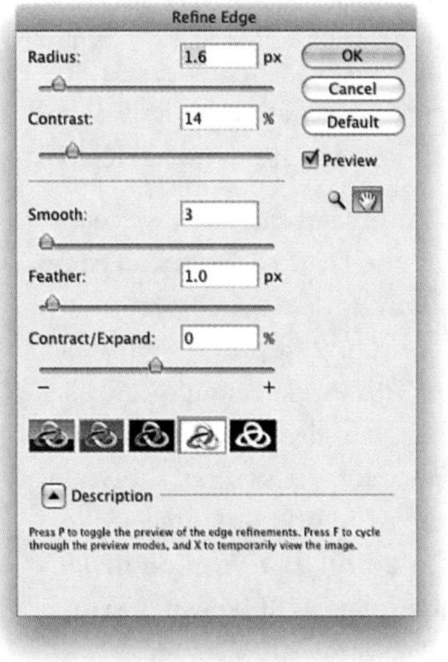

FIGURE 3.10
This dialog gathers together several powerful tools for making your selection just the way you want it.

The first two sliders in the Refine Edge dialog are Radius and Contrast. Use them to vary the quality of a feathered selection edge, including those created by the Quick selection tool and the Magic Wand. Increase the Radius setting to clean up the selection edge in areas with fine details or gradual transitions, and increase Contrast to make soft selection edges sharper and remove fuzz.

You can use the other three sliders with any selection. Drag the Smooth slider to the right to remove jagged angles along the selection edge and to eliminate 1- or 2-pixel "holdouts" in the middle of a selected area. The Feather slider, of course, works just like the Feather dialog box; increase the setting to blur the selection edge. And the Contract/Expand slider enables you to shrink or enlarge the selection while maintaining its shape; you can use this control to clean up the edges of an object you're silhouetting.

The buttons across the bottom of the dialog offer you several different Selection Preview options:

- ▶ **Standard selection border**—With this option, you see the typical "marching ants" marquee around the area you're selecting.

- ▶ **Quick Mask**—This button puts a translucent red mask over the areas of the image that aren't included in your selection. (To learn more about using Quick Mask to make and edit selections, turn to Hour 12, "Using Masks.")

- ▶ **Black background**—This button blacks out the areas of the image that aren't included in your selection.

- ▶ **White background**—This button places white over the areas of the image that aren't included in your selection.

- ▶ **White on black mask**—To see the selection itself, without the image getting in the way, click this button to display a white shape that corresponds to the selection against a black background.

Adobe's Photoshop experts recommend using the Smooth, Feather, and Contract/Expand sliders, in that order, on most selections for best results, and I concur. I've always used Smooth and Feather on most selections, and this dialog box makes it easy to apply both of those commands, combine them with others, and see what will happen to your selection before you click OK to finalize your changes.

Selecting Large Areas

You'll often find that you need to select a large part of the picture, such as the sky, so that you can darken its color or otherwise change it without changing the rest of the picture. Figure 3.11 shows a picture with a lot of sky and a very complicated object sticking up into it—namely, an iris blossom, standing in front of several buildings and trees. You can see gaps between the branches and leaves, and some of the highlights on the flowers and along the rooflines are close to the color of the sky. This isn't a situation you want to tackle with the Marquee or Lasso tools; selecting this complicated area calls for more subtlety.

FIGURE 3.11
Selecting just the sky, without including any of the leaves or flowers, is challenging.

You can download this picture from the Sams website mentioned in the Introduction. Look for iris.jpg.

To select the sky in this picture, follow these steps:

1. Choose the Magic Wand tool in the Tools panel.

2. Set the Tolerance in the Tool Options bar to 20, as shown in Figure 3.12. This enables you to select only similar shades of bluish gray. Be sure that the Contiguous box is not checked so that the Magic Wand can pick up the sky patches between the leaves.

Select a Large Area

FIGURE 3.12
You can set the Tolerance to any number between 0 and 255.

3. Click the Magic Wand on a typical piece of sky (see Figure 3.13).

FIGURE 3.13
You might need to click several times to include all of the sky in the selection.

4. Hold down the Shift key and select additional pieces of sky until the whole thing is included in the selection.

▼ TRY IT YOURSELF

Select a Large Area
continued

5. Look carefully at the selected areas. Have you selected areas of the image that aren't part of the sky? You've probably managed to get part of the roofs, some flag, and even a bit of flower lower down in the image. Change the tool to the Lasso, and press Option/Alt while you draw around pieces of the image that you want to deselect. You might have to do this several times.

6. Now you can change the color of the sky, press Delete to remove it, or do whatever else you like. Figure 3.14 shows the image with the sky completely gone.

FIGURE 3.14
The entire sky has been selected and deleted.

If you want some more practice, find another picture with a lot of sky and see how many steps it takes you to isolate the sky in a selection. It's not difficult, but it can be time-consuming. Remember, if you select more sky (or whatever) than you intended, Undo can deselect the last area selected, leaving the rest of the selection active.

You can also use the Quick Selection tool to select the sky in the iris image. You might find that you have to do a lot of "painting" with the tool to select all of the sky, and you'll almost certainly need to Option-click/Alt-click to deselect areas of the image that you *don't* want included. When the selection looks pretty good, you can use the Refine Selection Edge dialog to clean it up.

Advanced Selection Techniques

By now, you should really have this selection thing down. You know what selections are for, and you know how to make them. It's time to take your selection savvy to the next level with a look at a couple of advanced techniques, one for creating selections and one for editing them.

Selecting by Color

As you learned earlier in this hour, the Quick Selection tool and the Magic Wand create selections by searching out pixels of similar color and brightness level. To use them, though, you have to know where to click. If you're working on a complex image, it might be hard to spot all the areas of a particular color. Why not let Photoshop do that job for you? That's how the Color Range command works.

To get started, choose Select, Color Range. Click in the image window itself, or in the Color Range dialog's preview area, to choose the first area you want to include in the selection. If you want to select other areas, switch to the dialog's Add to Sample tool and click those, too. Then drag the Fuzziness slider to increase or reduce the number of colors included in the selection. When you've got the selection pretty much the way you want it, click Localized Color Clusters to reduce the likelihood that pixels farther away from where you clicked will be included in the selection. This helps get rid of selected areas in other parts of the image that just happen to match the *color* you're selecting but don't have anything to do with the *object* you're selecting. Use the Range slider to determine how much effect the Localized Color Cluster setting has. Now you'll probably have to use the Add to Sample tool to return some areas to the selection. When you're happy with the results, click OK.

You'll see that Color Range selects the chosen colors throughout the image, and it partially selects similar colors (see Figure 3.15).

FIGURE 3.15
A click in the middle of the blue sky created this selection; the clouds are white, but they reflect the sky's color, so they're partially selected.

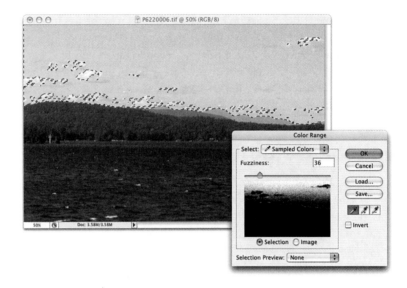

Transforming Selections

Transformations are different ways of reshaping objects within a picture, such as scaling, skewing, or rotating. You'll learn all about how to transform objects in Hour 10, "Using Transformations," but I want to take a minute here to let you in on a secret: You can transform selections, too.

That's right—though even some Photoshop power users don't realize it, you can use a special set of Transform commands to reshape a selection marquee without affecting the pixels within the selection. Why would you want to do this? Well....

Suppose you want to select a manhole cover in a street scene. You know the cover is round, but because it's parallel with the ground, it's not round in your picture. You could carefully trace around the cover with the Lasso tool, or you could use the Magic Wand to select it, but that's likely to be difficult because the cover's color is similar to the street's color. The quick and easy answer is to create a round selection using the Elliptical Marquee tool and then choose Select, Transform Selection to reshape the circle into just the right oval.

When you're ready to give this a try, read about using the Free Transform command in Hour 10. Select Transformation works exactly the same way, only on the selection marquee itself instead of on the selected area.

Saving, Loading, and Combining Selections

Suppose that you drop a complex selection and then realize that you forgot to make the slight color adjustment you had in mind for the selected area. No problem—just choose Select, Reselect, and you're in business again. Now suppose that you drop the selection, spend 20 minutes with the Clone Stamp tool editing out a particularly ugly parked car to one side of the image, and *then* realize that you forgot to make the color adjustment? At this point, either you bang your head against the wall for a while before sitting down to re-create the selection, or you reload the selection in about half a second because you were foresighted enough to save it.

Whenever you've got a selection that you might want to use again—or even if you don't think you'll use the selection again, but it took a long time to create—save it before you deselect it. Saved selections don't take up much space in a file, and it takes only a second to save a selection, so there's just no reason not to unless you're determined to keep your file size to a bare minimum. All you have to do is choose Select, Save Selection. In the Save Selection dialog box (see Figure 3.16), choose a document in which to save the selection (normally, the file in which you're currently working), give the selection a name, and click OK. That's all there is to it!

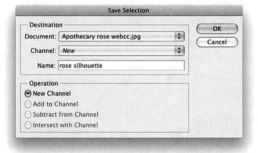

FIGURE 3.16
Saving the selection will ensure that I don't ever have to re-create it.

If you need to reselect the same area, just choose Select, Load Selection and choose the name of your saved selection from the Channel pop-up menu. You have several choices for what to do with the selection (see Figure 3.17). You can invert it so that everything *but* the formerly selected area is now selected. Or you can make it a new selection by itself, add it to an existing selection, subtract its area from an existing selection, or combine it with an existing selection so that only the overlapping area of the two is selected. Click OK, and the selection comes right back to life, in either its original form or one of these modified forms.

FIGURE 3.17
If I load the inverse of this saved selection, the image's background will be selected but not the rose.

When you save a selection, Photoshop turns it into a grayscale image and stores it alongside your picture's color channels in what's called an **alpha channel**. Some programs can use alpha channels to control the image's transparency; for example, if you make a selection that includes only the central figure in a photo and excludes the background, you can create an alpha channel from it that would hide the background, silhouetting the image, if you used the picture in an InDesign document.

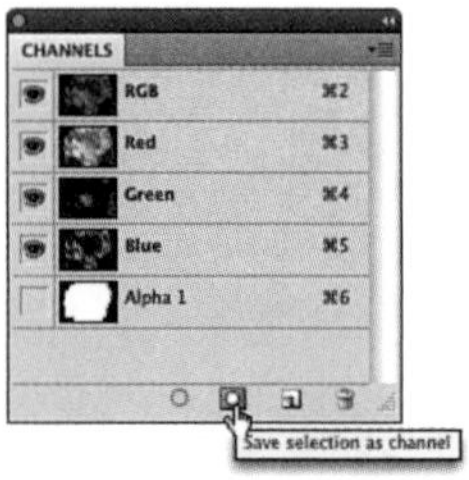

You can control channels, both color and alpha, using the Channels panel (see Figure 3.18). The first two buttons at the bottom of the panel enable you to load a selected channel as a selection or convert an existing selection into a new alpha channel, or you can Command-click (Mac) or Ctrl-click (Windows) a channel in the list to load it as a selection. Adding modifier keys when you Command-click or Ctrl-click enables you to add the channel to an existing selection (press Shift), subtract it from an existing selection (press Option/Alt), or select the intersection between it and an existing selection (press Shift and Option/Alt).

FIGURE 3.18
The quickest way to save a selection is to click this button in the Channels panel.

Cutting and Copying

The Cut, Copy, and Paste commands in Photoshop are identical to those in any other application. You'll find these useful commands in their usual place in the Edit menu.

Cutting, copying, and pasting enable you to borrow from one picture to add to another, or to enhance the first picture. The example that follows gives a lonely little girl some friends. Figure 3.19 shows the girl selected, with the feather amount set to 5 pixels to help her blend in when pasted. Next, you can simply use the Copy command (Edit, Copy), Command-C (Mac), or Ctrl+C (Windows) to copy the girl to the Clipboard.

You can now paste extra copies of the girl where they will fill in the empty space and improve the composition (see Figure 3.20). As long as she is on the Clipboard, you can make as many copies of her as you want (each copy is placed on a separate layer). A couple of the copies in Figure 3.20 are flipped horizontally to face the other way, disguising the fact that these kids are actually all the same. You can also scale the copies to different sizes or distort them a little so they look different. (Again, this is done using the Transform commands that you'll learn about in Hour 10.)

FIGURE 3.19
Before you can copy the little girl, you have to select her.

FIGURE 3.20
The new picture, with the added
kids, has turned this singleton into
quintuplets.

Cropping

Cropping is the artists' term for trimming away unwanted parts of a picture. You can crop a picture based on any selection (choose Image, Crop), or you can use the specialized Crop tool, which you'll find in the same Tools panel section as the Selection tools. When you use the Crop tool to drag a cropping box around the part of the image you want to keep, click Shield on the Tool Options bar to darken the rest of the image so that it's easier to see what' the uncropped portion of the image looks like (see Figure 3.21).

FIGURE 3.21
The Crop tool is simple to use, but the way you crop a picture makes a huge difference in its impact on the viewer.

To crop a picture, use any image and follow these steps:

1. Click in the Tools panel to choose the Crop tool or press C on the keyboard. (The Crop tool looks like two overlapped pieces of L-shaped mat board—the same improvised tool that artists use to help compose paintings.)

2. Click and drag across the picture with the Crop tool. When you release the mouse button, you'll see a selection marquee ("marching ants") with handles on the corners and sides.

3. Use the handles on the cropping box to fine-tune the selection. If the Shield box in the Options bar is checked, the area outside the cropping marquee is darkened.

4. When you have the cropping box sized and positioned the way you want it, double-click inside it (or press Enter, or click the Commit button, which looks like a check mark) to delete the area outside the box. If you decide to cancel the crop, press Esc or click the Cancel button.

TRY IT YOURSELF ▼

Crop a Picture

You can even use Photoshop's cropping tool to correct perspective. Drag the Crop tool over an image that needs perspective adjustment, such as the tilting house in Figure 3.22. After you've drawn the cropping box, click to select the Perspective check box and then click one of the corners of the box and drag it until the side of the cropping marquee is parallel to the side of the building. Repeat with the other side.

FIGURE 3.22
Use Perspective cropping to straighten warped buildings.

Click the button in the Options bar (it looks like a check mark) to apply the changes, or simply double-click inside the cropping window. Figure 3.23 shows the result. Now the building is in proper perspective, the walls are straight, and all is right with the world.

Open some of your own pictures and practice cropping them. Remember, if you crop too much of the picture, you can undo. If it's too late to undo because you have already done something else, just choose Window, History and click the step before you cropped the picture to return to that point in the image's life. You can also choose File, Revert to go back to the last saved version of your picture. As long as you don't close the file, you can keep cropping and using the History panel to undo as many times as you want.

FIGURE 3.23
With the house's walls straightened, the viewer is free to focus
on its Victorian design.

Summary

To exercise true power in Photoshop, you must master the Selection tools
so that you can choose the parts of an image that you want to change and
leave the rest alone. Developing a feel for when you can use selections can
save you a great deal of time that you might otherwise spend painstakingly applying edits one pixel at a time. Selections are most useful when you
need to fill a space with color or an image, when you need to manipulate
just a piece of an image, when you want to selectively brighten or adjust
part of an image, or when you need to extract a piece of an image from a
larger work. Selections themselves can sometimes take a bit of work to create, so be sure to save complex selections for reuse.

Q&A

Q. Can I combine selections made with different Selection tools?

A. Sure. Make a selection with any one of the tools, switch tools, and then press the Shift key before making a new selection; that ensures that the new selection is added to your existing selection. As long as you hold down the Shift key (making a tiny plus sign visible next to the tool's cursor), you can add to your selection as many times as you want.

Q. How can I deselect part of a selection?

A. The easiest way to do this is to press the Option (Mac) or Alt (Windows) key with any of the Selection tools active. A small minus symbol appears next to the tool's cursor. Click or drag, depending on which tool you're using, to select the part of the selection you want to remove. As soon as you release the mouse button, that area is removed from the selection.

Q. What about the Grow and Similar commands in the Select menu—what are they for?

A. Good question. When you have a selection active, no matter what its shape, choose Select, Similar to expand the selection to include all similarly colored pixels in the image, regardless of their location with respect to the original selection. Then, if you realize you need to include some related colors that weren't part of the original selection, choose Select, Grow to enlarge the selection by adding adjacent pixels with similar colors.

Workshop

Quiz

1. To change from the Rectangular to the Elliptical Marquee:

    A. Go back to the Tools panel and select it.

    B. Press Shift+M.

    C. Either A or B.

2. To select a single row or column of pixels:

   A. Hold down Ctrl+C and the Return key while double-clicking.

   B. Press Return as you drag the mouse.

   C. Use the Single Row or Single Column Marquee tool.

3. How do you make the Magic Wand more precise?

   A. Press Shift as you click.

   B. Set the Tolerance to a lower number.

   C. Set the Tolerance to a higher number.

Answers

1. **C.** If you want the Single Row or Single Column Marquee tool, however, you have to go to the Tools panel; these tools have no keyboard short-cuts.

2. **C.** Answer A isn't even possible unless you have three hands.

3. **B.** A lower Tolerance setting means that the Magic Wand will select only those pixels that are most similar in color to the one on which you clicked.

Exercise

Most pictures can be improved by careful cropping. Try this experiment: Scan or shoot a quick shot of your pet, child, or other favorite thing. Be sure to leave plenty of room around the photo's subject. Make two copies of the image file, then open all three in Photoshop. Crop the picture three different ways, placing the subject in the center, off to the side, and near the bottom of the image. See how different the three pictures look now? Which is your favorite? Why?

HOUR 4
Specifying Color Modes and Color Models

Color is infinitely variable; you only need to look out the window to realize that. Just try to count the different shades of green that you can see in a single tree's leaves or the myriad colors of the changing sky. Color is also subjective; an object can seem to be one color to one person and a completely different color to another person—and that's without even getting into all the imprecise ways we use language to describe color. So if you want to describe color objectively and consistently, you have to do it using math. But there's more than one way to do that.

Photoshop recognizes four different **color models**, in fact. Each of these is a way of defining a color by specifying its components. For example, we all learned in school that red, blue, and yellow are the primary colors, but many of us never realized two very important facts about that concept. First, red, blue, and yellow are just rough equivalents of the true primary colors of magenta, cyan, and yellow. Second, those colors are the **subtractive primaries**—the ones that you use when you're combining pigments. When you're creating colors on a computer screen, however, you're combining colors of light, not pigments, so the primary colors in that situation are different; they're the **additive primaries** of red, blue, and green.

So that gives you two different models right there: CMYK (which stands for cyan, magenta, yellow, and black) and RGB (which stands for red, green, and blue). Photoshop can also work with the HSB (hue, saturation, and balance) and CIE Lab color models. Each Photoshop image exists in one of these color spaces, and you specify which one by assigning each image a **color mode**. This image attribute controls which color model Photoshop uses to define the colors in that image.

This hour examines these models for displaying and describing color, and then turns to the Photoshop modes so you can see how all this color theory translates into your everyday dealings with color in Photoshop.

Color Models

In Photoshop, you use the Adobe Color Picker to specify colors in several different models (see Figure 4.1). You can reach the Color Picker by clicking either of the color swatches at the bottom of the toolbar. You'll see a color bar with a slider control alongside a graduated color field, which you can click to select a particular shade. The Color Picker also features text-entry fields that display the values for the chosen color in each of the four color models. If you know the numerical values for a color, you can enter those in the text fields, and the color fields and the color bar update themselves to show the specified color.

FIGURE 4.1
The Adobe Color Picker is designed to make it easy for you to define the colors you want to use.

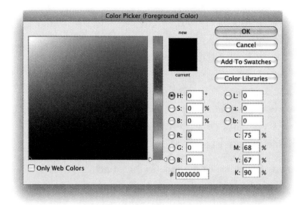

If the Color Picker isn't your cup of tea, you can define colors in Photoshop's Color panel (see Figure 4.2). If you don't see it on the screen, you can open it by choosing Window, Color. Its color field, along the bottom, covers the full color spectrum for the specified color mode, plus black and white. Clicking anywhere on it sets the Foreground color to that color and simultaneously adjusts the sliders and text-entry fields to reflect the values for that color. To see the controls for a different color mode, make a choice from the panel's pop-up menu.

FIGURE 4.2
The Photoshop Color panel's adjustable sliders show the same color value as its clickable color bar, which represents the full color spectrum in the specified color mode.

RGB

The RGB model, which computer monitors and TV screens use for display, defines colors in terms of their proportions of each of the three RGB primary colors—red, green, and blue—assigning a value between 0 and 255 to each. For example, pure green has red and blue values of 0 and a green value of 255. To get pure white in the RGB model, you must combine all three RGB primaries at their highest value of 255. In fact, that's why RGB is called additive color—because adding the three primary colors together produces white. Conversely, black is formed when all three of the RGB primary colors have a value of 0. And when the value of each RGB primary is 128 (half of 255), you get medium gray.

CMYK

The CMYK model describes colors according to their percentages of cyan, magenta, yellow, and black. These are the four colors of printing inks, both in your inkjet printer and in the high-resolution color printers and printing presses that you see in service bureaus and commercial print shops. A six-color inkjet printer adds light cyan and light magenta to the four basic colors to produce a wider overall range of colors.

HSB

Artists usually talk about color by using a set of parameters called HSB, and Photoshop can also use this color model. H stands for **Hue**, which is the basic color, as shown on a color wheel. It's expressed in degrees (0°–360°) that correspond to the positions on the color wheel of the various colors. For example, red is at 3 o'clock on the color wheel and is designated as the zero point. Directly across from red on the wheel is cyan, at the 9 o'clock position, with an H value of 180°.

In the HSB model, S stands for **Saturation**, or the strength of the color, and it's measured as 100% of the color minus the percentage of gray it contains. Pure color with no gray in it is considered to be 100% saturated. Neutral gray, with no color at all, is 0% saturated. Saturated colors are found at the edge of the color wheel; saturation decreases toward the center of the wheel. If you look at the Apple Color Picker in Figure 4.3, this makes a lot more sense. Finally, the B component in HSB is **Brightness**, the relative lightness of the color, and it is also measured as a percentage, with 0% signifying black and 100% signifying white.

NOTE

How Color Translates to the Web

Because web pages are displayed on computer screens, web designers use RGB to define colors. But they use a slightly different dialect: **hexadecimal notation**. In this method, each color is represented as a six-digit number in the hexadecimal system instead of the decimal system, with the first pair of digits indicating the amount of red, the second pair indicating the amount of green, and the third pair indicating the amount of blue. Hexadecimal numbers use the letters A through F to represent the numbers 10 through 15 with a single digit. This system results in values such as FFFF00 (bright yellow) and 66D2F6 (sky blue). Photoshop gives you the hexadecimal code for each specified color at the bottom of the Color Picker, just under the RGB text entry fields.

NOTE

Is Black a Primary Color?

As I explained earlier in this hour, cyan, magenta, and yellow are the subtractive primaries, which means that you have to subtract 100% of each color from black to get white. But how did black get to be one of the component colors in CMYK, too?

The CMYK model includes black purely as a matter of practicality. In theory, you can mix 100% cyan, 100% magenta, and 100% yellow to get black. In practice, when you do that, you get a smeary mess. So printers, both the electronic kind and the people who run printing presses, use black ink to get nice, clear black areas in their images. So black isn't a primary color at all, but it's definitely part of the CMYK color model.

FIGURE 4.3
The Apple Color Picker takes the
form of a standard color wheel.

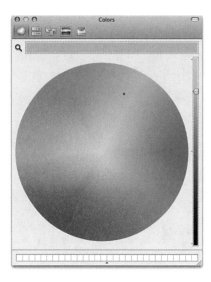

CIE Lab

The most encompassing of the color models Photoshop can work with is CIE
Lab. It defines a color **gamut** (a range of colors) that is broader than that of any
of the other models we've looked at so far. Because of its broad color gamut,
Photoshop uses the CIE Lab model to convert images from one color model to
another—sort of like a universal translation language. Lab colors are defined in
terms of luminance plus two components (a and b), which move, respectively,
from green to red and from blue to yellow. Lab color is designed to be device-
independent, meaning that the range of colors defined in this model isn't
restricted to the range that can be printed or displayed on a particular device.
However, you'll probably never run into a reason to actually use this model.

From Models to Modes

Now it's time to look at how you apply these color models to the images you
edit and create in Photoshop. First, forget about CIE Lab color unless you have
an extensive education in color theory. It's there—Photoshop uses it in the
background—but you don't have to worry about it. The other three models—
HSB, RGB, and CMYK—are much more relevant to your work in Photoshop.

The difference between modes and the models is simple: **Models** are methods
of defining color, and **modes** are methods of working with color based on the
models. HSB is the only model without a directly corresponding mode. CMYK
and RGB have corresponding modes in Photoshop, as does Lab. Photoshop
also has modes for black-and-white, grayscale, and limited-color images.

The Photoshop modes listed under the Image, Mode submenu are as follows:

- Bitmap
- Grayscale
- Duotone
- Indexed Color
- RGB Color
- CMYK Color
- Lab Color
- Multichannel

You'll do almost all of your work in Photoshop using just four of these modes: Grayscale, RGB, CMYK, and Indexed Color. Let's take a closer look at the big four.

Bitmap and Grayscale

Let's start with the most basic of the color modes that Photoshop has to offer: Bitmap and Grayscale. Images in Grayscale mode can contain up to 256 shades of gray, ranging from white to black and covering all the territory in between. Bitmap images use only two colors—black and white (see Figures 4.4 and 4.5 for examples).

FIGURE 4.4
What we think of as black-and-white photos actually use Photoshop's Grayscale mode.

FIGURE 4.5
Here's how the same image looks in Photoshop's Bitmap mode.

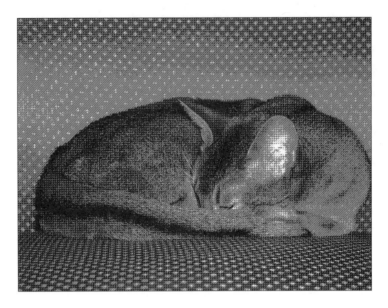

As you look at Figures 4.4 and 4.5, pay attention to the huge difference in quality. The Grayscale image's color shade gradually into each other, whereas the Bitmap image's colors don't. However, you have a number of ways to convert to image Bitmap mode that can compensate for the fact that it contains only two colors; we discuss those later in this hour.

Whenever you plan for a picture to be printed in black and white or grayscale—for instance, as part of a newsletter or brochure—it makes sense for you to work on that image in Grayscale mode. If you're starting with a color image, doing the conversion yourself (instead of sending a color photo to the printer) gives you the opportunity to make sure that the picture will print the way you want it to. You can tell by looking at the picture whether the dark parts of the image need to be lightened or the light grays need to be intensified to bring out more detail. You can both adjust the overall level of contrast in the photo and work on individual trouble spots. All this adjustment would take a lot of guesswork if you kept the image in a color mode instead of converting it to Grayscale mode.

The simplest way to convert a color photo to Grayscale is to choose Image, Mode, Grayscale. Photoshop asks you for permission to discard the color information. Click OK to confirm that this is what you want to do; the picture is converted to shades of gray. To convert a color picture to Bitmap mode, as you might want to for certain special effects, you must convert it first to Grayscale mode and then to Bitmap mode; you can't go directly from a color mode to Bitmap mode.

RGB

RGB is the appropriate color mode for working on pictures that will be viewed on a computer or television screen. If the pictures you're editing in Photoshop will end up as part of a web page, a presentation, or some other medium, stick with RGB for the best color rendition. If your work will eventually be converted to indexed color mode as part of saving it in GIF format, I still recommend doing the color adjustments in RGB and then converting the picture to Indexed Color when it has achieved its final form. That way, you can start with all the colors you need and reduce their number when your work is done. Also, if you work directly in Indexed Color mode, you can't use layers or any of Photoshop's filters, and that's out of the question.

CMYK

As you saw earlier, you should use CMYK mode only when your image is printed commercially. By converting to CMYK before you send an image to the printer, you can make sure that your nice yellow banana or flower doesn't end up a muddy brown, or your bright blue sky doesn't print as purple. Think of it this way: If you're writing a poem, you want to write it in the language in which it will eventually be published. You *don't* want someone else to ineptly translate the poem into a different language, thus changing your meaning and obscuring the beauty of your words. Along the same lines, if your picture will be printed in CMYK, you want to edit it in CMYK.

Desktop inkjet printers are an exception to this rule, however. Yes, they use cyan, magenta, yellow, and black inks, but their software drivers are set up to convert from RGB to CMYK in the most accurate way for their particular hardware. If you send a CMYK image to an inkjet printer, the driver actually converts it to RGB and then back to CMYK before printing it. Imagine what would happen to your poem if it were translated twice in this way, and you'll get an idea of how inaccurately a desktop inkjet printer can sometimes reproduce a CMYK image.

Indexed Color

Indexed color palettes are used to make images smaller by restricting the number of colors they can use. They're primarily used to produce GIF files for use on the Web, where the time it takes to download an image is always a concern; the smaller the image, the faster it can be transferred

TIP

Watch Your Gamut

Gamut refers to the range of colors that a particular color device can print. Some RGB colors are **out of gamut** for the combination of CMYK inks that desktop printers and commercial presses use and can't be printed accurately. Very bright colors, particularly oranges and greens, are often out of gamut. You can turn on a **gamut warning** to let you know that these colors won't print correctly.

With your image open in Photoshop, in the Transparency & Gamut section of Photoshop's Preferences, click the color swatch in the Gamut Warning area and choose a color that will stand out from the colors in your image. Then choose View, Proof Setup, Custom. In the Customize Proof Condition dialog, choose your printer from the Device to Simulate pop-up menu and click OK. Finally, click the View menu once more and make sure that Proof Colors and Gamut Warning are both checked.

After making these settings, you'll probably find that your picture is speckled with splotches of the gamut warning color, to a greater or lesser degree. Now you know what parts of the image won't reproduce correctly on your printer, and you can use the methods described in Hour 5, "Adjusting Brightness and Color," to modify these colors enough that the gamut warning disappears. Don't worry if some of the gamut warning color is still there when you're ready to print; as with guides and grid-lines, the gamut warning won't show up on a printout.

If you're choosing colors for type or other objects in the image, you can watch out for another gamut warning. It shows up on the Color panel and in the Color Picker as a small triangular traffic warning sign with an exclamation point in the middle. When you see it, you can click it to modify the color to the closest equivalent within your printer's gamut.

FIGURE 4.6
The Indexed Color dialog box offers you several ways to convert an image.

NOTE

Playing It Safe on the Web

One of the best-known pre-existing palettes is the Web Safe palette. This group of colors consists of the 216 colors that are part of the basic system palette on both Windows and Mac systems. The point of using the Web Safe palette is that the image's colors will remain consistent whether the image is viewed on a Mac or on a PC. The Web Safe palette is much less relevant than it used to be because most computer systems are set up to display millions of colors instead of the 256 colors many computers used in the old days. But if you're a better-safe-than-sorry type, or if you intend for your work to be used on older computers that display only 256 colors, using the Web Safe palette certainly won't hurt, and it might help keep your pictures looking the way you want them to.

from a web server to your computer so that you can view it. Because the colors in an indexed color image are limited, it's not a good idea to use indexed color for continuous-tone images (such as photographs), because they use a lot more colors than you might realize as each color shades gradually into the next. Indexed color is great, on the other hand, for logos, simple illustrations and charts, and clip art because these images generally use fewer colors than photos in the first place.

Photoshop offers you several ways to build a color palette when you convert an image into Indexed Color mode. You can choose how many colors the palette contains and determine how Photoshop chooses those colors, or you can even pick them all out yourself. From RGB mode, choose Image, Mode, Indexed Color to take a look at the Indexed Color dialog box (see Figure 4.6).

To reproduce colors that aren't included in their restricted palettes, indexed color images use a process called **dithering,** in which adjacent pixels of different colors are interspersed, visually blending onscreen to simulate a new color. If you zoom in on a dithered image, you can still see the pixels' original colors—or the closest index equivalent.

Your palette choices when converting to Indexed Color mode are as follows:

▶ **Exact**—This option takes all the colors that are in the RGB version of the image to build the indexed color palette. You'll see this option only if fewer than 256 colors are used in the original image.

▶ **System (Mac OS)**—This option uses the Macintosh System palette. Note that these colors might or might not be close to what already exists in the image, so using this option can change the image dramatically.

▶ **System (Windows)**—This option uses the Windows System palette. Again, these colors might or might not be anything like what the image is currently using, so proceed with care.

▸ **Web**—This palette uses the 216 colors in the Web Safe palette.

▸ **Uniform**—The Uniform option bases the colors in the palette on a sampling of colors at regular intervals along the color spectrum.

▸ **Perceptual**—This option creates a custom palette that's heavy on colors the human eye has the greatest sensitivity to. You can use a local palette, based solely on the colors in the current image, or a master palette that draws colors from this image and others in a group of images you plan to display together on a website or CD-ROM.

▸ **Selective**—The Selective option creates a color table (a list of colors) similar to one created by the Perceptual option, but this color table favors large areas of color and attempts to preserve web colors. Again, you can choose a local palette or a master palette.

▸ **Adaptive**—This is your best bet for most work in Indexed Color mode. During conversion with this option, Photoshop samples the most frequently used colors from the original image. An Adaptive palette usually provides you with the closest match to the colors in the original image. This option also comes in both local and master flavors.

▸ **Custom**—If none of the other options suits you, you can always build your own palette. When you choose Custom, a Color Table dialog opens. Click any of the color swatches in the custom palette to open the Color Picker and specify a different color. When you're done, click Save to save a copy of the color table you've created so that you can load it for future image conversions.

▸ **Previous**—This menu choice simply remembers and reverts to whichever option you chose the last time you converted to Indexed Color. It resets the dialog to the previous settings so you can see what they are before you click OK.

Converting Between Modes

All you have to do to convert an image from one color mode to another is choose Image, Mode and then choose the mode you want to use. Now, keep in mind that because different color models have different gamuts, Photoshop might have to change some of the colors in the image to fit it inside its new gamut. Photoshop uses the Lab color model, which has the broadest gamut and contains all the colors that other modes use, as a way to convert images between color modes. But this is no guarantee that your colors will look the same in another mode as they did in the original mode.

TIP

Choosing a Color Mode

I suggest that you do all your color work in Photoshop's RGB mode, regardless of whether your final image will be printed or viewed onscreen. I have a simple reason for this. Even if you specify CMYK as the color model, your monitor can display only RGB. It doesn't have cyan, magenta, or yellow pixels, except as combinations of RGB light. Instead of making Photoshop perform the CMYK-to-RGB conversion every time you change a piece of the image, wait and convert the picture when you're ready to print, *if* you're sending the image to a commercial print shop or fine arts Iris printer. If you're using a desktop inkjet, remember that it's designed to work best with RGB input, and skip the CMYK conversion altogether.

I'll bet you can guess what I'm going to say you should do to combat this fact of life: *Do your work in RGB,* even if you plan to have your images professionally printed. Convert a copy of your image to CMYK just before you send it to the print shop. First, though, use the Gamut Warning command (described earlier in this hour) to see whether all your colors are within the CMYK gamut. If you are going to publish your images on the Web, stick with RGB or use Indexed Color mode for files that you plan to save in GIF or PNG-8 format. Following these guidelines will save you many hours of wondering why the web page logo that looked great on the office Macintosh looks funky on the Windows machine you use at home, or why the yellow in your printed piece has a brownish cast.

▼ TRY IT YOURSELF

Get Started with Color Modes

By now, your head is probably jammed with new terminology and you're wondering when you'll actually get to see and play with some color. The time has come! Because the pictures in this book are in black and white, working through the steps in this exercise will give you a better understanding of the concepts that we've been talking about. Let's look at a colorful image and examine how Photoshop's different color modes affect the way the picture's color appears.

1. First, find a colorful picture and open it. (If you want to use the photo shown in Figure 4.7, you can download it from the Sams website; it's called peony.jpg.) 'Now take a look at the title bar at the top of your image window. If you don't see the letters RGB in parentheses after the filename, choose Image, Mode, RGB Color. This is your starting point. If your monitor is correctly adjusted, you should see very good color.

FIGURE 4.7
Color makes the image.

2. Choose Image, Mode, Grayscale. A dialog asks whether you want to discard the image's color information; click OK. Photoshop then examines your image and remaps all of its colors to 256 shades of gray that cover the whole range between white and black.

You can see in the status bar at the bottom of the image window how the size of your file diminishes. (If you don't see the file size at the bottom of the document window, choose Show, Document Sizes from the pop-up menu just to the left of the bottom scrollbar.) This reduction occurs because the amount of data in a color image is much greater than that required to display a grayscale image: Color images can contain millions of individual colors, but grayscale images can contain only 256 shades. In this case, the file size decreased by more than 1MB. (The second number is the size that the file will have if saved in Photoshop format.)

3. Before moving on, you need to return the image to its original RGB mode. Choose Edit, Undo.

This time, you're going to change the RGB image to CMYK. Getting this process right becomes enormously important if you'll be taking your images to a commercial printer. RGB can display a number of colors that CMYK, by the nature of its four inks, cannot reproduce. For instance, printing inks can only approximate neon colors.

Before making the mode change, let's take a closer look at some of the colors in this RGB image to see whether they can be reproduced in CMYK (see Figure 4.8).

TRY IT YOURSELF ▼

Get Started with Color Modes

continued

FIGURE 4.8
The triangle symbol means that the color is not part of the CMYK gamut.

▼ TRY IT YOURSELF

Get Started with Color Modes

continued

A. Click the Eyedropper tool in the Tools panel.

B. Next, open the Color panel by choosing Window, Color.

C. Use the Eyedropper to select (click) a color in the image. If you're working with the lily image from the book's website, try clicking the darker yellow stamens in the center of the peony.

D. Look in the Color panel. Do you see an out-of-gamut warning there? This little triangle indicates that the process colors of CMYK cannot precisely reproduce the selected color, which means the color will be converted to a different color when you change modes—you'll get a color that will definitely be similar to the original, but it might not be what you want. Click the warning triangle to see what Photoshop thinks is the nearest color that can be achieved in CMYK mode.

E. To get an idea of how far out of gamut your colors are, choose View, Gamut Warning. As you learned earlier in the hour, this shows you which colors will be lost or modified during the translation from RGB mode to CMYK mode. Figure 4.9 shows what the gamut warning looks like for this picture. Out-of-gamut areas are shown as gray patches. Remember, you can choose the gamut warning color in Photoshop's preferences, so feel free to change it to a color that stands out nicely from the rest of the picture.

FIGURE 4.9
The dark patches indicate out-of-gamut colors.

4. To change the mode from RGB to CMYK, choose Image, Mode, CMYK. Notice that the image's file size increases; this is because Photoshop has to keep track of four color channels instead of just three. We look more closely at color channels in the next hour.

5. After you've seen and perhaps printed the picture in CMYK mode, feel free to experiment with the other modes, too.

If you have a color printer, try reverting to RGB, and then print your picture and compare it to what you see onscreen. Does it look OK? If so, you're in luck—your monitor is accurately calibrated. If not, you need to calibrate your monitor so that the images onscreen accurately display the colors as they will print. Calibration is covered in the "What's Color Management?" section in Hour 23, "Printing and Publishing Your Images." If your monitor seems to need calibration, you can jump ahead to that section.

Color Bit Depth and Why It Matters

Bit depth is a way to describe how much color information is available about each pixel in an image. It's also called color depth—and, as you might expect, more is better. A higher bit depth (meaning more bits of information per pixel) yields more available colors and more accurate color representation in your digital images. Common values for bit depth range from 1 to 64 bits per pixel, but you will find that your color Photoshop images tend to be either 8-bit or 16-bit.

8-Bit Color

It's actually a little bit misleading to call 8-bit color by that name: What you really get with 8-bit color is 8 bits *per color channel*. So depending on the color mode you've chosen to work in, you have anywhere from 8 to 32 bits of information for each pixel. Because grayscale images have only one color channel, an 8-bit grayscale image really does have only 8 total bits of color data. In RGB mode, you have 8 bits each for the red, blue, and green color channels, making 24 total bits of color information. And in CMYK mode, you have 8 bits each for four channels, or 32 bits in all.

16-Bit Color

In older versions of Photoshop, not all of the tools and filters worked with 16-bit color. In Photoshop CS3, all tools and most filters became 16-bit compatible. Does this mean you should do all your work in 16-bit color? No. Technology moves forward in uneven leaps. Even though Photoshop can work in 16-bit color, your monitor can't show you all the millions of colors your image can contain at the higher bit depth. And your home/office inkjet or color laser printer can't possibly reproduce them. This could change eventually as new HDTV monitors and better printing

NOTE

Color Is Critical

Whether they realize it or not, people pay a lot of attention to color. For example, all the marketing done by ING Direct, the online bank, has made its orange logo so identifiable that the company now includes the word "orange" in the names of all its account types: Electric Orange for checking, Orange Savings Account for saving, and Easy Orange for mortgages. When people see that shade of orange, they think of ING, even if it's just subconsciously. And your eye for color might be even more accurate than you think it is; I'll bet if I handed you a couple red color swatches, you'd have no trouble telling Washington Redskins burgundy from Ohio State scarlet and Boston Red Sox true red.

NOTE

The Fine Print on Bits

The term **bit** is an amalgamation of the words "binary digit." Binary notation is a system of representing numbers that's based on two possible values for each digit: 0 or 1. By contrast, in our standard decimal notation, each digit can have 10 values: 0 through 9. So if you have 8 bits that you can use to describe a color, that's eight digits, each of which can have one of two values. That comes out to 256 possible values for that string of bits and, hence, 256 different colors or shades it can describe.

inks come on the market. The next frontier will be 32-bit color—but Photoshop's support for that at this point is still so limited that it's best to leave it alone.

You can find out what kind of color an image uses by checking the setting in the Image menu's Mode submenu. If the checkmark is next to 8 Bits/Channel, for example, then the image is in 8-bit color. Converting upward to 16-bit color won't make a difference, so the only time you should see a checkmark next to 16 Bits/Channel is when the image came to you that way.

Summary

Color is fun to play with, but a lot of technicalities are involved in working with it. Color models are a way of describing colors; there are a lot of them, but the four color models that Photoshop understands are HSB, RGB, CMYK, and CIE Lab color. Photoshop's color modes enable you to use different color models for different images. RGB is the most useful color mode because it's the way your monitor displays color. The CMYK and Grayscale modes, on the other hand, are used for printing.

In this hour, we discussed Photoshop's color modes and how Photoshop makes use of the different color models. We also looked at what happens when you convert an image from one mode to another.

In the next hour, you'll delve deeper into the world of color by learning how to make tonal adjustments and color modifications.

Q&A

Q. Is there ever a time when I would want to work in Lab color?

A. Professional photographers and prepress experts use the Lab color mode for very sophisticated color adjustments and conversions, but it's unlikely that you'll ever run into a need for it. Take it from me—I've been using Photoshop for almost 20 years, and I never use Lab color.

Q. I thought you said it was called CIE Lab, not just Lab. What does "CIE" mean?

A. It stands for Commission Internationale de l'Éclairage, which is French for International Commission on Illumination. As you probably know, the French have a commission for everything, and CIE is their governing body for standard methods of describing color. The CIE standards are used worldwide.

Q. Why isn't the CMYK gamut larger than the RGB gamut, when CMYK has four color channels instead of only three?

A. A color model's gamut doesn't include all the colors that can theoretically be described using that model; it includes only the colors that can *really* be achieved. Because pigments can go all muddy when you mix them together, some colors that you could produce with CMYK in theory just don't work in practical conditions. Colored light, the basis for the RGB color model, doesn't have that problem.

Workshop

Quiz

1. How many colors can an indexed color palette contain?

    A. 2

    B. 8

    C. 256

    D. Millions

   2. What primary color is directly opposite red on the color wheel?

      A. Cyan

      B. Green

      C. Yellow

      D. Blue

   3. True or false: HSB stands for hue, saturation, and blackness.

Answers

   1. **C.** But you can choose them from the millions of colors contained in the RGB gamut.

   2. **A.** Each of the RGB primaries is opposite one of the CMY(K) primaries; red is opposite yellow, and green is opposite magenta.

   3. **False.** The *B* in HSB stands for brightness, not blackness; however, a brightness value of 0 combined with any hue or saturation level does yield black.

Exercise

Here's a chance to get your own mental picture of which RGB colors just don't translate to CMYK. First, create a new blank document in RGB mode. Choose View, Swatches to bring up the Swatches panel; then switch to the Paint Bucket tool. (It's under the Gradient tool.) Click the first red swatch at the top of the panel and then click in the window to fill the image with red. Now choose Image, Mode, CMYK to switch to CMYK mode. See how the color darkens? Press Command-Z/Ctrl+Z to undo, and then fill the window with the first blue swatch at the top of the window (not the cyan one—we want royal blue, which is the blue from RGB). Switch to CMYK mode again. See the *huge* color change? These two colors, true red and true blue, just can't be reproduced exactly in CMYK. Now repeat this process with different colors from the Swatches panel, each time reverting to RGB mode before filling the image window. Note which colors change the most when you switch to CMYK and which ones change the least.

HOUR 5
Adjusting Brightness and Color

Messing around with color—and I do use the term "messing around" advisedly—is a little bit science, a little bit art. You can make some adjustments "by the numbers," such as darkening an image's darkest points so they're true white, but others have to be made by eye. When it comes right down to it, color is really all in your head—and that's a good thing. In this hour, we look mostly at ways to "fix" the color in your pictures, making it more lifelike and true to the original. Of course, you can use the same methods for more nefarious purposes; if you want to make the sky green and the grass purple, that's well within your reach using Photoshop.

Photoshop includes a full set of tools for making color adjustments, located on the Image, Adjustments submenu (see Figure 5.1). Some of these terms, such as Brightness/Contrast, might be familiar to you; others might not. Don't worry; you'll learn about them all in this hour.

WHAT YOU'LL LEARN IN THIS HOUR:

▶ Evaluating Your Color Adjustment Needs

▶ Adjusting by Eye with Variations

▶ Making Other Adjustments

▶ Preserving the Original with Adjustment Layers

▶ Understanding Channels

▶ Making Spot Fixes

▶ Converting Color to Black and White

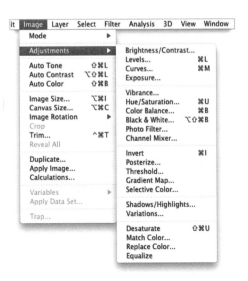

FIGURE 5.1
The Adjustments submenu gives you all the tools you'll need to produce a more (or less) true-to-life image.

Evaluating Your Color Adjustment Needs

Before you start to adjust color, you need to make sure the image uses the right color mode; to do that, you have to evaluate what kind of color the picture contains and how you'll eventually use the image. You learned about color models and color modes in the last hour, so you know that RGB mode is the way color is displayed on computer screens, and CMYK mode is the way color is printed. Because image colors can shift when you switch from one mode to another, it makes sense to adjust the color in a picture according to the way it will be displayed. For a picture that's going on a web page, you should work in RGB mode. If your picture will be printed on a four-color process commercial press, work in RGB to start with, but make your final adjustments (if any are needed) after you convert the image to CMYK mode. If you'll be printing on a home/office inkjet printer, stick with RGB, even though your printer uses CMYK inks. The software drivers for desktop inkjet printers are designed to convert from RGB to CMYK internally. Other kinds of color printers, such as color lasers, work fine with CMYK mode. On the other hand, if the picture is destined to be output or displayed in grayscale, forget about trying to make the sky a perfect blue; change the color mode to Grayscale and make the brightness and contrast perfect instead. Just keep these few rules in mind, and you won't go wrong. Table 5.1 helps you keep your options sorted out.

TABLE 5.1   Color Adjustment Matrix

Adjust Color In	If Output Is
RGB	Computer screen, the Web, or inkjet printer
RGB first, and then CMYK	Process color printing
Grayscale	Black-and-white printing

Adjusting by Eye with Variations

The most obvious way to make a color adjustment is to compare before and after views of an image, and Photoshop offers you a tool for doing just this— Variations. The Variations command combines several image-adjustment tools into one easy-to-use dialog, complete with thumbnail images that show you variations on the original image. You simply click the thumbnail that looks best to you, and Photoshop applies the corresponding adjustment. You can choose variations of hue and brightness and then see the result (which Photoshop calls **Current Pick**) side by side with the original.

Figure 5.2 shows the Variations dialog box. When you first open it, the Current Pick is the same as the original; as you click thumbnails to apply changes, the Current Pick updates to show your changes. The slider ranges from Fine to Coarse and determines how much effect each click has on the original image. Moving the slider one tick mark in either direction doubles or halves the previously specified amount, with the finest setting making changes that are so slight that they're almost undetectable. Use the coarsest setting only if you're looking for a really extreme effect. Normally, you'll want to stick with a setting somewhere in the middle.

TIP

Something Missing?

If Variations doesn't appear on the Adjustments submenu, check the Image, Mode sub-menu to make sure you're in 8-bit color mode and that you're not using Lab or Indexed Color mode. If those settings are OK, the Variations plug-in might not have been installed. Consult the Photoshop help system to learn more about using plug-ins.

FIGURE 5.2
The seven thumbnails at the lower left adjust hue, and the three on the right side adjust brightness.

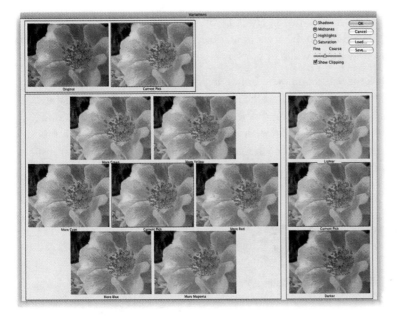

Adjusting Shadows, Midtones, Highlights, and Saturation

With Variations, you can adjust a color image's shadows, midtones, high-lights, or overall color saturation. **Shadows**, **midtones**, and **highlights** are Photoshop's terms for the darkest areas, the medium areas, and the lightest areas of the image, respectively; these are black, gray, and white in a grayscale picture. Depending on which you choose, your changes modify the color (hue) of the image's shadows, midtones, or highlights. The Saturation setting affects all three brightness levels at once, increasing or decreasing the intensity of the color without changing it.

The advantage of restricting color changes to one part of the picture is that you can adjust the midtones one way and the highlights or shadows another way, if you want. Each setting is independent of the others, so you can, for example, set the midtones to be more blue, thus brightening the sky, yet still set the shadows to be more yellow to compensate for their inherent blue tinge.

If a highlight or shadow color is adjusted so much that it becomes pure white or pure black, that's called **clipping**. If you check the Show Clipping box in the Variations dialog, you'll see a neon-colored preview of areas in the image that will be clipped by the adjustment; you can change your settings to minimize the amount of clipping that takes place. Clipping occurs only when you adjust highlights and shadows; it's not a problem when you're working solely with midtones.

Remember, as you learned in Hour 4, "Specifying Color Modes and Color Models," **hue** refers to the color of an object or selection. The **Brightness** value measures how much white or black is mixed into the color.

If you click the Saturation radio button instead of Shadows, Midtones, or Highlights, your changes affect the intensity of the color in the image; the thumbnails offer you only two choices: Less Saturation or More Saturation. Figure 5.3 shows what Variations looks like when you're adjusting saturation. Remember that you can apply the same correction more than once. For instance, if less saturation still leaves more color in the image than you want, click the Less Saturation thumbnail again to reduce the color intensity even more.

FIGURE 5.3
My increases in saturation are resulting in clipping, shown in all three thumbnails.

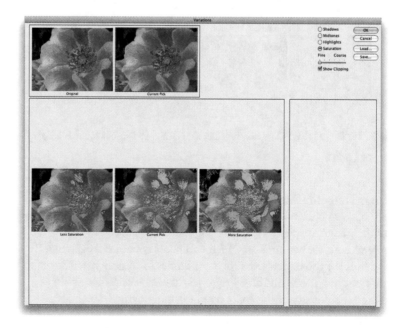

Adjust an Image Using Variations

Working with the Variations dialog is an excellent way to experiment with how colors work.

1. Open any color image and choose Image, Adjustments, Variations.

2. Click the appropriate radio button according to what you want to adjust: Shadows, Midtones, Highlights, or Saturation.

3. Use the Fine/Coarse slider to determine how much each thumbnail click will change the image.

4. Watch the Original and Current Pick thumbnails as you click different thumbnails. Here are some tips for achieving just the effect you want:

   ▶ To add more of a color, click the appropriate color thumbnail.

   ▶ To reduce a color, click the thumbnail opposite it, which increases the color's opposite on the color wheel. To reduce magenta, for example, click the More Green thumbnail.

   ▶ To adjust the picture's brightness, click the Lighter or Darker thumbnail on the right.

   ▶ If you're not sure exactly what you need to do, simply click the image that looks most correct to you.

   ▶ If you think you might have overdone your corrections and want to go back to the original image, press Option (Mac) or Alt (Windows) to change the Cancel button to a Reset button. Click the Reset button to restore the settings to 0 and revert to the original image. (*Note:* This fix works in all the adjustment dialog boxes.)

5. Click OK when you're done, or click Cancel to undo all your adjustments and leave the image untouched.

Saving and Loading Corrections

Two other buttons appear in this dialog box and in each of the other adjustment dialog boxes: the Load and Save buttons. If you have a whole series of pictures that need the same kind of corrections, you can save yourself a lot of time by applying the same settings to each image. Perhaps you used your digital camera to shoot several outdoor pictures with the same lousy light conditions, or maybe your scanner tends to make everything a little more yellow than you want. After you determine the settings that correct one picture perfectly, you can save your settings for the first image and then load them again to apply to each of the remaining images.

When you click the Save button, you'll see a typical dialog asking you to supply a name for your settings, such as foggy day fix or scanner correction. When you need to apply the same settings to another picture, click the Load button, and then locate and open the appropriate setting file. All the dialog settings instantly return to the values you applied to the original image, and clicking OK applies the correction.

Making Other Adjustments

Variations is a quick and intuitive way to adjust color, but sometimes it doesn't give you enough control. Other times you just want to experiment. These are the times when you'll want to work with individual adjustment settings.

Consulting the Histogram

Photoshop's Histogram panel was once a dialog box; now it's even easier to get to, and you can have it open on your screen all the time. As with the Info panel, the Histogram panel doesn't actually do anything, but if you learn how to use it, you can really improve the quality of your pictures.

If you ever studied statistics, you already know that a histogram is a type of graph. In Photoshop, it's a graph of the image that can show you the image's brightness levels overall or broken down by color. The height of the graph indicates the number of pixels at each brightness level from 0 to 255.

You might wonder why this is important. Mainly, you can tell by looking at the histogram whether there's enough contrast in the image to allow you to apply corrections successfully. If you're working with a photo that looks pretty bad at first glance, studying the histogram will tell you whether it's worth working on or whether you should trash the image and start fresh. If all the higher levels of the graph are bunched up at one end of the graph, and the image isn't supposed to be very dark or very light, you probably can't save the picture by adjusting it. On the other hand, if you have a reasonably well-spread-out histogram, there's a wide enough range of values to suggest that the picture can be saved. Watch out for gaps in the middle of the graph and for ends that cut off suddenly instead of tapering gently down to 0. Figure 5.4 shows the histogram for a reasonably well-exposed photo alongside the graph of a problematic image.

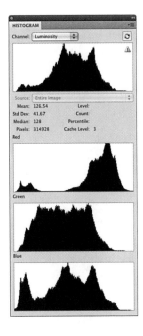 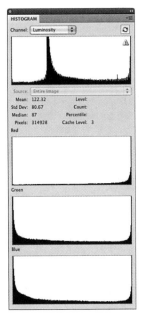

FIGURE 5.4
Can you tell which picture is probably beyond help from looking at these histograms? Answer: It's the one with the big spike in the middle of a flat graph.

Adjusting Levels

The Levels command gives you a method of adjusting the brightness of an image based on a version of the picture's histogram (see Figure 5.5). Setting the **black point** (the slider at the left of the histogram that represents absolutely saturated black) to match the concentration of darkest levels in the image, and setting the **white point** (the slider on the right, indicating completely unsaturated white) to match the concentration of the lightest levels in the image forces the rest of the levels to spread out more evenly across the graph. If you want to experiment with the photo I'm using in these examples, it's available on the book's website; the file is called pathway.jpg.

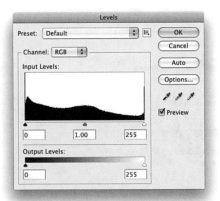

FIGURE 5.5
Be sure to check the Preview box so that you can see the effect of your changes.

Adjust Brightness Using Levels

When the colors are fine but the photo seems too dull or dark, adjusting the brightness can help. Follow these steps to make that adjustment using the Levels command:

1. Choose Image, Adjustments, Levels, or press Command-L (Mac) or Ctrl+L (Windows).

2. Check the Preview box so that you can see your changes in the image window.

3. Adjust the levels to improve the picture by moving each of the three sliders below the histogram to the left or right. Here are a few tips for getting the effect you're looking for:

   ▶ To set the black point (the darkest black) in the image, move the slider at the left side of the Input Levels histogram to the point at which the graph heads sharply upward.

   ▶ Set the white point (the whitest tone) by moving the right Input Levels slider to the point where the light pixels begin to rise.

   ▶ Adjust the midrange by watching the picture while you move the Input Levels middle slider left (to lighten midtones) or right (to darken midtones). Figure 5.6 shows the settings for this picture.

FIGURE 5.6
Adjusting the darks helps bring out shadow detail.

4. To reduce the contrast in the image, use the sliders on the Output Levels bar. The black slider controls the dark tones; moving it toward the center excludes all the dark levels to the left of the slider from the picture. The white slider controls the light tones; moving it toward the center darkens the lightest areas of the image by preventing them from being any darker than the shade shown on the slider at that point.

5. Click OK when you're done.

You can also use the Levels dialog's special Eyedropper tools to adjust the levels. Click the white Eyedropper (on the right) and click the lightest part of your image. Then switch to the dark-tipped Eyedropper (on the left) and click the darkest point on the image. To adjust the midtones, you can use the gray midrange Eyedropper (in the middle) to locate an area in the image that should be right in the middle of the brightness spectrum. Avoid using the midrange Eyedropper in a color image—stick to grayscale images—unless it has an area that's supposed to be a neutral gray—neither reddish (warm) nor bluish (cool); if you click in a colored area, Photoshop adjusts all the image's colors so that the area you clicked in doesn't have any color.

Adjusting Curves

Adjusting curves is much like adjusting levels, with a bit more control. You can use the Curves dialog box instead of the Levels dialog box to adjust the brightness. The big difference between using Levels and using Curves is that, with Curves, instead of adjusting at only three points (black, middle, and white), you can adjust at any point (see Figure 5.7).

Despite the name, the Curves dialog box doesn't display a curve when you first open it. Instead, you see a graph containing a grid overlaid with a diagonal line. The horizontal axis of the grid represents the original brightness values (input levels) of the image or selection, whereas the vertical axis represents the new brightness values (output levels). When you open the Curves dialog, the graph starts out as a straight diagonal line because no new values have been mapped; the input and output values are identical for all the pixels in the image. As always, be sure to check the Preview box before doing anything else so that you can see the effects of your changes in the image window.

NOTE

Channeling Colors

In a color image, you can adjust the composite RGB or CMYK color image (choose RGB or CMYK in the Channel pop-up menu), or you can work with the picture's individual color components by choosing a color channel from the Channel menu. For now, keep working with the composite. (You'll learn more about channels later in this hour.)

TIP

You "Auto" Try it

If you click Auto in the Levels dialog box or choose Auto Tone from the Image, Adjustments menu, Photoshop adjusts the levels based on its evaluation of the tonal range. Sometimes this works great; other times it produces an image that's too bright and too contrasty. Try it, but be prepared to undo if you don't like the results. You'll find that the Presets pop-up menu at the top of the dialog has more specific options; pick the preset that's closest to what you're trying to do and modify its settings until you get what you want.

FIGURE 5.7
On this kind of graph, the zero
point is in the middle.

As with the Levels dialog box, you can click Auto to have Photoshop make
the adjustment for you, you can choose an option from the Preset pop-up
menu, or you can use the Eyedroppers to adjust the values. Because the
Curves method of adjusting brightness gives you so much more control,
however, it's worth making your changes manually. Click and drag over a
portion of the image that needs adjusting. You'll see a circle on the graph
at the point representing the brightness level of the pixel under the cursor.
If you don't want to change certain points on the curve, click them now to
lock them down. For instance, if you want to adjust the picture's midtones
while leaving its dark and light areas alone, click the light and dark points
on the curve to fix them in place. Then click to add a point in the middle of
the curve and drag up or down until the image looks right to you.
Dragging up lightens tones, whereas dragging down darkens them (see
Figure 5.8). To remove a point, click and drag it off the grid.

FIGURE 5.8
You can add up to 16 points on
the curve.

In Photoshop CS4, Curves has a new feature: You can click the On-Canvas Adjustment button and then click and drag right in the picture to adjust the graph (see Figure 5.9). This way, when you click and drag in the image to locate the corresponding point on the graph, you can then go ahead and make the adjustment right there, without having to move your mouse over to the Curves dialog. One great application for this feature is fixing clipped areas: Click the Show Clipping box so that you can see where the clipped areas are; then click each area with the On-Canvas Adjustment tool and drag up or down to ameliorate the clipping.

If you're comfortable drawing freehand, you can also adjust the Curves graph by clicking the Pencil tool in the upper-left corner of the dialog and then clicking and dragging in the graph. This is an especially effective way to work if you're using a graphics tablet and stylus instead of a mouse, trackball, or trackpad; as you've probably noticed, it's quite difficult to draw neat curves with a mouse.

FIGURE 5.9
To make on-canvas adjustments, click the button labeled with a finger icon, and then click and drag right in the picture. Here I'm working on the iron planter at the left edge of the image.

It's Simple

To make the Curves dialog's grid squares smaller, Option-click (Mac) or Alt-click (Windows) the grid. Repeat to return to the default larger grid squares. Or, if you prefer, click the Simple Grid or Detailed Grid button in the Curve Display Options area to switch modes. The Simple Grid option divides the graph into quarters each way, and the Detailed Grid option gives you gridlines at 10% increments.

Click the disclosure triangle labeled Curve Display Options at the bottom of the Curves dialog to see a few choices you can make about how the graph is displayed. First, you can choose to display Light levels or Pigment/Ink levels; if dragging upward to darken the image and downward to lighten it makes more sense to you, then switch to the Pigment/Ink display. The four check boxes below enable you to hide or show channel overlays, the baseline (the graph's original line), the histogram (the graph of brightness levels), and the intersection line (the vertical and horizontal lines that appear when you move a point on the graph).

Adjusting Color Balance

To really understand color balance, you have to look at the color wheel (see Figure 5.10).

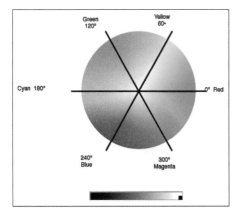

FIGURE 5.10
If the color wheel were a clock, red
would be at 3 o'clock and cyan
would be at 9 o'clock.

If you follow the line from any color on the color wheel through the center and over to the other side of the wheel, you reach that color's opposite. Cyan is opposite red, green is opposite magenta, and yellow is opposite blue. With the Color Balance dialog, you reduce one color by adding more of its opposite. Increasing cyan reduces red. Increasing red reduces cyan, and so on, around the wheel.

Color Balance is intended to be used to adjust color throughout an image, although, of course, you can use it with just part of the image selected (see Figure 5.11). For example, if you're dealing with a picture that has an overall color cast, such as an old, yellowed photograph, Color Balance makes it simple to remove the yellow without altering the rest of the colors in picture. Just use a light touch, and make sure you check the entire image before clicking OK, in case your changes have actually introduced a new color cast.

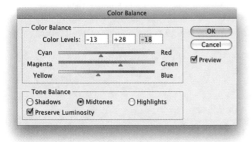

FIGURE 5.11
Drag the sliders in the direction of
the color you want to add to the
picture.

As with the Variations command described earlier, Color Balance requires you to indicate whether you want to work on an image's shadows, midtones, or highlights. And because color changes can affect an image's overall brightness, Color Balance provides you with a Preserve Luminosity check box; turn this on to make sure that your changes affect only the hue component of each color in the image, leaving the brightness as is.

▼ TRY IT YOURSELF

Apply Color Balance

Color balance can rescue pictures that have faded, and it can turn red roses blue or blue ducks red. It's fun to play with.

1. Open the image you want to work with; if you like, select the portion of the image to correct. Open the Color Balance dialog by choosing Image, Adjustments, Color Balance or pressing Command-B (Mac) or Ctrl+B (Windows).

2. Click a radio button for Shadows, Midtones, or Highlights. Generally, it's reasonable to start with midtones because midtones comprise 90% of most images. But if you know that you want to work with only the image's light or dark areas, click Highlights or Shadows, respectively.

3. Check the Preserve Luminosity box so that the color shifts you apply don't change the brightness of the image. If maintaining the brightness isn't important, don't enable the check box. If you're not sure, try checking and unchecking the box a few times after you make your changes, to see its effect. (Be sure to check the Preview box so that you can see your changes in the image window.)

4. Drag the sliders to adjust the image's colors. The numbers in the boxes change to indicate how much of a change you are making. They range from 0 to +100 (toward red, green, and blue) and from 0 to –100 (toward cyan, magenta, and yellow).

5. When you're happy with the midtones, adjust the shadows and then the highlights. You can keep modifying the corrections until the image looks correct to you; if you want to start over again, press Option/Alt and click Reset.

6. Click OK to apply the changes.

Adjusting Hue and Saturation

As you know, you can adjust the hue, saturation, and brightness of an individual color in the Color Picker. With the Hue/Saturation dialog, you can do the same to every color in the image (or in a selection) simultaneously. Don't be misled by the fact that "Brightness" isn't part of the command's name; it's included in the dialog nonetheless in the form of a Lightness slider.

First, look at the controls in the Hue/Saturation dialog box (see Figure 5.12). As with the Levels and Curves dialogs, Hue/Saturation offers you several prefab combinations of settings in the Preset pop-up menu. These make good starting points for your own adjustments. The second pop-up menu lets you choose either a single color to adjust or the Master option, which adjusts all the colors in the image or selection at the same time. For now, choose Master from the menu. Check Preview so that you'll be able to monitor the effects of your changes in the image window.

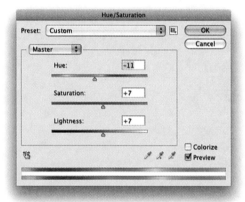

FIGURE 5.12
Minor adjustments to lightness and saturation are usually all you need to make a major improvement in an image.

Now let's take a look at the three sliders: Hue, Saturation, and Lightness:

▶ The Hue slider displays a flattened version of the color wheel. With Master selected, dragging the slider shifts all the image's colors the corresponding distance around the wheel. Starting with red (in the middle of the slider), you can move all the way left—through purple to blue or blue-green—or right through orange to yellow and to green.

▶ The Saturation slider starts out at 0%, in the center, and you can drag it right to 100% saturated (pure color, with no gray), or left to –100%, or completely unsaturated (no color).

▶ The Lightness slider lets you increase or decrease the image's brightness, from 0 in the center to +100 on the right or –100 on the left.

As you move each of the sliders, watch the two spectrum bars at the bottom of the dialog, as well as the image itself. The upper bar represents the current status of the image, and the lower one shows how each color in the

NOTE

Light Is Bright

Lightness is technically the
same as brightness; in fact,
you might run into the term
HSL, which stands for hue, saturation, and lightness, and
means the same thing as HSB.
Less common, but still synony-
mous with HSB, are the terms
HSI (hue, saturation, and intensity) and **HSV** (hue, saturation,
and value).

image changes according to the slider(s) you move. If you drag the Hue
slider to +60, for example, you can see by comparing the two spectrum
bars that the reds in the picture will turn quite yellow and the blues will
turn purple. In effect, you are skewing the entire color spectrum by 60°. If
you move the Saturation slider to the left, you'll see the lower spectrum
bar become less saturated. If you move the Lightness slider, you'll see its
effects reflected in the lower spectrum bar as well.

If you choose an individual color from the pop-up menu, instead of leaving
it set at Master, the Hue/Saturation dialog changes slightly, as you can see
in Figure 5.13. The Eyedroppers are now active, enabling you to choose the
colors you want to modify from the image, and adjustable range sliders are
centered on the color you've chosen to adjust. You can move these back and
forth to focus on as broad or narrow a range around that color as you want.

FIGURE 5.13
You can extend the range of colors
to be affected by dragging the
edges of the range selector
between the two spectrum bars.

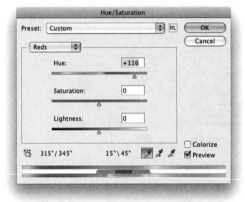

TIP

One Color, Two Color

The Colorize option applies a
monotone effect, using a single
color. For a similar but more
sophisticated effect, try choosing Image, Mode, Grayscale and
then Image, Mode, Duotone.
Chose Duotone from the pop-up
menu, and then click the color
swatches to choose "ink" colors. Most duotones use black
for the first color and any color
you like for the second color.
Click the curve swatch next to
each color swatch to change
how much of that color is
applied; most often, you'll want
to tone down the black (by dragging down on the curve's middle) and bump up the other
color (by dragging up).

You might have noticed the Colorize check box just above the
Hue/Saturation dialog's Preview check box. When you check this box,
Photoshop doesn't just shift the image's colors along the color wheel; it
applies shades of the chosen color to the entire image. Check the Colorize
box and take a look: You'll see that the Hue slider handle moves all the
way to the left, with a value of 0; the Saturation value changes to 25, and
the Lightness value stays put at 0, with its normal range of –100 to 100.
Meanwhile, the lower spectrum bar, indicating changed colors, changes to
a single color: the color that Photoshop is applying to the whole picture.

When you're using the Hue/Saturation dialog, be sure to check the entire image before clicking OK, instead of just focusing on the photo's main subject, in case your changes have had unintended consequences elsewhere in the image.

1. To get started, choose Image, Adjustments, Hue/Saturation, or press Command-U (Mac) or Ctrl+U (Windows). Check the Preview box to see your changes in the image window as you make them.

2. Use the pop-up menu to choose the color range you want to adjust, or leave it set at Master (the default setting) to adjust all the colors.

3. Drag each of the three sliders to the left or right. Here are a few tips for getting the effect you want:

   ▶ Drag the Hue slider left or right until the colors look the way you want. The numbers shown in the Hue entry field refer to the degree of rotation around the color wheel from the selected color's original location.

   ▶ Drag the Saturation slider left to decrease the saturation of the colors by moving them toward gray; drag the slider right to increase their saturation.

   ▶ Drag the Lightness slider to increase or decrease the brightness of the image.

4. As with the Curves dialog, the Hue/Saturation dialog now has an On-Canvas Adjustment tool. Click its button, in the lower-left corner of the dialog just above the spectrum bars, to adjust colors by dragging directly on the picture. The adjustments are applied to the color on which you click, wherever it appears throughout the image; dragging left and right adjusts the Saturation value, and Command-clicking/Ctrl-clicking and dragging left and right modifies the Hue value.

5. Click OK when you're done.

Adjusting Vibrance

New in Photoshop CS4, the Vibrance slider increases saturation in undersaturated areas of the image while leaving highly saturated areas alone. This differs from the Saturation slider in the Hue/Saturation dialog, which increases saturation uniformly throughout the image. Vibrance tends to leave skin tones alone, so you won't end up with orange or hot pink faces when you try to bump up the saturation in an image that has people in it.

Vibrance is particularly useful for fixing blown-out areas (too-bright high-lights) without overbrightening or oversaturating the rest of the picture.

To use Vibrance, choose Image, Adjustments, Vibrance (see Figure 5.14). You'll notice that the dialog has two sliders: Vibrance and Saturation. Drag the Vibrance slider to add or reduce saturation without making colors gar-ish; this control stays away from skin tones and concentrates on primary colors (both the RGB and the CMYK primaries). Use this more subtle ver-sion of the Saturation slider to increase saturation without risk of blowing out the image and turning it into pop art. It focuses only on colors that the Vibrance slider doesn't affect.

FIGURE 5.14
Use the sliders to adjust satura-tion more realistically.

Adjusting Brightness and Contrast

Photoshop's Brightness/Contrast function isn't new, but it has definitely improved in the last couple of versions. If you need to make a simple adjust-ment to the tonal range of an image that's too dark, the Brightness/Contrast dialog box (choose Image, Adjustments, Brightness/Contrast) seems like an easy way to accomplish just that (see Figure 5.15), right? However, in older versions of Photoshop, Brightness/Contrast applied the same correction throughout the image, meaning that if you made the image brighter, you ended up with gray shadows and stark white highlights along with your nice, bright midtones. Since CS3, however, that's all changed; Brightness/ Contrast now separately corrects the dark, middle, and light values.

FIGURE 5.15
Here I'm using Brightness/ Contrast to make it evening on the pathway.

Although the Brightness/Contrast dialog doesn't give you the same fine control that you would have if you made the adjustments using Levels or Curves, or even Variations, it's quick and easy. Sometimes it's all you need. Many images can be wildly improved by just raising the brightness and contrast by a couple points. As always, be sure to check the Preview box so that you can see the effect of your changes in the image window. So how is it done? Pretty simple: Dragging the sliders to the right of the middle point increases brightness or contrast. Dragging them to the left decreases it.

If you want to make everything in your picture lighter or darker, you can revert temporarily to the old version of the Brightness/Contrast function by clicking the Legacy check box.

Correcting Shadows and Highlights

One of the coolest features in Photoshop is the Shadows/Highlights command; I use it on pretty much every photo. It enables you to control the lightness levels in highlight and shadow areas independently. If you apply it to the pathway photo, for example, you can bring out shadow detail without making the sunny areas washed out, or darken the highlights a bit without making the shadows muddy. Be sure to check the Show More Options box to open the full set of sliders, as shown in Figure 5.16. Photoshop starts you out with what it thinks is an appropriate amount of correction the second you open the dialog, so be prepared to back off on that a bit for a less startling change. I click the Preview box off and on repeatedly to compare before and after versions of the image on the fly.

FIGURE 5.16
Experiment with these sliders on both high-contrast and low-contrast images.

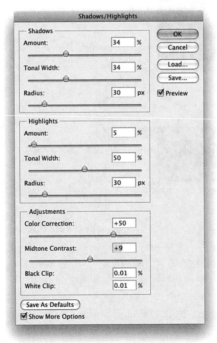

Applying Photo Filters

When traditional photographers want a special effect, they use colored filters over their camera lenses. With Photoshop's Photo Filters command, you can do the same thing to any image, whether it came from a camera, was scanned, or was created from scratch. To open the Photo Filter dialog, choose Image, Adjustments, Photo Filter. In Figure 5.17, I have expanded the menu of filters so you can see the many options available. Serious photographers will recognize the numbers after the warming and cooling filters, because they're the same as on the glass filters you can buy at a camera store. Use the Density slider to control the strength of the filter.

FIGURE 5.17
Photo filters apply a little (or a lot) of a specified color to the entire image.

What Else Is on the Menu?

It's almost time to wrap up your tour of the Adjustments submenu. Here's a look at a few commands in and near the Adjustments submenu that we haven't covered yet and that you might find useful.

You might recall the Auto Tone command from earlier in this hour; it applies Photoshop's best guess at the perfect Levels correction. Its relative, Auto Contrast (choose Image, Adjustments, Auto Contrast), is occasionally quite helpful. It automatically maps the darkest and lightest pixels in the image to black and white, causing highlights to appear lighter and shadows darker. It might not be the best way to make the necessary adjustments, but if you're in a hurry, it can save you some time.

Another Auto command, Auto Color, analyzes the color in an image and makes an educated guess of what it should be. If you're easily satisfied, it might be all the correction you ever need. As for me, I like things perfect, and Photoshop's sense of color is often different from mine. Still, if you want to give it a try (choose Image, Adjustments, Auto Color), often it can give you an idea of which direction to go in for a particular image. Then you can undo and work toward your own vision.

The Adjustment submenu's Desaturate command removes all the color from an image without changing the color mode. If you want a quick look at how something will reproduce in black and white, this is the command to use. Then simply undo it to go back to the colored version. (For a more sophisticated method of converting an image to black and white, check out "Converting Color to Black and White," later in this hour.

Preserving the Original with Adjustment Layers

When you apply a correction to the whole picture, it might improve some parts and make others worse, so you really need to look carefully at the end result and decide whether the good outweighs the bad. You might wish you'd applied the correction to only part of the image, or you might want to go back and try different settings. Fortunately, Photoshop provides you with an easy way to apply a correction and then change your mind as many times as you want.

As we've discussed, one of Photoshop's best features is the capability to work in layers. (You'll learn all about layers in Hour 11, "Creating Layered Images.") For now, you can think of layers as sheets of transparency film that you place over your image and paint or paste on. If you like what you see, you can merge the layers so that the additions become part of the image. If not, you can throw them away and try again. In addition to the layers that you paint on, Photoshop lets you create several kinds of special layers, including **adjustment layers**. These work like normal layers, except that instead of holding paint or pasted pictures, they hold the color adjustments that you make to the image.

You can add an adjustment layer to your image in a few different ways. First, and most logically, you can choose New Adjustment Layer from the Layer menu. You can also add an adjustment layer using the pop-up menu at the bottom of the Layers panel (look for the button with the half-black, half-white circle). Finally, Photoshop CS4 brings us the Adjustments panel, which enables you to add and modify all your adjustment layers in one place (see Figure 5.18).

TRY IT YOURSELF ▼

Add an Adjustment Layer

To create a new adjustment layer in your image, follow these steps:

1. Choose Window, Adjustments to open the Adjustments panel (see Figure 5.18).

FIGURE 5.18
The new Adjustments panel contains the same presets you'll find in individual dialogs such as Levels and Curves.

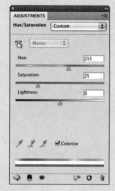

FIGURE 5.19
After the Adjustments panel has switched to displaying the adjustment controls, you can still access the presets for the specified adjustment from a pop-up menu.

2. Click a button to indicate the particular kind of adjustment that you want to make. The panel changes to show the same controls that you'd find in that adjustment's regular dialog (see Figure 5.19).

3. Make whatever adjustments are necessary. Later, in the Layers panel, you can delete the layer if you're not pleased with the changes, or change the layer's Opacity setting to effectively change the strength of the corrections you've made.

4. To change the settings, either click the adjustment layer in the Layers palette and open the Adjustments panel, or double-click the adjustment layer's swatch in the Layers panel. If you want to change the type of adjustment layer, click the back arrow at the bottom-left corner of the Adjustments panel to return to its initial view.

Understanding Color Channels

Photoshop's Channels panel offers the capability to look at each of the individual color components of an image. Each image has one or more color channels; the number depends on the color mode chosen. A CMYK image has four separate channels. One in RGB mode has three, and grayscale images have only one channel apiece. Each channel holds information about a particular color element in the image. Think of individual channels as something like the plates in the printing process, with a separate plate supplying each layer of color. You can often create interesting textures or special effects by applying filters to just one channel. Figure 5.20 shows the Channels panel (twice) with RGB and CMYK channels.

FIGURE 5.20
In the RGB image on the left, I've selected the mask from an adjustment layer; in the CMYK image on the right, the composite channel is selected, meaning that all the color channels are active.

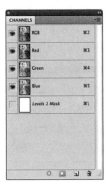

You learned about other channels called **alpha channels**, and their several uses, in Hour 3, "Making Selections." Alpha channels can define the placement of spot colors (Pantone, for example). They also contain the maps for selections you create and want to save with the image to which you have applied them, as well as adjustment-layer masks. Hour 12, "Using Masks," talks more about alpha channels.

Making Spot Fixes

As you know, any of the adjustment commands can be applied to an entire image (or the active layer) or to a selected area. The latter is how you avoid adjusting areas that are already fine, making sure your fixes go only where you want them. But another way to do that is to use Photoshop's retouching tools to apply fixes dab by dab, a bit at a time, just where they're needed.

The Toning Tools

Photoshop is primarily a digital darkroom program, so it makes sense that some of its most useful tools mimic the darkroom techniques that photographers have used for decades to lighten and darken portions of an image or to brighten colors. The Toning tools include the Dodge, Burn, and Sponge tools, each of which can use any of the brush tips available to the painting tools. Dodge and Burn are opposites, like Sharpen and Blur, but instead of affecting the contrast between adjacent pixels, they either lighten or darken the area to which the tool is applied. Sponging changes the color saturation of the area to which you apply it.

Dodge and Burn Tools

Dodging, in the photographer's darkroom, is accomplished by waving a dodge tool, usually a cardboard circle on a wire, between the projected image from the enlarger and the photographic paper. This blocks some of the light and makes the dodged area lighter when the print is developed. It's also called "holding back" because you effectively hold back the light from reaching the paper. Photoshop's Dodge tool, shown in Figure 5.21, looks just like the darkroom version.

FIGURE 5.21
The Toning tools—Dodge, Burn, and Sponge—can use the same range of brush tips as the painting tools.

Burning has the opposite effect of dodging—instead of lightening a small area, it darkens the area. In the darkroom, burning in is accomplished either by using a piece of cardboard with a hole punched out (the opposite of the Dodge tool) or by blocking the enlarger light with your hand so that the light reaches only the area on the print surface to be burned. Photoshop's Burn tool icon is a hand shaped to pass a small beam of light.

Click the Dodge tool and look at the pop-up menu in the Tool Options bar. As you can see, it gives you three choices:

- ▶ Shadows
- ▶ Midtones
- ▶ Highlights

These options indicate the types of pixels that the tool will affect. If you want to adjust the shadows, such as making them lighter and leaving the lighter pixels untouched, select Shadows. The default option for the Dodge tool is Midtones. This is a good choice when you want to affect the mid-tone pixels or when you are unsure of how to proceed. Select Highlights when you want to lighten already light-colored areas, leaving the darker areas untouched. Figure 5.22 shows the effects of dodging and burning on a picture shot outdoors in shade on a sunny day.

FIGURE 5.22
I lightened the tree and darkened
the overexposed leaves.

Sponging

Surprisingly enough, sponging is also a darkroom trick. When a picture in
the developing tray isn't turning dark enough or looks underexposed or
weak in color, the darkroom technician can often save it by sloshing some
fresh, full-strength developing chemical on a sponge and rubbing it directly on the wet print in the tray. The combination of the slight warmth from
the friction of the sponge and the infusion of fresh chemical can make the
difference between a useless picture and an acceptable one. It's no substi-
tute for a proper exposure, of course.

Photoshop's Sponge tool does much the same thing. On a color image, it
increases (or reduces, versatile tool that it is) the color saturation in the
area to which you apply it. On an image in Grayscale mode, it increases or
decreases contrast by moving the grayscale level away from or toward
middle gray. When you use the Sponge, you also need to adjust its setting
in the Options bar to determine whether it intensifies color (saturates) or
fades it (desaturates). The Vibrance check box prevents the Sponge from
oversaturating the image by restricting its effects to primary colors that
aren't already highly saturated. Figures 5.23 and 5.24 show before and after
views of a woodland scene with the Sponge applied.

FIGURE 5.23
Before using the Sponge, the colors are somewhat dull.

FIGURE 5.24
After using the Sponge, the colors are much brighter.

NOTE

Caught in the Middle

Have you ever wondered what's meant by **middle gray**? If you recall that the gray scale goes from 0% (white) to 100% (black), you'll realize that middle gray is the tone that's exactly 50%. In practice, highlights are anywhere from 0 to about 20%–25%. Shadows are 70%–100%. So anything between a 25% gray and a 70% gray is considered a **midtone.**

The toning tools are great for fine-tuning images and creating shadows or highlights. Use them in small doses to enhance the appearance of your images.

The Color Replacement Tool

The Color Replacement tool is one of the most useful tools in Photoshop. It functions like any other paintbrush, except that when you paint over an existing scene, it replaces the predominant color with whatever happens to be the foreground color in the Tools panel. More important, it changes only the color, not the saturation or value. If you had a blue sky with lots of white, fleecy clouds and you wanted an orange sky with the same white clouds, no problem. Choose your shade of orange and apply the brush to the sky. Go ahead and paint right over the clouds. The orange won't affect them except where they reflect blue from the sky; those areas will now be orange reflections.

Red Eye Tool

Similar to the Color Replacement tool, this tool is designed exclusively for fixing the photo problem known as red eye. You've seen it—glowing red "devil" eyes in portraits of people, and blue or green "alien" eyes in pictures of animals. It's caused by light reflecting off the back of the eye, and it usually happens only with flash photography or in a very bright light. To fix red eye with this brush, click right in the center of each red eye. We discuss this in greater detail in Hour 22, "Repairing Color Photos," along with special techniques for fixing animals' green eyes.

Converting Color to Black and White

It shouldn't surprise you to learn that multiple methods are available for converting a color photo to black and white (which, as you know, is technically called **grayscale**). You can choose Image, Adjustments, Desaturate, or reduce the Saturation value to 0 in the Hue/Saturation dialog. Either of these ends up in the same place. Or, logically, you can convert the image to Grayscale mode (you'll need to click OK when Photoshop asks if you're really sure you want to discard all the image's color data). This method gives you improved contrast over the Desaturate method. And there are other, more obscure techniques, involving converting an image to Lab Color mode and starting from the Lightness channel, or picking the best-looking of the red, green, and blue color channels.

All these conversion methods were rendered obsolete as of Photoshop CS3, when the Black & White command was introduced (choose Image,

Adjustments, Black & White). Using a dialog crammed with sliders (see Figure 5.25), Black & White gives you the opportunity to take complete control over just how each of the colors in a color photo is converted to grayscale. You can even make adjustments directly in the image, as you can with the On-Canvas Adjustment tools in the Curves and Hue/Saturation dialogs. And if it's too much bother to deal with all those sliders every time, you can take advantage of the comprehensive collection of presets Adobe has so thoughtfully included in the Black & White dialog.

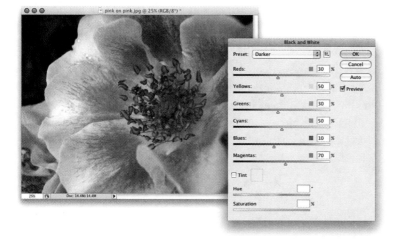

FIGURE 5.25
You can take advantage of the Black & White dialog's presets or create your own custom mix.

NOTE

Mixing Your Channels

The Black & White dialog works like the Channel Mixer (choose Image, Adjustments, Channel Mixer), which also enables you to adjust color channel by channel. The only difference is that Black & White is specially designed to make fabulous grayscale conversions easy.

As with Levels and Curves, Black & White has an Auto button; click this to use Photoshop's recommended settings for your image. The Auto function works better in Black & White than in the other dialogs in which it appears; it makes an excellent starting point for your own adjustments. The provided presets tend to be rather extreme and are most useful for special effects such as simulating an infrared image.

Working with the Black & White dialog is easy. Just click and drag any of the color sliders to change how objects of that color are converted to gray. If a red T-shirt is too dark with the default settings, drag the Reds slider to the right to brighten it. Or, if you prefer, click the T-shirt in the image window and drag to the right for the same results. To undo your changes without leaving the dialog, you can Option-click (Mac) or Alt-click (Windows) the Cancel button to reset all of the color sliders. To reset just one slider, Option-click (Mac) or Alt-click (Windows) its color chip.

Black & White and Color Too

If you plan to tint your newly minted grayscale image, you can save time by performing that function in the Black & White dialog as well. Click the Tint check box to turn on this option, then click the color swatch to open the Color Picker and choose a tint color. Drag the Hue and Saturation sliders to adjust the color.

Summary

During this hour, we looked at a multitude of ways to adjust an image's brightness and color, starting with Variations and ending up with a highly customizable way of converting a color photo to a black-and-white one. The Variations dialog is easy to use, enabling you to make seat-of-the pants corrections without worrying about numbers or channels or anything else technical. Other, more specific commands such as Curves and Color Balance give you precise control over every aspect of the brightness and color in your images. You can use the skills you've learned in this hour to make your pictures look more like the real world—or to make them look out of this world, with purple skies and orange grass.

The tools and commands covered in this hour will come in handy every time you use Photoshop. Some of them overlap in function; for example, most of the time you can use either Levels or Curves to achieve the same result. So practice, develop your own favorite techniques, and prepare yourself for a quantum leap in the quality of your photos.

Q&A

Q. If Levels and Curves are interchangeable, how do I decide which I want to use?

A. In theory, you can achieve pretty much the same results with Levels and Curves, although Curves is more powerful. In practice, I tend to use Levels when there's a color cast in the image—to fix it, click with the appropriate Eyedropper tool in an area that should be white, gray, or black. I use Curves when I want to modify only a small range of colors.

Q. What's the best way to add a sepia tint to an image?

A. You're right in assuming that there's more than one method—doesn't Photoshop have multiple methods for everything? You could use Hue/Saturation or make a duotone, but my favorite method is to use a Black & White adjustment layer. That way, I can always restore the image's color by just deleting the layer.

Q. Can I apply more than one adjustment layer to an image?

A. Sure, you can have as many as you want, and you can edit their layer masks so that the adjustments apply to the same parts of the image or to completely different areas. If you want to restrict the effects of an adjustment layer to the contents of one other layer, place the adjustment layer immediately above the other layer in the Layers panel and Option-click/Alt-click the line between the two.

Workshop

Quiz

1. How many channels does a CMYK image have?

    A. None; only RGB images have separate color channels.

    B. Two—one for the CMYK data and one containing RGB data, in case you want to convert the image to RGB mode.

    C. Four—one each for cyan, magenta, yellow, and black.

    D. Hundreds or even thousands, if it contains a lot of alpha channels.

2. **True or false:** The Burn tool lightens the image where it's applied, and the Dodge tool darkens the image.

3. Which of the following is not a kind of adjustment layer you can create?

    A. Vibrance

    B. Shadows/Highlights

    C. Curves

    D. Photo Filter

Answers

1. **C** or **D.** All CMYK images start out with four channels, but you can add as many alpha channels as you want.

2. **False.** The tools work the other way around; the Dodge tool lightens the image and the Burn tool darkens it. Use the Dodge tool to lighten shadows on people's faces; use the Burn tool to bring out underexposed details.

3. **B.** It's in the Adjustments submenu of the Image menu, but it's not available as an adjustments layer.

Exercise

Download some of the photos in this book from the publisher's website. Then see how much further you can go. Turn a cloudy day into a sunny one and then reverse the change. Experiment with all the different adjustment layer types. Try out some of the presets, and then see whether you can duplicate your efforts manually.

HOUR 6
Choosing and Blending Colors

Now that you know a little bit about different color modes and ways to adjust color, you need to know how to choose some colors to paint with. Even if you don't consider yourself an artist, sometimes you'll want to paint in a detail or paint over something in a photo. And if you *are* an artist, you're going to love painting digitally: Your color palette is infinite, as is the number of different brushes you can use. And you have complete control over how different colors combine with each other. In this hour, you'll learn about choosing and applying color and about blending modes, which affect the way colors (and layers) interact.

WHAT YOU'LL LEARN IN
THIS HOUR:

▶ Foreground and
  Background Colors
▶ Ways to Specify Colors
▶ Blending Modes

Foreground and Background Colors

At any given moment while working with Photoshop, you have two colors available. One's the color on your brush—the **Foreground color**—and the other's the color you'll see if you remove paint from the canvas—the **Background color**. The nice thing about painting with Photoshop is that you don't have to clean your brushes between colors, and you can change both the Foreground color and the Background color any time you want, unlike real-life canvas or paper, which tends to stubbornly stay the same color as you work.

Specifying Colors

The quickest way to choose a different paint or canvas color is to click the Foreground and Background swatches in the Tools panel (see Figure 6.1). The swatch to the upper left shows the Foreground color, and the one to the lower right shows the Background color. You can change either color by clicking its swatch.

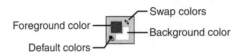

The small button at the upper-left of the swatches, which looks like a miniature version of the swatches, resets them to the default colors (black and white). The curved arrow at the upper right of the swatches swaps the Background and Foreground colors, whatever they might be at the moment.

> ### NOTE
>
> ### What's a Swatch?
>
> **Swatches** are the two little squares of color at the bottom of the Tools panel—like the swatch cards you get from the paint store. Photoshop sticks color swatches into panels and dialogs any time you can choose a color to work with.

To change the color of either the Foreground color or the Background color swatch, click the swatch to open the Color Picker that's currently selected in the General Preferences dialog (press Command-K/Ctrl+K to get there). If you haven't changed the setting, the Adobe Color Picker is active by default. Your other choice is either the Apple or Windows Color Picker, depending on which operating system your computer uses. The examples in this hour use the Adobe Color Picker because all Photoshop users, regardless of platform, have access to it.

The Color Picker

> ### TIP
>
> ### The Keys to Efficiency
>
> Knowing and using keyboard shortcuts saves you a lot of time that you'd otherwise spend mousing around your screen, freeing up that time to have more fun! So here are a couple of good ones: You can reset the default colors by pressing D. Press X to swap the Background and Foreground colors; press it again to switch them back.

Photoshop's Color Picker enables you to choose a Foreground or Background color in several different ways. Figure 6.2 shows the Color Picker dialog. The most common way to pick a color is to use the HSB model and click first in the vertical bar to set the hue component, and then in the color field to set the saturation and brightness components. If you'd rather specify a color by the numbers, you can enter values in any of the sets of entry fields for the different color models.

FIGURE 6.2
Photoshop's Color Picker works in several different ways.

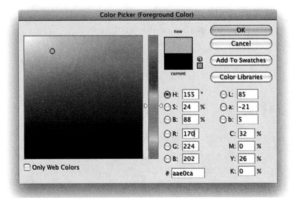

By default, the Color Picker opens to the HSB model, which (as you learned in Hour 4, "Specifying Color Modes and Color Models") stands for hue, saturation, and brightness. You'll always start with the Hue radio button active. This makes the vertical color bar into a spectrum in which you can choose a hue, and it enables the color field to show you all the possible saturation and brightness variations of the hue you've chosen. If you click anywhere in the color field, you'll see the Saturation and Brightness values to the right change, but the Hue setting remains the same; to change it, you have to click in a different spot along the Hue bar or drag the slider to a different location.

If you click the Saturation button, the color field changes to look like what you see in Figure 6.3. It shows you all the possible hues at the designated saturation value. If you click anywhere in the color field, Hue and Brightness values change, but the Saturation value stays the same.

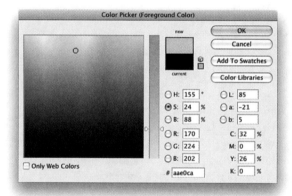

The HSB model is easy to understand, and it's the one that traditional artists use most often. You're not stuck with it, though. You can switch to RGB, Lab, or even CMYK, although CMYK doesn't have a clickable display mode; you just have to enter numbers. If you don't want to work with HSB, RGB makes a good second choice as a working model because that's the model that governs how your computer displays color. (It uses red, green, and blue light, just like a television.)

Choosing a color in RGB mode isn't quite as straightforward as it would be in HSB mode. Remember, in this model, colors are made from three components—red, green, and blue—in amounts from 0 to 255. The vertical slider bar represents the value of the color radio button that you've clicked—red, for example. Looking at the color field, you'll find the pure

NOTE

What's Hue, Pussycat?

Hue—Color, measured as its location on the color wheel in degrees (0°–360°). If you don't remember what the color wheel looks like, take a look at Figure 5.10 to jog your memory.

Saturation—The strength of the color, measured as a percentage between 0% (gray) and 100% (fully saturated color).

Brightness—The lightness of the color, measured as a percentage from 0% (black) to 100% (white).

FIGURE 6.3
This is the Color Picker's Saturation mode.

version of that color in the lower-left corner, with the other two components mixing in as you go up or right. In the upper-right corner, you'll see the result of adding both of the other RGB components at levels of 255: white. To get the chosen color's exact opposite (in the case of red, that's cyan), you remove all of your chosen color from white by dragging the slider all to the bottom, leaving the other two values at 255. So the RGB value of cyan is 0 red, 255 green, 255 blue. Figure 6.4 shows what this looks like in the Color Picker.

FIGURE 6.4
The chosen color (in this case, red) is mixed with varying amounts of the other two RGB primaries.

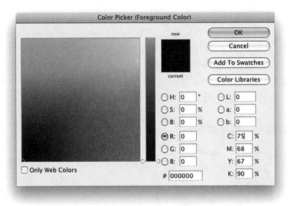

The best way to become comfortable with picking colors in RGB color mode is to practice with it. Open your Color Picker by clicking the Tools panel's Foreground color swatch and click a color. Then see how the numbers change as you click a different color. Try different radio button settings and see how they affect the color field and the color bar.

The Color Panel

The Color panel offers an alternative to using the Color Picker, with these differences:

- ▶ You can display it on your screen all the time, if you like, and because it's nonmodal, you can keep working while it's open. The Color Picker takes over when it's open; you must click OK or Cancel to perform other tasks.

- ▶ The Color panel doesn't have the color field and color bar combination for choosing colors. Instead, it has a bar at the bottom that can display an RGB, CMYK, or grayscale color ramp. Clicking anywhere in the ramp chooses the color at that spot.

- ▶ Next to the color value entry fields, the Color panel has sliders that you can use to change the value of individual color components.

For those who are mathematically challenged, the Color panel has fewer numbers to contend with than the Color Picker does, and the ones you see, as in Figure 6.5, are logically related to the sliders next to them. By default, the Color panel opens in whatever mode you used last, but you can set it to the color model you prefer to work in by using the pop-up menu, as shown in Figure 6.6. You can even choose web colors as a variant of RGB; the sliders are labeled R, G, and B, but their values are shown in hexadecimal.

FIGURE 6.5
The Color panel and its menu enable you to mix your own colors at any time.

FIGURE 6.6
If you're designing web graphics, use the RGB Spectrum color ramp and Web Color Sliders options, as shown here.

The menu also enables you to reset the color ramp at the bottom of the Color panel to match the color model you're working with. If your work will be printed and you want to avoid using colors that are **out of gamut** (in other words, they can't be achieved with CMYK inks), you can set the color ramp to the CMYK spectrum and know that any color you click will be printable. Similarly, if you click Make Ramp Web Safe, the only colors displayed on the color ramp will be the 216 colors in the Web Safe palette. (Flip back to Hour 4 if you've forgotten what the Web Safe palette is.).

FIGURE 6.7
The Swatches panel can display any of the color palettes shown in its pop-up menu.

The Swatches Panel

Here's the easiest way to choose colors of all the different methods Photoshop offers. The Swatches panel (shown in Figure 6.7) functions like a box of watercolor paints; you simply dip your brush in a color and paint with it. To choose a Foreground color, just click the one you want. To choose a Background color, Option-click (Mac) or Alt-click (Windows) to choose a color.

The Swatches panel opens by default, showing the current system palette, whether that's Mac OS or Windows. You can specify colors in the Color Picker to add to the Swatches panel, or you can choose a color system from the panel's pop-up menu, such as Pantone, Focoltone, TRUMATCH, or Toyo, and have an additional 700 to 1,000 or more printing-ink color swatches appended to those already shown in the panel. You can also add custom colors using the Eyedropper tool described in the next section, and you can save and reload your own palettes, or sets of custom colors.

▼ TRY IT YOURSELF

Add New Colors from the Color Picker to the Swatches Panel

Swatches are easy to work with, but Photoshop's choices of color won't always match yours. Here's how to add your own colors to those displayed in the Swatches panel.

1. Click the Foreground color swatch in the Tools panel to open the Color Picker.

2. Use the Color Picker to specify the color you have in mind; then click OK.

3. Open the Swatches panel (choose Window, Swatches). Drag it away from the edge of the screen if it's docked.

4. Click the lower-right corner of the Swatches panel and drag to enlarge the panel so that it resembles the one in Figure 6.8.

TRY IT YOURSELF ▼

**Add New Colors from
the Color Picker to
the Swatches Panel**
continued

FIGURE 6.8
Adding a new color to the Swatches panel takes just one click.

5. Move the cursor into the space below the existing swatches. It changes into the Paint Bucket tool.

6. Click anywhere in the unused space. Photoshop adds the new color after the existing colors and then asks you to give the new color a name. You can use a descriptive name (Logo Blue) or a poetic one (Lake Water Blue), or just leave the default name (Swatch 1).

If you use the same colors over and over, and they're not included in any of the palettes that ship with Photoshop, you can save them in your own custom palette, which you can then load any time you want and also pass along to other users to ensure that their colors match yours. You can copy colors from photos, from scanned artwork, and even from your desktop, or you can define colors "by the numbers" in the Color panel or pick them in the Color Picker. When you've added all the colors you want to include to the Swatches panel, choose Save Swatches from the panel menu. This saves you time and the headache of having to re-create all your favorite colors each time you open Photoshop. Color swatches are saved in the Presets folder within the Adobe Photoshop CS4 program folder.

The Eyedropper Tool

You saw the Eyedropper appear when you moved the mouse over a color swatch or over the color ramp in the Color panel. It also shows up in some of the adjustments dialogs, such as Levels and Hue/Saturation. You can use the Eyedropper to pick up a bit of whatever color you click it on, making that the active color. What's neat about this tool is that it works in the same way on a picture—you can pick up a bit of sky blue, grass green, or skin, without having to try to work out a match for it in the Color Picker.

You'll use the Eyedropper tool frequently when you're retouching a picture, so that you can duplicate the colors in it. Click it anywhere in the image, and the color under its tip becomes the new Foreground color. Option-click (Mac) or Alt-click (Windows) to pick up a Background color instead. If you drag the Eyedropper across an image, the Foreground or Background color swatch in the Tools panel changes each time the Eyedropper touches a new color; just stop moving the mouse when the swatch looks right. And if you begin dragging in the Photoshop image window, you can keep the mouse button down and drag anywhere on your screen to pick up colors from your wallpaper, icons, or other programs' document windows.

TIP

Hitting the Hot Spots

Remember that, as with all the tools, the Eyedropper is active only at its **hot spot**; in this case, that's right at the tip. If you find it hard to work with the hot spot, just go to Preferences, Display, and change the display to Precise in the Other Cursors area. You'll lose the cute little Eyedropper icon, but the targeting cursor that replaces it will be easier to position exactly where you want it.

When the Eyedropper is active, the Options bar (shown in Figure 6.9) contains two pop-up menus. The Sample Size menu enables you to specify how much of a sample to pick up with the Eyedropper. You can take a single pixel sample, or average the colors contained in a larger area (your choices are 3, 5, 11, 31, 51, or 101 pixels square). With the other menu, labeled simply Sample, you can choose whether to pick up colors found only in the current layer or whether to pick up colors from other layers as well.

FIGURE 6.9
The Eyedropper tool has just a few options, but they're vital.

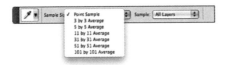

You can temporarily convert any Painting tool (except the Eraser, the History Brush, and the Art History Brush) into an Eyedropper to change your Foreground color on the fly by pressing Option (Mac) or Alt (Windows) while you're working. That's the same modifier you use with the regular Eyedropper to pick up a Background color, which means you can't choose a Background color unless you actually switch to the Eyedropper tool. My workaround: Pick up a color, then press X to swap the two swatches and make that color the Background color. Pick up another color as the Foreground color, and you're good to go!

Here's another way to add to the Swatches panel. Start by opening a photo from which you can borrow colors.

1. Click the Eyedropper tool in the Tools panel, or press I to switch to it.

2. Click within the image on a color you want to capture. Or, if you want to make the color a background color, Option-click (Mac) or Alt-click (Windows) the color you want.

3. Open the Swatches panel, if it's not already open. Place the Eyedropper over any empty (gray) space in the Swatches panel, and it turns into a Paint Bucket.

4. Click once to put a swatch of the Foreground color into the panel. If you want to save a swatch of the Background color, press X to swap the Foreground and Background colors, then click.

5. Choose Save Swatches from the panel's pop-up menu.

6. Give your swatch file a name, and then click Save to save it in the Color Swatches folder within Photoshop's Presets folder.

To load a saved swatch file, use the Swatches panel's pop-up menu again. Choose Load Swatches. Locate the swatch file you want to use, as shown in Figure 6.10, and click Load.

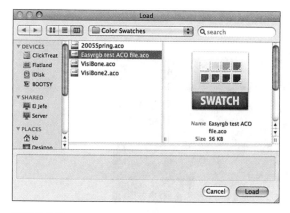

FIGURE 6.10
The swatch file has a swatch icon and an .aco extension.

TIP

Suite Swaps

Swatches can also be used to transfer colors between Photoshop and another Creative Suite application (such as InDesign or Illustrator). First, create your swatches. When you've got the colors you want, choose Save Swatches for Exchange from the Swatches panel's pop-up menu. Your file will end up in the same folder, but it will use a different format (Adobe Swatch Exchange, .ase) that the other Creative Suite programs can import.

▼ TRY IT YOURSELF

Use the Eyedropper and the Brush

Let's take a few minutes to practice with the Brush and Eyedropper. Find a picture with a variety of different colors and open it in Photoshop. Then perform the following steps:

1. Before you begin, choose File, Save As and save your picture with a different name and in Photoshop native format, to preserve the original; then you can play with this copy as much as you like.

2. Press B to switch to the Brush tool, then open the Brush panel and choose a medium-sized brush shape.

3. Place the Brush over a color in the picture, as I have in Figure 6.11. Press Option (Mac) or Alt (Windows) and click. The Brush turns into an Eyedropper and makes the color the Foreground color.

4. Release the Option or Alt key and drag in the image window to paint with the Brush using the color you've just picked up.

5. Open the Color panel (Window, Color) if it's not already open. Hold your brush over the color ramp at the bottom of the panel. Again, it turns into an Eyedropper.

6. Click to choose another color, and then paint something else into your picture. If you don't want to use the same brush, you can change brush tips in the Brush panel, switch to the Pencil (press Shift+B), or try the Airbrush option by clicking the button on the Tool Options bar. Experiment with different colors and brushes until you can't see the original image anymore.

7. When you run out of space to paint, choose File, Revert to go back to the original version of the picture so you can start over.

FIGURE 6.11
Click to copy the color.

Eyedropper cursor

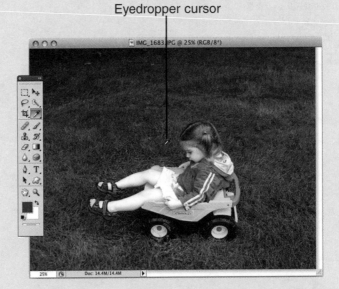

Blending Modes

In the real world, when you drag a brush full of paint over paint that's already there, the result depends on the color of the paint you're applying, how opaque it is, whether the original layer is wet or dry, and so on. In Photoshop, you can simulate all the possible combinations of two colors by using **blending modes**. You'll find them in a pop-up menu on the Options bar, as shown in Figure 6.12. Blending modes apply to all tools that can draw or paint, including the Pencil, Clone Stamp, and Gradient tools, as well as the more obvious ones such as the Brush. As you can see, there are quite a few blending modes. Let's take a quick look at the different blending modes and how they work.

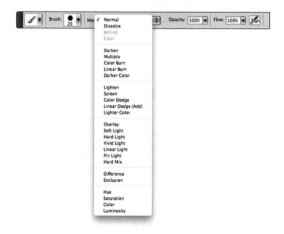

FIGURE 6.12
This list shows the Brush blending modes; other tools have similar choices.

Suppose that you're working with only two colors. One is the **base** color, the one that's already in place on the canvas. The second is the **blend** color, the one that you apply with a Painting tool . If you leave the blending mode set to Normal, you'll see only the blend color. But if you use a different blending mode, you'll get a third color, a **result** color that varies according to the method Photoshop uses to blend the first two colors.

Figures 6.13–6.37 show what happens when you choose each of the options. (The examples were painted with a firm brush in hot pink on a lime-green background, except for those with the letter *R*, which have the colors reversed.)

FIGURE 6.13
Normal—This is the default mode. The blend color replaces the base color.

FIGURE 6.14
Dissolve—A random number of pixels become the blend color. This gives a splattered or "dry brush" effect.

FIGURE 6.15
Darken—Evaluates the color information in each channel and assigns either the base color or the blend color, whichever is darker, as the result color. Lighter pixels are replaced, but darker ones don't change.

FIGURE 6.16
Multiply—Multiplies the base color by the blend color, giving you a darker result color. The effect is like drawing over the picture with a marker. Where the background is light, you see the original blend color.

FIGURE 6.17
Color Burn—Darkens the base color to match the value of the blend color.

FIGURE 6.18
Linear Burn—Darkens the base color to reflect the blend color by decreasing the brightness. Blending with white produces no change.

FIGURE 6.19
Darker Color—Works like Darken, but it uses all the color channels at once instead of operating on each channel separately. This is the opposite effect of Lighter Color, the other blending mode introduced in Photoshop CS3.

FIGURE 6.20
Lighten—Evaluates the color information in each channel and assigns either the base color or the blend color, whichever is lighter, as the result color. Darker pixels are replaced, but lighter ones don't change. This is the exact opposite of Darken.

FIGURE 6.21
Screen—Multiplies the base color by the inverse of the blend color, giving you a lighter result color. The effect is like painting with bleach. The symbol was drawn with the brush set to Wet Edges.

FIGURE 6.22
Color Dodge—Brightens the base color to match the value of the blend color.

FIGURE 6.23
Linear Dodge (Add)—Brightens the base color to reflect the blend color by increasing the brightness. Blending with black produces no change.

FIGURE 6.24
Lighter Color—Introduced in Photoshop CS3, this mode works like Lighten, but it uses all the color channels at once instead of operating on each channel separately. This is the opposite effect of Darker Color, the other new blending mode.

FIGURE 6.25
Overlay—Evaluates the color information in each channel and assigns either the base color or the blend color, whichever is darker, as the result color. Lighter pixels are replaced, but darker ones don't change.

FIGURE 6.26
Soft Light—Darkens or lightens depending on the blend color. The effect is said to be similar to shining a diffused spotlight on the image. With a light blend color, it has very little effect.

FIGURE 6.27
Hard Light—Multiplies or screens the colors, depending on the blend color. The effect is similar to shining a harsh spotlight on the image.

FIGURE 6.28
Vivid Light—Burns or dodges the colors by increasing or decreasing the contrast, depending on the blend color. If the blend color (light source) is lighter than 50% gray, the image is lightened by decreasing the contrast. If the blend color is darker than 50% gray, the image is darkened by increasing the contrast.

FIGURE 6.29
Linear Light—Burns or dodges the colors by decreasing or increasing the brightness, depending on the blend color. If the blend color (light source) is lighter than 50% gray, the image is lightened by increasing the brightness. If the blend color is darker than 50% gray, the image is darkened by decreasing the brightness.

FIGURE 6.30
Pin Light—Replaces the colors, depending on the blend color. If the blend color (light source) is lighter than 50% gray, pixels darker than the blend color are replaced and pixels lighter than the blend color do not change. If the blend color is darker than 50% gray, pixels lighter than the blend color are replaced and pixels darker than the blend color do not change. This is useful for adding special effects to an image.

FIGURE 6.31
Hard Mix—Combines the effects of Hard Light and Vivid Light modes.

FIGURE 6.32
Difference—Compares brightness values in the base and blend colors, and subtracts the lighter. Overlaps are interesting in this mode. They cancel the previous action.

FIGURE 6.33
Exclusion—Similar to the Difference mode, but has a softer effect.

FIGURE 6.34
Hue—Gives you a result combining the luminance and saturation of the base color and the hue of the blend color.

FIGURE 6.35
Saturation—Gives you a color with the luminance and hue of the base color and the saturation of the blend color. Unless you reduce the saturation of the blend color significantly, nothing shows in Grayscale mode.

FIGURE 6.36
Color—Combines the luminance of the base color with the hue and saturation of the blend color. Useful for coloring monochrome images because Color mode retains the gray levels.

FIGURE 6.37
Luminosity—Gives a result color with the hue and saturation of the base color and the luminance of the blend color. Opposite effect of Color Blend mode.

Two more blending modes that you'll occasionally run into are Behind and Clear. When you use Behind, you can paint only on the transparent parts of a layer; you can't paint over anything that's already on the layer. Clear, on the other hand, makes each pixel you paint over transparent, like using the Eraser. It works with the Shape tools, the Paint Bucket tool, the Brush and Pencil tools, and the Fill and Stroke commands. It's a convenient way to erase a specified shape or area.

Summary

All art is based on certain fundamental principles, including form, composition, and color. You spent this hour learning how to choose and paint with colors in Photoshop. We talked about the Foreground color and the Background color, and you used the Color Picker, the Color panel, the Swatches panel, and the Eyedropper to pick out colors for your work. Although it's the most powerful method of specifying colors, the Color Picker prevents you from doing anything else until you choose a color and click OK. The Color and Swatches panels, as well as the Eyedropper tool, are always available to you while you're working in Photoshop. We closed out the hour with a look at blending modes, the different ways two colors can combine to create a third color.

Q&A

Q. Is it better to use the Adobe Color Picker instead of the Apple or Windows version?

A. I think so. Even though the Apple Color Picker gives you a lot of different ways to choose colors, I think the Adobe version is easier to understand and use. The same is true of the Windows Color Picker.

Q. What happens when I have the Eyedropper set to sample an area containing more than 1 pixel, and it contains multiple colors?

A. Photoshop takes an average of the colors of each pixel in the area around where you clicked—in the case of a 5×5 sample, that's 25 pixels in the square—and makes the average the selected color. This often results in a more visually accurate color selection than choosing a color based on a single pixel, because your brain does exactly the same thing.

Q. Do all the Painting tools use the same set of blending modes?

A. For the most part, yes. But there are a couple of exceptions, such as the Color Replacement tool, which offers only Hue, Saturation, Color, and Luminosity. That's because when you use the Color Replacement tool, you've already specified the result color you want (the Foreground color).

Workshop

Quiz

1. True or False: Changing the Background color also changes the color of the existing canvas.

2. Which of the following is not a blending mode?

   A. Linear Burn

   B. Difference

   C. Combination

   D. Hard Mix

3. How do you swap the Foreground and Background colors?

   A. Option-click/Alt+click the Foreground color swatch in the Tools panel.

   B. Press X.

   C. You can't; you must respecify the Foreground and Background colors to accomplish this.

   D. Press D.

Answers

1. **False.** The Background color is the color you'll see if you use an Eraser tool or delete a selection on the Background layer. But any pieces of the original canvas that are still showing retain their original colors when you change the Background color.

2. **C.** All the blending modes produce combinations of the two colors involved.

3. **B.** If you press D, the Foreground and Background colors reset to their defaults of black and white, respectively.

Exercises

1. What's your favorite color? Click the Foreground swatch on the Tools panel and see if you can specify the exact color you love best in the Color Picker. When you're happy with it, make a note of its HSB and RGB values, then click OK. Switch to the Paint Bucket and click in the image window to fill it with your color. Now, using any of the Selection tools, make a selection of any shape in the middle of the image window and press Command-I (Mac) or Ctrl+I (Windows) to invert the color within the selected area. Press Option/Alt and click in the selected area, then click the Foreground swatch to go back to the Color Picker. How do the numbers correspond to those of the original color? Can you change the numbers to get back to the first color you chose?

2. Open a colorful image in Photoshop and zoom way, way in so you can see the individual pixels. Using the Eyedropper set to Point Sample in the Options bar, click a few areas of the image. Are the resulting colors what you expected to see? Now change the Eyedropper setting to 11 by 11 Average and click a few more times. Do the colors you're getting now seem more accurate?

PART II
Painting with Pixels

HOUR 7
Drawing and Combining Shapes

It may be a cliché, but it's true: You don't have to be able to draw a straight line—or a round circle, or a symmetrical square—to create digital art with Photoshop. That's because Photoshop provides you with a handy arsenal of predrawn shapes that you can use via the **Shape tools**. You can use the Shape tools to create filled shape layers or invisible paths, which you can then edit, stroke, fill, or even designate as clipping paths. After you create your shapes, you can resize and reshape them and place them wherever you need them. Photoshop has six Shape tools (see Figure 7.1): the Rectangle, the Rounded Rectangle, the Ellipse, the Polygon, the Line, and the Custom Shape tool, which can take on any of dozens of shapes included with Photoshop or even shapes that you design yourself.

The Tool Options bar offers more choices and is more important when using the Shape tools than with any other group of tools, except perhaps the Type tools. Settings on the Options bar control the color and style of each shape you draw, as well as how that shape relates to any other shapes in the image. When any Shape tool is active, you can access the others by clicking buttons on the Options bar. Of course, you can also switch to any Shape tool by pressing U, then Shift+U to cycle through the tools until you get to the one you want to use. In this hour, we'll use all the Shape tools and explore their options to learn how to get the most from them.

WHAT YOU'LL LEARN IN THIS HOUR:

▶ Drawing and Editing Shapes
▶ Combining Shapes
▶ Creating Your Own Shapes

FIGURE 7.1
The Shape tools can draw a wide
variety of filled or unfilled shapes.

TIP

Play It Again, Shape Tool

Tool presets for Shape tools
can include the shape's style
and, for the Custom Shape tool,
which custom shape you were
using at the time. So if you
want to create bunnies using
the Tie-Dyed Silk style in all
your documents, all you have to
is switch to those settings and
then create a tool preset using
them. You'll find the preset in
the tool presets menu at the
left end of the Options bar, as
well as in the Tool Presets
panel (choose Window, Tool
Presets).

Drawing and Editing Shapes

To draw a shape, first switch to the appropriate tool. If you are using the
Custom Shape tool, use the Shape pop-up menu on the Options bar to
choose one of the available shapes. Next, if you don't want to use the current Foreground color, click the color swatch on the Options bar and
choose a new color.

As you draw a shape, you can constrain its angle or shape. Press Shift
while dragging with a Shape tool to constrain a rectangle or rounded rectangle to a square, or to constrain an ellipse to a circle. If you press Shift as
you draw a line, it's constrained to 45° angles, and pressing Shift ensures
that your polygons stay level (see Figure 7.2). Press Option (Mac) or Alt
(Windows) as you drag to draw from the center of the object.

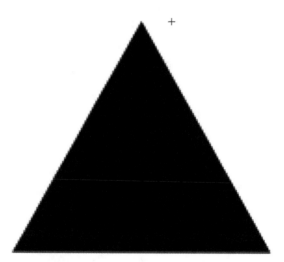

FIGURE 7.2
Pressing Shift as you draw with the Polygon tool keeps your shape lined up relative to
the rest of the image.

After you've drawn a shape, you can change its color to the Foreground
color by selecting the layer and pressing Option-Delete/Alt+Delete. Or
press Command-Delete/Ctrl+Delete to fill the shape layer with the
Background color. If you prefer, you can double-click the layer's color
thumbnail in the Layers panel to open the Color Picker and choose a new
color.

Choosing Paths or Pixels

When you draw a shape, you have a choice of three ways it can manifest: as a regular shape layer, as a path (which doesn't add a new layer), or as pixels (see Figure 7.3). What to choose? Here are your guidelines:

FIGURE 7.3
Click one of these buttons in the Options bar to control whether you create a shape layer, a path, or a rasterized shape.

▶ **Shape Layer**—When you want to draw a shape but you know you might want to modify its size or shape later, choose the Shape Layer option.

▶ **Path**—If you need to create a precise geometrical selection or you want to create a clipping path for use in an EPS file, go with Paths. This option won't create a new layer, and you won't be able to see the path if you print your image, but you can edit it and use it as a mask or as the basis for a selection. If you lose track of your paths, check the Paths panel to locate them (see Figure 7.4).

FIGURE 7.4
The Paths panel lists each path you create with the Shape tools.

▶ **Pixels**—If you know from the start that you're going to apply a filter to the layer right after you create it—or if you plan do something else that you can't do to a shape—choose this option to skip the step of rasterizing the shape layer. You'll still get a new layer, but instead of an editable shape, it will contain just pixels, as if you'd created a selection in the appropriate shape and filled it with color. When you use the Pixels option, Photoshop doesn't apply a layer style, but you can choose a blending mode and an opacity percentage in the Options bar before you draw the shape. You'll see a dialog before you start drawing, asking if you're sure you want to create a rasterized shape instead of a vector one.

TIP

From Shape to Pixels

If you decide you want to work with a shape layer as pixels after it's been created, you can rasterize it by choosing Layer, Rasterize, Shape. Sometimes Photoshop asks you if you want to rasterize a shape; this happens when you try to apply a filter to a shape layer. Other times, the commands you want (such as Image, Adjustments, Hue/Saturation) just aren't available in their respective menus until after you rasterize the layer.

Setting Shape Options

If you want to draw a shape that's a particular size or that uses specific proportions, click the triangle at the end of the row of Shape tools on the Tool Options bar. This opens a dialog containing a variety of options, which change depending on which Shape tool you're using (see Figure 7.5). Here's a look at what options apply to which tools:

FIGURE 7.5
Here's what the Shape Options look like for the Custom Shape tool.

▶ **Rectangle and Rounded Rectangle**—Unconstrained means you can draw the shape to any size and proportions you like. Obviously, Square constrains the shape to fit in a square area. Fixed Size and Proportional are similar: For Fixed Size, you enter measurements for the shape, and for Proportional, you enter a ratio (such as Width 2 and Height 1 for a shape that's twice as wide as it is tall). You can also choose to draw outward from the center, instead of from corner to corner, and you can force your shape to align perfectly with the pixels in the image, instead of drawing paths between two rows of pixels, so you'll be able to see exactly where the shape will be when the image is displayed or printed in its final form.

▶ **Ellipse**—As with the Rectangle and Rounded Rectangle tools, the Ellipse tool can produce unconstrained shapes, circles, fixed-size shapes, and proportional shapes. It can also draw from the center. Because it draws curved lines, the Snap to Pixels option isn't available; pixels are always arranged in straight lines, so there's no way a curved path can be aligned to the image's pixel grid all the way around.

▶ **Polygon**—Here the options start to get a little different. Before visiting the Shape Options dialog, enter the number of sides you want your polygon to have in the Options bar. Then you can choose a Radius value to produce a shape of a specific size. The Smooth

Corners option produces rounded corners instead of sharp angles, and you can specify whether you want the shape's sides to indent (as in a star) or not (as in a pentagon) by checking or unchecking the Star box. If you do want indented sides, just specify a percentage greater than 0 in the Indent Sides By field. You can also have the indented corners smoothed, if you prefer.

► **Line**—Start by assigning the line a Weight value to determine how heavy it is. Then, in the Shape Options dialog, you can give it arrowheads. Choose whether there should be arrows at the start, the end, or both. Then specify a Width (relative to the line Weight value) and Length (relative to the line Weight value) for the arrowheads. Set the Concavity value, which controls the flat end of the arrowhead, to a value between –50 and +50, with 0 giving you a flat line. Negative values indent the arrowhead's back, and positive ones poke it out toward the line (see Figure 7.6).

► **Custom Shape**—Here you'll find that the Unconstrained and Fixed Size options work the same way as they do for Rectangles and Ellipses. You can also choose either the Defined Proportions or the Defined Size option to constrain the shape to its original proportions or even its original size. Check the From Center box to draw from the center of the shape instead of from corner to corner.

After you set these options, click or click and drag in the image window to place the new shape. Then you can use the Tool Options bar to specify a blending mode and opacity for the shape.

Applying Shape Styles

Because shapes tend to be rather plain all on their own, Photoshop offers you the option of applying styles to them as they're created, instead of having to go back later to add styles. The Style pop-up menu that you see in the Options bar whenever a Shape tool is active (see Figure 7.7) contains the same styles as the Styles panel (choose Window, Styles). You can apply them either from the Options bar or from the Styles panel. Either way, you can also remove a style that you applied previously or switch a shape to a different style.

FIGURE 7.7
Shape layers were just made for styles!

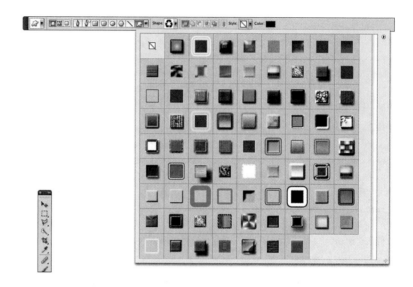

Apply a Style to a Shape

To apply a style to a shape you're about to draw, just choose the style from the Options bar before you draw the shape. Each new shape also gets the current shape color, as shown in the Options bar (this isn't necessarily the same as the Foreground color), and that underlying color affects some styles but not others. If the shape's appearance doesn't match the style thumbnail, try changing its color to white. To do that, or to apply a different style, follow these steps:

1. Click either of the shape layer's thumbnails in the Layers panel; clicking the layer's name doesn't work.

2. Click the Link button on the Options bar to activate it.

3. Choose a new style from the Style pop-up menu or click the color swatch to open the Color Picker and choose a color.

FIGURE 7.8
The Link button determines whether style and color changes apply to the current shape layer or to future ones.

The Link button is just to the left of the Style pop-up menu on the Options bar (see Figure 7.8). When you click it and select a shape layer, any changes you make in color or style are applied to the current layer. Otherwise, the changes apply to the next shape you draw. Again, you must click either of a shape layer's thumbnails—its color swatch or its vector mask thumbnail—to activate that layer. If you don't feel like fiddling with the Link button, you can simply drag a style onto any layer's entry in the Layers panel.

About Fill Layers and Shape Layers

A shape layer is really just a fill layer with a vector mask. Hour 11, "Creating Layered Images," covers fill layers, but there's not too much to know about them. They're special layers that contain a solid color, a pattern, or a gradient, and you can't directly edit their contents. You can change what they're filled with by applying a different color, pattern, or gradient. When they have masks, as shape layers do, you can edit their masks to change the apparent shape of the filled object. Fill layers can use either vector or raster masks. A vector mask is made of scalable paths instead of made by coloring specific pixels, and you can edit those paths in the same way you can edit any other path (see Hour 13, "Using Paths").

By default, each new shape is placed on its own layer, but you can draw more than one shape on a layer. To accomplish this, select the existing shape layer by clicking its color swatch or mask thumbnail in the Layers panel; then click the Add to Shape Layer button on the Options bar and draw your new shape. Keep in mind that when you put multiple shapes on a layer, they all have the same fill because each shape layer can contain only one color, pattern, or gradient. We talk more about combining shapes in the next section.

One way to use a shape layer doesn't display the shape's fill at all. You can use a shape as a **clipping mask** for an image layer by placing the image layer above the shape layer and Option-clicking/Alt-clicking the line between them (see Figure 7.9). You'll learn more about clipping masks in Hour 12, "Using Masks," along with how to create and edit other kinds of masks and which type to use when.

FIGURE 7.9
The shape acts as a clipping mask for the image layer directly above it.

NOTE

In Context

For quick access to shape layer functions, use contextual menus. In the Layers panel, Ctrl-click or right-click the shape thumbnail to access the normal Layers panel functions, including thumbnail size. If you right-click the layer's mask thumbnail, on the other hand, you'll be able to disable, delete, or rasterize the mask. Finally, right-click the layer's name to access a variety of other layer commands, including Disable Mask and Rasterize Layer.

Combining and Editing Shapes

One shape is fine, but you'll really be rolling with shapes when you create a bunch and then combine them to create more complex shapes. In this section, we look at a few different ways to change the outline of a shape created with one of the Shape tools.

Combining Shapes

To edit a shape after you've drawn it, first make sure that the shape layer is selected and then click one of the following buttons in the Options bar:

- ▶ Add to Path Area
- ▶ Subtract from Path Area
- ▶ Intersect Path Areas
- ▶ Exclude Overlapping Path Areas

If you choose Add and draw a second shape, they're both filled. If you choose Subtract and draw a second shape touching the first, you can cut out part of the filled shape where the two overlap. Intersect fills the shapes *only* where they overlap, and exclude fills only the area where the two shapes don't overlap. Figure 7.10 shows some examples.

FIGURE 7.10
These options aren't available until you've drawn the first shape.

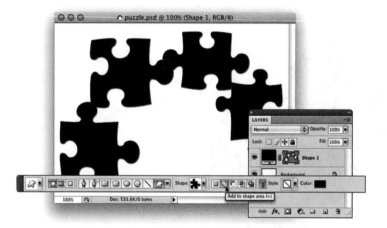

When you use these options, all the paths on the shape layer mask remain intact and editable with the Path tools; what you're doing just changes what shows through the mask. If you want to permanently combine or intersect shapes, select both paths with the Path Selection tool (the black arrow, not the Direct Selection tool's hollow arrow), click the appropriate button on the Options bar to do what you want to do with the paths, and then click the Combine button. Don't worry—the button says Combine even if you're intersecting or subtracting, but Photoshop will perform whichever function you chose.

Editing a Shape's Outline

To modify the outline of a shape, click the shape layer's vector mask thumbnail in the Layers panel or the Paths panel. Then change the shape using the Shape tools (as described in the previous section) or the Path tools. You might have to click the edge of the shape with the Path Selection tool or the Direct Selection tool to see the path. While you're editing a shape's path, press the spacebar while dragging to move the shape without changing its size or proportions.

If you've used Adobe Illustrator or another vector drawing program, you already know how to use Photoshop's Path tools. If not, hang on until Hour 13, when we go over their capabilities in detail.

Creating Your Own Shapes

My favorite feature of the Custom Shape tool is the capability to create my own shapes so that I can reuse them any time I want. This is great for logos or similar graphics such as "Happy Birthday!" To make a new shape, start by creating a shape using the other Shape tools, or select the path containing the shape you want to use. To add your shape to the Custom Shapes panel, open the Paths panel (choose Window, Paths) and make sure your chosen path is selected. Then choose Edit, Define Custom Shape and enter a name for the new shape in the dialog (see Figure 7.11). When you click OK, the shape is added to the panel.

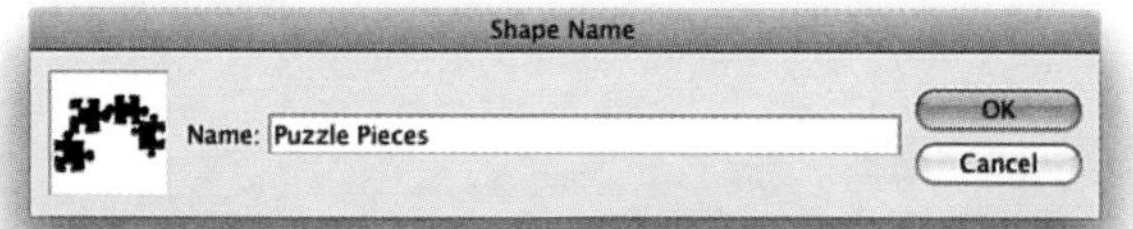

> **CAUTION**
>
> **One Step at a Time**
>
> Remember, combining shapes this way is a permanent change, so go slowly and be sure you're happy with the result before moving on; otherwise, you may find yourself having to undo more than just one step.

> **TIP**
>
> **Line 'Em Up**
>
> When you select shape paths with the Path Selection tool, you can use the Align and Distribute buttons on the Options bar to reposition them relative to each other. We cover this topic and lots more about editing paths in Hour 13.

FIGURE 7.11
Give the shape a name to add it to Photoshop's library of custom shapes.

TIP

Kicking It Up a Notch

You can convert any vector drawing into a custom shape by opening it in Illustrator, copying it, and pasting it into Photoshop. When Photoshop asks how you want to paste the data on the Clipboard, choose Shape Layer. Then choose Edit, Define Custom Shape and follow the procedure described earlier. You might find that you have to edit the drawing before it translates correctly to a shape layer; for example, "holes" in the drawing have to be real holes (you'll need to make a compound shape) instead of just white shapes in front of black ones.

To use your new custom shape, choose it from the pop-up menu in the Tool Options bar. If you want to save the new custom shape as part of a new library so that you can share it with friends or keep a backup, choose Save Shapes from the pop-up panel menu.

Summary

You don't have to be able to draw with a pencil or pen to draw perfectly shaped figures in Photoshop. The Shape tools offer a bevy of different shapes that you can use one at a time or in combination. You can fill shapes with any color, pattern, or gradient, and you can apply any of Photoshop's layer styles to them. After you create a shape, you can edit it and combine it with other shapes. You can even create shapes for use by the Custom Shape tool from your own vector drawings.

Q&A

Q. How many different shapes can you use with the custom shape tool?

A. Photoshop comes with libraries that include dozens of shapes. You can create your own shape libraries, using the custom shapes you create, and trade them with other people. So, really, there's no limit to the number of shapes the Custom Shape tool can use.

Q. What's the difference between layer styles and shape styles?

A. There is no difference! You can apply any layer style to a shape layer, and you can grab more on the Web; just Google "Download Photoshop layer styles."

Workshop

Quiz

1. What set of tools is used to edit the outline of a shape?

    A. Selection

    B. Type

    C. Edge

    D. Path

2. True or false: Any drawing created in Photoshop can be the basis for a custom shape.

3. Which of the following can't be created with a Shape tool?

    A. Shape layer

    B. 3D shape layer

    C. Path

    D. Rasterized shape

Answers

1. **D.** A shape's outline is really a path that defines a mask for a fill layer, so you can edit it just as you would any path.

2. **False.** Only path-based drawings can be used to create custom shapes.

3. **B.** You must have Photoshop Extended to create 3D layers; the commands you use to do so are in the 3D menu.

Exercise

Practice making shapes on new layers; then try putting more than one shape on a layer. See if you can create a combination of shapes that looks like a city skyline or a dog bone, or any other geometrical object. Then combine those shapes and use the resulting complex shape to create a new custom shape. Finally, switch to the Custom Shape tool and create some shape layers using your new custom shape; see how they look with a variety of layer styles and colors applied and at different sizes.

HOUR 8
Different Ways to Paint

Forget about all the complex color math and Shape tool geometry we've been talking about for the last few hours—it's time to break out the paints and have some fun! Although Photoshop was originally designed as an image editor—a program used for modifying and improving digitized photographs—it also draws a lot of its parentage from paint programs, such as MacPaint and Windows Paint. Remember the fun you had doodling around in those programs back in the day? Well, Photoshop offers you that same experience and much, much more in the way of art creation capabilities.

For one thing, you have complete control over your virtual paintbrush: It can be any size, shape, and texture you want. It can be hard-edged or soft-edged, and you can choose exactly how much paint it applies with each stroke—and even whether it responds to your pressure with a stylus on a graphics tablet. And, of course, you can paint with all sorts of tools in Photoshop, not just a brush (see Figure 8.1). You've got an airbrush, an eraser, a pencil, a bucket, and even your finger (it's called the Smudge tool). You can blur and sharpen details, you can paint previous incarnations of an image back into selected spots, and you can create perfectly shaded gradients containing as many colors as you desire. In this hour, we look at all these tools and techniques—and more.

WHAT YOU'LL LEARN IN THIS HOUR:

▶ Making the Most of Brushes

▶ Using Other Painting Tools

▶ Using the Focus Tools

FIGURE 8.1
These tools are designed for painting and drawing.

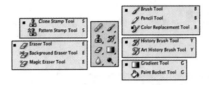

Making the Most of Brushes

Before we discuss specific brush configurations, let's take a brief look at the Brush picker, which is accessible from the Tool Options bar after you switch to any of the tools that use brush shapes. To open it, click the swatch on the Options bar that shows the current brush shape. Although each tool has its own set of options, the Brush preset picker (shown in Figure 8.2) works with most of the Painting tools, from the Brush to the Clone Stamp tool. (The Pencil's brushes are different, and the Paint Bucket and Gradient tools don't use brushes.) Using the Brush preset picker, you can choose any of Photoshop's preset brush shapes to use with the current tool.

FIGURE 8.2
The Brush preset picker shows the shape, size, and hardness of the selected brush tip.

Click to choose one of the built-in brush shapes. The size and shape displayed are the size and shape of the brush, unless you see a number underneath the brush shape. The number indicates the diameter of the brush in pixels. Drag the Master Diameter slider to change the size of the brush without changing any of its other characteristics. A brush can be up to 2,500 pixels wide.

Photoshop comes with many alternative sets of brushes. You can install one of the additional brush sets by choosing it from the pop-up menu on the Brushes menu. Photoshop asks whether you want to replace the current brush set with the new one or add the new brushes to what's already in the Brushes menu (Append). If you want to view the brush shapes by name instead of by the shape of the stroke they make, use the pop-up menu as well.

Choosing a Brush

Figure 8.3 shows the Brushes panel. Open the Brushes panel by first switching to any painting tool and then clicking the preferences button on the Options bar (it's the farthest button to the right), or by choosing Window, Brushes. You can drag the Brushes panel to a convenient spot on the screen or leave it "docked" at the right edge of the screen. If you move the panel out onto the screen, you can return it to the dock by dragging it back into its panel group with the Clone Source panel.

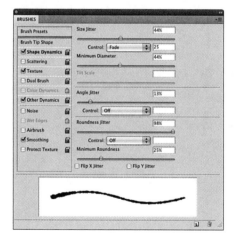

FIGURE 8.3
The Brushes panel has all the controls you need to design custom brushes.

The left column displays a list of brush attributes, from tip shapes to dynamics (characteristics that can change while you're painting). Clicking each of these items opens a different pane on the right side of the panel. (Shown in the figure is the Shape Dynamics pane.) With this panel, you can specify the qualities of each brush: the diameter, hardness, spacing, angle, roundness, and other characteristics of a brush, either starting from scratch or modifying a preset brush.

The first two brush attributes to consider are size and shape, which you set in the Brush Tip pane. Adjust the diameter with the slider, then drag the black dots on the brush tip proxy inward to determine its roundness (or lack thereof). Drag the arrow to set how far off horizontal the brush is angled.

Next, set the brush's hardness. The harder a brush is (closer to 100%), the sharper the edges of each paint stroke will be. A brush with a setting of around 20% makes soft-edged strokes.

The next option is for spacing. By clicking the Spacing check box, you can set a standard spacing of paint, no matter how fast you drag the mouse. If the Spacing check box is left unchecked, the speed of your mouse determines the spacing of discrete drops of paint. If you move more slowly, paint appears in a continuous line. If you move the mouse more quickly, dabs of paint shaped like your brush tip appear with spaces between them. If you prefer consistent spacing, a setting of about 25% normally yields a very smooth line of paint. As you increase the percentage (either by dragging the slider or by entering a number), the spaces expand. You can see the differences in the brush preview at the bottom of the panel as you drag the spacing slider (see Figure 8.4).

FIGURE 8.4
Here's what brush strokes look like with Spacing set at 25%, 100%, and 200%, respectively, from top to bottom.

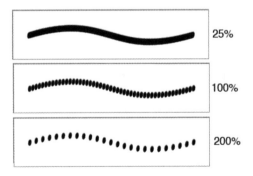

25%

100%

200%

Feel free to play around with these settings. With a little experimentation, you can end up with a brush that behaves just as a real brush does—painting thicker and thinner depending on the angle and speed of your stroke. When you create a brush you really like, save it. Click the New Brush button at the bottom of the panel and give your new brush a name in the Brush Name dialog. The brush will be available to you in the Brushes menu from then on (see

Figure 8.5). If you create an assortment of brushes, you can save them as a group. There's a pop-up menu on the right side of the Brushes panel. (Look for the right-pointing triangle.) Choose Save Brushes to save a brush set.

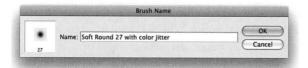

FIGURE 8.5
The Brush Name dialog.

Brush Options

In addition to the brush shape options, Photoshop gives you some options for brush behavior. Unfortunately, unless you have a pressure-sensitive graphics tablet, you won't be able to enjoy the full benefit of these options, but you don't need to have a tablet to use them. The brush behavior options appear in a list on the left side of the Brushes panel. Click the name of the action, such as Scattering, to reach the pane containing its settings. After you've made your adjustments, use the check box next to the action's name to turn the effect on or off.

Using the Wet Edges Setting

Wet Edges creates a sort of watercolor effect when you paint. Paint builds up at the edges of your brush, and, as long as you're holding down the mouse and painting, the paint stays "wet." In other words, you can paint over your previous strokes without building up additional layers of color. However, if you release the mouse button and begin to paint again, you add a new layer of paint, which creates an entirely new effect. Figure 8.6 shows an example of the same brush and paint with Wet Edges on and off. Notice the overlapped strokes in the figure.

CAUTION

Always Back Up

If you've created a bunch of custom brushes that you don't want to lose, be sure to save them in a set as a backup. Reinstalling Photoshop deletes your custom brushes, actions, and palettes—and, of course, a hard drive crash does the same thing.

FIGURE 8.6
The Wet Edges effect makes the middle of each stroke translucent, leaving the edge dark.

Setting Brush Dynamics

If you use a graphics tablet and stylus, you can get the same sort of fade-out effect that you'd get in the real world by easing off the pressure on a brush or pencil, and you can vary the color and shape of your brush by manipulating your stylus. You have five options for each of these settings: Off, Fade, Pen Pressure, Pen Tilt, and Stylus Wheel. Figure 8.7 shows the Color Dynamics pane of the Brushes panel and some sample strokes with the dynamics on.

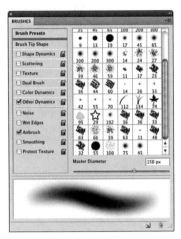

FIGURE 8.7
Each line is one brush stroke with different settings applied.

If you're not using a tablet and stylus, you can get a similar effect by choosing Fade from the pop-up menu shown in Figure 8.7; with this option, the effect is in full force at the beginning of a stroke and fades out as you continue to paint.

In the Color Dynamics pane, you can set an amount for your paint color to change during each stroke, called **jitter**. Foreground/Background Jitter, for example, makes blobs of the Background color appear within your stroke, while Brightness Jitter makes the color become brighter and darker as you paint. The Shape Dynamics options include Size Jitter, Angle Jitter, Roundness Jitter, and Flip X and Flip Y Jitter, by which you can flip the brush's shape horizontally or vertically while painting. This won't show if you're using a round brush, of course, but with other shapes it's a great way to add a naturalistic, random element to your painting. Finally, the Other Dynamics pane has two settings: Opacity Jitter and Flow Jitter. (We talk more about Opacity and Flow settings in "Using the Brush," later in this hour.)

Making Other Settings

We're not done yet; the Brushes panel has more to offer. I'll bet you never realized that designing a paintbrush could be so time-consuming, did you? The remaining settings in the panel are as follows:

▶ **Scattering**—These settings remove the restriction that brush tips must stick exactly to the line of your stroke, allowing them to float nearby at varying distances and adding another random element to your painting.

▶ **Texture**—Here you can add a pattern to your brushstrokes to make them look more natural. Click the pattern swatch to see a menu of other patterns you can use, and don't forget to check the Pattern menu's own pop-up menu for more preset groups of textures you can load.

▶ **Dual Brush**—Yes, yet another brush! Here you can set Photoshop to overlay another brush shape on top of the one you've already chosen, with the specified blending mode applied to the brush on top to determine how the two interact.

▶ **Noise**—Click this box—there are no settings to make—to add flecks of noise around your brush strokes.

▶ **Airbrush**—Check this box to turn on the Brush tool's Airbrush mode by default. You can still turn it off and on in the Options bar while you're using the brush, but you'll always start with it on.

▶ **Smoothing**—With this option turned on, Photoshop smoothes out your mouse's path, making your brush strokes into gentle curves instead of jagged lines.

▶ **Protect Texture**—This option ensures that all your patterned brushes use the same pattern and scale, so you get a consistent look throughout the image.

Using the Brush

Most often, when you're painting in Photoshop, you'll be using the Brush tool. Press B to switch to the Brush, or click it in the toolbox, then click and drag to paint; it's that simple.

When you're working with the Brush tool, the single most important setting in the Tool Options bar is Opacity. Enter a value or click and hold the triangle next to the Opacity field to enable the slider. A low setting applies a thin layer of paint—nearly transparent. The closer you come to 100%, the more concentrated the color is. Figure 8.8 contains some examples of different opacities. I've drawn lines on top of the gradient with both a soft and a hard brush, and I've changed the percentage of opacity for each set of lines.

FIGURE 8.8
These magenta stripes, painted over a blue gradient, vary in opacity; the opacity percentage for each one is listed below the stripes.

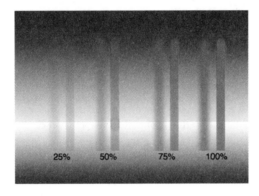

The Options bar's other settings include Blending Mode. All the blending modes you learned about in the last hour are available when you're using the Brush tool, although you can choose only Behind or Clear if you're on a layer other than the Background layer.

The Flow setting is similar to Opacity, but it enables you to vary the amount of paint you apply with each stroke by varying the amount of time you keep the Brush in that spot. The total amount of paint can't exceed the Opacity percentage, however, no matter what value you enter for the Flow value.

Can't draw a straight line? No worries. To paint a straight line between two points at any angle with the Brush or any other Painting tool, click the canvas once to set the first point, and then Shift-click to mark the endpoint. A line magically draws itself between the two points. If you need to draw a straight horizontal or vertical line, just press Shift as you paint to constrain the Brush's path. This trick also works with all the Painting tools, as well as the Toning tools. Figure 8.9 shows some work with the Photoshop brushes that uses both of these techniques. The picture began with a gradient. Then the artist used a smooth, moderate-sized Wet Edges brush, followed by a brush that simulates grass. These are all included in the default brush set.

FIGURE 8.9
This picture was painted with several different brushes.

Using Other Painting Tools

Now that you've mastered the Brush, it's time to turn your attention to the other Painting tools. Let's start by taking a good look at the Airbrush, Smudge, Eraser, and Pencil tools.

▼ TRY IT YOURSELF

Work with the Painting Tools

Before you get too immersed in the minutiae of these tools, take a break and try them out. Follow these steps:

1. Create a new file, making the canvas big enough that you have some room to move around. The default size, 7×5 inches, works fine for this task.

2. On the right side of the screen, look for the Swatches panel and click the tab to bring it forward, if necessary. If it's missing, open it from the Window menu. As you know from Hour 6, "Choosing and Blending Colors," the Swatches panel is your digital paint box, with built-in sets of paint colors for you to use. Start by clicking any color you like.

3. Press B to choose the Brush from the toolbox.

4. Click the Brush swatch in the Tool Options bar to open the Brush Preset picker, then choose a brush tip. Go wild—try some of the funky ones!

5. Press and hold the mouse button as you drag the brush over the canvas to paint.

6. Try the Pencil and Eraser tools, too. Press Shift+B to switch from the Brush to the Pencil; when you're done with the Pencil, press E to switch to the Eraser. Experiment with changing the options for each tool.

The Airbrush

Long ago, the Airbrush was a separate tool. Now it's represented by a button on the Tool Options bar when the Brush tool is active. Clicking this button makes the Brush work like an airbrush, which uses compressed air to blow paint through an adjustable nozzle. The Airbrush applies paint with soft diffused edges, and you can control how fast the paint is applied. You can adjust the Airbrush to spray a constant stream or one that fades after a specified period. You'll achieve notably different results with different amounts of pressure and different brush sizes and shapes. The longer you keep the Airbrush tool in a single spot, the darker and more saturated the applied color becomes, as if you were spraying paint with a real airbrush or from an aerosol can.

Figure 8.10 shows a drawing done with the Airbrush. The spotty effect comes from using a blending mode called Dissolve. (You' learned about blending modes in the last hour""; turn back and review, if you need to.)

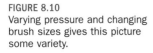

FIGURE 8.10
Varying pressure and changing brush sizes gives this picture some variety.

The Smudge Tool

It might not seem like a technical term, but **smudge** is the artist's term for blending two or more colors. The Smudge tool looks like, and works like, your finger, and you'll find it in the same toolbox compartment with the Blur and Sharpen tools. Just like your finger on wet paint, the Smudge tool picks up color from wherever you start to drag and moves it in the direction in which you drag. The Tool Options bar's Strength field controls the pressure of your smudging finger. At 100%, the finger wipes away the paint completely. At 50%, it smears it, and at 25%, the smear is less pronounced (see Figure 8.11 for examples of these different Strength settings). The Sample All Layers check box, also on the Options bar, determines how many layers you can smudge at once: only the current layer or all of them.

Photoshop considers the Smudge tool to be a brush, so you can set its width by choosing an appropriate brush size from the Brush menu.

You can also use the Smudge tool to mimic finger painting by checking the Finger Painting box on the Options bar. When this option is active, each stroke starts with the foreground color. You'll find it quite handy if you need to blend some color into an existing picture or soften the edges of an object.

Figure 8.12 shows the Smudge tool's Options bar. Click and hold the arrow next to the Strength setting to open the slider, then drag to set the Strength. If you'd rather not bother with the slider, type a single digit to set the Strength value to a multiple of 10. For instance, type **4** to set it to 40. Incidentally, that trick works with all of Photoshop's sliders, as long as only one relevant slider is visible at a time. If you like this shortcut but want more precise control, just type the digits of the measurement you want in quick succession.

FIGURE 8.11
Different Strength settings have markedly different effects on the existing paint.

FIGURE 8.12
The Smudge Tool Options bar includes the Brush Preset picker and a truncated selection of blending modes.

As usual, the blending modes are on a pop-up menu. This tool doesn't give you all the blending mode options you learned about in Hour 6, but you can choose Darken, Lighten, Hue, Saturation, Color, or Luminosity, or you can leave the menu set at Normal. Of these, Darken and Lighten are

TIP
Which Smudge Is Best?

If the Smudge tool doesn't achieve the effect you intended, you might try the Smudge Stick filter, which you'll learn about in Hour 16, "Applying Filters to Turn Your Picture into Art." **Filters**, in case you haven't encountered the term before, are commands that apply special effects to your picture, some artistic, others more prosaic, and still others just plain odd. Photoshop has dozens of filters, each of which applies a different effect to the image. These range from blurring and sharpening filters to one that adds clouds to a sky, another that lights up your backdrop, and yet another that turns the picture into a Japanese brush painting. You can adjust most filters in various ways before applying them, and you can use the Fade command on them afterward to increase or reduce their effects.

obviously the most useful. The Darken and Lighten modes affect only pixels that are lighter or darker, respectively, than the beginning color. So you can draw right over an existing object in Darken mode, and as long as the object's color is darker than the Foreground color you're using, it won't be affected. The reverse is true for Lighten mode—it will draw *only* on areas that are darker than the Foreground color.

The Eraser

The Eraser tool is unique, in that it can replicate the characteristics of the other tools. It can erase with soft edges as if it were a Brush removing color instead of adding it. It can erase a single line of pixels, as if it were the Pencil, or it can erase some of the density of the image, as if it were the Airbrush. Of course, it can also act as an ordinary rectangular eraser, removing whatever's there to reveal either the Background color or a transparent layer. The Eraser's Options bar settings enable you to determine how it works: whether it will be a block or a brush, how much you want to erase with each pass of the tool, and even whether you want to erase to a previous step on the History panel or to the Background color. Figure 8.13 shows the Eraser's Options bar.

FIGURE 8.13
The Eraser's options are the same as the Brush's, with the addition of the Erase to History check box.

The Opacity slider controls how much is erased—a setting of 50% removes half of the existing image, allowing whatever is behind it to show through. This is useful for blending separate images together, and it can help you create a watercolor effect.

Instead of erasing to the background, you can choose Erase to History. This check box in the Options bar hooks up the Eraser with the History panel, so your strokes of the Eraser can reveal an earlier version of the picture instead of allowing the background to show through. Before you begin to erase or make any other drastic changes to your picture, you can take a snapshot of it by choosing New Snapshot from the History panel. Then if you like the results of your changes in part of the image but not in other areas, you can use Erase to History to restore the snapshot's appearance wherever you don't like the changes. You'll find that this option can save you a lot of time when you're trying new techniques.

The Eraser has two roommates in its toolbox slot: the Background Eraser and the Magic Eraser. These tools make it easier for you to erase sections of a layer to transparency so that you can do things such as delete the background around a hard-edged object (called, in graphic arts terms, **silhouetting**).

With the Background Eraser, you can erase around an object to transparency as you drag along the object's edges. By specifying different Sampling and Tolerance options, you can control what color the Magic Eraser removes and the sharpness of the boundary between what's erased and what remains. In Figure 8.14, with the Sampling: Background Swatch option turned on in the Options bar, I've set the Background color to the predominant color of the background in my photo, so that the Background Eraser will remove only that color and those close to it. I'm using the Background Eraser to remove only the leaves surrounding the rose blossom. I can drag the tool right over the edges of the petals and remove only the green leaves next to the flower.

TIP

Not Fade Away?

The Fade option, found in the Control pop-up menu in the Brushes panel's Color Dynamics section, works with the Eraser just the way it does when you're using the Airbrush. When the Fade option is turned on, after a specified number of steps, the Eraser no longer erases. This is useful for creating feathering around irregularly shaped images. Set the Opacity slider to around 75%, set Fade to about eight steps, and then click and drag away from the object you want to feather.

FIGURE 8.14
Buttons on the Options bar offer you three ways to specify the color the Background Eraser should remove.

The Background Eraser can also take its cue for what to erase directly from the image; if you want to try this, click either the Sampling: Continuous or Sampling: Once buttons on the Options bar instead of the Sampling: Background Swatch button. The latter keys in on the color of the first pixel you click when you start each stroke; the former modifies the color it's looking for as you drag the Background Eraser across the image. Either way, the color the tool picks up is that of the one pixel directly under the cursor, so you'll get the best results with the Background Eraser if you use Precise or Normal Brush Tip cursors. (Change the cursor type for Painting tools and other tools in the Preferences dialog; press Command-K [Mac] or Ctrl+K [Windows] to get there, then click Cursors in the left column.)

Two other settings on the Options bar affect how the Background Eraser works: Limits and Tolerance. The Limits pop-up menu contains three choices; the second of these, Contiguous, is the most restrictive. With this option set, the Background Eraser removes only pixels that are directly under the cursor's crosshair when you click or drag, or pixels that are adjacent to the path of the crosshair. Set Discontiguous to allow it to delete pixels of the same color anywhere within the circle defining the Magic Eraser's area of influence. Find Edges, on the other hand, works like the Contiguous Option, but it looks farther afield to figure out where object edges are and maintain those clear boundaries. Finally, the Tolerance setting is a percentage between 1% and 100% that determines how far off from the original color a pixel must be for it to be erased; lower values erase fewer pixels and higher values erase more with each click or drag.

The Magic Eraser tool is very similar to the Background Eraser tool. When you click in the image, the Magic Eraser removes all pixels of that color throughout the image, without regard to their location; it doesn't try to figure out the foreground and background objects the way the Background Eraser does. This makes it the best possible tool for erasing large areas of similar colors, such as a boring gray sky; when you need to erase a detailed area containing multiple colors, the Background Eraser is a better bet. The Contiguous check box on the Options bar allows the Magic Eraser to erase throughout the image with one click; uncheck the box to restrict the tool to the pixels adjacent to where you're clicking. Two other useful settings appear in the Options bar for the Magic Eraser: Anti-alias, which softens the edges of the erased area to avoid a jagged-looking transition, and Sample All Layers, which enables the tool to base its work on all the visible layers, while erasing only on the current layer.

Why not give the Magic Eraser a try? I guarantee you'll be impressed. To practice with this tool, pick any image that has an area of fairly even color, such as the sky or a green field.

1. Switch to the Magic Eraser. The Options bar changes to show the tool's options.

2. Start by entering a Tolerance value; this defines the range of colors that can be erased. Use a low Tolerance value if you want to erase pixels within a range of color values very close to the color of the pixel you click. A higher Tolerance value erases pixels within a broader range of color.

3. Specify the Opacity to define how much of the erased pixels is removed. An opacity of 100% erases pixels to complete transparency. Lower opacity leaves pixels partially transparent.

4. Set up the remaining options as needed:

   ▶ Check the Sample All Layers box if you want to sample the erased color using combined data from all visible layers.

   ▶ Check Anti-alias to smooth the edges of the area you erased.

   ▶ Turn on the Contiguous option to erase only pixels of the same color contiguous to the one you clicked, or leave it unchecked to erase all similar pixels in the image.

5. Click in the part of the layer you want to erase. All similar pixels within the specified tolerance range are erased to transparency.

In Figure 8.15, you can see the results of using the Magic Eraser tool. First, I isolated the sky by lassoing the house and then inverting the selection; this ensured that the Magic Eraser wouldn't erase the light-colored house along with the light-colored sky. Then I clicked once in a white area between two tree branches to remove the entire white sky. Sometimes more clicks are required, but this time I got lucky. If the Magic Eraser misses any pixels, you might need to use the regular Eraser to clean up. In this case, once I removed the sky, I created a new blue and white sky using the Render Clouds filter, brightened up the image a bit with Shadows/Highlights, and warmed it up even more using the Photo Filter command and a warming filter. The result: a bright, cheerful photo instead of the gloomy shot I started with.

FIGURE 8.15
The Magic Eraser removes all pixels that are similar in color to the
one you click.

The Pencil

The Pencil tool works very much like the Brush tool, except that its strokes
are always hard-edged, even if the Hardness value in the Brush Preset
picker is set to 0%. You can't create soft-edged lines with the pencil as you
can with the Brush. Click the Pencil tool in the toolbox (it's located in the
same slot as the Brush and the Color Replacement tool) or press B to
switch to it. (Press Shift+B if the Brush tool or the Color Replacement tool
is active.) Figure 8.16 shows the Pencil's Options bar.

FIGURE 8.16
Even though the brush's Hardness
is set to 0%, the Pencil can produce only hard-edged strokes.

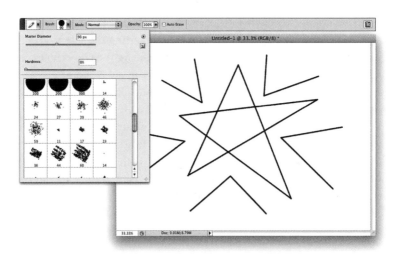

Most of the Pencil's options are the same as for the Brush: brush tip, blending mode, and opacity. The Pencil tool does have one option, though, that no other tool has. In the Tool Options bar, you'll find a check box labeled Auto Erase. When Auto Erase is checked, drawing over the current Foreground color (as shown in the toolbox) erases to the current background color until you release the mouse button instead of painting. If you click on any other color to start your stroke, the Pencil draws its line in the Foreground color as it normally would.

Using the Focus Tools

The Focus tools, Blur and Sharpen, are great for touching up an image, fixing tiny flaws, and bringing objects into sharper contrast. They can't save a really bad photo, but they can do wonders for one that's just a little bit off. Sharpen increases contrast to create the illusion of sharper focus, whereas Blur softens edges and can rid the background of unwanted clutter and de-emphasize parts of the picture that you don't want viewers to notice, such as facial wrinkles in head shots. Figure 8.17 shows the Focus tools.

FIGURE 8.17
The Focus tools share a toolbox slot with the Smudge tool.

The Blur Tool

Simply put, the Blur tool blurs your pictures by softening or evening out pixel values, reducing the image's contrast and, therefore, its sharpness wherever the blur is applied. Click the Blur tool in the toolbox; it doesn't have a keyboard shortcut. The Tool Options bar shows you the Blur tool's options (see Figure 8.18), which are the same as those for the Smudge tool except that there's no Finger Painting option. The Sample All Layers option is relevant only when your image has more than one layer. It enables the Blur tool to affect all the visible layers instead of just the active layer. You have the same choices of blending mode and the same Strength settings as with the Smudge tool.

NOTE

Back and Forth

While working with the Blur tool, you can temporarily switch to the Sharpen tool (and vice versa) by pressing Option (Mac) or Alt (Windows).

FIGURE 8.18
The Blur Tool Options bar looks pretty familiar if you've used the Smudge tool.

Figure 8.19 gives you a close look at the Blur tool's effect. This picture of a prize-winning donkey looked great, except that the car and horse trailer behind the beastie were rather distracting. So I applied some careful blurring to downplay the intrusive elements. Figure 8.20 shows the picture before and after retouching.

FIGURE 8.19
The Blur tool in use

FIGURE 8.20
Before (left) and after (right) blurring; the blurry background makes the donkey really stand out.

When you're blurring, be sure you don't miss any spots; a sharp, clear area really stands out in the middle of a blurry background. This can work for you—or against you, if the sharp area *isn't* the part of the picture you want to highlight. As you work, you can switch brush sizes to accommodate the area you're targeting, and feel free to zoom in and out as needed so that you can see clearly.

The Sharpen Tool

The Sharpen tool is the exact opposite of the Blur tool. Where the Blur tool softens color transitions by reducing edge contrast, the Sharpen tool brings edges and details into greater relief by increasing the contrast between adjacent pixels. Because of these two tools' equal-but-opposite relationship, they share a space on the toolbox, with a pop-up that lets you choose either one or the Smudge tool. Figure 8.21 shows a mushroom before and after having its surface sharpened.

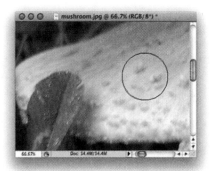 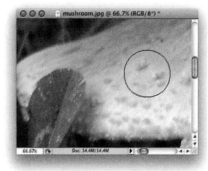

FIGURE 8.21
Here the Sharpen tool (being applied within the circle) increases contrast around the details of the mushroom's cap.

Sharpening is best done in very small doses. If you go over a section too many times or have the Sharpen tool's Strength set too high, you can end up burning the color out of an image and making it look worse than it did originally. See Figure 8.22 for an example of oversharpening.

TIP

A Touch of Retouching

One of the things you'll begin to notice as you become more accustomed to working with Photoshop is the use of image-manipulation techniques in advertising and even in editorial photos. You'll begin to recognize pictures that betray the work of a digital retoucher—and most of this work is done with Photoshop. When you see a picture that doesn't look quite right, or one that looks too good to be true, take a careful look at it and see if you can figure out how the pros created the image. Are details blurred? Are there extra highlights? Do surfaces look too perfect? The old saying "Pictures don't lie" is definitely obsolete these days. To see the dark side of Photoshop retouching, however, check out the Web site Photoshop Disasters (www.photoshopdisasters.com); it's full of retouched photos that couldn't exist in any universe I've ever heard of.

FIGURE 8.22
Too much sharpening produces nasty patterns based on the image noise that's normally nearly invisible.

Remember, too, that not even the magic of Photoshop can put back what wasn't there originally. Always work with the clearest, sharpest pictures you can manage. If your photo is fuzzy all over, instead of trying to sharpen it, set it aside until you start working with filters (see Hour 15, "Applying Filters to Improve Your Picture"). You may not be able to return to its full, lifelike glory, but it can still make good fodder for the funky and artistic effects that you can achieve with filters.

▼ TRY IT YOURSELF

Use the Focus Tools

Let's take a quick break here and try out these tools. Open any convenient picture in Photoshop and follow these steps:

1. Click the Zoom tool and then click once or twice in the image window to zoom in on the image.

2. Switch to the Blur tool and choose a soft-edged brush shape from the Brush Preset picker on the Tool Options bar.

3. Type **5** to set the Blur tool's Strength to 50%.

4. Drag the Blur tool across the picture. Notice the effect (see Figure 8.23).

FIGURE 8.23
Blurring a leaf with the image (and tool) enlarged

5. Switch to the Sharpen tool and choose a hard-edged brush. Drag it over a different part of the picture. Try to drag it along the edge of an object, and note the effect (see Figure 8.24).

needles.jpg @ 66.7% (RGB/8) *

66.67%   Doc: 9.00M/9.00M

TRY IT YOURSELF ▼
Use the Focus Tools
continued

FIGURE 8.24
Sharpening is more obvious than blurring.

6. Try sharpening the area you previously blurred. Can you restore it to its previous appearance? (Answer: no.)

7. Practice with these tools at different Strength settings and with different brushes. Use Revert (File, Revert) or click the snapshot at the top of the History panel to restore the picture if you run out of practice room.

Summary

In this hour, you took a look at the Brush tool and several of its colleagues: the Airbrush, Smudge, Pencil, and Eraser tools. Brush shapes apply to all these tools, not just to the Brush. You can alter the brush shape or its behavior using controls on the Tool Options bar, which vary depending on the tool you're using. You learned about some of the tool options and how they affect the quality of the brush stroke. You also learned to activate the Brush, Pencil, or Eraser by pressing a single keyboard letter.

Photoshop provides several ways to move paint around after you have applied it. The Smudge tool is one of these; it's useful for blending small areas of color and has the same effect as dragging your finger through wet paint. Sharpen and Blur, which share its space in the toolbox, are two sides of the same coin, so to speak. The Sharpen tool increases the contrast between adjacent pixels, whereas the Blur tool diminishes it. You can use both of these tools on photos you've taken or pictures you've painted.

Q&A

Q. Can I make a custom brush that's not round?

A. Sure. You can even make part of your image into a custom brush. Use the Rectangular Marquee to select a portion of an image, or use the Pencil tool to draw a brush shape and select that. With the selection active, choose Edit, Define Brush Preset. The new brush appears on the Brushes panel. Click it and then click Brush Tip Shape to set its spacing option and other variables.

Q. What's the difference between the Smudge tool and the Blur tool?

A. The main difference is in the way you apply them. Because smudging moves pixels from point A to point B, it tends to show the direction of that move. Blurring decreases the contrast between adjacent pixels, so they seem to blend together with no indication of movement.

Q. I understand the Sharpen tool, but there also seem to be Sharpen filters. When should I use the tool and when should I use the filters?

A. You peeked ahead, didn't you? You'll learn how to work with the Sharpen filters in Hour 15. For now, stick with the Sharpen tool when you have a small area that you want to sharpen so that it stands out more from what's around it. The filters are useful when you have a soft-focus image that needs all-over sharpening.

Workshop

Quiz

1. Are there other brush sets besides the ones I see in the Brushes panel and the Brush Preset picker? If so, where can I find them?

   A. No, but you can make your own.

   B. Photoshop comes with many sets of premade brushes. Check the pop-up menu on the Brushes menu.

   C. Brushes are available for purchase at www.coolestbrushesever.com.

   D. All over the Web: Just Google "Photoshop brush download" to find them.

2. What effect does 100% Strength have on the Smudge tool?

   A. None.

   B. It turns the smudges black.

   C. Instead of just smudging, the tool completely replaces color in the path of the stroke with the adjacent color.

   D. It renders the tool completely ineffective.

3. If you sharpen a piece of the picture too much, what happens?

   A. It turns into a seemingly random collection of black and colored pixels.

   B. It turns white.

   C. It turns black.

   D. It eventually starts to blur.

Answers

1. **B.** Actually, answer A is only partly wrong. You can make your own brushes and brush sets, and you can use the ones Adobe provides. Answer D is correct too. First, though, take a look at the brush sets you've already got.

2. **C.** If you have turned on the Finger Paint option, you can use the Smudge tool set at 100% almost like an eraser, dragging Background color over the object you want to smudge out.

3. **A.** It looks kind of neat, if you really go crazy with it.

Exercise

Here, you'll get some more practice with the Airbrush, Brush, and Eraser tools. Follow along with these steps:

1. Start by opening a new document, at least 6 inches square so that you have plenty of room to work.

2. Click the Brush in the toolbox. Set your opacity to 100%, choose a medium-sized, hard-edged brush, and draw a star.

3. Click the check box to turn on Wet Edges and draw another star.

4. Choose a soft-edged brush and draw another star.

5. Now turn off Wet Edges and draw another star with the soft-edged brush. Your result should look something like Figure 8.25, only, with luck, your stars are more symmetrical.

FIGURE 8.25
Four kinds of brush strokes produce four very different looks.

6. Now scroll to the top of the History panel and click the history state icon labeled New. This returns to your freshly opened page, minus stars. (It's a quick way to erase everything.)

7. Press B to activate the Brush, then click the Airbrush button on the Options bar. Set the Flow to 100% and draw a star.

8. Set the Flow to 50% by typing the number **5**, and draw another star. (You can change Brush Opacity settings by typing a number, too.)

9. Change brushes. If you've been using a soft-edged brush with the Airbrush, try a hard one, or vice versa. Draw more stars with different brushes and pressure settings.

10. Press E to bring up the Eraser. Set the Eraser mode to Brush and the Opacity to 50%. (Type the number **5**.) Try to erase one of your stars. Don't click the mouse more than once while you're erasing.

11. Change the Opacity to 100% and erase another star.

12. Experiment with different settings until you're comfortable with these tools.

HOUR 9
Advanced Painting Techniques

As you learned in the last hour, Photoshop can do more than fix photos; it can also help you create images straight from your imagination. In this hour, we look at ways to make an image in Photoshop look as though it was drawn or painted with real-world ink, charcoal, or paint. If you're already a skilled artist with conventional tools and materials, you'll be intrigued by Photoshop's capability to mimic some of those techniques, without all the mess—and with the capability to go back and undo your mistakes. If you're one of those who, like me, has never been able to get the hang of drawing or painting on paper or canvas, you'll love the ability Photoshop gives you to "fake it."

The techniques that we cover in this hour enable you to imitate traditional artists' media, such as chalk, charcoal, paint, and ink on paper. You'll create these effects with a combination of painting and using filters. But you can also create images that transcend the limitations of real-world media, combining effects and creating new ones. As with so much in Photoshop, experimentation is the key to mastery; your only limitation is your own creativity.

Simulating Different Media

One of Photoshop's remarkable tricks is simulating the appearance of real-world art media. You can achieve these effects by using a filter; we jump ahead a little in this hour and introduce you to some of Photoshop's "artistic" filters. You can also achieve these affects through judicious use of the Smudge and Blur tools, or by choosing or creating custom brushes and carefully applying color with a particular blending mode. You can create a picture starting with a blank canvas, or you can work with a photograph to

WHAT YOU'LL LEARN IN
THIS HOUR:

▸ Simulating Different Media
▸ Imitating Watercolor and Oil Paint
▸ Imitating Pencil, Charcoal, and Chalk
▸ Painting from Your History
▸ Using a Pressure-Sensitive Tablet

NOTE

Okay, It's Not Perfect

Let's back up for a minute and admit something: Photoshop wasn't actually designed to be an all-purpose graphics program. It lacks some of the precise drawing tools that you'll find in Adobe Illustrator or the natural-media painting tools featured in Corel Painter (to name just two of the best programs). However, Photoshop has such a wide range of features that you can use it very effectively to create many kinds of graphics. Because of its plug-in filters, which you'll learn about in a few hours, it can do some remarkable things with graphics, most of which lie far beyond the capability of an ordinary painting or drawing program. Should Photoshop be your only graphics program? Probably not, if you need to do a lot of drawing. But for digital darkroom work and retouching, nothing can top it—and its drawing and painting abilities are certainly nothing to sneeze at.

make it look like a watercolor painting, an oil painting in any of a half-dozen styles, or even a plaster bas-relief or fresco. Whatever method you choose, you'll find that you can achieve amazing results.

Watercolors

Artists who work in conventional media have a great deal of respect for watercolor painters because watercolor is considered to be one of the most difficult media to handle. Watercolorists must use a brush that's "wet" enough to blend colors smoothly but "dry" enough to prevent the image from turning to mud. Working with digital "watercolors" is much, much easier. We start with a filter technique that's intended to make a photo into a simulated watercolor painting.

Converting a Photograph to a Watercolor

Photoshop's Watercolor filter is one way to convert a picture to a watercolor painting. To apply the filter, choose Filter, Artistic, Watercolor submenu, as shown in Figure 9.1.

FIGURE 9.1
Watercolor is one of the 15 Artistic filters that come with Photoshop.

The Watercolor filter works best on pictures that contain large, bold shapes without too much detail. Because this filter tends to darken backgrounds and shadows quite a bit, you'll get the best results if you start with a picture that has a light background. (You can also use the techniques you learned in Hour 5, "Adjusting Brightness and Color," to turn a darker background into a lighter one.) The photo in the figures that follow features a perfect pink peony. When you choose the Watercolor filter (or virtually any other Photoshop filter, for that matter), you'll see a dialog like the one shown in Figure 9.2. This Filter Gallery contains a thumbnail view of your picture, a catalog of filters to choose from, and a different set of sliders for each filter that enable you to control the way in which the picture is converted. If you click and drag on the preview image, you can slide it around to see the effect of your settings on different parts of the photo, and you can enlarge and reduce it as well. Most Photoshop filters, even those that don't appear in the Filter Gallery, have dialogs and settings very much like this one. After you have used one, the rest will seem relatively familiar.

NOTE

Filters for Photoshop

Filters, in Photoshop terminology, are commands built into the program (or "plugged in" as added features) that apply specific effects to your images. For instance, one of Photoshop's filters converts your image to a pattern of dots, like a blown-up newspaper photograph. Another can turn it into a colored pencil drawing. Dozens of filters come with Photoshop, and others are sold by third-party vendors or distributed as shareware or freeware. In Hours 14–17, you'll learn more about what kinds of filters you can get and where to find them.

FIGURE 9.2
Use the + and − buttons below the preview to zoom in and out.

Filters can take anywhere from a few seconds to a minute or more to apply, even in the preview area. If you don't immediately see the effects of the filter on the preview, look for a progress bar in the status bar at the bottom of the filter window. It fills as the computer calculates and applies the Filter effect. When the bar disappears, the effect is in place.

The Watercolor filter has three sliders that control different aspects of the way it's created. The Brush Detail value can range from 1 to 14, with 14 retaining the most image detail and 1 yielding a splatter effect reminiscent of Jackson Pollock's work. Depending on the nature of the picture you are converting and your own preferences, I suggest that you start experimenting with Brush Detail settings in the neighborhood of 7–9. The Shadow Intensity slider ranges from 0 to 10, but unless you've lightened the picture ahead of time, leave it at 0 or 1. The Watercolor filter darkens shadows quite a bit, even at the 0 setting; with Shadow Intensity settings past 3 to 4, some pictures are almost totally black. The Texture setting can vary from 1 to 3 and produce a mottled effect that adds to the natural feel of the brush strokes. The effect is quite subtle; it's much more noticeable when you combine it with lower Brush Detail settings. In Figure 9.3 (in the following Try It Yourself exercise), you can see the differences among varying combinations of Brush Detail and Texture settings.

FIGURE 9.3
From top to bottom, these images use the following settings: Brush Detail 1, Texture 3; Brush Detail 14, Texture 1; and Brush Detail 7, Texture 7.

▼ TRY IT YOURSELF

Convert a Photograph to a Watercolor

You might not want to convert all your photos into imitation watercolors, but the Watercolor filter does amazing things with some images.

1. Choose one of your own pictures that you think would look good as a watercolor, or download the one shown here from the book's website. It's called `pinkpeony.jpg`. Open the downloaded file in Photoshop and make any color and brightness adjustments you think necessary. I lightened the background quite a bit using Shadows/Highlights and then increased the Vibrance setting to the maximum. (If you've forgotten how to adjust the image's colors, turn back to Hour 5 to refresh your memory.) Remember not to let the colors get too dark before you start applying filters. Photoshop filters, in general, tend to add more black to the image. To avoid too much distracting detail in the picture's foreground, I also blurred the grass below the flower.

2. Choose Filter, Artistic, Watercolor.

3. In the Watercolor filter dialog, which you saw in Figure 9.2, use the sliders to settle on a combination of Texture and Brush Detail values that you like the looks of. Set the shadow intensity to 0, unless you want a lot of black in the image (see Figure 9.4).

4. Move the thumbnail image to check details by clicking and dragging the hand symbol that appears when you place your cursor in the thumbnail window and zooming in where necessary by clicking the + and – buttons.

5. When you're done, click OK to apply the changes.

6. If the picture seems drab, you can use the Sponge tool set to Saturate, to intensify the colors.

TRY IT YOURSELF ▼

Convert a Photograph to a Watercolor

continued

FIGURE 9.4
Brush Detail has been set to 2, Shadow Intensity to 2, and Texture to 3.

Watercolors from Scratch

Sometimes you don't have a photo of what you want to paint or perhaps you're looking to achieve a different effect than the Watercolor filter can produce. With some careful brushing, you can produce watercolors that you'd almost swear were painted with a real brush on real paper.

You learned about working with the Brush tool in Hour 8, "Different Ways to Paint." As I'm sure you recall, using the Tool Options bar, you can switch from a large brush to a small one, or change the opacity of the paint

Sort Your Panels

If you drag the tabs at the top of the panels, you can move them around so that you can use the Layers, History, Color, and Swatches panels all at once, or any combination of panels you need. Close the panels you aren't using to make more room, and dock the panels you're most likely to need—for instance, Brushes, Layers, Color, and History—in the dock at the right side of your screen.

the Brush applies, with just a click. I also like to open the Swatches panel, add the colors I want to paint with, and use it as a paint box to choose colors, instead of going to the Color Picker each time I want to switch paint colors. Feel free to flip back if you need to review any of these techniques.

Transparency is one of the distinguishing features of real watercolor. To make a "synthetic" watercolor, you'll want to set the Brush opacity at no more than 75%, which means that your paint will be 25% transparent—about right for watercolors. Try the brush on a blank canvas, and you'll notice that painting over a previous stroke darkens the color. Click the Wet Edges check box in the Brushes panel for even more authentic-looking brush strokes. This option adds extra color along the edges of a stroke, making it look as if the pigment gathered there the way it does when you paint with a watery brush.

Watercolor artists painting on paper often start with an outline and then fill in the details. Figure 9.5 shows a "watercolor" painting of Doolittle the tiger cat. Painting in her stripes was time-consuming but easy, and when I was done, I added some texture to make the picture appear to be done on real paper. While working, I switched brushes often, zoomed in and out, and used the Smudge tool to keep my details soft and wet looking.

Another useful trick for creating a watercolor is to use the Eraser as if it were a brush full of plain water, to lighten a color that you have applied too darkly. Set the Eraser to a very low opacity to lighten a color slightly or to a high opacity to clean up around the edges of the picture where needed. Don't forget that the Eraser always erases to the Background color, which might or might not match the "paper" color you're using. If you have been changing colors as you paint, be sure to set the Background color to what you want to see when you erase, or keep your painting on a separate layer from the Background layer.

FIGURE 9.5
Use soft-edged brushes for the most realistic results.

Most real watercolors are painted on heavily textured watercolor paper, like the surface I created in Figure 9.5. If you want yours to have the same character, you can use the Texturizer filter (choose Filter, Texture, Texturizer) to add a simulated watercolor paper texture to the picture after your painting is completed. Don't apply the filter until you're sure you're done painting, though, because additional changes you make will obscure the texture. Figure 9.6 shows the Texturizer filter being applied.

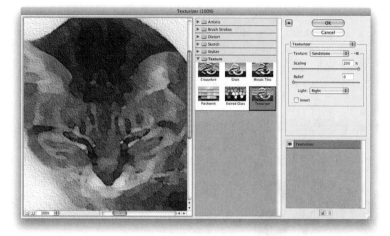

FIGURE 9.6
The direction of the light controls the shadows that make it possible for the viewer to see the texture.

The Canvas texture comes the closest to replicating watercolor paper, especially if you fiddle with the Scale to make it appropriate for the resolution of your image. Sandstone works well, too; that's what I used for the painting of Doolittle. Use the sliders to experiment with different combinations of Relief and Scaling values.

Oil Painting

Oil paint has a very different look from watercolor, and it's a look that's much easier to duplicate with Photoshop. The qualities that distinguish works in oil are the opacity of the paint, its thick texture, and the textured canvas, which adds a definite fabric grain to the image. To get the full effect in Photoshop, you can combine several techniques. We start, as artists do, with underpainting.

NOTE

Take One Tablet

For painting in Photoshop, a pressure-sensitive graphics tablet is darn near required. Drawing with a stylus is far more natural than drawing with a mouse or trackball, and the pressure-sensitivity of most tablets permits you to make trailing brush strokes that look far more realistic than anything you can produce without a tablet.

TIP

Keeping It Real

Try applying the same texture a second time, with the light coming from the opposite direction, to produce a really good imitation of textured paper. Or you can try printing your images on real watercolor paper; you should find that lighter-weight papers run through a desktop inkjet printer just fine.

Underpainting

When an artist begins an oil painting of a landscape, she often sketches the subject with a few lines, often working with charcoal or a pencil, to position the horizon and the major masses. Then she dips a big brush in thinned-out paint and begins the process of underpainting, which blocks in all the solid areas: the sky, the ground or the sea, and any obvious features, such as a large rock, a tree, or whatever else will make up the picture. Underpainting creates a foundation for the picture, establishing the colors and values of the different parts of the image. After that, the artist must fill in the details.

Photoshop's Underpainting filter analyzes the image to which you're applying it and converts it to solid patches of color. In Figure 9.7, I'm applying the filter to a photo of an iron gate in an elaborate garden. If you want to download this photo and work along, it's called gardengate, and it's at the Sams website.

FIGURE 9.7
The preview area shows you exactly what result your current settings will yield.

Using the Underpainting filter requires making some settings decisions. The Texture settings are exactly the same as in the Texturizer filter I used on the watercolor of Doolittle earlier in this hour. Here, however, you want to bring out more of the texture, so you'll use a higher Relief value and possibly a greater Scaling value as well. You can paint on canvas, burlap, sandstone, or brick, or on textures that you import from elsewhere. The Brush Size setting ranges from 0 to 40. Smaller brushes retain more of the detail in the original image, and larger brushes give somewhat blotchy coverage and remove more detail. Texture Coverage also varies on a scale from 0 to 40. Lower numbers here reveal less texture; higher numbers bring out more. In real-life underpainting, the texture is visible only where there's paint, not all over the canvas.

TRY IT YOURSELF ▼

Turn a Scene into an Oil Painting

Let's apply the oil paint technique to a photo and see how the results differ from those you can achieve with watercolor techniques.

1. As always, start by preparing the picture. Adjust the brightness and colors if necessary, rotate the image if it's not straight, and crop as needed.

2. Choose Filter, Artistic, Underpainting to open the Underpainting filter dialog.

3. Set the Brush Size slider to 10 and the Texture Coverage value to 6; these settings will retain most of the detail in the picture.

4. Set the Texture to Canvas and Scaling to somewhere around 100%. You want to keep the texture small so that it doesn't interfere with the detail you will be adding to the picture later, but big enough to show.

5. Set the Relief slider to 3 and the Light Direction to Top Right. This shows just enough texture to establish that your painting is on canvas instead of stone. The Light Direction matches the position of the sun in the original photo.

6. Click OK to apply the filter. Figure 9.8 shows the result so far.

FIGURE 9.8
The scene with just the Underpainting filter applied

Overpainting

The Underpainting filter is the first step in the "oil painting" process; the second step is to overpaint the areas that need to have detail, so that's what you'll do to complete this garden scene.

Because oil paintbrushes tend to be rather stiff, choose a hard brush instead of a soft-edged one. Make sure that Wet Edges is turned off in the Brushes panel. Although the Normal blending mode will work fine for some parts of the painting—wherever you want to make sharp strokes of paint—Dissolve might be a more useful mode for working into the trees. Use it, as shown in Figure 9.9, to stipple colors into the underpainting. (**Stippling** means to paint with the very end of a hard round brush, placing dots instead of strokes of paint. Dissolve replicates this effect very well.) Vary the Brush Size and Opacity settings to add more or less paint with each stroke.

FIGURE 9.9
I've restored texture to the trees and bushes, and put back some of the gate's details.

You can go on painting in this picture until it looks exactly like an oil painting, or you can use it as a basis for experimentation with other filters and effects. In Figure 9.10, I've reapplied the Texturizer filter (Filter, Texture, Texturizer) to restore the texture lost during the overpainting process.

FIGURE 9.10
Restoring the canvas texture in this image makes it look much more like an oil painting.

Pencils and Pens

The Pencil tool has been part of every graphics program since the very first ones, and it definitely deserves its place. It shares a space in the toolbox with the Brush tool and the Color Replacement tool. You can draw with it just as you would with a real pencil, except that you can specify its width by choosing a brush tip, or you can use it (or any of the Painting tools) in a sort of connect-the-dots mode. Click where you want a line to begin, and Shift-click where it should end; Photoshop draws the line for you. Keep Shift-clicking to add more line segments. If you click the Auto-Erase function on the Tool Options bar, the Pencil tool can also serve as an eraser. With Auto-Erase enabled, when you click the Pencil on a colored pixel that is the current Foreground color, you erase it to the current Background color. This fact can save you a lot of time switching between the Pencil and the Eraser when you're drawing.

The Pencil is great for retouching and drawing simple shapes, but it's difficult to use for a more complex drawing. You'll find that it's easier to use, however, if you zoom in to 200% so that you can see the individual pixels in the image. Setting your mouse acceleration to Slow also helps, but it's better to use a graphics tablet instead of a mouse (see "Using a Pressure-Sensitive Tablet," later in this hour, to learn more).

If you want to get the look of a pencil drawing without all the effort, start with a photo and try the Colored Pencil filter (choose Filter, Artistic, Colored Pencil) or the Crosshatch filter (choose Filter, Brush Strokes, Crosshatch). The Colored Pencil filter, shown in Figure 9.11, turns your original image into a light, somewhat stylized drawing using the Foreground and Background colors. If you convert the drawing to grayscale (using the Black & White adjustment command) after applying the filter, it looks as though it were done with black pencil instead of colored pencil. The Crosshatch filter, applied to the same image in Figure 9.12, retains much more of the original image's color and detail, but the result still looks like a pen-and-ink drawing.

FIGURE 9.11
The Colored Pencil filter gives images a light, airy feel.

FIGURE 9.12
Crosshatching emulates a different, more detailed drawing style.

Chalk and Charcoal

Charcoal is one of the oldest known art media, and chalk is pretty darn close. Some of the earliest cave drawings were done with charred sticks pulled from a fire, and early artists soon learned to mix charcoal with grease to make paint. If you've never seen any of these very old drawings, check out the pictures at the Bradshaw Foundation's web pages about Cosquer Cage in France (www.bradshawfoundation.com/cosquer/).

Chalk and charcoal are still beloved by artists today for their ease of use and versatile lines. You can make sharp lines or smudged ones, depending on how you hold the chalk or charcoal stick. And modern chalk drawings can be found on virtually any surface, from grained paper to brick walls and concrete sidewalks. You can put your "chalk" drawings in Photoshop on sandstone, burlap, or a texture that you've imported from another source.

Chalk and charcoal are both linear materials, meaning that they're used to draw lines instead of fill in large flat areas, like paints. Choose pictures to apply the Charcoal and Chalk & Charcoal filters to with that fact in mind. Of course, you can apply shading as a pattern of lines or crosshatching, and you can smudge to your heart's content. If you're drawing from scratch, start with a fairly simple line drawing and expand on it. If you're converting a photo into a chalk or charcoal drawing, choose one that has strong line patterns and well-defined detail.

The Chalk & Charcoal Filter

When you apply the Chalk & Charcoal filter (choose Filter, Sketch, Chalk & Charcoal), you'll see that it reduces your picture to three colors: gray plus the Foreground and Background colors that you have set in the toolbox. Chalk uses the Background color and Charcoal becomes the Foreground color. Areas that aren't colored appear in gray. Experimentation will help you find the right colors for each image, but you'll probably want to stick with a light Background color and a darker Foreground color; otherwise, the image ends up with dark and light areas reversed, like a photo negative.

Figure 9.13 shows the Chalk & Charcoal dialog, which controls how this filter works. In it, you can set values for the amount of Chalk and Charcoal coverage. These sliders have a range from 0 to 20. Start somewhere in the middle and adjust until you get a combination that works for your picture. The Stroke Pressure varies from 0 to 5. Unless you want the picture to turn into areas of flat color, keep the setting at 1 or 2. Intensity builds up very quickly with this filter. The Foreground color for this image is black, but the Background color is a light peach.

FIGURE 9.13
Use the preview window to see the filter's effect on every part of the image before clicking OK.

▼ TRY IT YOURSELF

Convert a Photograph to a Chalk and Charcoal Drawing

The Chalk & Charcoal filter looks great with any reasonably high-contrast subject. Try it on a portrait.

1. Open the image, set your Foreground and Background colors, and then choose Filter, Sketch, Chalk & Charcoal.

2. Set both the Charcoal and Chalk Area sliders to 10 or less. When you work with a filter for the first time, always start in the middle of the settings range to get an idea of what the filter does, and increase or decrease as necessary. It's often also useful to set all the sliders at their lowest point and then at their highest point, too.

3. Set the Stroke Pressure slider to 1 or 2. Move on to step 4 if you like the view in the preview area, or experiment with other numbers until you're happy.

4. Click OK to apply the filter. Study the result. Decide what areas need touching up.

5. Switch to the Eraser tool and erase some of the extraneous charcoal, to bring up more of the Background color.

6. Select the Brush tool to apply more of the Foreground color, also known in this situation as chalk. Press X to swap the Foreground and Background colors quickly.

7. Use the Eyedropper to select the gray, if you need to apply it elsewhere. (The gray is an arbitrary color this filter uses and can't be adjusted within the dialog—but you can use the techniques you learned in Hour 5 to modify it afterward.)

8. When you're satisfied with the drawing, save it (see Figure 9.14).

TRY IT YOURSELF ▼

Convert a Photograph to a Chalk and Charcoal Drawing
continued

FIGURE 9.14
After applying the filter, I erased and redrew various areas of the image until I liked the result.

The Smudge tool works particularly well with the Chalk & Charcoal filter. Use it exactly as you would use your finger or the side of your hand on paper to soften a line or blend two colors. You can also use Photoshop's Blur and Sharpen tools to define edges or to soften a line without smudging it.

The Charcoal Filter

Use the Charcoal filter (choose Filter, Sketch, Charcoal) to convert a photograph to a reasonably good imitation of a charcoal drawing. Because charcoal doesn't come in colors, your "charcoal" drawings will be most realistic if you set the foreground to black and the background to white, or to another pale color if you want the effect of drawing on colored paper. Figure 9.15 shows the Charcoal filter dialog. You can adjust the thickness of the charcoal line from 1 to 7, and the degree of detail it retains from 0 to 5. The Light/Dark Balance setting ranges from 0 to 100 and controls the proportion of Foreground to Background color in the filtered image.

NOTE

Lots to Learn
Photoshop CS4 includes more than 100 filters! If you master one each week, in a couple of years, you'll know them all— and by then a new version of Photoshop will be out, with new features and filters for you to learn.

FIGURE 9.15
As with most of Photoshop's filters, you'll need to experiment with
these settings to find the right
combination for each image.

Figure 9.16 shows a portrait converted using the Charcoal filter and lightly
retouched with the Brush, Blur, and Sharpen tools. Using a graphics tablet
instead of a mouse makes it much easier to reproduce the filter's crosshatched lines with the Brush.

FIGURE 9.16
A bit of retouching brought back
the details that were lost in translation.

Painting from Your History

Sometimes you'll apply a filter and get perfect results—in 90% of the image. Elsewhere, you wish you could back off just a bit, or even just revert those areas of the image to the way they were. That's what the History Brush is for. If you get heavily into using combinations of filters, you'll find this tool indispensable. And the Art History Brush is a neat twist on the basic concept, applying swirling brush strokes to the image as it paints.

Using the History Brush

The History Brush comes in handy when you're making changes in an image and aren't sure exactly how much change to make or where to make it (which describes most artists most of the time). It enables you to apply a bunch of changes and then selectively restore parts of the picture by choosing a brush size and painting over the new image with the old one. In Figure 9.17, I applied the Glowing Edges filter to a photo of the Golden Gate Bridge, and then I used the History Brush to undo the effect of the filter in a few areas of the photo.

FIGURE 9.17
I restored the original details of the sun, the water, and the misty hills in the distance.

To use the History Brush, click the box at the left side of the History panel (choose Window, History) next to the history state you want to use as the source. To produce Figure 9.17, I clicked the original image because I wanted to restore parts of it in the altered version. Then switch to the History Brush, choose a brush shape and size, and start painting.

Using the Art History Brush

The Art History Brush shares a slot in the toolbox with the History Brush, and you can press Shift+Y to toggle between the two. The Art History Brush tool paints with a variety of stylized strokes, but—like the History Brush—it draws its source data from a specified history state or a snapshot. If you don't want to paint in an older version of the image, just click next to the latest history state in the History panel. The Art History Brush offers a menu of different kinds of strokes. After you've chosen a stroke and a brush size, you can paint onto the image with the chosen stroke, turning your image into something perhaps resembling an Impressionist watercolor, a Pointillist oil, or some other artistic style. Figure 9.18 shows the Art History Brush's Styles pop-up menu on the Tool Options bar.

FIGURE 9.18
Curls imitate van Gogh at his wildest, Dab does Monet, and Loose Medium resembles a Renoir.

In Figure 9.19, I've applied the Art History Brush to a photo, and then I've gone back into it with the History Brush to restore some of the edges and detail.

FIGURE 9.19
Combining the Art History Brush and the History Brush enables you to restore some of the original image's details after you've changed it.

Try out the Art History Brush by following these steps:

1. Start with an open image that you've modified extensively since you opened it (such as by applying a filter). On the History panel, click the left column next to the state you want to use as the source for the Art History Brush tool. You'll see the Art History Brush's icon appear next to the name of the state.

2. Click the Art History Brush; you'll find it grouped with the History Brush tool in the toolbox.

3. Set Mode to Normal for now (we talked about blending modes in Hour 6, "Choosing and Blending Colors") and set Opacity to 75%. You can change both of these settings as you work.

4. Choose an option from the Style menu to control the shape of the brush strokes.

5. In the Area field, enter a value to specify the area around the cursor that the paint strokes will cover. Larger sizes mean larger areas covered and more paint strokes produced, with fewer clicks on your part.

6. Enter a Tolerance value or drag the slider to limit the regions where paint strokes can be applied. A low Tolerance lets you paint unlimited strokes anywhere in the image. A high Tolerance limits paint strokes to areas that differ significantly from the color in the source.

7. Choose a brush shape and start painting.

The Art History Brush can produce some really nice effects, if you spend time learning to work with its settings. Even more than most tools in Photoshop, it takes practice to use correctly.

Using a Pressure-Sensitive Tablet

As you become more accustomed to creating art in Photoshop (or in any other graphics program, for that matter) you'll realize that dragging a mouse around your desktop isn't the best way to draw, to put it mildly. As for using a trackball or a touchpad—well, they're even more difficult. These tools simply weren't designed for creating artwork.

The natural way for people to create a picture is to pick up a pencil, pen, or brush and draw on something. People have been doing it for thousands of years, all the way back to the cave painters I mentioned earlier in this hour, who used crude crayons made of animal fat and colored clays; the ancient Sumerians, who created images using a sharpened stylus and a slab of wet clay; and the ancient Egyptians, who wrote and drew with squid ink and feathers on papyrus, a paperlike material made from fibrous plant stems.

Today we have something much better: graphics tablets that are designed specifically to work with Photoshop and other programs like it. These consist of a flat drawing surface, sometimes tethered to the computer by a cable and sometimes wireless, and a stylus about the size and weight of a ballpoint pen, sometimes having an eraser at its top end. The drawing surface is sensitive to the stylus's motion and pressure, and translates that information into the movements of the cursor on your screen. A tablet such as the Wacom Bamboo (www.wacom.com/bambootablet/) costs less than $100 and will save you a good deal of time and frustration when you're trying to draw or paint in Photoshop. Try one at your local computer store, and you'll quickly be as hooked on it as I am.

Summary

Although Photoshop wasn't originally designed as a true paint program—it's really an image editor—digital painting is definitely within the program's capabilities. You can create drawings and paintings from scratch or convert digital photos to simulated natural-media works using filters. Photoshop's myriad filters and Painting tools enable you to turn your work into a decent imitation of an oil painting, watercolor, or drawing. The Artistic filter set, in particular, includes filters that can do much of the work of conversion for you. For best results, though, you'll nearly always want to touch up the picture after the filter has done its magical work. For this touch-up phase, choose tools and colors that are appropriate to the medium you're trying to imitate. You can even use the History Brush to restore lost detail, and the Art History Brush to apply sweeping brush strokes to an image.

Q&A

Q. Is there any way to "juice" photos beforehand to produce the best results with artistic filters?

A. Absolutely. I almost always do some prep work before applying the filters we've discussed in this hour. A typical series of steps might include increasing the contrast, increasing the brightness, increasing the vibrance, and using the Blur tool to obscure unwanted details.

Q. I just can't get started drawing on Photoshop's utterly sterile canvas. Help!

A. Some people just need a pen in their hand and a piece of paper in front of them to get the creative juices flowing. If this describes you, try basing your art on a paper sketch that you scan and bring into Photoshop. This isn't a violation of the digital artists' bylaws, I promise!

Q. I'm having trouble with the Art History Brush; it just seems to turn my picture into a pile of mush.

A. First, undo what you've done and let's start over. Try reducing the Tolerance value and the brush size, and increasing the Area value; then try different Style settings. It's vanishingly rare for someone to get good results with the Art History Brush when picking it up for the first time, so don't feel bad; just keep practicing!

Workshop

Quiz

1. The Watercolor filter works best on pictures with

    A. Large, flat areas

    B. Lots of detail

    C. Dark backgrounds

2. Oil paintings and watercolor paintings look

    A. Very different

    B. Very similar

    C. A lot like colored pencil

   3. Charcoal comes in many colors.

    A. True

    B. False

    C. True only in Photoshop

Answers

   1. A. Detail tends to get lost in a watercolor, and the process darkens the image somewhat, so lighter ones come out better.

   2. A. In Photoshop, as in the real world, oils emphasize texture, whereas watercolor is flat. Try the techniques you've learned in this hour and see for yourself.

   3. C. You want pink charcoal? Or purple? Pea green? Go for it.

Exercise

Find a picture with a good range of light and dark colors and moderate detail. Apply the filters discussed in this hour to the picture, and be sure to experiment with different Background and Foreground colors, as well as with various settings for brush width, pressure, and so on. After working with the original photo, try prepping it as described earlier in the Q&A section, and see if your changes make a difference in the results you achieve.

PART III
Photoshop Power Tools

HOUR 10
Using Transformations

When you transform something, you change it completely without turning it into something else. This concept applies in design, math, and even Photoshop. Transformations in Photoshop are geometric changes that you can make to an entire image or to just part of it, without turning it into something it's not. They include rotating, scaling, flipping, skewing, and more—and it's time for you to learn how to use them for your own purposes. You might need to make an object bigger or smaller, or you might need to straighten a tilted horizon. Perhaps you simply need to make your photo's subject face left instead of right or flip an object upside down. With a few mouse clicks or a couple of simple commands, you can make all this happen.

WHAT YOU'LL LEARN IN THIS HOUR:

▶ Resizing
▶ Rotating
▶ Flipping
▶ Skewing, Distorting, and Changing Perspective
▶ Using Free Transform
▶ Warping and Liquifying

Resizing

Technically, moving an object counts as transforming it, but in Photoshop, the most basic transformation you can perform is to resize an object, whether you're making it smaller or larger. You can resize the entire image, or you can select part of the image and resize just the selected area. Or you can resize the image's canvas, which leaves the image the same size but gives you more room to work with around its edges.

Resizing an Image

To resize an image, start by choosing Image, Image Size; you can see the Image Size dialog in Figure 10.1. The Pixel Dimensions area shows you the current size of the picture in either pixels or percentages; choose the unit you prefer from either pop-up menu, and the other pop-up changes to match. Below that, you can see the image's print size in inches, centimeters, millimeters, points, picas, or columns, based on the specified resolution, and also as percentages of the current size. For example, an image that's 600 pixels wide at a resolution of 300 pixels per inch will be 2 inches wide when printed, so you'll see a Width value in the Document Size area of 2 inches. As with the Pixel Dimensions pop-up menus, the Width and Height unit pop-ups always match each other—if you change one, the other automatically switches along with it.

FIGURE 10.1
The Image Size dialog shows you how big the image is in terms of pixels, along with the size at which it will print based on its current resolution.

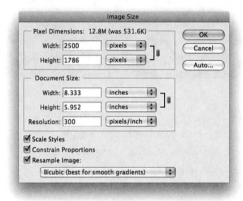

When you first open the Image Size dialog, if you set the Width and Height dimensions in either the Pixel Dimensions area or the Document Size area to Percent, you'll see the default setting of 100%. To enlarge or reduce the image, just make sure that Constrain Proportions is checked at the bottom of the dialog, and then enter a new percentage in one of the fields and click OK. Because you've elected to constrain the image to its existing proportions, the other number changes to give you the correct percentage of enlargement or reduction. For now, don't worry too much about the Resample Image check box; just make sure that its pop-up menu is set to Bicubic. You'll learn more about resampling in Hour 23, "Printing and Publishing Your Images."

The third check box at the bottom of the Image Size dialog controls an essential feature if you have applied a style such as a drop shadow or embossing to an object in your picture. When you check the Scale Styles box, Photoshop makes sure that the size of the shadow or the height of the embossing remains proportional to the rest of the resized picture. You'll want to leave this box checked 99.9% of the times you use the Image Size dialog.

As you make changes in the Document Size area, Photoshop automatically updates the numbers shown in the Pixel Dimensions area at the top of the dialog, and vice versa. You can use either set of entry fields to make your changes; the result is the same either way.

Resizing a Canvas

Resizing the canvas instead of the image itself enables you to add a frame around an image or even change its proportions—remember, you don't have to add the same amount of extra space on all four sides. To resize the canvas, choose Image, Canvas Size and specify the height and width you want for the canvas in the dialog (see Figure 10.2). You can specify a measurement unit using the pop-up menus, just the way you can in the Image Size dialog. Photoshop calculates and displays the new file size as soon as you enter revised numbers in the dialog's New Size area.

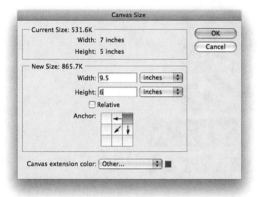

FIGURE 10.2
The Canvas Size dialog enables you to enlarge or reduce the image's canvas without affecting the size of objects within the picture.

Click an Anchor proxy box to determine how the image will be positioned within the resized canvas. If you click in the middle, the picture is centered on the enlarged canvas. Click in any of the other boxes to indicate where you want the existing image to be placed relative to the enlarged or reduced canvas area. Figure 10.3 shows the result of anchoring an image at the top center of the canvas. The image size hasn't actually changed, but the canvas is bigger, making room for the type I've added. The final result is on the right.

Resizing a Selected Area

You can also resize an object on a layer or a selected area of an image. To do so, first activate the layer or select the part of the image that you want to resize. If you're creating a selection, use whichever Selection tool is most appropriate for the object you're trying to select. With the selection marquee active, choose Edit, Transform, Scale. A box with corner and side handles—it looks like the cropping box—appears around your selected object (see Figure 10.4). Drag any of the corner "handles" on the box while pressing Shift to change the size of the selection while maintaining its proportions. If you drag the side handles of the box, you'll stretch the selection's height or width accordingly.

FIGURE 10.3
I started designing this logo with a square image of a fancy tile. Then I increased the image's canvas size as shown to make room for the type in the final logo.

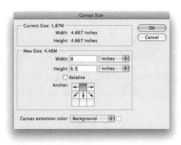

FIGURE 10.4
I drew a selection marquee around the metal tag on one of the jars and dragged the lower-right corner to enlarge it.

Content-Aware Resizing

One of the coolest new features in Photoshop CS4 is the seemingly miraculous ability to resize images without resizing their contents. Content-aware scaling is based on work done by scientists Ariel Shamir and Shai Avidan, who turned the normal way of resizing images on its head. Ordinarily, image data is removed in rows and columns of pixels. Shamir and Avidan figured out how to calculate which areas of the image contain the least detail and then remove winding paths of pixels within those areas instead of straight lines of pixels. Basically, when you use this method of resizing, the major elements of the photo stay the same size while the spaces between are enlarged or reduced.

To scale a selection or layer using this method, first make the selection or activate the layer, then choose Edit, Content-Aware Scale. Drag the handles around the selection to enlarge or reduce it (see Figure 10.5). Press Shift as you drag if you want to maintain the selection's existing proportions. When you're done, click the Cancel or Commit button.

FIGURE 10.5
As it scales this image of two derelict buses (left), Photoshop is smart enough to figure out that I won't mind if it reduces the size of the road, the trees, and the utility pole (right), because the buses are what I really care about.

Several options are available when you're using content-aware scaling. The first half of the Options bar looks just the way it does when you're using Free Transform, but then you'll see some new settings:

- ▶ **Amount:** You can use a combination of content-aware scaling and normal scaling by entering a percentage for content-aware scaling.

- ▶ **Protect:** If you want to make sure that specific areas in the image are protected, create an alpha channel that's white in those areas and then choose it from the pop-up menu.

- ▶ **Protect Skin Tones:** This button, which looks like a little person, tells Photoshop to try to preserve the shapes of regions that contain skin tones; this is intended to keep people from being transformed.

NOTE

The Bad News

Content-aware scaling doesn't work on adjustment layers, layer masks, individual channels, Smart Objects, 3D layers, video layers, or layer groups, and you also can't use it when you have more than one layer selected in the Layers panel.

NOTE

They Have Been Transformed

If you have used a much older edition of Photoshop, you might look for the Transform commands on the Layer menu. But since Photoshop 5, they've lived in the Edit menu.

Rotating

You might need to rotate an image for many reasons. If you have a scanned picture or a digital camera image that should be vertical but opens as a horizontally oriented picture, rotating it 90° corrects the problem. Then again, because you're not a computer, you might not have been holding your camera level when you took the picture. In this case, you'll need to rotate the picture by just a few degrees to fix it.

Rotate 180° and 90° Clockwise or Counterclockwise

To rotate the entire image, choose Image, Image Rotation and pick an option from the submenu shown in Figure 10.6. Choose 90° clockwise (CW) or counterclockwise (CCW) if you simply want to straighten a sideways image, or 180° if you've somehow brought in the picture upside down.

FIGURE 10.6
The Image Rotation submenu seems compact, but it contains all the commands you'll need to rotate or flip your entire image.

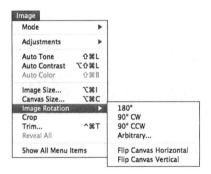

Rotate by Degrees

To rotate the canvas by a number of degrees other than 90° or 180°, choose Image, Image Rotation, Arbitrary to bring up a dialog like the one shown in Figure 10.7. Enter the number of degrees to rotate the image. If you're not sure, guessing is okay. If your first try doesn't pan out, you can always undo and try again with a different number of degrees or a different direction. Click a radio button to indicate the direction of rotation: clockwise (CW) or counterclockwise (CCW). Then click OK to rotate the picture.

If there's a good straight horizontal line in your picture, you won't need to guess at the right number of degrees. You can use the Ruler tool to determine the exact amount of rotation needed. Switch to the Ruler tool and

draw a measuring line along the image's horizon or another line that
should be level; then choose Image, Image Rotation, Arbitrary. Photoshop
inserts the right number of degrees in the Angle field, based on your measurement, so all you have to do is click OK.

FIGURE 10.7
You can even rotate by fractions of
a degree.

Using the Arbitrary command is an easy way to correct a picture that needs
to be straightened. The picture in Figure 10.8 was shot just as the photographer dodged an annoyed bumblebee. Fortunately, fixing tilted horizons is an
easy task for Photoshop. You can download this photo from the book's website and work along, if you like; it's called foxglove.jpg.

TRY IT YOURSELF ▼

Level the Horizon

FIGURE 10.8
This picture would look a lot nicer
if it weren't tilting to the left.

You can tell from a cursory glance at the picture that it needs to rotate clockwise a few degrees. To straighten it out, follow these steps:

1. Switch to the Ruler tool (you'll find it under the Eyedropper in the
   Toolbox) and click at one end of a line that's supposed to be horizontal
   or vertical—in this case, the neatly mulched ground. Drag along the
   line, releasing the mouse when the Ruler's line is parallel to the line
   you're following. (The longer the line you draw with the Ruler, the more
   accurate your measurement will be.) Choose Image, Image Rotation,
   Arbitrary to open the Rotate Canvas dialog.

Level the Horizon
continued

FIGURE 10.9
You can see the white background color in the corners of
the rotated image.

2. The number of degrees of rotation the picture needs is already entered;
click OK to apply the rotation. Now the image's contents are level, but
the picture itself is tilted (see Figure 10.9). Cropping will square up the
corners again and improve the composition at the same time.

3. Choose the Crop tool from the toolbox or press C to switch to it. Drag
across the picture to position the cropping box; then use the handles to
fine-tune your cropping. Figure 10.10 shows the cropping box in position.

4. If the horizon still isn't perfectly straight, you have another chance to
correct it at this point. Click just outside the cropping box. When you
see a double-pointed curved arrow, you can click and drag to rotate the
cropping box itself until the image looks level.

5. When the picture looks the way you want it, double-click inside the cropping box or press Enter. Figure 10.11 shows the corrected horizon.

FIGURE 10.10
Drag the cropping box to fix the image's crooked sides.

FIGURE 10.11
The flower bed is level now, and the image's composition has improved along the way.

TRY IT YOURSELF ▼

Level the Horizon
continued

Rotate a Selected Area

You can rotate a selection (as opposed to turning the whole canvas) essentially the same way you resize one. First, select the area you want to rotate. Then choose Edit, Transform, Rotate; again, Photoshop puts a bounding box around your selection. Drag any of the corner handles to rotate the selection around its center point, indicated by the target-shaped object in the middle of the selection in Figure 10.12. To rotate the selection off-center, drag the center point to where you want it, and then drag a handle to rotate the selection. The center point stays where it is, even if it's no longer really at the center of the selection, and the rest of the selection rotates around that point.

NOTE

Now You See It

Don't worry about the Ruler tool's measuring line obscuring your image, by the way. As soon as the Rotate Arbitrary command is executed, the measuring line disappears.

FIGURE 10.12
Drag any corner point to rotate the
selection.

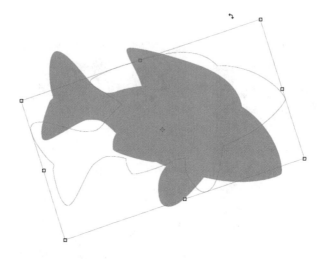

Flipping

When you **flip** an image, you reverse it so that you see a mirror image. You
can flip a selection or an entire image horizontally or vertically. Figure
10.13 shows both; note that flipping an image vertically does *not* yield the
same result as rotating it 180°.

FIGURE 10.13
The top pair of words has been
flipped horizontally, and the bottom
pair has been flipped vertically.

Flipping (also called flopping in the printing industry) is different from
rotating because it changes the orientation of the image, turning it backward
relative to the original. Of course, sometimes you need to both flip and
rotate an image or selected object to get it oriented the way you want it. For
comparison purposes, Figure 10.14 shows the effects of rotation. To make
this composition, I typed the word *Rotate* and copied it, rotating each copy.

FIGURE 10.14
For each copy of the word *Rotate*, I chose Edit, Transform, Rotate, and then moved the center point of the selection to the center of the image so that the copies would fan out from the middle.

To Flip or Not to Flip

You can safely flip almost any image, as long as nothing in it that would give the viewer a clue. You can't flip a picture that has type or a clock in it, obviously. You should also be careful when you flip pictures of people wearing shirts with a pocket on one side, a wristwatch, a wedding ring, a single earring, or another telltale item. And don't forget to watch out for words on signs in the background and in reflections. If you do need to flip a picture that contains one or more of these giveaway elements, you'll probably want to use some Photoshop magic to delete or obscure the offending objects. You'll learn how to do this in Hour 22, "Repairing Color Photos."

Skewing, Distorting, and Changing Perspective

Skew, according to my trusty *American Heritage Dictionary*, means "to turn or place at an angle." So far, that sounds just like rotating. But skew also means "to give a bias to; distort." Now that's more accurate for our purposes. When you skew an object in Photoshop, you can do more than just slant it; you can twist, stretch, and distort it as if the object were on a sheet of rubber instead of just depicted on your computer screen. The Skew command (choose Edit, Transform, Skew) enables you to twist the selected object in all possible directions by just clicking and dragging the handles. When you're happy with the results of your labors, double-click inside the selection or press Enter/Return to apply the transformation.

Skewing is related to the Perspective crop function and can be used to serve the same purpose: restoring warped perspectives. The big difference is that, because it's used on a selected area instead of the whole canvas, you can straighten individual objects. Figure 10.14 shows a couple of kids checking out a tilting tower at a local children's museum. Something about the angle of the photo makes the whole thing appear to be slanting. In Figure 10.15, I've selected the entire tower with the Polygonal Lasso.

FIGURE 10.15
In this snapshot, the kids and their tower seem to be tilting to the right.

Now I can apply the Skew function (choose Edit, Transform, Skew) to the selected area to straighten it. Figure 10.16 shows this step.

Now all I have to do is fill in the "holes" in the rug along the entrance to the tower, and I'm done. That just takes a few swipes with the Clone Stamp; you can see the result in Figure 10.17.

As you've seen so far, all the transform commands operate very similarly, with subtle differences in how each one moves or reshapes the selected object. The Distort command (choose Edit, Transform, Distort) has similarities to both the Scale command and the Skew command, but instead of changing the size of the image, Distort crushes or stretches the image. The big difference between Distort and Skew is that when you use Distort, you can angle the four sides of the selection any way you want—nothing has to remain parallel to anything else. Figure 10.18 shows a cute scooter owned by the New Orleans Police Department and the way it looked after I applied a few distortions to it.

FIGURE 10.16
It usually doesn't take much to straighten a tilting line.

FIGURE 10.17
Now the kids aren't about to topple over.

FIGURE 10.18
The Distort command can turn this
police scooter into a pretzel.

FIGURE 10.18
The Distort command can turn this police scooter into a pretzel.

Select an object in one of your pictures and practice skewing and distorting it. Remember that you must have an active selection to apply either of these commands.

The Perspective command can't be beat for changing the apparent viewing angle of an image. Its movement is completely intuitive. When you drag a corner handle, the opposite corner mirrors the handle's movement—if you click an anchor and drag the mouse away from the selection, the opposite corner moves away. When you drag the anchor inward, the opposite corner moves inward as well.

The difference between Perspective and Distortion is that when you apply Distortion, you can do it to only one corner of the selection. Perspective automatically adjusts both corners when you drag one. In Figure 10.19, I'm applying perspective to what I'm pretty sure is a Dominique hen. In this case, I want to make it look as though she's going straight for me—killer chicken!

FIGURE 10.19
Apply the Perspective command to a selection to create false perspective.

Using Free Transform

You can use Edit, Free Transform to make any of the changes described. Drag the handles as you press modifier keys to rotate, skew, scale, or distort as much as you want. You can also access the numeric transformations in the Tool Options bar. To distort relative to the center of the bounding box, press Option (Mac) or Alt (Windows) as you drag. To distort freely, press Command (Mac) or Ctrl (Windows) instead. To skew, press Shift-Command (Mac) or Shift+Ctrl (Windows). Press Shift to scale the selection while maintaining its proportions. If you change your mind, press Esc to cancel the transformation.

Warping and Liquifying

Not all transformations have to be useful. The Liquify command, which does exactly that to an image, doesn't have too many productive uses—but you'll have a great time playing with it anyway. You can swirl the image, make it bulge or shrink, and generally have fun with it. Pick a photo, or just draw a squiggle on a blank canvas and play with it yourself by choosing Filter, Liquify. Here's my attempt (see Figure 10.20) at liquifying a vintage fire truck. Of course, you can also use it "seriously" to turn a frown into a smile or to widen a photo subject's squinting eyes; it's actually very popular for retouching magazine cover shots of "beautiful people." Use light pressure, and don't overdo it.

FIGURE 10.20
Dr. Seuss would have loved this.

Another semiuseful but extremely entertaining feature that was introduced back in Photoshop CS2 is the Warp command. Select any portion of an image, or activate any layer, and choose Edit, Transform, Warp. Then go to town! You can drag the "handles" around the warp area's edges to make them bulge or flow, and you can drag the intersections of the interior grid to do the same for the inner portions of the selection or layer (see Figure 10.21).

FIGURE 10.21
More methodical than Liquify, Warp still enables you to push pixels around to your heart's content. Here, we can turn the level New Orleans skyline into a scene from hilly San Francisco.

Summary

Transformations are an important function in Photoshop, especially when you're combining elements from different pictures. You might need to shrink or enlarge an object within the picture or the entire image. Use the Image Size and Canvas Size dialogs to adjust the size of the image or the work area, respectively. Photoshop also enables you to transform selected objects by stretching, distorting, or applying perspective to them. You can do any of these by choosing the appropriate menu command and then dragging the sides or corners of the transformation box.

Q&A

Q. What exactly does "constrain" mean?

A. To constrain an action means to restrict its possible outcomes. In the case of the Transform commands, you can constrain rotation to increments of 45° and resizing to maintain the selection's proportions.

Q. The selected area looks fuzzy when I'm transforming it. Is that okay?

A. Sure. Photoshop creates a low-res version of the selection each time you adjust the transformation box; it waits until you apply the transformation to make the high-res version from the image's original pixels.

Q. What's the difference between using Free Transform and using the individual Transform commands?

A. Nothing, so feel free to use whichever works for you. Personally, I use the Free Transform command for all my scaling and rotation needs.

Workshop

Quiz

1. Which of the following is *not* a Transform command?

   A. Scale

   B. Rotate

   C. Modify

   D. Flip

2. True or false: The Warp and Liquify commands do the same thing, but with a different interface.

3. Which key do you press while dragging a handle to constrain a transformation?

   A. Shift

   B. Ctrl

   C. Esc

   D. Option/Alt

Answers

1. **C.** You can think of the Free Transform command as a way to modify the selection.

2. **False.** The Warp tool doesn't stretch adjacent pixels, meaning that there will be blank spaces next to the selection you're warping unless it occupies its own layer.

3. **A.** If you press Esc, the transformation is canceled.

Exercise

Create a new canvas. Paint a squiggle on it and select the squiggle. Practice scaling, flipping, skewing, distorting, and rotating it. Then choose Edit, Transform, Free Transform or press Command-T/Ctrl+T and use the modifier keys to apply all those kinds of transformations at once.

HOUR 11
Creating Layered Images

When Photoshop 2.5 first introduced layers, the concept was revolutionary. Layers made it possible for artists to make changes while preserving the underlying image by isolating different elements on their own layers. For example, suppose you place a butterfly image on a transparent layer, with a flower garden image on the Background layer. You can use all the Transform commands you learned about in the last hour on the butterfly without messing up the flowers behind it. Or you can change its colors to suit your lightest whim—again, without affecting anything else in the picture. You can hide and show the butterfly layer to help you decide whether the picture looks better with or without it. You can run filters on the Background layer without affecting the butterfly. The list of possibilities is endless.

In the years since layers were introduced, Adobe has thought of lots more ways that Photoshop can make use of them, to help you create more complex images in less time with less effort. Now there are several special kinds of layers, including the following:

▶ **Fill layers** contain a single color, gradient, or pattern. You could always create a layer and fill it with a particular color, or a gradient or a pattern, but fill layers are a bit easier to change. You just click a fill layer's color swatch in the Layers panel to open the Color Picker. Choose a new color, click OK, and you're all set; there's no need to fill the layer with the new color. We looked at creating fill layers in Hour 7, "Drawing and Combining Shapes."

▶ **Shape layers** are simply fill layers with an editable vector mask in the form of the chosen shape. You can modify the mask using the Path tools, and you can transform the shape in any way you like without blurring its details because it's defined by paths instead of pixels. Hour 7 also covered creating shape layers.

WHAT YOU'LL LEARN IN THIS HOUR:

▶ Using the Layers Panel
▶ Working with Multiple Layers

▶ **Type layers** contain editable type that you can search and even spell-check. Of course, you can also go back and change the font, size, and other attributes at any time. Hour 18, "Adding Type," shows you everything you need to know about using type and type layers in Photoshop.

▶ **Adjustment layers** are just about as cool as it gets. You can create an adjustment layer for any of kind of image modification in the Image, Adjust submenu (Levels, Curves, Vibrance) so that the adjustment is not only easily removable (just delete the layer), but also editable (you can go back and change the settings at any time). We used adjustment layers back in Hour 5, "Adjusting Brightness and Color," to make this kind of nondestructive change.

▶ **3D layers** are a new feature that you'll find only in Photoshop CS4 Extended. If you're into 3D modeling, you'll love the capability to create and animate 3D scenes right in Photoshop. Skip ahead to Appendix B, "A Quick Walk on the Extended Side," for a few more details about 3D and 3D layers in Photoshop CS4.

▶ **Video layers**, like 3D layers, are only available in Photoshop CS4 Extended. As the name implies, they can hold video footage that's integrated into your projects.

Despite all these special types of layers, the plain old transparent layer remains one of Photoshop's most powerful features. In this hour, we look at how to create and edit layers, how to keep them organized, and what kinds of projects you might want to use them for.

Using the Layers Panel

Sometimes the best way to learn something is to jump right in, so let's spend some time experimenting with layers. The first step is to create a new image file (the default size is fine) and then open the Layers panel, if it's not already visible. Just choose Window, Layers, or, if you see the Layers panel icon docked on the edge of your screen, click the button at the top of the dock to switch it out of icon mode. The Layers panel (see Figure 11.1) is where you control your layers' behavior—you can create, add, delete, hide, or show them. The small versions of your images on the left of the panel are layer **thumbnails**. Each of these small rectangles displays a tiny version of the contents on that layer. For the moment, because you haven't added any new layers to the image, you should see only one blank thumbnail in the Layers panel. That's the Background layer; if you stuck with the default white background fill when you created this image, the Background layer's thumbnail is white.

FIGURE 11.1
The Layers panel provides access to most of Photoshop's layer-related functions.

NOTE

Deep Background

The biggest difference between the Background layer and a regular layer is this: When you erase pixels on a regular layer, the erased area is transparent; when you erase on the Background layer, the erased area is filled with the background color shown in the toolbox.

If the thumbnails are too small for you to be able to tell what's on each layer, choose the Panel Options command from the panel's menu (click the arrow in the upper-right corner to pop it out) and change the size to suit your needs (see Figure 11.2).

You can choose from three sizes or choose no thumbnail image at all; it's up to you. Of course, the smaller the thumbnail, the less space the panel takes up on your screen. This won't matter much at the moment, but if you end up working with more than a few layers at a time, you'll find that being able to see more layers in the Layers panel at one time is worth reducing the thumbnail size.

Creating and Copying Layers

You can add new layers to an image in more than one way. The most obvious of these, of course, is to click the New Layer button at the bottom of the Layers panel. This gives you a new, empty layer positioned just above the layer that was active when you clicked the button. You can also duplicate an existing layer by clicking its thumbnail and dragging it to the New Layer button. Again, the copy is placed just above the original in the list of layers.

FIGURE 11.2
You can choose a size for layer thumbnails and have them display the entire layer or just the objects each layer contains.

▼ TRY IT YOURSELF

Create a New Layer

It's time to dip your toe in the water; let's make some layers. First of all, we'll put something on the Background layer, just to make it easier to keep track of. Follow these steps:

1. Create a new document; if the one you created for the previous section is still open, that will work just fine. Use the Elliptical Marquee to select a large circular area on the page. Remember, press Shift as you drag out the marquee to constrain it to a circular shape. Choose a new Foreground color and switch to the Paint Bucket, then click in the circular selection to fill it with the color. Press Command-D (Mac) or Ctrl+D (Windows) to get rid of the selection marquee.

2. Look at the thumbnail labeled Background. (It's the only one on the panel.) It should look like Figure 11.3.

3. Click the small page icon at the bottom of the Layers panel. You've just added a layer, so now your panel should look like the one shown in Figure 11.4.

FIGURE 11.3
The Background layer is your blank canvas when you open a new document—an empty starting point.

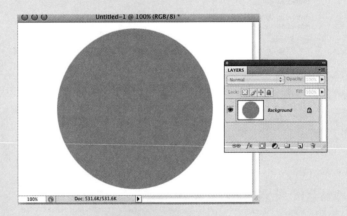

FIGURE 11.4
The newly added layer is active.

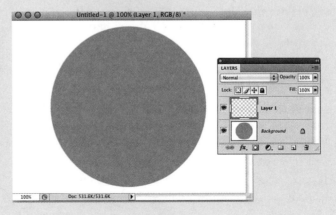

Let's pause and take a look at the new layer's thumbnail. Its double frame and the highlight color indicate that this is the **active** layer. When you paint, only the layer or layer mask with the double frame receives the paint. Similarly, when you make edits or adjustments—colorizing or blurring, for example—they'll be applied only to this layer. Of course, the active layer's entry in the Layers panel is also highlighted.

To change the active layer, click the name of the layer you want to work on. Figure 11.5 shows what the panel looks like after the active layer change has been made.

FIGURE 11.5
Changing the active layer takes just one click.

Let's make some layers to see how they work. Download the following files from the book's website: Plate, Cake Layer, Jam, Frosting, and Candle. Then follow these steps to make a layer cake:

1. Open the files called Plate and Cake Layer. Bring the cake layer image to the front, if needed, by clicking it. Copy the cake by dragging over it with the Quick Selection tool. If you overshoot and end up selecting the entire image, Option-click/Alt-click on the white background to remove it from the selection. When the cake layer is selected, press Command-C (Mac) or Ctrl+C (Windows) to copy it. Bring the plate image to the front. Press Command-V (Mac) or Ctrl+V (Windows) to paste the cake onto the plate, and then look at the Layers panel. You've added a new layer! Close the Cake Layer file.

2. Now open the file called Jam. Notice that a checkerboard pattern surrounds the jam, indicating that this part of the layer is transparent; there's no Background layer in this file. Move the two image windows so that you can see both at once. Switch to the Move tool, then click the jam and drag it onto the plate. Use the Move tool to center it on the cake layer. If you take a look at the Layers panel (see Figure 11.6) you'll see that the jam is also on a new layer.

TRY IT YOURSELF ▼

Get Started with Layers

▼ TRY IT YOURSELF

**Get Started with
Layers**
continued

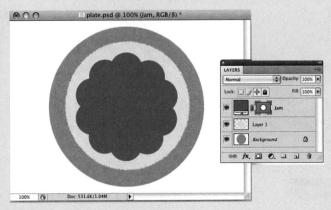

FIGURE 11.6
Drag the jam onto the cake. It appears as a new layer.

3. The jam's color is right (it's strawberry, of course), but it's too flat-looking. Let's add a layer style to give it a bit more dimension. (See Figure 11.7.) Under the Layer menu, choose Layer Style, Bevel and Emboss. Set Style to Emboss, and set Technique to Smooth. Make Depth 21% and Size 54 pixels. Soften should be at 9. In the Shading area, change the Gloss Contour to the one shown in Figure 11.7 and the Opacity for the shadow to 0%.

FIGURE 11.7
Applying a style to the layer gives it more dimension.

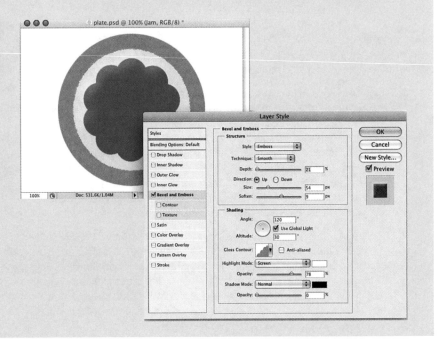

TRY IT YOURSELF ▼

Get Started with Layers
continued

4. The jam still looks too opaque, so let's change the opacity on the Layers panel to 80%, as shown in Figure 11.8.

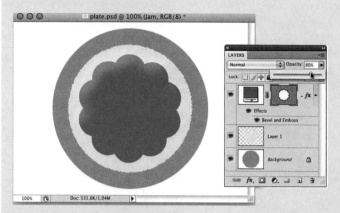

FIGURE 11.8
Use the slider to change the opacity, or double-click the Opacity entry field and type **80**.

5. Click the cake layer to activate it. Choose Layer, Layer Properties and change the name of the lettuce layer from its current default name to First Cake Layer. (There's no good reason to make this change now, except to show you that you can name your layers.) Figure 11.9 shows the Layer Properties dialog.

FIGURE 11.9
The ability to name your layers comes in handy when you have a lot of them.

6. Drag the First Cake Layer layer onto the New Layer button to duplicate it. Click on the new layer and drag it upward in the layer list until it's at the top of the cake. With this second cake layer still active, click the first of the Lock buttons at the top of the Layers panel; then change the Foreground color to chocolate brown and use the Paint Bucket to fill the layer. Notice that the transparent areas of the layer stay transparent; that's because you've locked the layer's transparency. If you later want to paint in this layer's transparent areas, you'll need to go back and uncheck the Lock Transparency box.

7. Now open the Frosting file and switch to the Move tool. Start dragging the frosting onto the top of the cake; then press Shift before you release the mouse button. This forces the frosting to take the same relative position within the image window that it occupied in the Frosting file.

▼ TRY IT YOURSELF

Get Started with Layers
continued

8. Time to top off the cake! Open the Candle file and press Command-A/Ctrl+A to select all. Press Command-C/Ctrl+C to copy the selection, then switch to the cake image and press Command-V/Ctrl+V to paste it onto the top of the cake (see Figure 11.10).

FIGURE 11.10
The finished cake image has six layers.

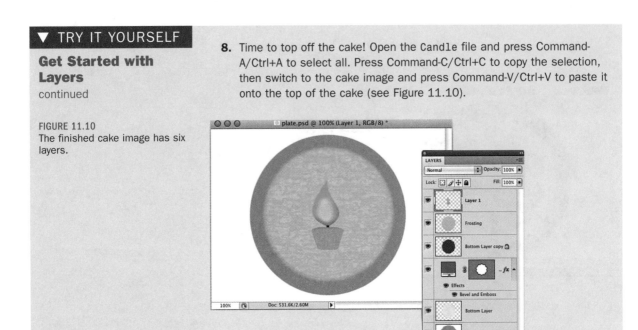

You can move, add to, or erase anything on the active layer, but those actions won't affect layers above or below the one you're working on. For instance, if you make Layer 1 the active layer, you can use the Move tool to reposition the candle, but you can't move the jam until you make its layer active.

Reordering Layers

As you saw in step 6, you can also change the order of the layers. Because new layers are always created above the current active layer, you'll sometimes need to move them to a more appropriate position in the layer stack. Let's review the steps to do that:

1. In the Layers panel, click and hold the thumbnail of the active layer.

2. Hold down the mouse button and drag the layer up or down to a different position in the stack. (Note that you can't move the Background layer—by definition, it has to stay at the bottom of the stack unless you convert it to a regular layer by double-clicking it.)

If you want to move a layer up or down one level, you can select it in the Layers panel and press Command-] (Mac) or Ctrl+] (Windows) to move it up, or press Command-[(Mac) or Ctrl+[(Windows) to move it down.

Hiding and Showing Layers

As you've seen, using layers enables you to avoid painting where you don't want to paint. You can also hide layers so that you can concentrate on one part of your image. To the left of each layer thumbnail, there's a small icon in the shape of an eye. This indicates that a layer is visible. If you see the eye, you can see the layer—logical enough. If you click the eye, the eye disappears and the layer becomes hidden. In Figure 11.11, you can see that I've turned off the frosting, but the plate, cake, jam, and candle are still visible.

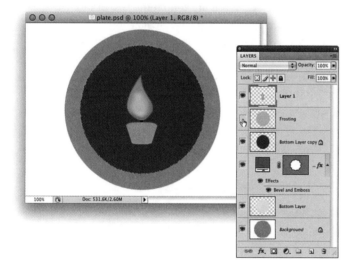

FIGURE 11.11
To make a layer visible again after hiding it, click the space where the eye was.

Why don't you try it? Click the eye icon next to your own frosting layer. The icon disappears, as does the corresponding layer in your image. Click again and the icon reappears—with the layer. While the layer is hidden, you can't paint on it or do anything with it except drag it up or down (or use the commands detailed previously) to change its order.

Removing Layers

The easiest way to remove a layer is to click to make it active and then click the Delete Layer button at the bottom of the Layers panel—it looks like a trash can. Or you can choose Layer, Delete, Layer or the Delete Layer command in the Layers panel pop-up menu. If you use any of these three methods, you'll see a warning dialog asking whether it's really okay for Photoshop to delete the layer, and you'll need to click OK. To skip the warning, Option-click (Mac) or Alt-click (Windows) the Delete Layer button or drag the layer to the panel's button instead of clicking the button. To bring back the layer, choose Edit, Undo, assuming you've done nothing else in the meantime. If you have made other changes to the image, you'll need to use the History panel to return to a previous state.

Working with Multiple Layers

You have seen how to create, move, and remove layers, but we still haven't really addressed the question of what they're good for. Layers are useful in many situations, especially whenever you are combining two or more images (in Photoshop terms, **compositing**). Each of the elements you paste or drag into the background image from another document is added on a separate layer. You can use the Layers panel to control exactly how these elements combine to form the whole image. Although a layer itself always remains transparent, you can control the opacity of objects that you paste onto the layer or paint that you apply to it. You can also control the blending modes that affect how the colors on one layer combine with the colors of the layers beneath it, just as you can when painting over an image or background.

Layer Opacity and Fill Opacity

As you saw in our cake-making session earlier in the hour, the Layers panel's Opacity slider controls the opacity—the opposite of transparency—of the active layer. You used it briefly to change the opacity of the jam. You can make the slider appear by clicking the triangle to the right of the percentage entry field. You can adjust the value adjusted from 0% to 100% by dragging the slider. If you'd rather not mess with the slider, enter a value without even clicking in the entry field by just typing 0 for 100%, 1 for 10%, 2 for 20%, and so on. For more precise control, simply type the digits of the measurement you desire (57, for instance) in quick succession. This trick works with any active tool that doesn't have its own Opacity setting—if you're currently using a tool that *does* have an Opacity setting, using the keyboard adjusts the setting for the tool instead of for the layer.

Time for some more practice with the Opacity slider. You should still have the layer cake image open. Hide the candle, frosting, and top "cake layer" layers, and then make the jam layer active and drag the Opacity slider (by clicking and holding the arrow to make it appear) to about 25%. Can you still see the jam? Yes, but it's spread very thin—not the kind of cake we like to eat in my house. Drag the slider down to 10% and then to 0%. Then move it back to 100% again. You can change opacity as often as you like, with no permanent effect on the layer's contents.

You can't use the Opacity slider to change the opacity of the Background layer. By definition, the Background layer always remains 100% opaque. To get around this, you have to convert the Background layer into a regular layer; that's accomplished by double-clicking its thumbnail and then clicking OK in the resulting dialog. If you look at the Layers panel, you'll notice that the former Background layer is now called Layer 0, indicating that you can change its opacity.

You can create a document with a transparent background by choosing File, New. From the Background Contents pop-up menu, choose Transparent, as shown in Figure 11.12. When the image window opens, you'll see a checkerboard pattern, indicating that the layer is transparent. And if you look at the Layers panel, you'll see that the image's only layer is called Layer 1 instead of Background. Anything you paint on that layer will have a transparent background. Anything you copy from another source and paste in will go on a new layer that's also transparent wherever it doesn't contain image data.

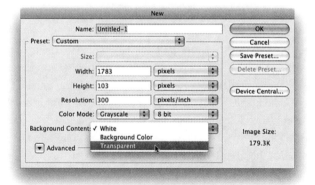

FIGURE 11.12
You can create a new image without a Background layer.

NOTE

Changing the Way You Look at Transparency

If you have trouble distinguishing the transparency checkerboard from the rest of your image, you can change its color and size in Photoshop's preferences. Press Command-K/Ctrl+K and click Transparency & Gamut in the left column. You can choose None, Small, Medium, or Large for the size of the checkerboard's squares, and you can pick from the color choices in the Grid Colors pop-up menu or click the color swatches below it to choose your own colors using the Color Picker.

Layer Blending Modes

In Hour 6, "Choosing and Blending Colors," you learned about blending modes and how they affect the way paint is applied. Almost the same set of modes can be applied to layers to control how their colors combine, and they produce the same general effects, but only on the layers beneath the one to which you have applied the blending mode. (If you're not clear on what the effects are, refer back to Hour 7.) The color of the layer to which you're applying the blending mode is called the blend color, and the color of the image below is called the base color. You'll find all the layer blending modes on a pop-up menu at the top of the Layers panel.

Just as a reminder, the blending modes for layers are the following:

- Normal
- Dissolve
- Darken
- Multiply
- Color Burn
- Linear Burn
- Darker Color
- Lighten
- Screen
- Color Dodge
- Linear Dodge (Add)
- Lighter Color
- Overlay

- Soft Light
- Hard Light
- Vivid Light
- Linear Light
- Pin Light
- Hard Mix
- Difference
- Exclusion
- Hue
- Saturation
- Color
- Luminosity

You can apply blending modes directly from the Layers panel or by using Layer, Layer Style, Blending Options. This opens a dialog that gives you a great deal of control over the way blending happens. Along with the usual opacity and blending mode controls, the Blending Options dialog contains the Advanced Blending controls, which enable you to determine which color channels are affected and whether a layer's special effects contribute to its blending attributes (see Figure 11.13).

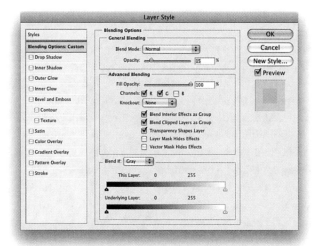

FIGURE 11.13
The best way to learn your way around the Advanced Blending Options is to experiment. Have fun!

Linking Layers

If you select more than one layer in the Layers panel (Command-click or Ctrl+click), you can click the Link Layers button at the bottom of the panel to tie the layers together. Each linked layer has a piece of linked chain next to its name. This indicates that the layers are linked together, meaning that if you move the contents of the active layer, all the layers that are linked to it move with it. Figure 11.14 shows the Layers panel with the jam and frosting layers linked to the cake.

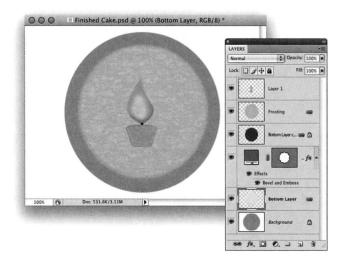

FIGURE 11.14
Layers linked to the active layer move with it. In this case, the jam filling and the frosting will also move if you slide the cake off the plate, but the candle will stay where it is.

TIP

Group Half-Empty or Half-Full?

You can create an empty layer group by clicking the New Layer Group button at the bottom of the Layers panel (it looks like a file folder). Drag layers onto the group's name to move them into the group.

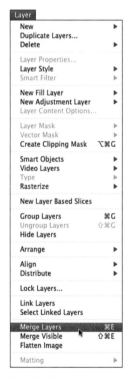

FIGURE 11.15
The Merge commands in the Layer menu are context sensitive.

Grouping Layers

When you start working with a lot of layers, you'll need some help keeping them organized. That's what layer groups are for: managing collections of layers. After you create a group to contain related layers, you can collapse the entire group or reveal its contents as necessary, without actually flattening the image, and you can hide and show the entire group as one. With the cake example, you could have designated all the edible components as a group. If you needed to move the individual layers or change the size of the objects they contained, you could do so to the whole group instead of having to work with one layer at a time. Layers in a group have to be contiguous; you can't group layers 1, 3, and 5 together unless you move layers 2 and 4 to above or below the layer group. To create a layer group, Command-click or Ctrl+click to select the layers you want to group, and then choose Layer, Group Layers. To make the group easier to locate, you can double-click its entry in the Layers panel and assign it a color in the Group Properties dialog. The assigned color surrounds the group's folder icon and the visibility icons of each layer in the group.

Merging Layers

Merging layers combines them into a single layer so that you can apply layer effects, mask, and edit them as a unit. The Layer menu contains different Merge commands depending on which layers are active: Merge Layers, Merge Down, Merge Group, and Merge Visible (see Figure 11.15). The latter is always available and applies to all layers that aren't hidden; Merge Layers appears when more than one layer is selected, and Merge Down is available only when a single layer is selected. Merge Group, as you might guess, appears in the menu when you've selected a layer group in the Layers panel.

Flattening an image combines all its layers with the Background layer. You can make this happen at any time by choosing Layer, Flatten Image; if you save in a format that doesn't support layers, the image is automatically flattened. Formats that do support layers include the two native Photoshop formats as well as TIFF, PDF, and Dicom (which you'll almost certainly never see or use). However, if you're saving in TIFF or PDF, you're most likely sending the file somewhere else to be printed or otherwise output, which means you're probably done editing it. In this case, you can make the file smaller by flattening the layers before you save it in TIFF or PDF format. Both merging and flattening reduce file size, but beware: After you merge or flatten and close the file, you can't go back. Those layers are gone.

Using Layer Comps

A comp is a mock-up made so that a client can see how a design for an ad, a web page, or product packaging will look. It includes rough illustrations, sample type, the company's logo, and so on. Often several comps are made of the same design, with elements in different colors or different positions, to see which version looks best.

Photoshop's Layer Comps panel gives you the capability to create and save layer comps, each of which records the visibility, layer style, and positions of selected layers. So when you're working up a design in Photoshop, whether it's for a big business client or for your holiday newsletter, instead of needing to create a half-dozen examples as six separate documents, you can create just one image file and then add as many comps as you need. To save a layer comp, first open the Layer Comps panel by choosing Window, Layer Comps. When the image is set up the way you want it, with the right layers showing and the others hidden, click the New Layer Comp button at the bottom of the panel. (It looks just like the New Layer button on the Layers panel.) You can name the layer comp and choose which attributes it should preserve in the resulting dialog, shown in Figure 11.16. You can also add notes about this version of the image in the Comment field.

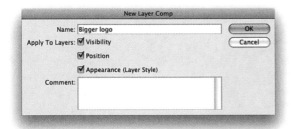

In Figure 11.17, I've created a bunch of different versions of my cake. They are all listed on the Layer Comps panel. If you look at the Layers panel as well, you can see that they are simply different combinations of visible layers.

TIP

The Key to Merging

Pressing Command-E/Ctrl+E executes whichever Merge command is appropriate in the current situation. If only one layer is selected, that layer is merged into the layer below it. If multiple layers or a layer group are selected, those layers are merged together.

FIGURE 11.16
Giving layer comps names that make sense to you helps you keep track of which is which.

FIGURE 11.17
To switch to a different comp, click next to its name on the Layer Comps panel.

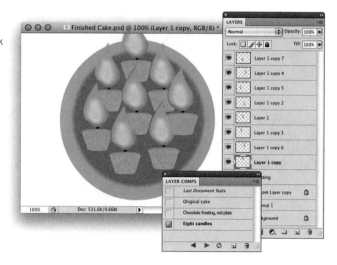

Applying Layer Styles

Photoshop also includes customizable **layer styles**, a number of automated effects that you can apply to layers, including drop shadows, glows, bevels, embossing, and a color fill effect. You've already tried the Emboss style on the jam in our cake. Figure 11.18 shows Photoshop's Layer Style submenu.

FIGURE 11.18
Most of these styles are best used with type or with a transparent layer containing an object.

You'll apply these effects to type and to composited images in Hours 17, 19, and 20.

Summary

In this hour, you learned how Photoshop handles layers and what you can do with them. You used the Layers panel to create, delete, and move layers. You also learned about layer comps. Layers are an important part of the Photoshop interface, and knowing how to apply them will get you a great deal closer to being a master user, especially when you work with type and composite images later.

Q&A

Q. Can I add a Background layer to an image that doesn't have one?

A. Yes. Use Layer, New, Background from Layer to convert the active layer into a Background layer. If you don't want to convert one of your existing layers to a Background layer, create a new layer for that purpose.

Q. Can an image have more than one Background layer?

A. Nope; you're stick with one per document.

Q. How many layer groups can I create?

A. As many as you have layers; for all practical purposes, there's no limit on the number of layers or layer groups.

Q. When I tried to open the Layers Panel Options dialog to change the size of the thumbnails, I also pressed the Option/Alt key by mistake. Something strange happened. What was that about?

A. That, my friend, was an Easter Egg, a little goodie put in by the programmers to add some extra fun for users (and to entertain themselves during late-night programming sessions. You discovered Merlin, who's also featured in the Layers Panel Options dialog in the thumbnail examples.

Workshop

Quiz

1. How can you put the Background layer at the top of the layer stack?

    A. You can't.

    B. Convert it to a transparent layer, then drag it to the top of the Layers panel.

    C. Press Option/Alt as you drag it to the top of the Layers panel.

    D. Choose Layer, Float Background to Top.

2. How many blending modes can you apply to each layer?

   A. One

   B. Three, but they must all be in the same group in the Blending Mode pop-up menu

   C. Up to 256

   D. As many as you want

3. True or false: Flattening an image merges all its layers down into the Background layer.

Answers

1. **A,** technically, but you can go with **B** if you really need to move the Background layer.

2. **A.** You can apply only one blending mode to each layer—but you can paint on a single layer with as many different modes as you want.

3. **True.** This happens automatically when you save to most image formats, and you can make it happen any time you want by choosing Layer, Flatten Image.

Exercise

Let's do some more experimenting with layers. First, click the Background color swatch in the toolbox and choose a medium-light color for a background. Then create a new image. Be sure to choose Background Color from the Background Contents pop-up menu so that the image is filled with the color you picked out. Choose a contrasting Foreground color, create a new layer, switch to the Brush tool, and use a medium-sized brush tip to write the number 1. Add layers, with a number on each, until you have about 10. Then, starting with the first one, apply different blending modes. Try changing the transparency of a layer. Move the number 5 to the upper-left corner of the screen. Merge Layers 2 and 3. Play around until you feel that you really understand how the layers are working.

Using Masks

You can use Photoshop for years and never use a **mask**—but you'll get a lot more done if you learn how to create and apply masks. Painting or cloning next to an object you don't want to change? Be sure to mask the object so you won't accidentally paint over it, just the way you mask woodwork when you're painting a wall. Changing the color of the sky? Mask the rest of the image so you don't turn *it* pink. You can use selections as temporary masks; any time a selection is active, you can paint or apply filters and adjustments only within its bounds. Selections are easy to accidentally drop, however, so Photoshop provides you with other kinds of masks that stay active while you do other things, until you specifically delete or hide them. These semipermanent masks include vector- and pixel-based layer masks.

You can use layer masks to hide things that you're not entirely sure you want to delete from the image; you might need them for another version of the design, or you might change your mind about hiding them later. Layer masks can also give a particular shape or type of edge to an image without actually deleting the parts of the image outside that shape.

Masks show up in a couple different places within Photoshop: the Layers panel (layer masks and clipping masks) and the Channels panel (alpha channels made from saved selections and Quick Masks). Layer masks—including those for adjustment layers, shape layers, and fill layers—also show up in the Channels panel whenever their layer is the active layer. There's even a kind of mask that you can't see anywhere: transparency masks. Every transparent layer has one of these, and you can convert it into a selection by Command-clicking (Mac) or Ctrl+clicking (Windows) the layer's thumbnail in the Layers panel.

With all these kinds of masks, how are you supposed to learn how to work with them all, much less which kind to use for what? Relax; that's what we're doing in this hour. Just follow along, and I promise you'll be a mask expert by the end of the hour.

Applying Masks

First, let's take a look at what masks are and, in general, how you use them. Masks can hide either a selected object or the background around that object, and they can be opaque, semitransparent, or even completely transparent, although a completely transparent mask doesn't mask anything. Most masks—and channels, which you'll learn about later—are actually grayscale images. Opaque areas of a mask are black, 50% transparent areas are 50% gray, and transparent areas are white.

In Figure 12.1, I have a nice photo shot in Arizona that somehow managed to capture a cloudy sky. (I know, I didn't think they had clouds in Arizona, either.) To my eye, this picture would be a lot more interesting if I could do something with that boring white sky. The rest of the image is accurate for color, as nearly as I can remember, so I don't want to change it. If I select just the sky, I can work on it without affecting the rest of the photo.

FIGURE 12.1
I've done my best to select the sky so I can work on the background without disturbing the rest of the image.

Creating a selection like this is the most basic kind of masking. It's not always perfect, though. In Figure 12.2, you can see that making a selection using the Quick Selection tool didn't really give me an accurate mask. The edges aren't very smooth, and some of the bluish hills in the distance are included in the selection with the sky. I'm definitely going to need a way to edit this selection—and it's called Quick Mask.

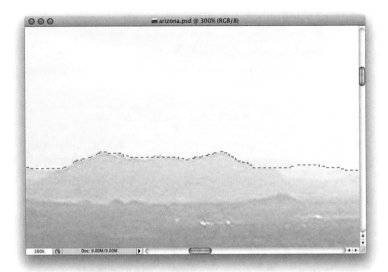

FIGURE 12.2
Up close, you can see that the
selection isn't very accurate.

Using Quick Mask

Photoshop provides a quick and easy way to make a temporary mask that
can be edited: **Quick Mask**. One of its advantages over working with selections is that you can see both the image and the mask, including partially
masked areas, at the same time. You can start with a selection such as the
one in Figure 12.2 and use the Painting tools to add to or take away from
it, or you can create the mask from scratch entirely in Quick Mask mode.
Let's apply a Quick Mask to an image.

TRY IT YOURSELF ▼

Create a Quick Mask

Quick Masks are the quickest, easiest way to create a mask. Follow these
steps to create and edit a Quick Mask.

1. Find a photo with a subject that stands out clearly against the background. If you want to use the same image I'm working on, you can download arizona.jpg from the book's website. Using whichever Selection
   tool seems appropriate, or a combination of tools, select the part of the
   image you want to change—in this case, the background. It's okay if your
   selection isn't perfect; you're going to edit it in Quick Mask mode anyway.
   If it's easier, feel free to select the object and then invert the selection.

2. Click the Quick Mask Mode button at the bottom of the toolbox or press Q.

   Quick Mask puts a color overlay indicating the mask over the protected
   area—the area that wasn't selected. In Figure 12.3, you can see that
   the mask has covered the hill and valley below with a red layer. By

▼ TRY IT YOURSELF

Create a Quick Mask
continued

FIGURE 12.3
Activating Quick Mask mode masks the area outside your selection.

default, the mask is 50% opaque red. If your image contains a red object or red background, you can change the mask's color by double-clicking the Quick Mask Mode button in the toolbox and choosing a different color in the Quick Mask Options dialog.

3. If the mask needs editing, as this one does, click the Brush tool, or press B to activate it, and choose an appropriate brush size from the Brushes panel. You can use any of the Painting tools to modify a mask.

   Because masks are essentially grayscale images, painting with black adds to the mask. Painting with white (or erasing) takes it away. Painting with gray gives you a semitransparent mask. You can also use any of the Selection tools to select parts of the image and fill them with black, white, or gray. The Foreground and Background colors automatically change to black and white when you enter Quick Mask mode. Figure 12.4 shows the edited mask.

4. When the mask is edited to your satisfaction, press Q or click the Quick Mask Mode button in the toolbox again to return to Standard mode. The unprotected area (in this case, the background), which was clear in Quick Mask mode, is surrounded by a selection marquee (see Figure 12.5). Now you can apply any change you want to make to this area without affecting the picture's foreground; two quick fixes are increasing the area's vibrance (choose Image, Adjustments, Vibrance) or using the Brush tool's Airbrush mode to spray some color into the sky at a low Opacity setting. Taking a different tack, I chose to create a new layer

and fill it with the Render Clouds filter; because my selection was active when I added the new layer, it automatically turned into a layer mask that allowed only the sky layer to show within the selected area.

Create a Quick Mask
continued

FIGURE 12.4
The mask is touched up and ready to use.

FIGURE 12.5
Here I've applied the Clouds filter to give the sky more oomph.

TIP

Keep It Straight

If you need a straight edge on your mask, use the Line tool (one of the Shape tools in the toolbox) to draw a line. It takes on the mask color as long as you are in Quick Mask mode when you draw it.

NOTE

Not on the Background

You can't add a layer mask to the Background layer. If the part of the image that you want to mask is on the Background layer, double-click the Background layer in the Layers panel and rename it to turn it into a regular layer. Then you'll be able to mask that layer.

FIGURE 12.6
The Layers panel shows that the BLOOM type layer is masking the shot of a field of white flowers.

If you think you might need to use the same mask again, you can save it after you've returned to Standard mode by clicking the Save Selection as Channel button at the bottom of the Channels panel. (It looks just like the Quick Mask button.) This saves your mask as an alpha channel; you can take a look at it by clicking its thumbnail in the Channels panel. Now you can turn that channel back into a selection any time you want by Command-clicking (Mac) or Ctrl-clicking (Windows) the channel's thumbnail in the panel.

Working with Layer Masks

A layer mask hides and reveals parts of a single layer without deleting any of that layer's contents. Layer masks, like Quick Masks, can be edited; unlike Quick Masks, however, they don't prevent you from editing the area they mask—just from seeing it. If you don't like the result, simply discard the mask, and your image is left untouched. If you do like what you see, you can just leave the mask in place or apply the mask to make the changes permanent. Most of the time, you'll create and edit pixel-based layer masks. But if you like working with the Path and Shape tools, Photoshop now lets you use those tools to create vector-based layer masks. You'll learn how to create both kinds of layer masks in this section.

A Different Kind of Layer Mask

Clipping masks enable you to mask the contents of one layer with the shape of another layer. For example, you might mask an image, gradient, or pattern layer with a type layer to give the effect of type filled with an image while maintaining the type as editable text (see Figure 12.6).

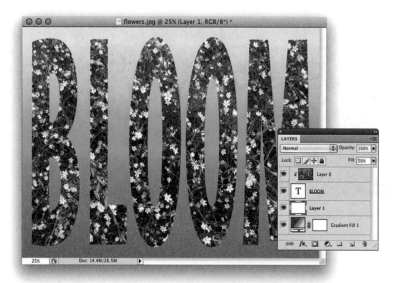

To apply a clipping mask, first you have to correctly position the layers involved. You can use as many layers as you want; they'll all be masked by the one layer at the bottom of the stack. Together, the mask layer and the layers it's masking are referred to as a **clipping group**.

In the case of my type example, you'd start by moving the type layer below any layers that you want it to mask. Then Option-click (Mac) or Alt-click (Windows) the line between the type layer and the layer immediately above it in the Layers panel. To add more layers to the clipping mask, just drag them so they're adjacent to the upper layer in the clipping group and Option-click or Alt-click again between the two layers.

You can use any layer you want as a clipping mask. The contents of the mask layer won't be visible—only its shape will. Transparent parts of the mask layer hide corresponding areas of the other layers in the clipping group, while opaque areas enable the other layers' contents to show through.

Creating a Layer Mask

To make a pixel-based layer mask, select an area of the image to mask and click the Add Layer Mask button (the second button from the left) at the bottom of the Layers panel. When you do, you see a layer mask thumbnail next to the layer's image thumbnail (see Figure 12.7). In the thumbnail, black indicates the portions of the layer that are hidden and white shows the parts that are revealed. If the mask were made to be semitransparent, the partially masked areas would be shown in gray. This happens if you turn a feathered selection into a layer mask, for example.

FIGURE 12.7
The mask hides the background that I pasted in with the brindle greyhound (#3).

Creating a vector-based layer mask works slightly differently. Instead of creating a selection, you start by drawing a path. You can use the Pen tool or any of the Shape tools; either way, you need to make sure that the Paths button at the left end of the Options bar is active instead of Shape Layers or Fill Pixels. When your path or shape is complete, choose Layer, Vector Mask, Current Path to convert it into a layer mask. Not surprisingly, the mask thumbnail in the Layers panel looks just like the thumbnail for a shape layer. By default, vector masks either hide completely or show completely; there are no partially transparent pixels in a vector mask.

Whether you're working with a pixel mask or a vector mask, you'll see links between the two thumbnails in the Layers panel, indicating that the mask is linked to the layer. After you create the mask, you can edit it by clicking the mask icon. For a pixel-based layer mask, the Foreground and Background colors revert to the defaults. You can then paint with black to add to the mask or with white to remove parts of it. To edit a vector mask, switch to one of the Path tools and modify the path. (I show you how to work with paths in the next hour.)

If you create your mask using the Layer menu, you can choose whether the selected area will be shown (and the rest of the image masked) or masked (and the rest of the image shown). Choose Layer, Layer Mask, and choose either Hide Selection or Reveal Selection, depending on whether you want to mask the area around the selected piece of image or the image itself. Figure 12.8 shows the menu for pixel-based layer masks; the commands for vector masks are immediately below these in the Layer menu.

Hide Selection hides the area that you have selected so you can work on the rest of the image. You can re-create the selection from this mask at any time by Command-clicking (Mac) or Ctrl+clicking (Windows) the mask's thumbnail in the Layers panel; that protects the unselected part of the picture while you work on the rest. The Reveal Selection, as you might imagine, does just the opposite of Hide Selection. This command hides everything on a layer *except* that area within the Marquee selection. The other commands, Hide All and Reveal All, work a little differently. As their names suggest, these commands create masks that are entirely opaque or entirely transparent across the entire layer.

In Figure 12.9, I've masked the beach and water and then scribbled across the entire picture. The writing is visible only in the unmasked area.

FIGURE 12.9
The black area of the mask hides
the image; white areas of the
mask allow the image to show
through.

NOTE

Only One to a Customer

Each layer can have only one
layer mask of each type. If you
need to do additional temporary
masking on a layer that already
has a pixel-based mask, activate the layer and use Quick
Mask (press Q).

Add a Pixel-Based Mask to a Layer

The business of making masks can seem very confusing, so it's best to work through the process step by step.

1. Open the Layers panel, if it's not already visible.

2. Click to activate the layer to which you want to add a mask. Make sure that the layer doesn't already have a mask—remember, each layer can have only one pixel-based mask at a time—and that it's not the Background layer.

3. To hide the entire layer, choose Layer, Layer Mask, Hide All. Or, to show the entire layer, choose Layer, Layer Mask, Show All. You'd do this, for example, if you plan to edit the mask later by drawing on it.

4. To make a mask that hides or reveals a selected area, first make the selection on the active layer.

5. Choose Layer, Layer Mask, Hide Selection, or choose Layer, Layer Mask, Reveal Selection, whichever is appropriate for your needs. After you've created the mask, you can edit it with the Painting and Selection tools.

Take some time now to open an image and practice applying masks. Try working with Quick Mask first, and then make a selection and turn it into a layer mask. If you practice these skills while they're fresh in your mind, you'll remember them later when you need to do a quick color change or preserve an object while swapping out its background.

Editing a Layer Mask

FIGURE 12.10
The Masks panel offers quick access to editing functions for masks.

Photoshop CS4 comes with a brand-new Masks panel designed to make it easier for you to select and modify masks (see Figure 12.10). Here's a brief tour of the new panel:

▶ In the top-right corner of the panel, you'll see two Select/Add buttons, one for pixel masks and the other for vector masks. If the current layer doesn't have either type of layer mask, clicking one of these buttons adds the corresponding mask. If the layer is already masked, clicking a button selects the corresponding mask so you can edit it.

▶ Below that is a Density slider. This value works just like a layer's Opacity value; lowering it from 100% allows the masked layer to show through somewhat.

▶ Next comes a Feather slider. Drag this to blur the appearance of the mask's edges without actually modifying it. You can go back and change this value as many times as you want until you're happy with the mask's appearance.

▶ In the Masks panel's Refine area, you'll find three buttons. The first, Mask Edge, opens a dialog that's identical to the Refine Selection Edge dialog you learned about in Hour 3, "Making Selections." Use the controls in this dialog to expand, shrink, or soften a pixel-based mask's edges; none of the Refine controls works for vector masks. Under that is the Color Range button, which opens another familiar dialog: the Color Range dialog, which was also featured in Hour 3. Here you can modify the mask by adding or removing areas based on their colors. Finally, you can click the Invert button to turn the mask's black areas white and its white areas black.

▶ Along the bottom edge of the Masks panel are four more buttons: Load Selection from Mask, which creates a new selection based on the mask; Apply Mask, which deletes the mask and makes its effects permanent; Disable/Enable Mask, which temporarily hides the mask and shows it again; and Delete Mask—I'll leave it to your imagination what that last one does.

To target a layer mask so that you can modify it, either click its thumbnail in the Layers panel to make it active, or click the layer itself and then click the appropriate button in the Masks panel to select the mask you want. If you're working in the Layers panel, when a mask is active, you'll see the thumbnail outline move from the layer thumbnail to the mask thumbnail. This lets you know that any edits you perform will be applied to the mask instead of the layer content.

If you're working with a pixel-based mask, you can Option-click (Mac) or Alt+click (Windows) the mask's thumbnail in the Layers panel to display just the mask in the image window, hiding the layer's contents. Choose a Painting tool and paint the mask with black to add to the mask, with white to subtract from the mask, or with gray to make the layer partially visible. As you work, the mask thumbnail (either in the Masks panel or in the Layers panel) displays your changes. Figure 12.11 shows a mask being edited.

CAUTION

Your Permanent Record

Unlike with the Feather setting, the changes you make to your mask using the Mask Edge and Color Range buttons can't be quickly undone with a click. They're permanent; to undo them, you have to re-create or re-edit the mask.

FIGURE 12.11
Here, the mask will hide the portion of the text that would overlap the sea and land.

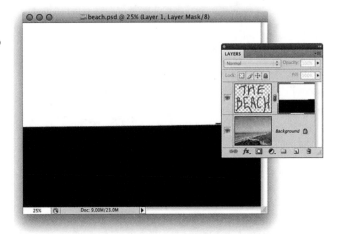

To edit a vector mask, activate it the same way, by clicking its thumbnail in the Layers panel or clicking the Select Vector Mask button in the Masks panel. Instead of painting or erasing to make changes, you can modify the path itself using the Path tools. In the next hour, you'll learn how to use these tools to add and delete corner points, modify curves, and move line segments.

To go back to editing the layer instead of its masks, click its thumbnail in the Layers panel. In addition to clicking the Disable/Enable button in the Masks panel, you can turn off the layer mask by choosing Layer, Disable Layer Mask, or by Shift-clicking the mask's thumbnail in the Layers panel. When you've disabled the mask, Photoshop puts a large red X through the mask thumbnail so that you know it's inactive (see Figure 12.12). You can still paint on a mask while it's inactive, though, so be careful!

FIGURE 12.12
The mask is temporarily disabled.

Removing a Layer Mask

When you're done with a layer mask or you want to start over, you can get rid of it in two ways. The first way, and the easiest, is simply to drag the layer mask's thumbnail onto the Delete button (which looks like a trash can) at the bottom of the Layers panel. You also can get rid of a layer mask by choosing Layer, Layer Mask, Delete, or Layer, Layer Mask, Apply (see Figure 12.13); or, if it's a vector mask, choose Layer, Vector Mask, Delete. If you drag the mask to the trash, you are presented with the dialog shown in Figure 12.14, in which you are prompted to apply the effects of the mask or discard the mask without applying it.

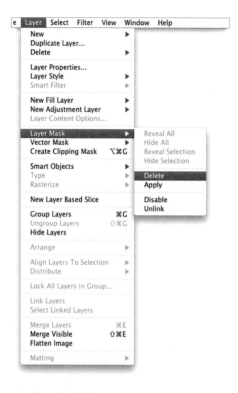

FIGURE 12.13
Apply the layer mask or delete it
without applying it.

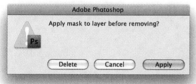

FIGURE 12.14
Choose Delete, Cancel, or Apply.

Making Layer Masks Visible with Channels

Each mask that you add to an image creates a new channel in your image,
called an **alpha channel**. You can see all these channels in the Channels
panel. Channels are Photoshop's way of storing both color and mask information. If you add a mask to a layer and choose Window, Channels, you'll
see something like the example in Figure 12.15.

Click the eye icon to the left of an alpha channel in the Channels panel;
the mask appears in the image window as red, representing a transparent
red plastic film called rubylith (a carryover from the old days when this
stuff was done with paper, glue, and X-Acto knives in the real world). You
can also target the mask for editing in the Channels panel. More important,

FIGURE 12.15
The Channels panel with a layer
mask at the bottom.

you can save it by choosing Duplicate Channel from the panel menu. You'll get a dialog like the one in Figure 12.16, letting you save the mask either as part of the document or as its own document. To turn a selection into an alpha channel, choose Select, Save Selection, or click the Save Selection as Channel button at the bottom of the Channels panel. It's another quick and easy way to make a mask.

FIGURE 12.16
If you click New, the alpha channel becomes a new channel in the current document.

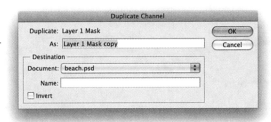

Summary

In this hour, you looked at using masks. Masking enables you to apply changes selectively, while protecting parts of the picture that you don't want to change, or to hide parts of an image without deleting them. You learned about modifying selections using Quick Mask mode and how to edit a mask with the Brush and Eraser. Then you learned about layer masks, both pixel-based and vector-based. You learned how to view your mask and how to save it as an alpha channel.

Q&A

Q. Remind me again—does black on a mask show or hide the layer contents?

A. The black area of the mask hides the image; white areas of the mask allow the image to show through. Don't feel bad; I always have trouble keeping it straight, too. The esteemed technical editor of this book, Doug Norris, uses the mnemonic "Black blocks," which I think makes perfect sense.

Q. Why would you delete a layer mask and apply it, rather than just keeping it in place?

A. Well, that depends on your situation. If you're trying to keep your file size way down, you'll want to delete as many "extras" as possible, including channels and layers that you're not using. The same goes for when your Layers and Channels panels get overcrowded and you're trying to pare things a bit so you can keep better track of what you're doing. On the other hand, I'm a conservative sort, so I don't like deleting *anything,* and most computers these days have plenty of hard drive space and plenty of RAM, as well as fast Internet connections, so large files just aren't the problem they once were.

Q. What's the difference between the Feather slider in the Masks panel and the Feather slider in the Refine Mask dialog?

A. Simple: Changes you make with the former are undoable simply by dragging the slider back the other way. Changes you make in the Refine Mask dialog, on the other hand, are permanent.

Workshop

Quiz

1. A mask can hide:

   A. An object

   B. The background

   C. Either the background or an object

2. True or false: Masks can be opaque, semiopaque, or transparent.

3. True or false: You can have up to 12 masks on a single layer.

4. Masks are saved with the picture and, therefore, increase file size. To save disk space, always:

   A. Apply and discard the masks when you're sure you're done with them.

   B. Flatten the image.

   C. Hide the layer masks.

Answers

1. **C.** Masks hide anything you want to protect.

2. **True.** However, if the mask is transparent, it's not hiding anything. Some might say that it's not really a mask, in that case, but we'll leave that topic to our friendly neighborhood philosophers.

3. **False.** Sorry, you can have only one layer mask of each type per layer. Use Quick Mask for additional masking.

4. **A and B** both work. Flattening the image compresses the layers into a single Background layer and applies the masks.

Exercise

Find a picture with several similar objects in it. Mask them separately and experiment with changing the colors of the objects, one at a time, without changing the background. Try using both vector- and pixel-based layer masks. You'll find that vector masks are great for masking geometric objects, whereas pixel masks work better for complex objects and soft-edged selections.

Using Paths

Way back in Hour 3, "Making Selections," you learned how to make selections that can isolate the part of the image so that you can work on it without affecting the rest of the image. Then in the last hour, you learned how to convert selections to masks to hide the parts of your image that you don't want to show and to preserve selections so you can recall them later. The problem with selections is that it can be difficult to achieve a precise shape. Photoshop has all kinds of tools for creating selections based on the image content, by following object edges or choosing similarly colored areas, but what if you need to select a very smoothly curved area? Or a triangular area?

Paths offer you a way out of this dilemma. Using paths, you can create and save selections for future use, the same way you can save a mask to preserve a selection. Paths are saved right within the Photoshop file, along with layers, layer masks, channels, and all the rest. And because paths are vector based instead of pixel based, you aren't restricted to the shapes you can create with the Selection tools. You can draw very precise shapes and smooth curves with the Path tools. Then you can use these shapes as the basis for selections, stroke and fill them as objects or lines in your picture, or turn them into vector masks.

Let's start by exploring the different ways to create paths. Then we'll look at techniques for editing and using them in Photoshop.

Creating Paths

You can create paths in three different ways (or you can use a combination of these methods):

What You'll Learn in This Hour:
▶ Creating Paths
▶ Editing Paths
▶ Using Paths

▶ Create a path based on a selection.

▶ Create a path from scratch by using the Path tools to draw the path by hand.

▶ Create a path using the Shape tools, which you learned about in Hour 7, "Drawing and Combining Shapes."

Paths via Selections

Making a selection and converting it to a path is often the most efficient way to create a path. Let's look at an example. Figure 13.1 shows the test image, a tire gauge. I'll select the object and make what's called a **clipping path** to clip it out of the background. Without Photoshop, you could achieve the same effect with a photographic print and a pair of scissors.

FIGURE 13.1
My goal is a clipping path that outlines the gauge.

As you remember, you can create selections using several different tools. For this image, I selected the background with the Quick Selection tool and then cleaned up the selection using Quick Mask mode. Other objects might be selected more easily by using a combination of the Elliptical Marquee and the Polygonal Lasso. You might even need to use several Selection tools in turn to achieve the selection you need. Just keep the Shift key pressed as you apply each new tool, to merge the selections into one. Figure 13.2 shows my final selection.

FIGURE 13.2
The tire gauge is now selected.

Convert a Selection to a Path

Starting with a selection of your own, follow these steps to convert it to a path:

1. First, make sure that the Paths panel is visible. If you don't see it, choose Window, Paths to bring it up.

2. Choose Make Work Path from the Paths panel's pop-up menu (see Figure 13.3).

FIGURE 13.3
The pop-up menu on the Paths panel.

3. The only option that you can set in the Make Work Path dialog is Tolerance (see Figure 13.4). **Tolerance**, measured in pixels, refers to how closely Photoshop follows the outline of your selection in creating the path. The lower the Tolerance value, the more exactly the path conforms to the bounds of the original selection.

For this image, I first tried a Tolerance of 5 pixels. As Figure 13.5 shows, the results were nowhere near what I wanted. Photoshop's approximation of the selection at this setting was way too loose; you can see in the figure that the path doesn't follow the outline of the valve stem closely enough.

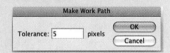

FIGURE 13.4
The Make Work Path dialog.

▼ TRY IT YOURSELF

Convert a Selection to a Path
continued

CAUTION

It's a Long and Winding Path

Be aware that complex paths with lots more points and angles can be resource intensive; images that contain them are larger, save and open more slowly, and take longer to print

FIGURE 13.5
When the path doesn't match the selection closely enough, the Tolerance is set too high.

When this happens, the answer is simple: Undo. Then try the path conversion again with a lower Tolerance value. After some experimentation, I found that a value of .5 pixel worked quite well for this picture (see Figure 13.6).

FIGURE 13.6
When the Tolerance value is set correctly, the path matches the selection closely.

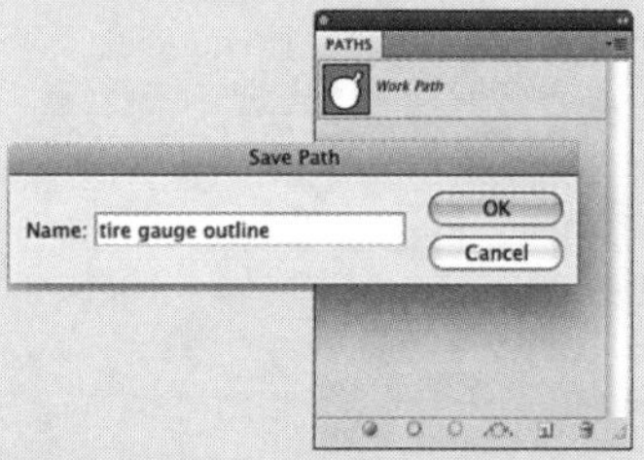

FIGURE 13.7
You can give paths more logical names using the Save Path dialog.

4. Once created, the path appears in the Paths panel (see Figure 13.7). Photoshop names it **Work Path**, but you can rename the path by double-clicking it in the Paths panel. In the Save Path dialog, type the new name and click OK, as shown in Figure 13.7.

5. Now that you've created the path and given it a name, all that remains is to choose Clipping Path from the Paths panel pop-up menu and specify the path you just created as the clipping path.

Although renaming the work path isn't required, it's a good idea to make this a habit, especially if you might need the path again. If you leave the path labeled as a work path and then start a second path, one of two things will happen. First, if the work path is still active in the Paths panel, the new path will be added to it as a **subpath**. Second, if the original work path is *not* active in the Paths panel, it will disappear and the new path will replace it. You can choose Undo or use the History panel to go back and recover the original path, but it's easier to simply rename it at the time of creation, turning it into a regular path that only you can delete.

Paths via the Path Tools

Sometimes making a selection is too difficult or requires too much work on a certain image, particularly if you want it to include smooth, complex curves. In that case, you can use the Path tools to draw the path by hand.

If you've used vector-based illustration programs, such as Adobe Illustrator, you're already familiar with Bézier-based drawing tools such as Photoshop's Path tools. If you haven't used these kinds of tools, however, you should know that mastering them takes a little practice—but the pay-off is well worth the effort. In addition to the standard tools that draw a straight or curved line and add or remove points on the line, Photoshop provides the Freeform Pen tool. This tool gives you the power to draw any kind of line you want—straight, curved, or squiggly—and turn it into a path. When used with the Magnetic option, the Freeform Pen tool makes drawing around a complicated object much easier.

Each end of a **Bézier curve** is defined by three points: one on the curve and two outside the curve at the ends of handles that you can use to change the angle and direction of the curve. If this sounds confusing, don't worry; you'll see some examples soon.

TIP

Another Path to Travel

Photoshop offers a short-cut to create a path from a selection: Make a selection and then click the Make Work Path button at the bottom of the Paths panel. The path is created automatically using the same Tolerance setting you used for your last conversion.

TRY IT YOURSELF ▼

Use the Pen Tool

The best way to learn how to use the Pen tool is simply to play around with it in a new Photoshop document. Let's take some time to do that now.

1. First, create a new Photoshop document that's big enough to give you some working room. Photoshop's default size (7×5 inches) should work fine, and a plain white background will enable you to see the Pen's paths easily.

▼ TRY IT YOURSELF

Use the Pen Tool

continued

FIGURE 13.8
Just two clicks create two corner points and a straight line between them.

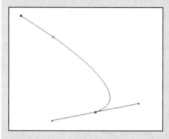

FIGURE 13.9
Clicking and dragging creates a smooth point and a curved line.

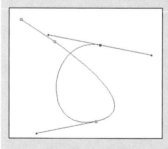

FIGURE 13.10
Click and drag to create another smooth point along the same path.

2. Switch to the Pen tool (its button in the toolbox looks like a fountain pen nib) and make sure that the Paths panel is visible.

3. In the Tool Options bar, click the Paths button—it's the middle one in the first group of three at the left end of the Options bar.

4. Click somewhere near the left edge of the page to begin your path. (Notice that Photoshop immediately creates a path called **work path** in the Paths panel. You can rename this path later in the same way described in the previous "Try It Yourself.")

5. To draw a straight line, move your cursor anywhere else on the canvas and click. (Don't hold down the mouse button while you're moving; we get to that technique in a bit.) You've just created a **corner point**, which means that Photoshop connects this point and the first one you drew with a straight line (see Figure 13.8).

6. To continue the path with a curved line, move your cursor to the bottom of the window and then click and *drag* left. You'll see a curve immediately appear and change as you drag (see Figure 13.9). You've just created a **smooth point**, which means that Photoshop creates a smooth curve where two curved line segments meet. After you click to position the point, your dragging positions its handles, which control the angle and degree of its curve.

7. To make this clearer, add another smooth curve to your path. Move your cursor to a point above and to the right of the second point, then click and drag to the right and a bit down. Another smooth point and another curve are created (see Figure 13.10).

   Stop and take a look at the point you created in step 5. It forms a nice smooth curve between the point you just created and the point you created in step 4. That's what a smooth point is all about.

   As you have no doubt noticed, each smooth point has two handles positioned 180° from the other. You can use these handles to change the angle and direction of a curve after you've established it. You'll learn more about how to modify curves in the "Editing Paths" section, later in this hour.

8. Switch to another tool or click your starting point to end the path. Unlike selections, paths don't need to be closed.

Okay, by now you should have the basic idea: You create straight lines via corner points and make curved lines using smooth points. But you have to know more about each kind of point to use it effectively.

Corner Points

Corner points are easy. No matter what kind of lines a corner point connects, the result is always an angle, not a curve. If a curved line ends in a corner point, the smooth point at the other end of the line controls the curve's angle (see Figure 13.11), because corner points don't have any handles that you can use for adjusting curves.

TIP

Restraining Order

If you want to constrain corner points so that each one appears only at a 45° or 90° angle from the last point you created, press the Shift key as you click to create the new point.

FIGURE 13.11
Corner points surround smooth points.

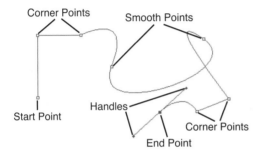

Smooth Points

As you saw in this hour's first Try It Yourself exercise, the behavior of smooth points is a bit more complicated than that of corner points and takes some getting used to. A smooth point always creates a smooth curve between two lines (see Figure 13.12), and its direction handles are always directly opposite each other.

FIGURE 13.12
Smooth points do their utmost to create curves out of any situation.

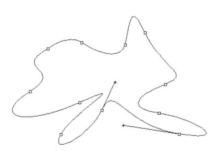

You can call upon one last kind of point when you need it; Adobe calls it a corner point with independent direction handles, but it's also often called a **combination point**. It's what you get when you put a corner point between two curves.

Create a Sharp Curve

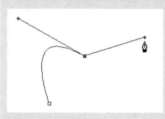

FIGURE 13.13
Here I'm creating a sharp curve. The rightmost line is the handle I just created by using the Option or Alt key.

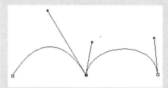

FIGURE 13.14
The final path, made of curves, smooth points, and a combination point.

Curves with a combination point in the middle can look like a stick seagull. The following steps show you how to create one:

1. Set up a new Photoshop document and begin a path by clicking to set an initial point.

2. For the second point, create a smooth point as you normally would: by dragging after you click to set the point, making a curved path.

3. Now move the cursor so that it's exactly over the smooth point you just created. Press Option (Mac) or Alt (Windows) as you click and drag the mouse in the direction of the intended "bump" in the new curve. Release the key and the mouse button. Your path should now look fairly close to what you see in Figure 13.13.

4. Move the cursor to the position where you want the line to end; then click and drag in the opposite direction than the way you dragged in step 3. The line will curve neatly from where you ended the first arch to where you just clicked at its endpoint. As you drag, the curve expands farther upward. Figure 13.14 shows the resulting path, containing two smooth points (at either end) and one combination point (in the middle). If your 'curve doesn't match this configuration, click on each point in turn and use the point's handles to reshape the curve.

Previewing the Path

While you're clicking and dragging to create all these points and lines, you might think that a preview feature would be very helpful. Fortunately, Photoshop provides one. Look at the Tool Options bar and locate the downward-pointing triangle at the right end of the strip of tool buttons. You'll see an option called Rubber Band; click the check box to turn it on. Activating this feature enables you to preview both straight lines and curves before you click to create them. Experiment to see this feature at work; if you don't like it after all, you can go right back to the same menu to turn it off again.

Completing the Path

To complete a path, you have two choices: *close* the path by connecting the final point to the initial point, or leave the path *open*.

A **closed path** is a loop with no beginning or end. To close a path, follow these steps:

1. Use the Pen tool to draw a path, using whatever points you want.

2. After you've clicked to place the last point, move your cursor right on top of your initial point. You'll see a tiny circle appear next to the Pen cursor.

3. Click to turn this final point into a corner point, or click and drag to create one last curve (see Figure 13.15).

An **open path**, on the other hand, has a beginning and an end. Figures 13.8–13.14 all show open paths. To finish off a path that you want to keep open, follow these steps:

1. Use the Pen tool to draw a path, using whatever points you want.

2. After you've clicked to place the last point, click the Pen tool button in the toolbar or the Options bar, or switch to any other tool. The path now ends at the last point you created.

   The next time you click in the image window, you'll start a new path instead of continuing your previous path. And if you didn't save your previous path with a new name, the new path will replace it.

FIGURE 13.15
The starting and stopping point is the gray one.

NOTE

Real, but Not Real

One point to remember when you're working with paths is that any path you create is not really part of the image, even though paths are saved in the file along with the image. 'A path is not the same as a line drawn on the canvas; until you add color to it, it's merely a theoretical line. When you stroke a path, it becomes a visible line. If you fill a path, it becomes a shape.

Editing Paths

Whether you create a path by converting a selection or by drawing with the Pen tool, it usually won't be perfect. No matter how good you are with the Selection or Path tools, every path needs a little tweaking before it's ready for prime time. You've probably realized this while working through the Try It Yourself exercises in this hour. Fortunately, you can easily alter paths after they are created. Again, you use the Pen tool (and the other Path tools) to do this kind of work.

The Path Tools

First, let's take a look at the different Path tools Photoshop offers. Click and hold the Pen tool's button in the toolbox (see Figure 13.16).

FIGURE 13.16
Photoshop's Path tools, including both the Pen tools and the Path Selection tools.

TIP

It's Magnetic...

Remember the Magnetic Lasso that automatically formed a selection marquee around the object you were trying to select? The Freeform Pen has a magnetic option, on the Tool Options bar, that works just the same way. You can use it to draw a path that traces the boundaries of a shape. To turn on this option, click the check box labeled Magnetic to the right of the tool buttons in the Tool Options bar.

▶ **Pen tool**—You've already met this tool; it's used to create new paths.

▶ **Freeform Pen tool**—As its name implies, you can use this tool to draw a freeform path in any shape. Photoshop adds points and handles as you go, so you can go back later and adjust any part of your path that's not quite what you had in mind. This tool is best used with a graphics tablet, if you've got one.

▶ **Add Anchor Point tool**—Use this tool to add new points to an existing path.

▶ **Delete Anchor Point tool**—Use this tool to remove points from a path while leaving the path itself intact.

▶ **Convert Point tool**—Use this tool to change a point's type after you've created it. For example, you can turn a corner point into a smooth point, a smooth point into a combination point, and so on. You'll learn more about how to use this tool in the next section.

Two Path Selection tools also help you work with paths: the Path Selection tool and the Direct Selection tool. They're found in the toolbox just below the Type tools. The Direct Selection tool (represented by a hollow arrow) can select and move individual segments of a subpath. The Path Selection tool (the black arrow), on the other hand, always selects and moves all the components of a subpath at once. If you have several subpaths within the same path, the Path Selection tool will move one path at a time. To select all the subpath components of a path at once, Option-click (Mac) or Alt+click (Windows) its thumbnail in the Paths panel.

You can switch between the Pen tool and the Freeform Pen tool in one of two ways: either by clicking and holding down the Pen tool in the toolbar so that the menu of other Path tools appears, or by pressing Shift+P on the keyboard. Press A to switch to the Path tools, and press Shift+A to switch between the Direct Selection tool and the Path Selection tool. If you're already using a Pen tool, press Command (Mac) or Control (Windows) to temporarily switch to the Direct Selection tool.

Basic Path Techniques

Here are a few basic techniques for navigating among and using paths:

- ▶ To activate a path, simply click its name in the Paths panel, just as you would click a layer to activate it. Active paths show up in your image, as you would expect.

- ▶ To deselect a path, click its name again or click in the empty area of the Paths panel. This makes the path disappear from the main window.

- ▶ To delete a path, select the path's entry in the Paths panel and drag it to the trash button at the bottom of the panel, just as you would to delete a layer.

- ▶ To create a new path, you can do one of four things: Your first option is just to start drawing with one of the Path tools in the image window. This creates a new work path or, if an existing path is selected, adds to the existing path. If you want to name the path before you draw it, choose New Path from the Paths panel's menu before you begin. You can also click the Create New Path button at the bottom of the panel to place a new path on the Paths panel. Finally, as you know, you can create a selection and then use the Make Work Path command or button to turn it into a path.

- ▶ To duplicate a path, click its entry in the Paths panel and drag it to the Create New Path button. This works the same way as duplicating a layer.

Using Paths

What can you do with paths after you've gone to all the trouble of creating them? Quite a lot, actually. Paths can represent selections that you want to use repeatedly. You can **fill** a path area or give it a **stroke** with your choice of color and width, and you even have a tool to apply the stroke. Stroking adds a stroke of paint on the current layer along the path, filling places inside the path with a color or pattern. Figure 13.17 shows a freeform path that has been stroked with red and filled with a pattern. Finally, you can use a path to hide whatever's outside its bounds, either within Photoshop (a vector layer mask) or when the image is brought into another program, such as Adobe InDesign (a clipping path).

NOTE

Use the Active Layer

When you fill or stroke a path, you are adding pixels to the active layer of your picture. Make sure that you've activated the layer you want to put the paint on before you apply the fill or stroke.

FIGURE 13.17
A filled and stroked path.

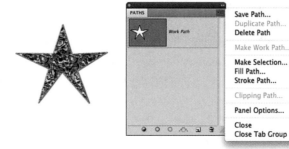

Turning Paths into Selections

In Photoshop, turning selections into paths is one way to make your selections more easily editable. This can be incredibly helpful when you want to tweak a selection edge or move part of it without moving the rest. When in doubt, create a path so that you can edit the selection one point at a time.

▼ TRY IT YOURSELF

Convert a Path into a Selection

You've already learned how to turn a selection into a path. The following steps show you how to convert a path into a selection, whether the path was initially created from a selection or by drawing with the Pen tools:

1. Start by creating a path using whatever method you prefer.

2. Click the path you want to convert in the Paths panel to activate it.

3. Choose Make Selection from the Paths panel's menu (see Figure 13.18), or click the Load Path as a Selection button at the bottom of the Paths panel. (The latter option bypasses the dialog described in the next step, so if you choose it, you're done! Photoshop uses the settings you last entered in the dialog box.)

FIGURE 13.18
Turning a work path into a selection.

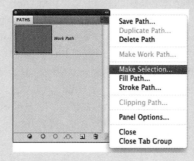

4. In the Make Selection dialog, set a value for how much feathering, if any, Photoshop should apply to the resulting selection (see Figure 13.19). The higher the Feather Radius setting is, the more partially selected pixels will appear along the edges of the selection.

Convert a Path into a Selection
continued

FIGURE 13.19
The Make Selection dialog

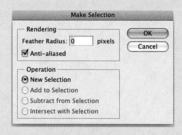

5. Click OK, and the new selection appears. The path is still there in the Paths panel, and you can use it again any time you want.

Filling a Path

Filling a path means just what you expect. Choose a path in the Paths panel and choose Fill Path from the panel menu; you'll get the same options you see when you fill a selection, plus a couple of extras. In the Fill Path dialog (see Figure 13.20), you can choose a color, a pattern, or a snapshot to fill the area. You can also choose a blending mode and an opacity percentage, and you can opt to preserve any transparent pixels within the path, filling only pixels that are already painted. You can turn on anti-aliasing, and you can also set a feathering value. If the path consists of two or more subpaths, only the one you select with the Path Selection tool will be filled or stroked.

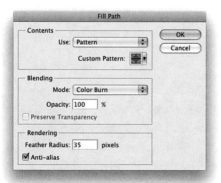

FIGURE 13.20
The Fill Path dialog has many options.

Stroking a Path

Stroking a path affects the outline of the path, not the entire area that it encloses. Select a path, and then choose Stroke Path from the Paths panel menu. The Stroke Path dialog offers you a choice of tools with which to apply the stroke, from Pencil and Brush to History Brush and Color Replacement tool (see Figure 13.21).

Stroke Path

- Pencil
- Brush
- Eraser
- Background Eraser
- Clone Stamp
- Pattern Stamp
- Healing Brush
- History Brush
- Art History Brush
- Smudge
- Blur
- Sharpen
- Dodge
- Burn
- Sponge
- Color Replacement Tool
- Quick Selection Tool

OK
Cancel

Whatever tool you pick, Photoshop uses that tool's current settings to create the stroke. So, for example, if you want to airbrush the path outline with only 60% pressure, make sure that you switch to the Brush tool, turn on the Airbrush option, and set that Flow value in the Tool Options bar *before* you choose Stroke Path.

Using a Path to Clip an Image

In the last hour, you learned how to create vector layer masks from a path; now you have the skills you'll need to draw that path in the first place. A layer mask, whether vector-based or pixel-based, hides parts of a layer while letting other parts show through. In the case of a vector mask, everything within the path's bounds shows, and everything outside the path is hidden.

Vector masks work great in Photoshop, but they often don't translate into other programs that don't support Photoshop's transparency. For example, if you look back at the pressure gauge image at the beginning of the hour (see Figure 13.1), you'll see that its image window is square. I can use the path I created around the gauge to create a vector mask that will make everything around the gauge transparent, so that a background I place behind it will show around the edges. But if I save this image as a TIFF file and then import it into QuarkXPress, all those transparent pixels will be replaced with white ones.

To make sure that transparency is preserved when you're using an image in another program, you need to do two things: Designate a clipping path and save your image in EPS format. To assign a clipping path to an image, make sure you've given the path a name, and then choose Clipping Path from the panel menu and pick the path you want to use. Then, when you save the image, choose Photoshop EPS for its format.

Summary

Paths are the key to true precision when creating selections, masks, and shapes in Photoshop. Because they're based on mathematical equations, not pixel locations, they stay the same shape when you scale them up or down, and they're infinitely adjustable. You can use paths to save selections for future use, turn them into complex filled and stroked shapes, and mask parts of your image with them. You can create paths from scratch with the Path tools or generate them by converting selections. Either way, editing those paths is a sometimes arcane art that requires you to get used to manipulating curves without actually touching them—but mastering it is a worthwhile pursuit because of the artistic freedom it gives you.

NOTE

You Do Have Options, But...

Some design programs support several methods of representing transparency. In addition to clipping paths, you can use alpha channels or layer masks, and, in this case, you're not stuck with saving the image in EPS format. On the other hand, some older programs can use only EPS with clipping paths for transparency. So to be on the safe side, use the EPS-with-clipping-path method for saving nonrectangular images.

Q&A

Q. What's a Bézier curve, and why should I care?

A. Bézier curves are a type of curve that can be described exactly by specifying the positions of the curve's two endpoints and those endpoints' four direction handles. They were first used in 1962 by a guy named, surprise, Pierre Bézier, a designer for the Renault car company. The nice thing about Bézier curves is that you don't have to know the math behind them to use them, and if you master them, you'll be well on your way to becoming an Illustrator expert as well as a Photoshop expert.

Q. I'm not clear on the connection between paths and shapes. Can you explain?

A. It's simple: They're the same thing. Think of shapes as fill layers with vector masks, and each vector mask is composed of a path. When you use a Shape tool to create a shape layer, you're really just dropping in a prebuilt path as the vector mask for that layer. That brings us to a wonderful revelation: You can turn your own paths into custom shapes. Just choose a path in the Paths panel, and choose Edit, Define Custom Shape. Now you can drop that exact shape into any document you like, with whatever fill you desire. If the path wasn't a closed path, Photoshop will close it to create the custom shape.

Q. How do I know what tolerance to set when I convert a path to a selection?

A. That depends on how smooth—or how accurate—you want the finished path to be. A tolerance of 1 pixel or less (.5 pixels is as low as the setting can go) makes the path follow the selection as precisely as possible. A tolerance of 5–10 produces a smoothed-out path, following your selection within 5 to 10 pixels rather than exactly.

Workshop

Quiz

1. What does it mean to *stroke* a path?

    A. Using the points and direction handles to carefully massage its shape

    B. Adding a color to it to paint a line

    C. Painting over it with short strokes

2. How do you turn a selection into a path?

 A. Make the selection and press Command-P (Mac) or Ctrl+P (Windows).

 B. Choose Make Work Path from the Paths panel menu.

 C. Line it with bricks.

3. What does the Pen tool's Rubber Band option do?

 A. Makes your paths visible as you click the mouse

 B. Makes paths spring back to a straight line when clicked

 C. Makes lines "stretchy" so that you can edit them without using the direction handles

Answers

1. **B.** Think of stroking the length of the path with a paintbrush or any of the other Painting tools.

2. **B.** Don't try A unless you want to print your image.

3. **A.** All paths are visible as you draw them (while you drag to set the handles), but Rubber Band mode makes the path visible as you move the mouse.

Exercise

Create a new image file and use the Pen tool to draw both a star-shaped path and a freeform path with a lot of curves. Stroke each of these paths with a color. Then use the Freeform Pen tool in Magnetic mode to trace around them. Notice that as long as you stay close to the original line, the Pen tool places a path right at the edge of the stroke. Fill the new shapes with a color. Draw two more paths inside these shapes, and fill them with a different color. Practice with the Path tools, adding points and refining your paths until you're comfortable with them all.

PART IV
Fantastic Filters

HOUR 14
Getting Started with Filters

Ah, filters! They offer the Photoshop user the most bang for the buck, that's for sure. With a filter, you can instantly turn a blurry picture into a faux oil painting, create fluffy clouds from thin air, or remove dust and scratches from an old photo. And there's more—oh, so much more.

But before you go wild with filters in the next few hours, I'd like you to take just one hour to learn a few things that will make your filter adventures even wilder and woollier. Did you know, for example, that you can apply more than one filter at a time using the Filter Gallery? Or that you can make any filter a Smart Filter whose settings you can adjust at any point after you apply it—yes, even years later? When you master these techniques, in addition to the Fade command, you'll be ready to move on to actually applying some filters. So hang in there.

Using the Filter Gallery

If you've skipped ahead and applied some of Photoshop's more artistic filters, you've already met the Filter Gallery (see Figure 14.1). This very large—but resizable—dialog houses the Artistic, Brush Strokes, Distort, Sketch, Stylize, and Texture groups of filters. If you take advantage of all this dialog has to offer, you'll find that you have more control over these filters and their limitless possibilities than you ever imagined. Let's take a quick tour.

WHAT YOU'LL LEARN IN THIS HOUR:
▶ Using the Filter Gallery
▶ Applying and Editing Smart Filters
▶ Combining and Fading Filters

FIGURE 14.1
You can spend hours experimenting with Photoshop's filters and still never leave the Filter Gallery.

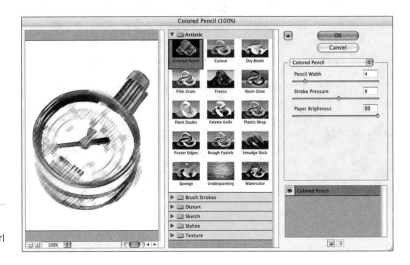

The Filter Gallery's first, and most obvious, advantage over other dialogs is its huge preview area. Although you can't resize the preview area itself, you can make it larger by enlarging the whole Filter Gallery dialog or by simply hiding the column of thumbnails. Zoom controls in the lower-left corner of the preview area enable you to change its view percentage so that you can focus on details as you experiment with filters.

Next to the preview area is a list of filter groups; clicking one displays all the filters in that group. This gives you access to 47 filters in a single dialog— how's that for efficiency? In addition, each filter name is accompanied by a small thumbnail showing you the results of applying that filter to a sample image. If you don't need to see the thumbnails and filter group labels, you can hide this list by clicking the inverted triangle to the right of the list.

Moving farther right again, you'll notice the filter settings area under the OK and Cancel buttons. The controls you see here, of course, vary depending on which filter you're currently working with. At the top of the settings area is a pop-up menu that lists all the filters in the Gallery; this is how you switch filters if you've hidden the filter list to enlarge your preview area.

Below the settings area is another list that looks similar to the Layers panel. Here, in the **effect layers list**, is where things get really interesting. When you click a filter name, a new entry appears in the list, complete with an eye icon that you can click to hide the filter's effects. At the bottom of the list are two familiar-looking buttons: a trash button that removes the filter and its effects, and a New Effect Layer button that enables you to add another filter on top of the first one. Using this list, you can create combinations of filters and settings in literally infinite numbers.

To see and change the settings of an effect layer, click its entry in the effect layers list, or click and drag an effect layer to change its stacking order. Be sure to experiment with these capabilities—the possibilities are endless (see Figure 14.2).

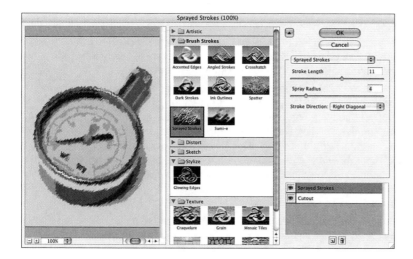

FIGURE 14.2
Try putting filters with blurry, blocky effects on the bottom of the layer stack and filters with sharp detail on the top.

Applying and Editing Smart Filters

Now that you've been wowed by the power of the Filter Gallery, prepare to be wowed some more. Smart Filters, first introduced in Photoshop CS3, are one of the coolest features to be added to Photoshop in a very long time. And they're not even new filters; they're simply a new way of using the filters that have been in Photoshop all along.

Smart Filters have elements in common with adjustment layers, which you learned about in Hour 5, "Adjusting Brightness and Color," and with layer styles, which we covered in Hour 11, "Creating Layered Images." After you apply a Smart Filter to a layer, you can return to that filter's dialog at any time and change its settings.

You can apply as many Smart Filters to each layer as you like. They're displayed in the Layers panel under the layer's name, just the way layer styles are (see Figure 14.3). Applying Smart Filters works just like applying

FIGURE 14.3
The Layers panel shows you which Smart Filters have been applied to each layer.

regular filters, with one difference: You must first convert the layer you're working with to a Smart Object. To do that, choose Filter, Convert for Smart Filters. Then choose the filter you want to apply from the Filter menu—any of Photoshop's native filters other than the Liquify or Vanishing Point filters, and any of your third-party filters that have been updated to work as Smart Filters.

What's a Smart Object, Anyway?

You can turn any existing layer into a Smart Object (choose either Layer, Smart Objects, Convert to Smart Object, or Filter, Convert for Smart Filters)—or you can place other files within your image as Smart Objects (choose File, Place). All the changes you make to a Smart Object are shown onscreen, but they're not actually applied to the object until you output the image by printing it or saving it in a format other than Photoshop's native format.

What's the point? Using Smart Objects not only gives you greater creative freedom (because you can change your mind repeatedly), but also improves the quality of your images. For example, suppose you use the Transform, Scale command to shrink an object within an image but then later you change your mind. If you scale it back up to its original size, you'll have a fuzzy image that's nowhere near as sharp and detailed as the original, because the original pixels were deleted when the object was scaled down. However, if you convert that layer to a Smart Object before scaling it down, you can rescale it as many times as you want without loss of quality.

As a bonus, if you duplicate a Smart Object's layer, the copy of the object remains linked to the original version of the object, and any changes made to either one are also applied to the linked Smart Object.

What can you do with a Smart Object? You can scale, rotate, or warp it. You can change its layer blending mode or opacity, apply a layer style to it, and, of course, apply filters to it.

And what *can't* you do with a Smart Object? You can't erase it, smudge it, or paint over it. If you try, Photoshop asks you if you want to rasterize the Smart Object, which means turning it back into a regular layer.

Here are some of the cool things you can do with Smart Filters after you've applied them:

▶ Change filter settings by double-clicking a Smart Filter's entry in the Layers panel to return to the filter's dialog.

▶ Click the eye icon next to a Smart Filter or a group of Smart Filters to hide the filter effects or to show them again when they're hidden.

▶ To change the stacking order of Smart Filters, drag their entries in the Layers panel. This changes the way they affect the image, so be sure to try different combinations.

▶ To copy a Smart Filter to another Smart Object, press Option (Mac) or Alt (Windows) and drag the filter's entry over the Smart Object's entry. If you want to copy all the Smart Filters from a layer, Option-drag or Alt-drag the "Smart Filters" line itself.

▶ Block the effects of a Smart Filter or group of Smart Filters on parts of a layer by editing the layer's **filter mask**. Filter masks work just like the masks associated with adjustment layers (see Hour 5). Wherever the mask is black, the effect of the filter is eliminated, and where it's white, the effect shows. Gray areas let the effect show partially. To edit a filter mask, click its icon (next to the Smart Filters entry in the Layer panel) and paint with black, white, or gray (see Figure 14.4).

FIGURE 14.4
A filter mask enables you to restrict the effects of a Smart Filter to a particular area on a layer.

Combining and Fading Filters

By now, you've probably realized that there's much more to using a filter in Photoshop than simply applying the filter to your picture. You can try different settings, you can go back and change those settings, and you can combine filters to create whole new effects, as well as change the opacity of filter effects *after* you've applied them.

Using Multiple Filters

You don't have to be satisfied with a single filter; I rarely am. The coolest filter effects are achieved by stacking multiple filters on top of one another.

That's one of the reasons Adobe invented the Filter Gallery and Smart Filters, as well as the History panel. These features enable you to experiment as much as you want without worrying about doing permanent damage to your image. And you'll find that if using one filter is great, using two filters (or more!) is even better. Take a look at Figure 14.5, for example. It shows the before version and two after versions of the same photo; I could have applied millions more combinations of filters to this image, to achieve millions more different effects.

FIGURE 14.5
I started with a simple still life and turned it into a painting and a charcoal sketch with different filter combinations. The painting uses the Palette Knife and Dry Brush filters, while the sketch was produced by applying the Smudge Stick and Charcoal filters.

Fading Filters

The Fade command (Edit, Fade [last filter or adjustment]) fades the effect of the filter or adjustment by reducing its opacity, using a percentage setting ranging from 0% to 100%. You might think that this would have the same result as simply using lower settings in the filter's original dialog—but you'd be wrong. Using Fade gives you a completely different result from lowering the settings in the original filter or adjustment dialog. (Note that the Fade command doesn't work with Smart Filters.)

Take a look at the example in Figure 14.6. I applied the Crystallize filter with a Cell Size of 15 to the paw print on the left. Then I selected the other paw print and applied the same filter with the Cell Size doubled, to 30. Finally, I chose Edit, Fade Crystallize and entered an Opacity of 50%. You can see that the effect of the filter isn't halved by the Fade command; instead, it's as though Photoshop duplicated the original paw print, dropped it under the new Crystallized paw print, and set them both to 50% opacity.

FIGURE 14.6
Fading a filter has a very different effect from using lower filter settings in the first place.

TRY IT YOURSELF ▼

Fade a Filter Effect or Color Adjustment

Let's try putting the Fade command to practical use.

1. Open any convenient image. Apply a Blur filter or make any color adjustment (Image, Adjustments).

2. Choose Edit, Fade. (The command gives the name of the filter you applied in step 1—for example, Fade Gaussian Blur.) If you're working on a selection instead of the whole image, don't deselect it.

3. Set the Preview option so that you can see the effect of the fade.

4. Drag the slider to adjust the opacity.

5. Choose a blending mode other than Normal, if you want a particular effect.

6. Click OK. Deselect the selection, if necessary.

Summary

During this hour, you experienced the wonders of filters, in preparation for learning about the filters themselves. You explored the Filter Gallery, which enables you to experiment with combining filters and changing their settings before you actually apply them to your image. You learned about Smart Filters, which enable you to return to a filter dialog at any time to tweak your settings. And you learned about how filters can work together to produce a greater combined effect, as well as how to alter the intensity of a filter's effect by using the Fade command.

Q&A

Q. I applied a filter, but it affected only part of the image. What did I do wrong?

A. Probably nothing. You can apply filters to only one layer at a time, so if part of your image is on one or more other layers, that part won't be filtered. Click each of the other layers in turn and press Command-F (Mac) or Ctrl+F (Windows) to apply the filter to those layers as well. Or, if your layers are Smart Objects, just Option-drag (Mac) or Alt-drag (Windows) the Smart Filter entry from the Layers panel onto each of the other layers. Of course, the problem might just be that you have an active selection.

Q. Can I make a third-party filter into a Smart Filter?

A. You can if it has been updated to work as a Smart Filter. Incidentally, you can also apply the Shadow/Highlight adjustment as a Smart Filter.

Q. This Fade command is so neat—I'm having a great time just dragging the slider back and forth and watching the image change. Are you sure there isn't something else fun I can do with this command?

A. It sounds as though you've been so focused on the Fade dialog's Opacity slider that you've overlooked its Mode pop-up menu. Try changing a filter's blending mode for different effects. You'll be amazed at what a difference you can make by switching from Normal to Linear Dodge, for example. And this is the only way you can set a filter's blending mode; you can't do it when you first apply the filter—you can do this only after the fact with the Fade command.

Workshop

Quiz

1. What command opens the Filter Gallery?

    A. Filter, Gallery

    B. Window, Filter Gallery

    C. Any of the commands in the Artistic, Brush Strokes, Distort, Sketch, Stylize, and Texture submenus of the Filter menu

2. Which of the following filters can't be applied as a Smart Filter?

   A. Liquify

   B. Reticulation

   C. Median

3. When you fade a filter, you change its _____.

   A. Intensity

   B. Opacity

   C. Blending mode

Answers

1. C. And when you've entered the Filter Gallery, you can access any of the filters in these groups without ever leaving the dialog.

2. A. The other filter that you can't use as a Smart Filter is Vanishing Point.

3. Either **B** or **C** is correct; you have the option of changing both of these attributes using the Fade dialog, although you can choose to change just one.

Exercise

With a colorful photo open, view the Filter Gallery by choosing any of the commands in the Artistic, Brush Strokes, Distort, Sketch, Stylize, or Texture submenus of the Filter menu. Choose a filter and tweak its settings, and then switch to a different filter. When you like the way your image looks, add another filter on top of the first one and experiment with its settings. After you've clicked OK to apply the filter, choose Edit, Fade. Drag the slider to reduce the opacity of the filter effects. Try different blending modes, too. You'll go much further with the filters you'll encounter in the next few hours if you've first mastered these tools for applying filters with maximum virtuosity.

Applying Filters to Improve Your Picture

When you get right down to it, Photoshop is really all about math. That's right—I know some of you don't want to hear it, but it's true. All the actions that you can perform on an image in Photoshop rely on complex calculations of pixel color and position with respect to other variables that you specify. That's why we let the computer do the heavy lifting, but it's also why there are so many filters for you to play with. Each filter is a combination of changes to your image based on its underlying numbers, and since numbers are infinite, so are the possible combinations. In this hour, we look at some of the ways Photoshop can use its math prowess to sharpen, blur, and clean up your pictures.

Sharpen Filters

One of the most common problems photographers face is the out-of-focus picture. A picture can turn out fuzzy for many reasons; the subject or the photographer might have moved slightly when the picture was taken, or maybe the camera focused on something other than the photo's real subject. Regardless of how it happened, what you want to know is whether the picture can be saved.

If a photo is way out of focus, there's not much you can do to bring it back. But if it's only slightly soft, Photoshop can create the illusion of sharper focus. It does this with a set of filters called **Sharpen**, located in their own submenu on the Filter menu (see Figure 15.1).

WHAT YOU'LL LEARN IN THIS HOUR:

▶ Sharpen Filters
▶ Blur Filters
▶ Noise Filters

FIGURE 15.1
The Filter menu showing the
Sharpen filters.

Sharpen and Sharpen More

The simplest of the Sharpen filters, Sharpen and Sharpen More, provide different levels of the same basic function. They work by finding areas in the image where there are significant color changes, such as at the edges of an object. Then Photoshop increases the contrast between adjacent pixels in those areas, making the light pixels lighter and the dark pixels darker. Figure 15.2 shows three versions of a picture of a neat bell I saw in Ohio. The top example is before sharpening. The middle example has had Sharpen applied, and the bottom example has had Sharpen More applied. If you don't enlarge the picture too much, the Sharpen effect looks quite good. The Sharpen More effect, however, is a bit much; it exaggerates the already grainy appearance of the bell's surface.

Be careful not to overdo the sharpening. As with the Sharpen tool, which we looked at in Hour 8, "Different Ways to Paint," you must apply all the Sharpen filters with a light touch. Because of the way the filters enhance contrast in adjacent pixels, you might be just a click away from turning your photo to patchwork, as in Figure 15.3.

By the way, the Sharpen More filter has approximately the same effect as applying the Sharpen filter twice in a row. Most filters don't have a "More" version, but you can always apply a filter more than once any time it has less than the desired effect. There's even a keyboard shortcut to do just that; press Command-F (Mac) or Ctrl+F (Windows) to apply whatever filter you applied last, using the same settings (if applicable).

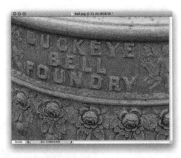

FIGURE 15.2
A Buckeye bell, before and after sharpening.

FIGURE 15.3
This image has been seriously oversharpened.

Try the Sharpen filter on one of your own fuzzy pictures and see what you think. Does it help? Try the Sharpen More filter as well. Both are great for quickly and painlessly adjusting slightly out-of-focus photographs or scans. They can't really bring the picture back into focus, but they can provide the illusion of focus, and sometimes that's good enough. Don't forget that you can apply filters selectively, using selections to keep the filter from affecting unselected parts of the image.

Sharpen Edges

Sharpen Edges doesn't affect the whole image, so its effect isn't as extreme as that of Sharpen More. Instead, Sharpen Edges picks out and enhances the contrast wherever it finds an edge in the image—anywhere there's a sharp delineation between two colors. Figure 15.4 shows before and after versions of the bell, using Sharpen Edges. Sharpening the edges has a slight but noticeable effect on the quality of the photo.

FIGURE 15.4
You can really see the Sharpen Edges effect around the letters of the company's name.

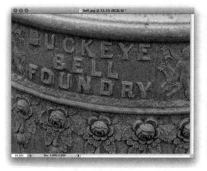

Unsharp Mask

Unsharp masking is a traditional technique that has been used in the printing industry for decades. Photoshop's version of it is probably your best bet for precision sharpening. The Unsharp Mask filter locates every two adjacent pixels with a difference in brightness values greater than the Threshold value you've specified and increases their contrast by an amount that you also specify. Being able to control which areas are sharpened and how much sharpening is applied gives you real control over the process.

Choose Filter, Sharpen, Unsharp Mask to bring up the Unsharp Mask dialog shown in Figure 15.5. The Radius slider determines how far out from each pixel Photoshop looks for contrasting pixels to which the program can apply the sharpening effect. You'll generally want to keep the Radius value fairly low—around 2.0 for most images, and slightly higher for high-res pictures. The Threshold setting controls how much contrast there has to be between the pixels for them to be affected. The lower the setting, the more similar the pixels can be and still be affected by the filter. The higher the setting, the fewer parts of the image will be affected. Be sure to check the Preview box so that you can see the effect of your changes in the image window as you work.

Many Photoshop experts recommend applying the Unsharp Mask filter to every image that you process, whether it will be printed or used on the Web. You should certainly *try* it on every image, to see whether you like the effect.

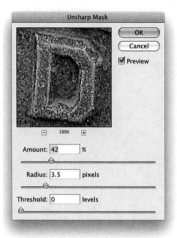

FIGURE 15.5
The preview area lets you see the effect of your settings.

Smart Sharpen

For the ultimate in sharpening power, you can turn to the Smart Sharpen filter, which Photoshop CS2 introduced. With this filter, you can choose different sharpening algorithms, or styles, for different kinds of images, and you can control the amount of sharpening in dark and light areas of your image.

Choose Filter, Sharpen, Smart Sharpen to see the Smart Sharpen options (see Figure 15.6). First, choose an option from the Remove pop-up menu. To fix a generally soft image, choose Gaussian Blur, which uses the same sharpening technique that the Unsharp Mask filter uses. If your image has a lot of detail and needs a pretty hefty amount of sharpening, choose Lens Blur to sharpen edges without adding "sharpening halos" (as shown back in Figure 15.3). And if your camera moved just as you shot the photo, choose Motion Blur and set the angle to match the angle of the blur you see in the image. Finally, unless you're in a hurry, check the More Accurate box so that Photoshop will take a little more time on its calculations and produce the best possible result.

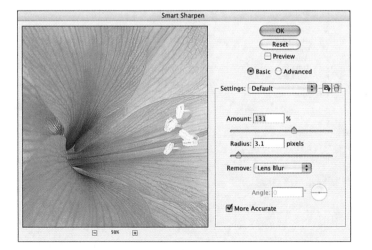

FIGURE 15.6
The Smart Sharpen filter packs a lot of power into a single dialog.

In Advanced mode, you'll see two tabs in addition to the Sharpen tab, where you've just made your basic settings. If you're seeing too much effect from the basic settings, but only in the shadows or only in the highlights, drag the Fade Amount slider to the left to reduce the amount of sharpening just in those areas. Drag the Tonal Width slider back and forth to determine how much of the image constitutes "shadows" or "highlights"—the higher the setting, the greater the area affected by your Shadow and Highlight tab settings. And the Radius slider controls how much of the area around each pixel Photoshop uses to decide whether that pixel falls into the category of a shadow or a highlight; unless you're feeling adventurous, you can leave this setting alone and get perfectly fine results.

Blur Filters

The Blur filters (Filter, Blur) are useful tools when you're going for a soft-focus effect, whether you're starting with a photo or working on a painting. As with the Blur tool, blurring can smooth a harshly lit portrait or, when used on a selection instead of the whole image, can throw a background out of focus so that it doesn't distract viewers from the picture's subject. Figure 15.7 shows the Blur filters.

FIGURE 15.7
The Blur submenu contains quite a few more filters than the Sharpen submenu.

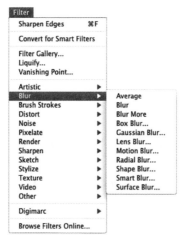

Blur and Blur More

As with Sharpen and Sharpen More, there are two basic Blur filters: Blur and Blur More. They do exactly what their names suggest. Blur is very subtle, and Blur More is a bit less so, about like applying the Blur filter twice in succession. Figure 15.8 shows a comparison of the two filters in use, against an unblurred original. As you can see, the changes are minor. Blurring doesn't make much difference, but it can smooth out wrinkles in a portrait or soften a hard edge.

FIGURE 15.8
Blur is applied on the top left; Blur More, on the top right. You have to look carefully to see the effect.

Gaussian Blur

You can apply the Blur filter several times to get the effect you want, or you can move right on to Gaussian Blur (Filter, Blur, Gaussian Blur), which lets you determine precisely how much the image is blurred. This filter uses a mathematical formula (the Gaussian distribution equation, which results in a bell curve) to calculate the difference in color and brightness between each pair of pixels. Most of the blurred pixels, therefore, end up in the middle of the two colors or values instead of at either end of the spectrum. This results in a generalized blur that neither darkens nor lightens the image.

The Gaussian Blur dialog (see Figure 15.9) lets you determine exactly how much blur to apply by setting a Radius value from 0.1 to 250. You can also use it to antialias the edges of an object on a layer so that the object will blend better with the background, and to blur dark shapes to create shadows. Even at fairly low settings, it has quite a dramatic effect.

FIGURE 15.9
Smaller numbers result in less blur.

Gaussian Blur is a useful retouching tool when applied to a selected area within the picture that you want to de-emphasize. In Figure 15.10, the brindle greyhound puppy is overwhelmed by the long grass in the image on the left. If I select the dog and apply a mask to hide him, I can blur the rest of the scene and call attention to the puppy (see the image on the right).

FIGURE 15.10
Selective blurring helps the subject of a photo stand out from its background.

A quick application of the Blur tool, with Strength set to 75%, helps blend the blurred background into the unblurred area near the dog.

Smart Blur

The Smart Blur filter (Filter, Blur, Smart Blur) is particularly useful for photo repair and for cosmetic retouching. It blurs everything in the image, or in the selected area of the image, except the edges. Smart Blur locates boundaries between color regions and maintains those boundaries while blurring everything within them. It's the perfect filter when you need to take 10 years off a portrait subject's face or get rid of the texture in a piece of cloth without losing the folds.

Figure 15.11 shows the Smart Blur filter dialog. The original photo is in the background, and you can see the change in the filter window. You can set the Radius and Threshold sliders to determine how much blur is applied and choose a Quality setting to determine how the effect is calculated.

The Smart Blur filter has three modes:

▶ In Normal mode, the filter blurs as you would expect.

▶ Edge Only shows you edge boundaries that Smart Blur detects, hiding the rest of the image.

▶ Edge Overlay shows the boundaries as white lines overlaid on the image.

TIP

Which Blur, When?

Use the Blur filters when you have a large area to blur. Use the Blur tool when you want to soften just a small area, because you can control its effect more precisely and target just the pixels you want.

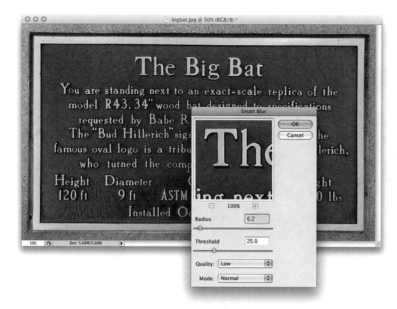

FIGURE 15.11
The plaque's texture is distracting
from the text, so I decided to blur
it away.

You can use the Edge Overlay or Edge Only mode to help you determine which Threshold value to set. Then switch the mode back to Normal and finalize your Radius setting before you click OK to apply the effect.

Surface Blur

Even more than Smart Blur, this filter blurs an image's surfaces and background areas without obscuring edges. It's a good way to get rid of "noise" in old or rescanned photos, although it doesn't offer as much control as Smart Blur. The controls work just like those in the Gaussian Blur dialog.

Radial Blur

The Radial Blur filter can produce two different kinds of circular blur effects: Spin and Zoom. The Spin option produces a blur that looks as if the image is spinning around its center point. Zoom mode is intended to look as though the camera is zooming into or away from the image.

In the Radial Blur dialog, shown in Figure 15.12, you can set both an amount for the blur effect (from 1 to 100) and a quality level (Draft, Good, or Best). Amount refers to the distance that the pixels are moved to create the blur. You can see a representation of the Amount setting in the Blur Center area as you drag the slider. You can click and drag in the Blur Center area to determine a center point for the blur effect. In Figure 15.12, I moved the center point so that it was located on the baby's face.

FIGURE 15.12
This poor baby is being spun right 'round like a record.

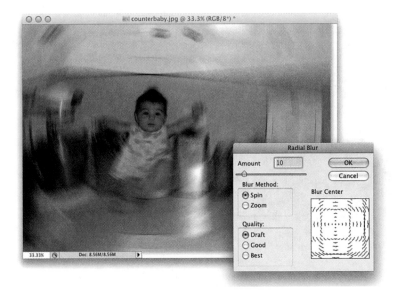

The Quality settings determine the manner in which the blur effect is calculated; you can choose Draft, Good, or Best. There's very little difference between Good and Best in the resulting images. The biggest difference, in fact, is not in the image quality, but in how long it takes Photoshop to compute and apply the blur in each mode. You're likely to notice a difference only if you're working on a large image. But because Radial Blur doesn't have a preview, you might find that you have to apply the filter repeatedly, undoing each time, to arrive at the right settings for your image. In that case, you'll probably want to use Draft until you get the settings the way you want them, then switch to Best.

Motion Blur

When we see lines drawn radiating from the back of an object or a person in a drawing, we instinctively know that the subject is supposed to be in motion. Those lines represent **motion blur**, which is actually a photographic mistake caused by using a slow shutter speed on a moving subject. The image's subject appears blurred against the background because it kept moving during the fraction of a second that the camera shutter was open.

In the early days of photography, motion blur was a common occurrence, primarily because cameras' shutter speeds were slow and film was less sensitive, and therefore, required a longer exposure. Today motion blur in snapshots is unusual; you're more likely to see it when the photographer is capturing the subject this way on purpose by using the least sensitive film available or by using a small lens opening and a correspondingly slower shutter. You don't need to mess with shutter speed to achieve this effect in your pictures, however; in the Motion Blur filter, Photoshop gives you a tool that can do it.

The Motion Blur filter (choose Filter, Blur, Motion Blur) can simulate the appearance of motion by adding a directional blur to an image. In the Motion Blur dialog, shown in Figure 15.13, you can set both the Distance and the Angle of the blur according to how fast and in what direction you want the object to appear to be traveling. The Distance slider controls how far each pixel in the original image or selection is "moved" to create the blur effect; the Angle value sets the direction of the blur. The trick to getting a realistic result, however, is to select the right area to which to apply Motion Blur. To get a convincing blur, you need to blur either the subject of the photo or its background, but not both. Whatever remains unblurred in the image seems to be stationary, in contrast with the moving elements of the picture.

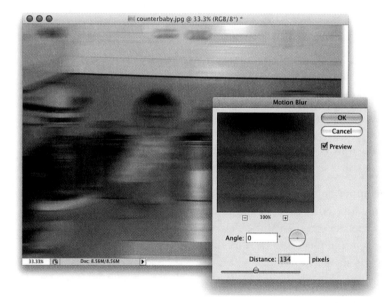

FIGURE 15.13
Using the Motion Blur filter is tricky, at best.

The Motion Blur filter doesn't do much for most photos. After all, blurring the whole image with this filter replicates the blur caused by the camera shaking, and that's the kind of thing we usually try to avoid, not add. But for some special effects, and for doing tricks with type, it has interesting possibilities. Figure 15.14 shows one possible use. First, I carefully selected the background of the image, around both vehicles, and then I applied Motion to the selected area.

FIGURE 15.14
The halftrack and motorcycle appear to be moving even though they're standing still, because of the motion blur applied to the background.

Lens Blur

The Lens Blur filter attempts to reproduce the "real-world" phenomenon in which lens flares and highlights take on the shape of the camera iris. Depending on the number of leaves in the camera shutter, the shape can be a hexagon or a pentagon. Photoshop takes it a step further, letting you choose to have anywhere from three to eight sides on the highlight and specify how much of the image is involved. You can apply this filter to the entire photo, to a selection, or to a layer.

The most important thing to know about lens blur is that it can vary the amount of blur in different parts of the image based on the current selection or, if you prefer, on an alpha channel. This adds depth of field to the image, so you can focus attention on the objects in the foreground and blur the objects in the background.

Average Blur

Taking blurring to the max, the Average Blur filter mixes all the colors in an image or the selected area to come up with the color that's the average of them all. Among other applications, it's a great way to choose a color that goes with everything to use for backgrounds and type.

Shape Blur

If you have some time to play around, consider devoting some of it to this fil-ter. Shape Blur bases its blur on an irregular shape of your choosing, repeating that shape throughout the image and applying the blurring effect more in darker areas of the shape. This results in a very subtle effect—for example, a slight starry sparkle can show up in an image blurred using a star shape. In addition to choosing a shape, you can determine how large the "kernel" image is using the Radius slider. The larger the kernel, the greater the blur effect.

Box Blur

I'm really not sure what Adobe intended Photoshop users to do with this fil-ter. It works like the Gaussian Blur filter, and it does pretty much the same thing, only less smoothly. An image blurred using Box Blur has more pro-nounced detail than the same picture blurred using a Gaussian blur with the same radius setting. The esteemed technical editor of this book, Doug Nelson, likes to use Box Blur for removing dots from scanned newspaper images. If you've got another favorite use for this filter, drop me an email!

Noise Filters

The Noise filters (choose Filter, Noise and pick one from the submenu) are useful for adding and removing noise from your images. What's noise? Well, zoom way in on one of your photos. When you get to an area that should be a solid color, do you see random specks of black, white, and other colors? That's noise; the extraneous colors are color noise, and the variance in brightness levels within a color is luminance noise. If there's too much of it, your image looks grainy. When there's not enough, pictures can look flat and fake. Adding noise helps blend in edits, and it can be an interesting special effect, particularly if you're going for a vintage or distressed look. Figure 15.15 shows the Noise filters.

FIGURE 15.15
The Noise submenu

Add Noise

When you want to make your picture noisier, this is where you should head. The Add Noise filter inserts random dots throughout your image, either randomly colored or all shades of gray (if you check the Monochromatic box). The Amount slider determines just how much noise Photoshop adds, with settings ranging from 0.1% to 400%. The only other thing you have to decide is whether you want to use the Uniform or

Gaussian setting for Distribution; the former creates randomly colored noise, while the latter is more likely to use colors similar to those in your picture, creating a more natural effect.

The Add Noise filter is a great starting point for experimenting with filters, most of which need to have some kind of image to work on. (Render Clouds, for example, is an exception to this rule.) If you want to create a background texture, Add Noise is usually the first filter to apply—you can get creative from there (see Figure 15.16). Add Noise also has a tremendously useful application; if your prints are showing bands of colors in areas that should be smooth, apply a tiny bit of noise before printing to tone those bands down.

FIGURE 15.16
The History panel shows the steps I took after applying the Add Noise filter (shown on the left side of the image) to create this texture.

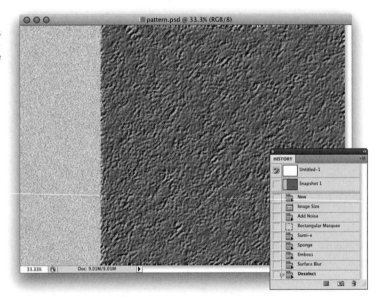

Despeckle

Want an easy filter to apply? Here you go. Despeckle has no options and no dialog; it just does its job. And what is that? Despeckle detects the edges of objects in your picture and blurs all of the selected area or image except those edges. So if you've got a noisy picture that's full of sharp color transitions, give Despeckle a try. On the other hand, if you apply Despeckle to an image that contains a lot of similarly colored objects that don't contrast strongly with each other, the whole thing will end up blurry.

Dust & Scratches

This filter is specifically designed for dealing with flaws in scanned images and vintage photos; you'll probably never need to use it for an image shot with a digital camera. It's like the Despeckle filter, but it offers slightly more control; you can set the blur Radius and Threshold, just as you can when using the Smart Blur filter.

Threshold controls how different pixel colors must be for the filter to affect them. Radius, on the other hand, determines how far around each pixel Photoshop looks for unusual specks or scratches. For the maximum change, you'd drag Threshold down to 0 and Radius all the way up to 16, its highest value. In the real world, however, you don't do that, because you'll blur the image beyond recognition. Here's the typical procedure to follow with Dust & Scratches:

▶ Drag the Threshold slider all the way left, to 0. This turns it off so that the filter affects the entire image.

▶ Now drag the Radius slider left or right, or enter a value between 1 and 16. Keep adjusting it until you find the lowest value that gets rid of the objects you want to clean up.

▶ Finally, drag the Threshold slider slowly to the right and stop at the highest value at which the image's problems are still fixed, according to the preview (see Figure 15.7).

FIGURE 15.17
This old family portrait can use some help from the Dust & Scratches filter.

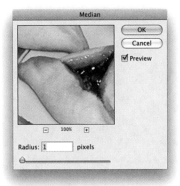

FIGURE 15.18
To apply the Median filter, just drag the Radius slider until you like what you see in the preview.

As you can see, using Dust & Scratches requires that you perform a balancing act, and it's not perfect; it won't do magic. But it's an incredibly useful tool to anyone who's using Photoshop to restore older photos.

Median

If you need to smooth out a photo of a moving object, Median is the filter for you. It reduces image noise by averaging out the brightness of the pixels in the image or selection. Its only control is a Radius slider (see Figure 15.18).

Reduce Noise

If you've got a particularly noisy photo, or one that you want to get just right, try the Reduce Noise filter (choose Filter, Noise, Reduce Noise). It has a range of controls so you can be very precise, and you can choose to apply its changes to each color channel at a different level for the most subtle effect. Reduce Noise is the best filter for removing noise without losing image detail, and it's the only way you can address color noise and luminance noise separately.

You'll find four different sliders and a check box in the main section of the Reduce Noise dialog, all with interlocking effects on the noise in your image:

- ▶ **Strength** controls how much luminance noise reduction the filter applies to the image or selection.

- ▶ **Preserve Details** attempts to keep the filter from blurring edges and fine image details. The higher the value, the more detail you preserve, but the less noise you allow the filter to remove.

- ▶ **Reduce Color Noise** removes color noise to a greater or lesser degree, depending on the slider setting.

- ▶ **Sharpen Details** applies sharpening to the image after the noise-reduction process. If you prefer, you can leave this setting at 0 and sharpen the image using any of the Sharpen filters when you're done with the Reduce Noise filter.

- ▶ **Remove JPEG Artifacts** attempts to remove halos around objects caused by low-quality JPEG compression (see Figure 15.19).

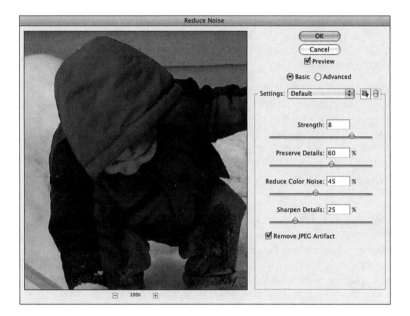

FIGURE 15.19
Since most digital cameras use JPEG format, you'll probably want to check the Remove JPEG Artifacts box every time you use Reduce Noise.

TIP

Change the Channel

Color noise, obviously, shows up in all of a picture's color channels. Luminance noise, on the other hand, tends to be worse in one channel, which usually turns out to be the blue channel. By using the Reduce Noise filter's Advanced mode, you can apply noise reduction only to that channel, which helps keep image details from being blurred because they're still completely clear in the other color channels. First, check each of the color channels in the Channels panel and decide which one you want to work on. Then choose Filter, Noise, Reduce Noise and click the Advanced radio button. Then click the Per Channel tab and choose that channel from the pop-up menu. Finally, adjust the Strength and Preserve Details sliders to produce the best results.

Summary

In this hour, you looked at some Photoshop filters that can help you rescue a bad photo or bad scan. The Sharpen filters can salvage out-of-focus photographs by increasing contrast between adjacent pixels. The most powerful of these is the Unsharp Mask filter, which lets you set the parameters for how it finds and adjusts contrasts.

Blur filters are most useful for putting unwanted parts of the picture out of focus and for softening hard edges. The Motion Blur filter enables you to create the illusion of movement in stationary objects, and the Radial Blur filter is a fun special effect.

Finally, we looked at the Noise filters, which either increase or reduce the amount of color noise and luminance noise in an image. Noise is a fact of life with today's digital cameras, so knowing how to reduce its effect on an image is a useful skill. Adding noise to an image, on the other hand, is a great start for a variety of special effects, and the Add Noise filter can even be used on a blank canvas as a starting point for creating textures.

Q&A

Q. Which filters are closest to the effects created by using the Sharpen and Blur tools?

A. Not surprisingly, those are the plain old Sharpen and Blur filters. If you don't feel like fiddling with Radius and Threshold values, however, and you need to sharpen or blur only a small area, you're better off using the tools than the filters because you can control the amount of sharpening or blurring by how many times you click or drag over an area.

Q. Why don't some filters have previews?

A. Good question. I like to play with the Radial Blur filter, but it's frustrating to work without a preview, so I have to keep undoing and going back to the dialog to try different settings. When Photoshop was much younger, desktop computers were much less powerful, and applying filters like this took much longer. The most complex filters didn't have previews because it would take too long to generate those previews. I think Adobe could probably add previews to a few of these golden oldies, however—and maybe that will happen in the *next* release of Photoshop.

Q. Can I reduce noise by cleaning my camera lens or scanner surface?

A. Sorry, but the answer is no. Image noise occurs because digital cameras have small sensors (so that the cameras are small and convenient), and the only way to reduce its frequency in your images is to get a better-quality camera. If it's really starting to annoy you, consider upgrading to a **digital SLR** (single lens reflex) camera.

Workshop

Quiz

1. Sharpen More applies _____ as much correction as Sharpen.

   A. Exactly

   B. Twice

   C. Half

2. Gaussian Blur uses a _____ to determine how blur is applied.

   A. Mathematical formula

   B. Random memory algorithm

   C. Prismatic crystal filter

3. Many experts advise applying which filter to every photograph you bring into Photoshop?

   A. Sharpen

   B. Gaussian Blur

   C. Unsharp Mask

Answers

1. **B.** To get the same effect, apply the Sharpen filter twice in succession.

2. **A.** The blur follows the Gaussian distribution (commonly known as the bell curve).

3. **C.** The Unsharp Mask filter is especially likely to improve scanned images.

Exercise

Find or shoot a picture of yourself or a friend, and open it in Photoshop. (If you don't have a digital camera or scanner, download a news photo from the Web or a portrait from the book's website—see the Introduction for the URL.) Use the Blur and Sharpen filters to improve it. Find and remove wrinkles, eye bags, uneven complexions, and any other flaws. (In Hour 21, "Repairing Black-and-White Photos," you'll learn more techniques for improving photos.)

Applying Filters to Turn Your Picture into Art

In Hour 9, "Advanced Painting Techniques," we looked at ways Photoshop's filters can help you imitate real-life media, such as colored pencil sketches, oil and watercolor paintings, and chalk and charcoal drawings. Now it's time to delve even deeper into Photoshop's Artistic, Brush Strokes, and Sketch filters: 37 filters that you can apply alone or in combinations to turn a so-so image into a masterpiece. Every time I sit down to play with these filters, I achieve new results that delight me, and I hope you have as much fun working with them in this hour as I had writing it.

Artistic Filters

Artistic filters always obscure some of the detail in your image. How much depends on which filter you're using and, of course, on how you set the filter's controls. With many of the filters that we look at in this hour, you'll set Brush Size, Detail, and Texture values. The Brush Size setting determines the width of the simulated brush strokes that Photoshop applies to the image. Detail determines how large a "clump" of pixels must be for the filter to affect it. Texture, not to be confused with the effect of the Texturizer filter, simply adds random smudges here and there in your image to make them look more natural and less perfect. Although you can't see the effects of your settings in the image window until you click OK, the Filter Gallery (and most of Photoshop's other filter dialogs) features a good-sized preview area where you can see what's happening as you work. To move the image within the preview area, just click and drag. The cursor turns into a hand, enabling you to slide the picture around to check out the filter's effect on each part of the image. Click the plus or minus button to reduce or enlarge the preview zoom level; it's always a good idea to preview your image at 100% before you click OK. And if you

WHAT YOU'LL LEARN IN THIS HOUR:

▶ Artistic Filters
▶ Brush Strokes Filters
▶ Sketch Filters

NOTE

Try It Anyway

You won't find any step-by-step "Try It Yourself" exercises in this hour because you apply all these filters in the same way: Choose Filter, Filter Gallery; pick the filter you want to use; and play with the settings until you like what you see in the Filter Gallery's humongous preview window. The key to success with any of these filters is to experiment until you get the effect you want. If you don't like the results after you apply a filter to the whole picture, you can undo the filter, revert to the last-saved version of the image, or fade the filter to tone down its effects. Choose Edit, Fade to reduce the strength of the filter, or any other tool or effect, by a percentage you set with a slider.

change settings and the preview doesn't change right away—this is more likely to happen with slower computers and larger images—you'll see a progress bar at the bottom of the window; just wait for it to complete.

One of Photoshop's more useful features is the Filter Gallery. It's a special dialog that shows up when you're using Photoshop's more "artistic" filters, and it shows you how the various filters look when applied to a fairly typical photo. If you would rather see a larger preview pane and skip the thumbnail images, clicking the triangle just to the right of the gallery pane toggles the thumbnails on and off.

For the sake of consistency, I'm going to apply all the Artistic filters to the same picture, an atmospheric shot of an outdoor staircase. See Figure 16.1 here and in the color plate section for the original version of this photo.

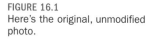

FIGURE 16.1
Here's the original, unmodified photo.

Colored Pencil

As you saw in Hour 9, the Colored Pencil filter goes over the photo with crosshatching (see Figure 16.2). It retains most of the original photograph's colors, but it converts any large, flat areas to "paper" color, which you can set to any shade of the current Background color. The filter's dialog, shown in Figure 16.3, asks you to choose Pencil Width and Stroke Pressure values. Paper Brightness can be set on a scale of 1–50, with 50 being the lightest shade of your Background color and 1 being the darkest.

FIGURE 16.2
The Colored Pencil filter applied.

FIGURE 16.3
Colored Pencil filter settings.

Using a narrow pencil (a lower Pencil Width value) produces more lines, and greater stroke pressure picks up more detail from the original image. In Figure 16.2, I used a wide pencil and heavy pressure. To produce Figure 16.4, I tried a compromise: a smaller pencil and lighter pressure. As you can see, the resulting picture is much lighter and more delicate.

FIGURE 16.4
Less pencil width, less stroke
pressure.

Cutout

The Cutout filter can transform a picture to something resembling a cut
paper collage or a silkscreen print. The filter accomplishes this by averaging
all the image's colors and shades and retaining only a handful of them to
color the entire picture. You can decide how many colors the filter uses by
setting the number of levels from 2 to 8 in the dialog. You can also set Edge
Fidelity (1–3) and Edge Simplicity (1–10) in the dialog, shown in Figure 16.5.

FIGURE 16.5
The Edge Simplicity setting controls how much objects' shapes
are simplified.

Medium Edge Simplicity and Low Edge Fidelity settings produced the picture in Figure 16.6, which shows just one of the many variations you can achieve with this filter and photo combination. It's important to experiment with different settings every time you apply a filter to a new photo; what works with one picture might be completely wrong for another image that's more or less detailed, lighter or darker, or even just more saturated. Don't forget, though, that you can also use the Adjustment commands to *make* any picture darker or lighter, or modify its colors so that it will work better with the filter you want to apply to it.

FIGURE 16.6
The Cutout filter applied.

Dry Brush

Dry brush is a watercolor style in which a brush is loaded with highly concentrated pigment and dabbed, instead of stroked, on the paper. Figure 16.7 shows the Dry Brush dialog with medium values for Brush Size and Brush Detail. You can see the result in Figure 16.8.

FIGURE 16.7
Dry Brush filter settings.

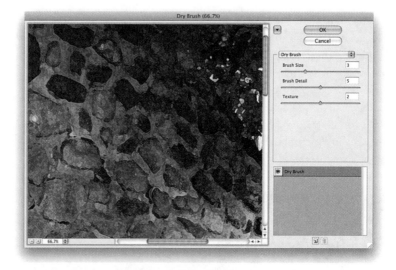

FIGURE 16.8
Used on the right image, the Dry
Brush filter can look very painterly.

Film Grain

One reason many commercial photographers have switched to high-resolution digital photography is to avoid the problems caused by film grain, the inevitable result of manufacturing film by applying a layer of chemicals to a piece of plastic. When a picture is blown way up, you can see the tiny particles embedded in the chemical layer as specks in the picture.

If you want to simulate film-based photography, you can use the Film Grain filter to add interesting texture to your pictures. You can even apply the Film Grain effect to selected areas instead of to the whole photo. Figure 16.9 shows what happens when it's misapplied.

FIGURE 16.9
Film Grain adds a spotty texture that's more pronounced in dark areas.

The Film Grain filter exaggerates the textures of the trees' leaves and the stone wall (see Figure 16.10), making the picture look very gritty. The specks tend to concentrate in flat areas. If I tone down the settings, it works much better.

FIGURE 16.10
Grain applies dark specks to dark areas and light specks to highlights.

Fresco

Fresco is an Italian term for a mural painted on a freshly plastered wall, where the plaster isn't dry yet. Photoshop's Fresco filter doesn't produce results that look anything like classical fresco works. It gives a spotty but nicely abstract feeling that I actually quite like. The Fresco filter adds a good deal of black to the image in the process of abstracting it, so it's a good idea to start with a picture that's very bright, even too bright for your normal tastes. Figure 16.11 shows an example of the Fresco filter applied to our garden step picture.

FIGURE 16.11
A fresh approach, but not exactly a fresco.

In the case of this picture, I like the extra darkness; I think it makes the steps look even more moody and atmospheric than they do in the original photo. Other photos might need to be lightened before applying the Fresco filter. If you've forgotten how to do this, or if you jumped ahead to the fun chapters, go back and review Hour 5, "Adjusting Brightness and Color." Remember, too, that if a filter doesn't seem to work for you with the picture as is, you can change the filter's settings and try again.

Neon Glow

Cool though it might be, the Neon Glow filter has no resemblance whatsoever to neon. As you can probably tell in Figure 16.12, the Neon Glow filter
reduces the image to shades of two colors (the current Foreground and
Background colors) and adds highlights around the edges of objects in a
third color. You can choose a color in the dialog and specify the width and
brightness of the glow. With a very light color or gray, it can produce an
interesting watermark effect. Applied with bright blue, it turned my garden steps into a very eerie scene.

FIGURE 16.12
Neon Glow filter settings.

TIP

That's a "No Glow"

The Neon Glow filter looks its
best when used on type or
blocks of color or shapes. It
doesn't do well with images
that contain a lot of detail or
recognizable subjects (such as
people).

Paint Daubs

The Paint Daubs filter transforms the image into a soft-edged,
Impressionistic painting. You can set Brush Size and Sharpness values, and
you have a choice of several brush types. I used the Simple brush in Figure
16.13. You might need to do even more experimentation with the settings
for this filter than for others. In this example, I used a Brush Size of 32 and
set the Sharpness to 40.

FIGURE 16.13
Paint Daubs filter settings, including a Simple brush.

FIGURE 16.13
Paint Daubs filter settings, including a Simple brush.

Palette Knife and Plastic Wrap

Normally, a painter uses a palette knife to mix paints on a palette, producing a far broader range of colors than can be achieved with the original
pure oil paints. But sometimes a painter uses a palette knife to paint, and
the result is large areas of smudged color that blend at the edges. It's hard
to achieve this result with the Palette Knife filter, but it can be done. I get
the best look with a high Stroke Detail setting and a low Softness setting.

Plastic Wrap is one filter that I very seldom use. It places an unattractive
gray film over the whole picture and then adds white highlights around
large objects. The Plastic Wrap filter is supposed to look as if you shrink-
wrapped the scene. It really looks more as though you poured craft glue all
over it. The overall effect can be pretty drab. I've had better luck combining it with other filters to produce more interesting effects; for instance, it
can make a good basis for a metallic effect.

Poster Edges

Here's a filter that I love playing with. Poster Edges locates all the edges in
your image by finding areas with the greatest amount of contrast between
adjacent pixels, and it **posterizes** the areas around them, placing a dark line
along each edge. It looks pretty cool in the sample photo I'm using, as you
can see in Figure 16.14. But it works less well with images that contain
large, flat areas, such as the sky; the posterizing process tends make these
areas look pretty patchy. If you run into this problem, try applying Poster

Edges to a selected part of the photo instead of to the entire image. For instance, the best way to use the filter on a seascape might be to apply it to the ocean and the ground, but not to the sky, or perhaps to just the boat and the lighthouse, but not the rest of the picture.

FIGURE 16.14
Poster Edges filter applied.

Rough Pastels

Rough Pastels is a neat filter with an interface that's a little bit more complicated than the others because you can specify canvas texture as well as values for Stroke Length and Stroke Detail; you can see the Rough Pastels dialog in Figure 16.15. Choose from the supplied textures (Brick, Burlap, Canvas, and Sandstone) or import a grayscale image of your own to serve as a custom texture.

The Stroke Length and Stroke Detail settings seem to give the most realistic results in the low to middle portion of their respective ranges, but, as always, you'll need to experiment to see what works best for your image. Figure 16.16 shows the Rough Pastels filter applied to the sample image.

FIGURE 16.15
Rough Pastels filter settings.

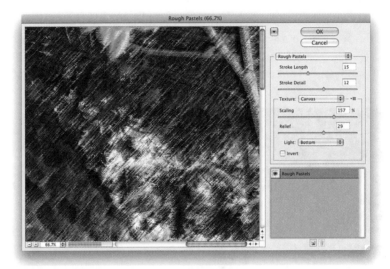

FIGURE 16.16
Rough Pastels filter on Canvas.

Smudge Stick

On light-colored areas, the Smudge Stick filter adds a subtle, blotchy texture. And on dark areas and at edges, it also includes a smudge, making the lines heavier and the edges soft. Figure 16.17 shows an example. I like this filter, but you'll want to watch out for overly cartoony colors when you use it.

FIGURE 16.17
Smudge Stick filter applied.

Sponge

Sponge painting isn't just for faux surfaces anymore; now you can turn your pictures into sponge paintings. They have a blobby look that can be really attractive with the right picture. It doesn't work particularly well on portraits, but it's definitely worth trying on landscapes. On large, flat areas, the Sponge filter gives a good imitation of a coarse, natural sponge (not the rectangular kind you buy at the grocery store!). In detailed areas, the sponge automatically resizes itself downward. You can set Brush Size, Definition, and Smoothness values in the Sponge filter dialog (shown in Figure 16.18).

FIGURE 16.18
Sponge filter settings.

Underpainting

The Underpainting filter, which you read about in Hour 9, reduces an image to a less saturated, lighter, and blurrier version of itself. You'll mostly use it as an intermediate filter on the way to an effect rather than by itself. I like to duplicate an image's background layer, apply Underpainting to the lower layer, and then reduce the opacity of the upper layer to put some detail back.

Watercolor

In Hour 9, you learned how to make a photo look like a watercolor, both with manual brush strokes and by applying the Watercolor filter. Figure 16.19 shows this filter applied to the sample image. The look isn't really watercolor, but it has its uses. If you like the general effect of the Sponge filter but it distorts your picture too much, try the Watercolor filter instead. It produces smaller clumps of color for a more refined look. Both of these filters— Watercolor and Sponge—tend to darken the image quite a bit, which works fine for this moody image but might not work so well for other pictures. If so, feel free to lighten the picture before applying the filter..

FIGURE 16.19
Watercolor filter applied.

Brush Strokes Filters

Sure, the Brush Strokes filters are artistic, too, but Adobe had to do something to break its filters into manageable groups. Breaking out the ones that
simulate specific brush techniques seems as good a way to do that as any.
Figure 16.20 is the original picture of the charming side entrance to a New
Hampshire cottage, and it's about to get filtered to within an inch of its life.

FIGURE 16.20
The original image of a rustic
porch is a bit blurry, so it's no
good for display as it now stands.

Accented Edges

The Accented Edges filter enhances contrast at object edges. It can be sub-
tle and classy, or brazen (which is the way I chose to go in Figure 16.21).
The dialog has sliders for Edge Width, Edge Brightness, and Smoothness.
The Brightness setting darkens edges if the amount is 25 or less; from 26 to
50, it progressively lightens them. In the example, I went with a fairly high
Brightness value to give the image a surreal quality.

FIGURE 16.21
Accented Edges filter applied.

Angled Strokes and Crosshatch

Both of these filters produce a crosshatched effect, similar to but darker than the one applied by the Colored Pencil filter. The Angled Strokes filter is less dramatic than the Crosshatch filter; Figure 16.22 shows both. Not being the subtle type, I tend to prefer Crosshatch, but you can try them both on your own images and make your own choice.

FIGURE 16.22
The Angled Strokes filter applied on the left and the Crosshatch filter applied on the right.

Dark Strokes

The Dark Strokes filter tends to turn the whole picture black; you'll probably find yourself turning the Black Intensity all the way down and the White Intensity all the way up, even with a relatively light picture. Figure 16.23 shows a carefully balanced application of dark strokes. My settings were Balance, 4; Black Intensity, 1; and White Intensity, 5.

FIGURE 16.23
Dark Strokes filter applied.

Ink Outlines

The Ink Outlines filter draws first a white line and then a black line around every object edge that it can locate (see Figure 16.24). You can set Stroke Length and both Dark Intensity and Light Intensity in the dialog. Applied to a still life or a landscape, the Ink Outlines filter can give you the look of an old woodcut or steel engraving. Used on a portrait, however, all those cool blips and blobs can turn into warts, so proceed with caution.

FIGURE 16.24
Ink Outlines filter settings.

Spatter

Remember how we used the Dissolve blending mode in Hour 9 to add some texture to an "oil" painting? The Spatter filter has much the same effect, only to a greater degree (see Figure 16.25). My settings were Spray Radius 16 and Smoothness 1. Applied with a light touch, the Spatter filter is a great way to add realistically random texture to images processed with another filter, such as Underpainting.

FIGURE 16.25
Spatter filter applied.

Sprayed Strokes

Sprayed Strokes looks like Spatter, but it's less messy and more artful because it applies directional strokes instead of just splattering paint everywhere. You can even control the direction of the spray. Figure 16.26 shows what it does to the cottage porch. The settings for this variation were Stroke Length 13, Spray Radius 22, and Direction, Right Diagonal.

FIGURE 16.26
Sprayed Strokes filter applied.

Sumi-e

Sumi-e is Japanese for brush painting, and the best sumi-e work out there is truly wondrous. The results of the Sumi-e filter aren't always so exquisite. This filter turns any area with any sort of detail almost completely black, even at the lowest settings. It renders all dark areas in black angled strokes. One way to make use of this filter is to apply it to rescue a very light picture.

Sketch Filters

Again, Photoshop's filter groupings don't always make sense—since when is bas relief a form of sketching? But you'll find that the 14 filters found in the Sketch submenu are still fun to play with. Some of them, such as Conté

Crayon or Chalk & Charcoal, even mimic actual sketch media. Figure 16.27 shows the sample image: a rather poorly focused and grainy image of some antique clay pots. Remember, as long as the colors and brightness levels are workable, you can almost always get away with filtering blurry and grainy images, and you'll end up with something much nicer than what you started with.

Bas Relief

The Bas Relief filter uses the Foreground and Background colors to create a low-relief rendering of your picture, rather like a stone carving. If you choose the colors you use carefully, it can even look like copper foil or hammered metal. Because it seizes upon every scrap of texture, the Bas Relief filter is best used on pictures that have contrasting textures, or a textured subject against a flat background; otherwise, your subject will blend right into the background. Figure 16.28 shows what the filter does for my pots. Needless to say, this is *not* the kind of image on which I recommend using Bas Relief. The leafy background makes it too hard to pick out the pots' shapes.

FIGURE 16.28
Use a dark Background color for best results with the Bas Relief filter.

Chalk & Charcoal

Because the Chalk & Charcoal filter reduces the image to just three tones, you'll get the best results if you set the Foreground color to a dark color and the Background color to a light one. The third color, by default, is a medium gray, so be sure you choose colors that work with gray. This filter can produce really beautiful drawings. Figure 16.29 shows the filter applied; notice the realistic shading around the tops of the pots.

FIGURE 16.29
Chalk & Charcoal filter settings.

Charcoal

The Charcoal filter does much the same thing as the Chalk & Charcoal filter, but it uses only the Foreground and Background colors and adds no gray, which makes it more difficult to control. Experiment until you are satisfied. It helps if you bump up the contrast in the image before applying the filter, especially if you want to make sure that details are preserved.

Chrome

As with the Plastic Wrap filter I showed you earlier in the hour, the Chrome filter is generally not particularly successful. As you can see in Figure 16.30, it doesn't really produce realistic chrome. To me, it looks more like hammered silver. The Chrome filter automatically desaturates the image when it's applied, but you can go back and paint in colors, if you like, or tint the image using Hue/Saturation. As with Neon Glow, this filter is most useful on type or large, simple shapes with flat backgrounds.

FIGURE 16.30
The pots almost disappear against the busy background.

Conté Crayon

Conté Crayon works very much like the Chalk & Charcoal filter described previously, but with the addition of background textures, using the same interface that the Rough Pastels dialog uses. Figure 16.31 shows the pots rendered in Conté Crayon on a canvas background. Real conté crayons are always made in black, brown, or a range of red tones, because they're made by mixing wax with charcoal, graphite, or clay. But don't let that stop you from creating a masterpiece done in lime green conté crayon. With Photoshop, almost anything is possible.

FIGURE 16.31
Conté Crayon filter settings.

Graphic Pen and Halftone Pattern

These two filters do very similar things, starting with the fact that both reduce the image to whatever Foreground and Background colors you set. Graphic Pen then renders the image in slanting lines, whereas Halftone Pattern renders it in overlapping dots. I've spent years trying to get the Graphic Pen filter to produce something that really looks like a pen-and-ink sketch, with no luck. I like to use Halftone Pattern, however, for a funky retro effect.

Note Paper and Plaster

The Note Paper filter (see Figure 16.32) uses the Background and Foreground colors to produce an embossed effect, plus shades of gray for shadows. I have no idea why it's called Note Paper; if anyone out there knows, please email me and fill me in! Meanwhile, the Plaster filter is very similar to Note Paper, except that it doesn't have the same grainy surface; it looks more like freshly poured plaster.

FIGURE 16.32
The Note Paper filter applied with
a fairly low relief setting.

Photocopy, Reticulation, Stamp, and Torn Edges

These four filters have a lot in common. As with many of the filters in this set, they all convert your image to a two-color version of itself. The Stamp filter eliminates most of the detail, attempting to replicate a rubber stamp. Photocopy, on the other hand, retains most of the detail, resulting in the rather interesting image shown in Figure 16.33. Reticulation adds dot grain to the Stamp filter, so it looks as if you've stamped the picture on coarse sandpaper. Finally, Torn Edges is the Stamp filter again, only with the edges of objects in the image roughened.

FIGURE 16.33
The Photocopy filter applied.

Water Paper

The last filter in the Sketch set is Photoshop's version of the wet-in-wet technique of painting with watercolors, in which wet paint is applied to wet paper. Unlike most of the filters in the Sketch set, Water Paper retains the colors of your original picture, adding crosshatching in the background and softening edges appropriately. The crosshatching is the only part of this filter that I don't like; otherwise, it does a fairly good job of simulating wet-in-wet painting. (Not to be confused with wet-*on*-wet painting, which is done with oils.) Figure 16.34 shows this filter applied my pots.

FIGURE 16.34
The Water Paper filter applied.

Summary

Filters are definitely fun to play with; they're the part of Photoshop that's most like a puzzle. What happens when I do *this*? What effect will *that* setting have? But they're also a way to rescue a flawed image or turn a decent picture into a lot more than that. In this hour, we looked at a multitude of ways to make your pictures look like art created using real-world media; in the next hour, we'll have even more fun with some really bizarre filters.

Q&A

Q. Is there a way to tone down a filter that does what I want, but does too much of it?

A. Yes. Choose Edit, Fade to bring up a handy little dialog whose slider enables you to change the strength of the filter from 100% all the way down to 0%. You'll find the Fade command particularly useful for restoring details after applying a filter that went too far in blurring or posterizing the picture.

Q. Are the filters that come with Photoshop all there are?

A. No, not at all! By now, there must be thousands of filters that individuals or companies have created. You can locate tons of them by Googling "Photoshop filters." You can also whip up your own filters by choosing Filter, Other, Custom and entering random numbers in the dialog's entry fields (see Figure 16.35). If you get an effect you like, click Save to preserve it for future use.

FIGURE 16.35
Modifying these numbers enables you to make custom changes to an image, then save your settings and reapply them to any other image.

Workshop

Quiz

1. The Colored Pencil filter applies:

    A. Colored outlines around edges

    B. A crosshatched effect

    C. The color-wheel opposite of any color to which you apply it

2. Sumi-e is Japanese for:

   A. Ink painting

   B. Raw fish and rice with a sweet sauce

   C. Digital imaging

3. Photoshop Artistic filters, in general, tend to _____ an image.

   A. Lighten

   B. Darken

   C. Sharpen

Answers

1. **B.** Try applying it twice with the image rotated 90° between applications. You might be shocked by what a difference this technique makes.

2. **A.** Although you could certainly create a digital painting of some sushi using the Sumi-e filter....

3. **B.** If an image is quite dark to start with, it might turn completely black.

Exercise

Use a picture you already have, or download one of the three used in this hour (`steps.jpg`, `sidedoor.jpg`, and `pots.jpg`) from the Sams website. Try out each of the Artistic, Brush, and Sketch filters. Experiment with different settings and then try applying the same filter a second time, and even a third. Also, give the Fade command a try and see how fading a filter can make its effect more useful. Try applying a different filter over the first. Some combinations work better than others. See whether you can find a combination that turns your photo into a work of art. Make sure you remember the settings you use; some artists even enter that data in the File Info before saving the final file (choose File, File Info).

HOUR 17
Applying Funky Filters

Some of Photoshop's filters, such as Reduce Noise and Smart Sharpen, are unequivocally utilitarian. Others, including Plastic Wrap and Stamp, are less so. With any luck, you'll find the filters we cover in this hour to be the least useful of all—which should also make them some of the most fun to play with! We also look at three groups of filters:

- **Distort**—These filters alter the geometry of an image, twisting, folding, and, yes, even spindling your picture.

- **Pixelate**—Here you'll find more than half a dozen different ways to break up your picture into tiny pieces.

- **Stylize**—The nine filters in this group represent various unrelated ways to modify an image; the submenu is really a catch-all for filters that just don't seem to belong anywhere else.

Be sure to spend plenty of time trying out different settings with each of these filters; more than any others, they depend on the numbers you give them to determine their final effects. Without a doubt, the hours you spend working with the funky filters we're about to look at will be some of the least productive time you'll spend in Photoshop—and some of the most enjoyable.

Distort Filters

To distort an image is to bend, twist, or stretch an image, sometimes until it's unrecognizable. That's what you'll get from this first group of filters, for sure. You can melt your picture, twirl it around, or even turn it inside out. We'll try out all these modifications on the image shown in Figure 17.1, which shows a crab-steaming business's truck in Baltimore.

WHAT YOU'LL LEARN IN
THIS HOUR:

▶ Distort Filters
▶ Pixelate Filters
▶ Stylize Filters

Diffuse Glow

Oddly, the very first Distort filter doesn't actually distort an image. Instead, it adds a foggy glow in the Background color in the lighter areas of a picture. I think this is another case of Photoshop's designers not having any *other* place to stick this filter; regardless, it's pretty neat-looking when applied to the right image.

Diffuse Glow is one of three Distort filters that you can apply via the Filter Gallery, which I think is far superior to the old-style dialogs of filters such as Displace. Its settings include sliders for Graininess, Glow Amount, and Clear Amount. It's usually simplest to start with Glow Amount and Clear Amount, and try to achieve a reasonable balance between the two. If you're looking for a soft glow, keep the Graininess setting low, to avoid a somewhat speckled look. In Figure 17.2, I set white as my Background color before applying the filter with a Graininess value of 2, a Glow Amount value of 9, and a Clear Amount value of 4 to turn a sunny Baltimore day into a foggy one. Using white as the glow color and a low Graininess setting gives you "fog"; more grain would make the picture look more like a snowstorm.

You can get a surreal effect by increasing the image's saturation all the way up to 100% before you apply the glow. The result is somewhat posterized, more colorful, and definitely fantastical.

FIGURE 17.2
The Diffuse Glow filter applied.

Displace

To apply the Displace filter, you need to have a **displacement map**, which works sort of like a texture map. To apply a displacement map, choose Filter, Distort, Displace and then set the Horizontal and Vertical Scale amounts, which can range from –999 to 999 and influence how much distortion is applied. The default value is 10, and you'll generally want to stay fairly close to that. After you set these values and click OK, Photoshop asks you to choose a displacement map; you can use any Photoshop-format file as a displacement map. The effect the Displace filter produces depends entirely on which map you choose. One common use of Displace is to wrap text or a flat image snugly to the contours of an image below. In Figure 17.3, you can see the displacement map I used to map the truck image onto a cobblestone layer below it (shown in Figure 17.4). I made the displacement map by duplicating the cobblestone layer, converting it to grayscale, posterizing it to three brightness levels, and then blurring it to smooth it out.

FIGURE 17.3
The Displace filter revamps the truck image to map these contours.

FIGURE 17.4
The truck layer uses the Multiply blending mode to enable the cobblestones to show through.

Glass and Ocean Ripple

The Glass and Ocean Ripple filters can have similar effects on an image; they both create displacements that make the image appear to be viewed through textured glass or moving water.

The Glass filter (see Figure 17.5) features a choice of glass texture, including Frosted, Tiny Lens, or Canvas. If you prefer, you can load a texture of your own instead; just choose Load Texture from the pop-up menu at the bottom of the dialog and open any Photoshop-format file.

FIGURE 17.5
Glass filter settings.

Use the Smoothness slider to reduce the angularity of the effect. Keeping the Distortion value low and the Smoothness value high creates a subtle effect; the opposite gives you much more distortion. The Scaling slider adjusts the scale of the distortion relative to the image itself, from 50% to 200%. The Invert button at the bottom of the dialog replaces the light areas of the texture with dark areas and vice versa, making low areas appear high and high areas appear low.

The Ocean Ripple filter is quite similar to Glass; it makes your image appear to be under water (see Figure 17.6). This filter is easier to use than the Glass filter because it has only two sliders: Ripple Size and Ripple Magnitude. The former determines how big the ripples are relative to the image, and the latter controls how many ripples are applied.

FIGURE 17.6
Ocean Ripple filter settings.

FIGURE 17.6
Ocean Ripple filter settings.

Pinch, Spherize, and ZigZag

The Pinch, Spherize, and ZigZag have very similar interfaces. Figure 17.7 shows the dialog for the ZigZag filter, which features a gridlined proxy that shows you the true shape of the zigs and zags you're applying to the image with this filter. The Pinch and Spherize dialogs also make use of a grid proxy to show you their geometry.

The Amount slider controls the size of the ripples, and the Ridges value determines how many waves are applied to the picture. Choose a Style option to change the shape of the overall ripple pattern (see Figure 17.8 to see the results of the settings shown in Figure 17.7).

FIGURE 17.7
ZigZag filter settings.

FIGURE 17.8
The ZigZag filter applied.

Although their interfaces are similar to that of the ZigZag filter, Spherize and Pinch produce a completely different type of distortion. When you apply Spherize, Photoshop creates an elliptical bulge in the middle of the image, with the size of the bulge controlled by the Amount Slider. The Mode pop-up menu contains Normal, Horizontal Only, and Vertical Only options, with the latter two restricting the bulge to the specified dimension. Pinch does almost the same thing as Spherize, except that it pulls the image inward instead of bowing it outward. It doesn't have a Mode menu—only an Amount slider.

Shear

This filter takes its name from an engineering term referring to horizontal stress on an object. As you might expect, it warps images horizontally, in relation to the vertical line shown in the Shear dialog (see Figure 17.9). The preview area shows the effect of your changes to the line. Note that not only can you drag the line's top and bottom points to angle it, but you can also add more control points on the curve by clicking it. You can drag each control point independently to redirect the motion of the curve.

Figure 17.10 shows the results of the Shear filter. I've set the image to Repeat Edge Pixels, so it looks as if the warping left a smudge of pixels behind.

FIGURE 17.9
Shear filter settings.

FIGURE 17.10
Here the Shear filter makes the picture look as though it's being blown right out of the image window.

TIP

One Way

The Shear filter works only horizontally, not vertically. If you want something to shear vertically, you need to rotate the image before you apply the filter (choose an option from the Image, Image Rotation submenu). Then rotate the picture back again after you've applied it.

Twirl

If you want your picture to be swirling down the drain, a quick application of the Twirl filter will fulfill your desire. There's just one control to worry about: an Angle slider that ranges from –999° to 999°. Drag the slider to twirl the picture a little or a lot; the grid proxy next to the slider gives you an idea of what the filter's geometry actually looks like. Take a look at Figure 17.11 to see what –394° of twirling does to the truck picture.

FIGURE 17.11
The Twirl filter applied.

Pixelate Filters

Pixelation happens when similarly colored pixels within an image are clumped together to form larger units, which can be square (like the pixels from which they're formed), rounded, or polygonal. You'll see pixelation when you print a picture at too low a resolution; the too-large pixels form angular, blocky shapes. And in traditional art, you've seen pixelation whenever you've looked at a mosaic or a Pointillist painting.

Photoshop's Pixelate filters work best on simple subjects and images with strong contrast, such as the photo of workers hosing down a baseball field in Figure 17.12.

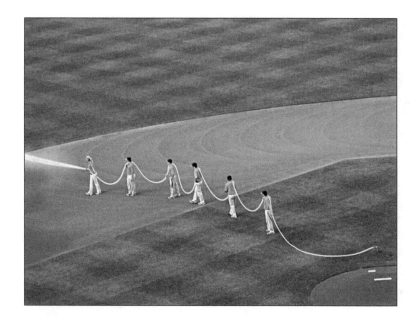

FIGURE 17.12
Green grass, red dirt, and people
hauling a hose around—must be
baseball!

Color Halftone

When a color photo is processed for printing, it's turned into a collection of variably sized dots, each colored cyan, magenta, yellow, or black. The size of the dot and the corresponding amount of whitespace around it determines the apparent intensity of the color at that point in the image, and colors other than cyan, magenta, yellow, and black are simulated by clustering together different-colored dots to fool the eye. This kind of image is called a **halftone**; if you look at a magazine ad or the photos in this book using a magnifying glass, you'll be able to see the images' halftone dots.

Now that you know much more than you ever expected to about color printing processes, let's take a look at the Color Halftone filter. You guessed it—this filter turns your image into a color halftone, generally with much larger dots than you're actually likely to see anywhere other than on the side of an 18-wheeler (see Figure 17.13). You've probably seen a similar effect used in Pop Art images such as paintings by 20-century painter Roy Lichtenstein. The Color Halftone filter isn't needed to prepare images for printing, but it can give your pictures a fun sort of quirky, retro look. Its dialog enables you to control the maximum diameter of the dots, as well as the angle at which each of the four colors of dots is applied to the image.

FIGURE 17.13
Color Halftone isn't for everyone, but it can be interesting with the right image.

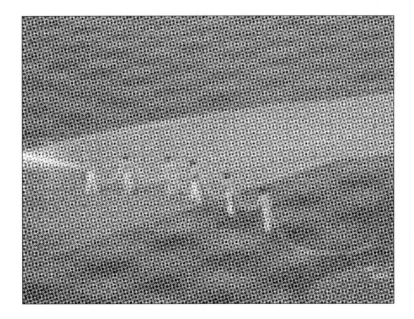

Crystallize

Most of the Pixelate filters look best if the effect is applied using a rather small Cell Size. Otherwise, the clumps of color, whatever their shape, are so big that the image is unrecognizable. In Figure 17.14, I applied the Crystallize filter with a Cell Size of 8. This setting adds an interesting amount distortion without obscuring the basic forms in the image. In Figure 17.15, I pushed the Cell Size up to 50, completely destroying the picture. You can set the Cell Size as high as 300, but doing that might turn the entire picture into just one or two cells, depending on the image's resolution. An extremely hi-res image might require a Cell Size in the hundreds; the picture I'm using here is only 800 pixels by 600 pixels, so a value that high would divide it into just a dozen or so cells.

FIGURE 17.14
The Crystallize filter applied.

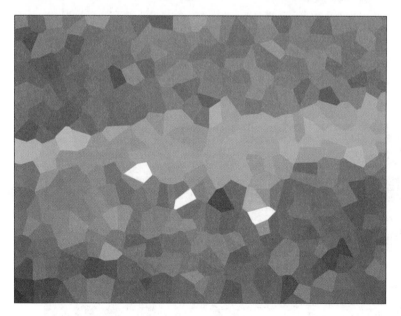

FIGURE 17.15
The same filter, overapplied.

Facet and Fragment

In my opinion, neither of these two filters is much to speak of. Neither has a dialog, and their effects don't seem particularly attractive or useful to me. You, on the other hand, might love them—so, by all means, give them a try.

As with the rest of the Pixelate filters, the Facet filter clumps like-colored pixels together into faceted shapes. The problem is that it does so on such a tiny level that the effect is nearly impossible to see. This filter would be much more usable if you could control the clumps' size.

Fragment, on the other hand, is rather unusual for a Pixelate filter: It doesn't create clumps; instead, it gives your image a really (really!) bad case of camera shake, turning each object into four ghostly copies of itself, each slightly offset from the others. If you come up with a good use for this one, please do email me and tell me all about it!

Mezzotint

In this venerable print-making method, a copper printing plate is roughened more in areas of darker color, less in areas of lighter color, and not at all in areas that are to print white. The roughening process produces tiny pits in the metal that hold on to the ink and then deposit it onto the paper. Photoshop's Mezzotint filter converts your image to a random pattern of dots or lines (choose a pattern from the filter dialog's Type pop-up menu, its only control) and bumps up the saturation all the way (see Figure 17.16).

FIGURE 17.16
The Mezzotint filter can do good things for images with strong shapes and few details.

Mosaic and Pointillize

The Pixelate filters include a couple more real-life media analogs: Mosaic and Pointillize. The former is supposed to create an analog of tile mosaics. In reality, though, it works similarly to Facet, except that it makes larger "pixels" out of the original smaller ones because it produces only square clumps. The result is the sort of thing used to hide the faces of the people who refused to sign the release forms on all those reality shows (see Figure 17.17).

FIGURE 17.17
The Mosaic filter can make your pictures appear to be built out of Lego blocks.

The Pointillize filter, on the other hand, can look quite convincing. Comparing the work of Georges Seurat to that of some of the "sloppier" French impressionists can be quite a revelation. Seurat's dabs of paint, all neatly clustered, form elegant scenes from a distance and form equally elegant abstract patterns up close. This is the effect that Photoshop's Pointillize filter is going for, with varying results.

The key to making the Pointillize filter work is choosing the right Dot Size value for your picture; expect to do some experimentation. You might have to use a larger value than you expect, to distinguish dots of "paint" from image noise or film grain. The example in Figure 17.18 was created with a Cell Size value of 5 pixels. A neat twist is that Photoshop uses the current Foreground and Background colors to create the dots; you won't notice this if you stick to the defaults of black and white, but the effect gives an interesting color cast if you choose other colors.

FIGURE 17.18
Larger dots obscure image detail;
smaller ones don't stand out
enough.

Stylize Filters

To stylize something is to give it a distinctive style that's often clearly arti-
ficial. That's what the Stylize filters are all about. These nine filters provide
a wide variety of different looks that don't replicate natural media and
don't attempt to look like anything but what they are: the result of funky
Photoshop filters. We'll take a look at these filters applied to this dramatic
photo of a cathedral (see Figure 17.19).

Diffuse

First up in the Stylize submenu is the Diffuse filter, which can lend a soft
appearance to an image that's subtly different from a blur. The only problem is that you can't control its radius, so on high-resolution images, it
tends to be pretty much invisible. The filter actually rearranges pixels with
a view toward softening the focus, in one of four different ways:

- Normal shuffles pixels completely randomly within the filter's limited radius.
- Darken Only replaces light pixels with darker ones, diffusing the
  image and darkening it at the same time.
- Lighten Only replaces dark pixels with lighter ones, lightening the
  image as it diffuses it.
- Anisotropic shuffles pixels so that there's the smallest possible
  amount of color shift, which results in a much smoother effect.

FIGURE 17.19
This church is about to go where
no church has gone before.

As with Facet, Diffuse is hard to see in high-resolution images (see Figure 17.20). To get a more pronounced effect, sometimes I reduce the image's resolution, apply the Diffuse filter, and then resample the image back to its original resolution (see Figure 17.21).

FIGURE 17.20
Diffuse turns the picture slightly
dotty…

FIGURE 17.21
…but Diffuse on a lower-res image
does twice as much.

Emboss

The Emboss filter doesn't do much for most photos. It turns an image into a bas relief, although not as well as the Bas Relief filter does. In the process, the Emboss filter also converts most of the image to medium gray. The Emboss filter has only three options: Shadow Angle, Height, and Amount. Figure 17.22 shows our church image after the Emboss filter has been applied, with an Angle of 135°, a Height value of 8 pixels, and an Amount value of 100%.

FIGURE 17.22
This picture takes embossing better than most.

A better way to use the Emboss filter is on a duplicate layer with a different blending mode or Opacity value (see Figure 17.23). In the example shown here, I duplicated the Background layer and applied the Emboss filter to the copy using the same settings as I did to create Figure 17.22. Then I changed the embossed layer's blending mode to Overlay.

FIGURE 17.23
By combining the embossed layer with the original image to retain the color, I've achieved a more useful effect.

Extrude

If you're into faux 3-D effects, you'll just love the Extrude filter. It breaks up a picture into simulated cubes or pyramids of varying apparent height, based either on the brightness level of that area of the image or on a random distribution. You can set the size of the cubes or pyramids as well as their average height. It's…interesting (see Figure 17.24).

FIGURE 17.24
You won't use Extrude often, but someday it might be just the effect you're looking for.

Find Edges, Glowing Edges, and Trace Contour

These three effects sound as if they should look alike, and they do—to an extent—simply because they all locate edges within an image and outline them in some way. I definitely count them in the category of filters I like to combine with other filters, just to see what happens.

The first of the three, Find Edges, removes most of the colors from the object and replaces them with a line around each edge contour. The color of the lines depends on the value at that point on the original object, with the lightest points in yellow and the darkest points in purple. The picture looks like a rather delicate-colored pencil drawing. Find Edges works best, naturally, on photos that have a lot of detail for the filter to find. In Figure 17.25, I've applied it to the cathedral image.

Find Edges becomes darker and more intense if you apply it multiple times to the same picture. If you don't like the result of a single application, try it again before you move on to a different filter, or undo and then increase the contrast in the original photo before you reapply the filter. You can also touch up areas afterward with the Sponge tool, to bring out colors you hardly knew were there. And I find that if I pump up both the vibrance and the contrast in a picture before applying Find Edges, the result retains more detail and has more robust color.

Unfortunately, you can't set the sensitivity of the Find Edges filter; there are no controls. You can prepare the picture before you trace it, however, to try to improve your results. Start by running the Despeckle filter (choose Filter, Noise, Despeckle) so that Photoshop won't attempt to outline every piece of dust in the picture. If you don't want the background to show, select and delete it, or select your object and copy it to a new layer (choose Layer, New, Layer Via Copy to do this in a single step). After applying Find Edges, you can also choose Edit, Fade to back off the strength of the filter. Using this filter on duplicate layers with different blending modes can produce some spectacular effects, too.

Glowing Edges is even more fun because it's prettier (at least, I think so) and because you can adjust it to have maximum impact on your specific picture. Glowing Edges draws brightly colored lines along areas of color transition, against a black background. The effect is more than a little reminiscent of neon signs. In the Glowing Edges dialog (which is the only Stylize filter dialog in the Filter Gallery), you can vary the intensity of the color and the thickness of the lines.

In Figure 17.26, I've applied Glowing Edges to the church picture again. This filter works especially well with busy pictures that contain a lot of edges. The more it has to work with, the greater impact the filter has.

Similar to several of the filters we've talked about in this hour, Trace Contour sometimes benefits from being applied several times (see Figure 17.27). The Trace Contour dialog features a slider that controls the level at which brightness value differences are translated into contour lines, much like those you see on geological survey maps. Drag the slider to set the threshold at which the values (from 0 to 255) are traced. Experiment to see which values bring out the best detail in your image; this varies a lot in different pictures. The Edge option in the Trace Contour dialog determines how Photoshop uses the Level value, Lower outlines areas in which the color values of pixels fall below the specified level, and Upper outlines areas where the values of the pixels are greater than the specified level.

Solarize

Here's another filter that doesn't have any options for you to set; just choose Filter, Stylize, Solarize and go! The result combines a negative version with the original positive version of the image (see Figure 17.28). Again, you *can* manipulate the results of this filter, but you need to do it by altering the image before applying the filter. Try experimenting with different contrast, brightness, and saturation settings.

FIGURE 17.27
I applied Trace Contour to five copies of this image with a different Level value each time; then I combined the five images using the Soft Light blending mode.

FIGURE 17.28
Solarize is supposed to look like what you'd get if you flipped on the lights in your darkroom briefly while developing a print.

Tiles

If you've been longing for a way to cut up your picture into squares and then shuffle them just a bit so you can see gaps between them, this is a great day. That's exactly what the Tiles filter does, and it gives you four choices of what can go in the gaps between tiles: the Background color, the Foreground color, an inverted version of the image, or slices of the original image itself. Used on its own, Tiles isn't very interesting. Combined with, say, Diffuse and Emboss, it might be just what you need.

Wind

The Wind filter creates a directional blur that's intended to evoke, you guessed it, wind. You can control the Direction (From the Left or From the Right) and the intensity of the wind effect (Wind, Blast, or Stagger) in the filter's dialog (see Figure 17.29). This is a great filter for creating the illusion of movement and for applying to type. It works best when applied to a selected area instead of to the entire picture. When I was working on a previous edition of this book, one of the editors told me, "My favorite Wind filter effect is making a brushed metal look by adding noise to the basic metal color and then hitting it with wind from both directions, followed by a bit of tweaking for the perfect illusion." Thanks for the tip, Jon!

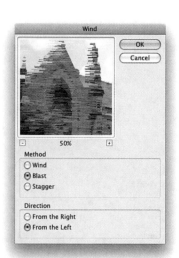

FIGURE 17.29
The Wind filter's dialog offers just two groups of settings.

Summary

This hour has been devoted the Distort, Pixelate, and Stylize filters. They're not for everyone—and they're certainly not for every image—but they're fun to play with and can occasionally create some unusual and beautiful effects. Don't hesitate to apply a second and even third filter over the first; often the second filter or a second application of the original filter can make a real difference, and you can always undo if you don't like the results.

And now, here's one final reminder to keep experimenting. You never know what a filter or combination can do to a particular picture until you try it, even if you've used that filter extensively with a different image. The criteria on which Photoshop bases the effects of its filters means that some filters can look very different, according to the kind of picture to which they are applied. You can't always predict what will happen, but that's what makes it fun.

Q&A

Q. Does the Glass filter include more than one kind of glass?

A. This is Photoshop; your choices are virtually unlimited. In addition to the textures provided, which include that beloved classic Glass Brick, you can choose Load Texture from the dialog's pop-up menu and open any Photoshop-format document to apply as a texture. Try taking close-up pictures of lots of different textures—grass, leaves, stones, rivets, whatever you like—that you can apply with the Glass filter.

Q. I like all the different Type options available in the Mezzotint dialog, but I want to know which is the most authentic.

A. That's Fine Dots. Check out the Wikipedia article on mezzotint printing to see some amazing examples of fine art prints created using this method.

Q. I like the effect of Glowing Edges, but I don't want my background to be completely black.

A. You've got a couple options here. First, you can apply the filter to a selected part of the image so that your background remains its previous colors. Or you can try applying Find Edges and then inverting the image (choose Image, Adjustments, Invert). This gives you a dark background, but one with much more texture and detail than Glowing Edges yields.

Workshop

Quiz

1. A displacement map is:

    A. Another name for a texture map

    B. A pattern who brightness values determine the movement of individual pixels in an image

    C. A chart showing how colors shift between your monitor and printer

2. The Spherize filter makes your picture appear to bulge _____.

   A. Outward (convex)

   B. Inward (concave)

   C. Either way

3. Pointillism is a painting style originally introduced by introduced by:

   A. Georges Seurat

   B. Leonardo da Vinci

   C. Jean-Luc Picard

4. **True or False:** The Shear filter can be used either vertically or horizontally.

Answers

1. **B.** You can definitely use a displacement map to simulate texture, though, so **A** is correct as well.

2. **C.** It depends on how you apply it.

3. **A.** See an example at www.ibiblio.org/wm/paint/auth/seurat/baignade/.

4. **False.** If you want to apply it vertically, you need to rotate the image first.

Exercises

1. Start with one of the pictures used in this hour—`pots.jpg`, `sidedoor.jpg`, and `steps.jpg` are all available for download on the book's website—and apply filters one after another until you can't recognize the image. See how many filters you can stack up before the picture completely disappears.

2. Go back to the original picture save a copy to preserve the original, and apply the Find Edges filter. This should give you an interesting image. Save it. Try the other filters over it until you find at least three that work well with the Find Edges filter. Whenever you have time, repeat this exercise, starting with a different filter.

PART V
Using Text and Special Effects

HOUR 18
Adding Type to Pictures

No matter how great the image, there usually comes a time when it needs a few explanatory words to accompany it. That's why Photoshop has the Type tools, and in this hour you'll learn to make the most of them. Photoshop enables you to add type directly to an image, edit it just as you would in your word processor, and control its leading, tracking, and kerning. (Don't worry if those terms aren't familiar to you; we cover them later in the hour.) You can set type vertically as well as horizontally, and you can warp it into a predetermined shape or set it along a curving or angular path. When your type is shaped the way you want it, you can apply dozens of layer styles and special effects designed just for type. But let's start with the basics. Here are a few important things to know about type in Photoshop:

WHAT YOU'LL LEARN IN THIS HOUR:

► Using the Type Tools
► Setting Type
► Creating Special Effects with Type
► Checking Your Spelling

► Each time you click the Type tool in a new location in the image window, Photoshop creates a separate type layer to hold the type you're about to enter.

► Point type starts from where you click the Type tool, and it begins a new line only if you press Return or Enter. To create a bounding box to contain type (this is called paragraph type), click and drag out a rectangle in the image window with the Type tool.

► Type must be **rasterized** (or converted to a Smart Object—see "Applying and Editing Smart Filters" in Hour 14, "Getting Started with Filters") before you can apply filters.

► You don't need to rasterize type to apply gradient fills and layer styles such as drop shadows, bevels, and embossing.

NOTE

Types of Type

At this point, it seems like a good idea to get a couple of terms straight. In Photoshop, you work with two kinds of type: vector type and bitmapped type. Vector type consists of mathematically defined shapes that can be scaled to any size without changing their shape in the least. Bitmapped type, on the other hand, is composed of individual pixels, just like a digital photo. The sharpness of bitmap type depends on the type's point size and on the resolution of the underlying image. If you scale bitmapped type to a larger size, it will have jagged edges, or **jaggies**.

When you type letters in the image window in Photoshop, they're vector type. This means that you can edit the text, reshape the letters, and modify their style attributes as much as you like. However, images don't often stay in Photoshop forever, which means that they have to be saved in other formats that don't support vector type, such as JPEG and TIFF. To make the type part of the picture in these formats, Photoshop converts it from vectors to pixels, or **rasterizes** it.

Think of it this way: Vector type that you place on a type layer is still text. It's easy to edit words or to move letters closer together just the way you would in Adobe InDesign or Microsoft Word. When you rasterize type, you are, in effect, turning it into a picture of type—it's no longer text, and Photoshop can no longer manipulate the individual letters, only the pixels they're drawn with.

Using the Type Tools

As with all of Photoshop's tools, the Type tools have a bunch of basic controls on the Tool Options bar. But they also have two extra panels, Character and Paragraph, that contain other settings just for type, such as the amount of vertical spacing between lines, or **leading**. In this section, we look at all three of these locations for type controls, starting with the Options bar (see Figure 18.1).

FIGURE 18.1
The Type Options bar.

Starting at the left end of the bar, you'll see the Type Orientation button—a capital *T* with two arrows. You can create horizontal type with the Horizontal Type tool and vertical type with the Vertical Type tool, but this button can change a type layer's orientation from horizontal to vertical and back after the fact.

After that come menus listing all the fonts installed in your system, all of their styles, and a range of point sizes from 6 to 72 points. You can set larger or smaller type by typing the point size right into the entry field at the top of the menu. Next, you can set the kind of antialiasing, or edge smoothing, to apply: None, Sharp, Crisp, Strong, or Smooth. Antialiasing makes type appear to be smoother type by partially filling the edge pixels of the letters, making them appear to blend into the background. For images that you'll view onscreen, antialiased type always looks better, especially if you're working with very small type sizes; in printed images, it just looks blurry. Crisp makes your type somewhat sharper; Sharp makes it as sharp as possible. Smooth makes it smoother, and Strong makes it look heavier.

The next set of three buttons enables you to choose an alignment option for the type: flush left, centered, or flush right. Clicking the color swatch next to the alignment buttons opens the Color Picker so you can set a color for the type.

Moving rightward along the Options bar, next we come to the Warp Text button, represented by a warped *T* with a curved line under it. This option gives you access to 15 preset shapes, ranging from arcs and a flag to a fisheye lens, any of which you can apply to a type layer. You'll learn more about warping type later in the hour.

Finally, a button called Panels opens the Character and Paragraph panels; we get to these panels soon, but first let's set some type.

Create a new image in Photoshop. Make it the default size and give it a white or colored background, whichever you prefer.

1. Click the Horizontal Type tool.

2. On the Tool Options bar, choose a font, a style, a point size, and a color that contrasts well with the background.

3. Click the Left Align Text button.

4. Click the Type tool somewhere in the left side of the image window. You'll see a blinking black line—the insertion point, just like a word processor's.

5. Type your name.

6. Click and drag the cursor along the type to select the whole line.

7. Click the color swatch in the Tool Options bar and choose a new color for the type.

8. Keeping the type selected, change the point size in the Options bar.

9. Now change the font to something completely different.

10. Click the Commit button to finalize the type, or click Cancel to delete the text and start over.

11. Click near the top of the canvas (be careful not to click in your name), and click the Text Orientation button. Now type your name again—it's vertical!

12. In the Layers panel, click any type layer, then click the Text Orientation button. That type turns vertical, too; you don't have to select the type itself to change its orientation—just make its layer active.

The Character Panel

Now let's check out the more sophisticated type settings you'll find in the two type panels. First, the Character panel (see Figure 18.2) gives you control over kerning, tracking, and shifting the baseline, in addition to the font, style, color, and size options also found on the toolbar. There's also a selection of type styles that aren't related to the chosen font, such as underlining. You can set type options on the Character panel before you set the type in the image window, or you can use the panel to reformat type you've already entered and selected.

FIGURE 18.2
The Character panel gives you very
fine control over the appearance of
your type.

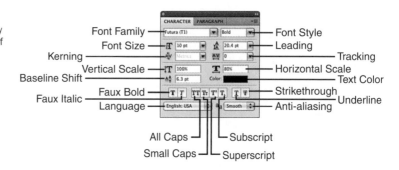

The buttons, menus, and entry fields on the Character panel give you
access to your system's installed fonts, the styles associated with those
fonts, and a range of font sizes, just like the ones on the Tool Options bar.
You've got a few more precision settings to accompany those as well.

The entry field labeled A\V controls **kerning**, or the amount of space
between each pair of adjacent letters. Most fonts, especially when they're
used in larger sizes, need some kerning to adjust the spaces between letter
pairs such as AV and WA so that you don't see a gap between the letters.
The default kerning setting is Metrics, which means that Photoshop applies
the kerning information built right into the font. If you don't like the looks of
this, you can override it by choosing Optical from the pop-up menu (which
lets Photoshop decide how much kerning to apply) or by positioning your
cursor between two letters and entering a Kerning value in the field.

Tracking is similar to kerning, in that it involves spacing between letters,
but it refers to the amount of space between each pair of letters in an entire
word or phrase instead of just between a single pair. Tracking can be tight
(enter negative numbers) or loose (enter positive numbers). Entering 0 in
the Tracking field means that no tracking is applied; the letters are spaced
according to the information in their font files.

Leading (pronounced to rhyme with "bedding") is the amount of vertical
space between lines of type. If you're setting a single word or line of type,
you don't need to worry about the leading value. As soon as you add a
second line, however, leading becomes important. Because Photoshop
measures leading from the baseline of a line of text to the baseline of the
line above it (*not* the line below it), the amount of leading must be equal to
or greater than the point size of the type, to keep the lines from touching
or overlapping. (The **baseline** is the invisible line on which type sits.) If
you don't specify a leading value, Photoshop uses its default Auto setting,
which is 120% of the type's point size. So, for example, 10-point type has
12-point leading if you use Auto.

Below the Kerning and Tracking fields are entry fields for Vertical and Horizontal Scale values. Type designers hate to think that people will stretch their perfect letterforms, but in the real world, you've got to do what you've got to do. If you need to scale your type vertically (to make it taller or shorter) or horizontally (to make it wider or narrower), here's where you go. The default value is 100%; enter a larger value to stretch the selected letters or a smaller value to squish them. You can also set a baseline shift value, which enables you to move type above and below the baseline by the specified amount.

Finally, there's a row of buttons at the bottom of the panel for type styles, and menus for language and antialiasing. In addition to faux bold and faux italic, you can apply several other styles: all caps, small caps, superscript, subscript, underscore, and strikethrough. The language menu lets you choose fonts with special characters and makes sure that Photoshop uses the appropriate dictionary when you check spelling. (You'll learn more about Photoshop's spelling checker later in the hour.)

The Paragraph Panel

In Photoshop terms, any line followed by a carriage return is a **paragraph**—which isn't exactly the classic definition, but let's go with it for now. In the Paragraph panel, you can set options relating to an entire paragraph, such as alignment, justification, and indentation (see Figure 18.3).

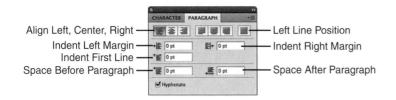

Align Left, Center, Right —— Left Line Position
Indent Left Margin —— Indent Right Margin
Indent First Line
Space Before Paragraph —— Space After Paragraph

FIGURE 18.3
On the Paragraph panel, you can set alignment and indentation for an entire paragraph.

The buttons in the upper-left corner of the panel show the possible alignments: left, centered, and right. These same buttons also appear on the Tool Options bar. Four additional buttons let you specify that the last line of a justified paragraph should align to the left, to the center, or to the right, or be spread out and fully justified. These latter options are available only if you have set paragraph text in a bounding box; they don't apply to point type. **Justified**, for those not familiar with the term, means that the spacing within the type is stretched or compressed as necessary to make all the lines exactly the same length. The opposite of justified is ragged, which is what you get when each line is a different length.

The other buttons and entry fields on the Paragraph panel are for setting the amount of first-line indents, right indents, and left indents, as well as adding space before or after a paragraph. Obviously, these are most useful when you're dealing with a block of text instead of just a few words or a line or two.

Setting Type

Long, long ago, in the days when type consisted of blocks of metal or wood with letters sculpted in reverse on their surfaces, you had to be able to read backward to set type. And that was just one of the special skills of a printer or typesetter back them. Today, of course, that's no longer true. But you do have to learn a few ins and outs to work with type in Photoshop. Ready? Let's go!

Typesetting Principles

Of course, putting letters on a page—or in a Photoshop image—is easy; anyone can do it. Doing it right is another matter entirely. Typesetting is a centuries-old craft, and it has rules. Of course, today's designers break all the rules, and that's fine, but you should know the rules before breaking them.

First of all, thousands of typefaces are available. You've probably got dozens of fonts that came with your computer or with programs you've installed on your computer. You can buy more in CD-ROM collections, download them online, and so on. Trying out new and exciting typefaces can be so much fun that you lose sight of the goal: to communicate. When you've chosen a font because it looks pretty, look again and make sure you can actually read it. And follow these guidelines:

- ▶ Stick to a plain, legible font for longer chunks of text, and go wild with the headings. Studies show that if type is too hard to read, people stop trying and move on to the next thing.

- ▶ Don't use too many typefaces in one design. It just looks like a yard sale; you want your designs to look more like perfectly designed department store display windows.

- ▶ If you're stuck for a good combination, try mixing one serif font (the kind with little "sticks" at the ends of the strokes) with one sans serif font (the kind without).

▶ Remember to use "curly" quotes and apostrophes instead of the straight kind.

▶ Avoid using underlining for emphasis; instead, use italic or bold type—that's what they're for.

▶ Don't set script in all caps. It's too hard to read, and it violates the intent of script fonts, which generally have connected letters like cursive handwriting.

Before finalizing a design, print a sample and examine it with an eye toward making it more readable. That might be a simple matter of making the type larger or giving the lines of type more space (leading). You might need to rethink your background or add an outline around the letters. A drop shadow might help—or might make matters worse. Try combinations of different type and image treatment. And if you end up sticking with your original concept, that's fine—sometimes you do get it right the first time.

Creating Type Layers

As I mentioned earlier, you can set type in Photoshop in two ways. The first is just to click in the image where you want the type, creating a new layer and starting a line of point type. If you choose flush left alignment on the Tool Options bar or the Paragraph panel, your text heads right from the insertion point. If you select centered, Photoshop centers the words around your insertion point as you enter them. Flush right makes the text run to the left from your right-side insertion point. Figure 18.4 shows examples of each.

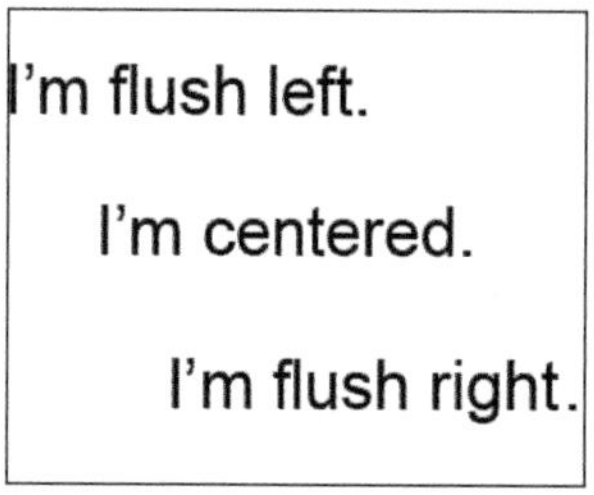

The other way to create type, when you have to set a lot of it or when you need to fill a specific area, is to drag out a bounding box for paragraph type. Switch to the Type tool, click it to create the corner point of the box, and then drag until the box is approximately the right size and shape (see Figure 18.5). You can go back and resize the box at any time later, so don't worry if it's not precisely where you want it or not quite the right size. Then enter your text by typing it or by copying and pasting from another program.

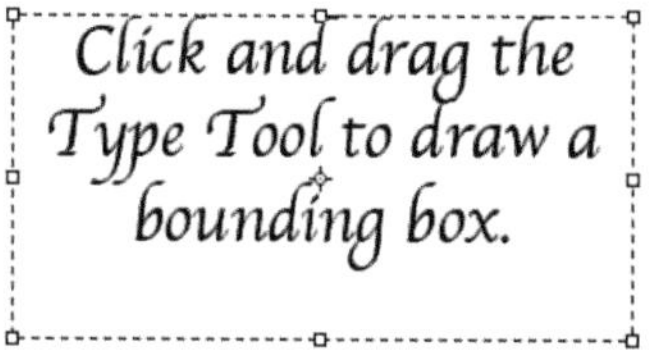

Type always appears on a new layer. Type layers are indicated in the Layers panel by a large letter *T*, as you can see in Figure 18.6. They're named according to the first new word you type, but you can change a type layer's default name by double-clicking it and entering a new name. To edit the type itself, switch to the Type tool and click anywhere in the text. Double-clicking the *T* also selects all the type on that layer so that you can apply changes. If you've set paragraph text in a bounding box, now's the time to adjust the leading, paragraph spacing, and indents, if any.

I'm flush left.

I'm centered.

I'm flush right.

FIGURE 18.4
Text flows from the insertion point.

Click and drag the Type Tool to draw a bounding box.

FIGURE 18.5
The type bounding box determines the shape of the block of text. Photoshop automatically breaks each line at the edge of the bounding box, just like a word processor.

FIGURE 18.6
Each line of type occupies its own
type layer.

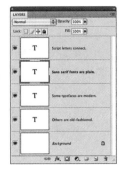

Type layers are special in several ways: You can edit their text and insert new text or delete some. You can make changes in the text itself or in its font, style, or size. You can change the orientation of the type from horizontal to vertical. You can apply or change the type of antialiasing. But as with any layers, you can also move their contents, copy them, or change their stacking order, and you can change the layer options of a type layer as you can for a regular layer. You can use layer styles on type layers, and you can apply to type layers most of the Transform commands from the Edit menu—except Perspective and Distort. Those two commands require type layers to be rasterized before you can apply them, which brings us to our next topic.

Rasterizing Type

You can do a lot with "live" type in Photoshop, but some functions require you to turn a type layer into a regular layer, one composed of image pixels instead of editable type. As you just learned, you need to do this before you can apply the Perspective or Distort commands; you also need to rasterize a type layer to transform just part of it, or to apply some of Photoshop's many filters. Many filters can be used as smart filters, which enables you to leave your type editable; this is clearly the choice that leaves you the most leeway for making changes later (see "Applying and Editing Smart Filters" in Hour 14 for instructions). But if the filter you want to use won't work as a smart filter, or if you're convinced that you're done editing the type and want to lock it down, you can rasterize it.

Rasterizing, in effect, turns type into a picture of type. After the type is rasterized, you can't go back and edit it again. To rasterize type, click the type layer in the Layers panel to activate it and choose Layer, Rasterize. You can rasterize type layers one at a time or do all the layers at once by selecting multiple layers in the Layers panel. Or you can simply flatten the image (choose Layer, Flatten Image) if you're sure that you're finished making changes to the wording and no longer need the image elements to be on separate layers.

After you've rasterized a type layer, you can have some real fun with it. Apply filters to your heart's content. Pour paint into selected letters, or fill them with patterns or gradients. Texturize the type. Select the type and distort it. Figure 18.7 shows just a few of the things you can do.

FIGURE 18.7
Filtered, distressed, and distorted type.

NOTE

Fat Faces Are Good

Filters tend to be most successful on bold typefaces. Thin, delicate strokes in a letter can easily get lost. And if you can't read the type, it's not saying anything.

Creating Special Effects with Type

So much for black words on a white page; in Photoshop, type can be just as decorative as any other part of an image. In this section, we look at several ways to add punch and appeal to type.

Creating Drop Shadows

Arguably the most common special effect applied to type these days, a drop shadow adds dimension because it makes the object producing the shadow appear to be closer to the viewer than the background. Because this effect is used so often, apply it sparingly—but don't let that scare you away from this simple way to make type stand out from the image that contains it.

Here are a few tips for using drop shadows most effectively:

NOTE

Drop or Cast?

A **drop shadow** is the kind of shadow produced by an object that's floating above the surface on which the shadow appears. It's called a drop shadow to distinguish it from a **cast shadow**, in which the shadow-casting object touches the surface on which the shadow is cast, like a tree casting a shadow on the ground.

▶ Choose the objects to which you're applying shadows carefully. If you use too many shadows, *everything* pops forward, and the shadows don't draw attention to any one particular object.

Too Dark

Too Fuzzy

Too Far Away

Just right!

FIGURE 18.8
A drop shadow needs to be light
enough that it's distinguishable
from the type, but positioned so
that it appears to be part of a unit
with the type.

▶ Make sure that all the shadows in a particular image have the same density, and if you use shadows on multiple objects that are near each other, make sure that the shadows all go the same way. If the shadows are inconsistent, viewers will notice; although they might not realize what the problem is, they'll sense that the picture is somehow wrong.

▶ Don't make drop shadows too dark. It's easy to go overboard and create deep, saturated shadows that overwhelm the foreground image. Keep shadows fairly light and subtle. Figure 18.8 shows what can go wrong (and right) with drop shadows on type.

Photoshop's collection of layer styles includes a powerful and easy drop shadow function, along with the Glow, Bevel, Emboss, Satin, and Overlay styles, that you can apply to type layers and image layers alike. You will find all these effects in the Layer, Style submenu. Remember that you can use drop shadows and other layer styles on any object that's on its own layer, as well as on type.

▼ TRY IT YOURSELF

**Create a Drop
Shadow for Text**

Follow these steps to see how Photoshop applies drop shadows to type layers.

1. Create a new Photoshop image file with a white background.

2. Switch to the Type tool, click in the image window, and enter some words—whatever you want. Choose any font that appeals to you, and don't worry about color, kerning, or any other stylistic niceties. Figure 18.9 shows an example of a basic line of point type.

FIGURE 18.9
Plain black type is just a starting
point...

URGENT

3. Choose Layer, Layer Style, Drop Shadow to open the Layer Style dialog, shown in Figure 18.10. Check the Preview box so that you can see how the image changes as you modify the settings. I've found that the trickiest part of this operation is actually getting the screen arranged so that you can see both the dialog and the type you're working on. (Situations like this are a great argument in favor of hooking up more than one monitor to your computer.)

4. Set the Blend Mode pop-up menu to Normal, Multiply, or Darken. Otherwise, you won't see the shadow against the white background. Click in the color swatch next to the Blend Mode menu to open the Color Picker so you can change the color of the shadow.

5. Adjust the shadow's Opacity and Angle until you're happy with what you see in the image window, by clicking the slider and dragging the angle proxy to change the angle, or by typing numbers into the boxes.

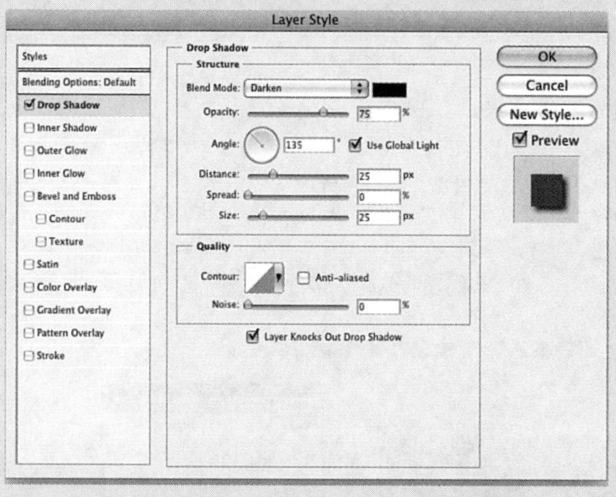

TRY IT YOURSELF ▼

Create a Drop Shadow for Text
continued

FIGURE 18.10
The Layer Style dialog's drop shadow settings aren't as complicated as they might seem.

6. Set the Distance to determine how far the shadow will be from the word or object. Drag the Size slider to control the amount of shadow that's visible, and set the Spread slider to make the edges of the shadow more or less distinct. Click OK when you like the looks of your drop shadow. You can go back and change the settings at any time, of course, unless you merge the layer that contains the shadow with another layer. I've added a little bit of art to create the finished effect you see in Figure 18.11. (I used the Shape tool to draw a lightning bolt, and then I filled it with an appropriate color and added the same drop shadow that I used on the type layer.)

FIGURE 18.11
Adding just a bit of art and a drop shadow makes a huge difference.

Of course, drop shadows in the real world occur not just over white or solid-color backgrounds, but over all kinds of objects. You can make a drop shadow appear to fall on a texture, an image, or anything else that strikes your fancy.

▼ TRY IT YOURSELF

Place Drop Shadows on a Background

Follow these steps to apply drop shadows from text onto a background image and add depth to the background itself.

1. First, create the Photoshop image. I started with a photo of the World's Cutest Baby™. I added some type and put the baby photo on its own layer, deleting part of the background to allow a gradient to show through as a backdrop. The important thing to remember is to create a *new layer* for each element for which you want to have a drop shadow (see Figure 18.12). For a refresher on layers, refer to Hour 11, "Creating Layered Images."

FIGURE 18.12
The original image before drop shadows. I've included the Layers panel so that you can see the separate layers.

2. Add a shadow to the text first, by following the steps in the previous section (see Figure 18.13). If the background and the lettering are similar colors or values, consider adding a bit of outer glow as well.

   Notice how you can actually see the texture of the background right through the new shadow. The result is a pleasant, realistic effect. You can make even more of the background show through by adjusting the Opacity slider in the Layers panel. Give it a try.

TRY IT YOURSELF ▼

**Place Drop Shadows
on a Background**
continued

3. Now create some depth in the background itself. I start by adding a drop shadow to the baby layer. Then I scale the effect (choose Layer, Layer Style, Scale Effects) so that it's more in proportion to the size of the baby. Figure 18.14 shows the final version.

   Notice how the text casts a shadow on the baby and the bed; the baby, in turn, casts a shadow on the background.

FIGURE 18.13
A drop shadow applied to the text.

FIGURE 18.14
Drop shadows at work.

Cutting and Filling Type

So far, you've seen type placed in front of an image. But another fun trick to play with type is to put an image *inside* it. You can do this if you're using a nice bold typeface that leaves plenty of room for your picture (or pictures!) to show through. In this case, I'm using a photo of a cobblestone street. You could use a single photo or a collage of several photos.

First, I click the Type tool and hold down the mouse button to select the Horizontal Type Mask tool, which is used for making type-shaped selection marquees. I've selected a bold face called Impact; you've probably

TIP

Drop Shadows Should Drop

I find that shadows almost always work best if they're *below* the original image—that is, if the light source appears to be *above* the object instead of below it. When the shadow falls downward, the object appears to be popping upward instead of heading away from the viewer.

FIGURE 18.15
Faux Bold adds extra boldness to any character, whether it's already bold or not. This can distort delicate letterforms, but it doesn't do much harm to the simple, blocky characters of Impact.

seen it before. To make it even bolder, I'll click the Faux Bold button at the bottom of the Character panel, shown in Figure 18.15.

When I position the cursor and start to place my letters, Photoshop enters Quick Mask mode and the image window turns pink. As I type the letters, they appear to be in a contrasting color, but when I finish typing and deselect the Type tool (or press Enter on the numeric keypad), they turn into a selection marquee and the Quick Mask goes away. Figure 18.16 shows how this looks onscreen.

FIGURE 18.16
The letters have turned into an active selection.

Now I can press Command-X (Mac) or Ctrl+X (Windows) and cut out the letters. I'll create a new image file right away and paste my filled type into it for safekeeping. Figure 18.17 shows the cutout lettering.

I'm going to use these letters as part of the title slide for a keynote presentation. So I'll use the Texturizer filter to make a nice sandstone background, tint the background with colors picked up from the original cobblestone image, and add a couple layer styles to the cut-out image: Emboss and Drop Shadow, both of which give it a three-dimensional appearance. Figure 18.18 shows the final logo, after all these tricks.

FIGURE 18.17
The type is cut out of the photo.

NOTE

It's Automatic

If you open a new image file after copying or cutting out a selection, Photoshop automatically inserts the selection's dimensions in the New dialog box and chooses the right color mode, so you can just press Command-N/Ctrl+N and click OK immediately.

FIGURE 18.18
The letters jump right out.

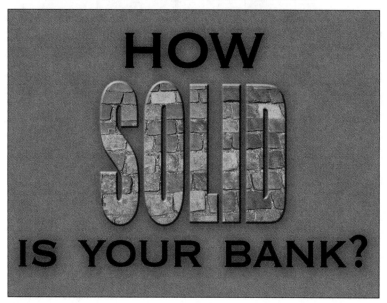

Adding Glows

After all this talk about drop shadows, I wouldn't blame you if you thought that's the only layer style Photoshop can do. Of course, you'd be mistaken. Remember, in the last example, I needed to emboss my type as well as add a drop shadow to separate the letters from the background. Here, we'll play a little with glow styles. You can use a layer style to place a glow—really, in the case of Outer Glow, an outline—around your type. You can also apply an Inner Glow effect to make it appear as if the letters themselves are glowing. Both of these are great for adding emphasis to a piece of text or making it stand out from a busy background. Figure 18.19 shows a fairly ordinary text and photo combination that could use some of this kind of help.

In Figure 18.20, I've applied a subtle Outer Glow to the letters. It's simply another way of defining them from the background, one that's particularly useful when a drop shadow isn't appropriate. Other objects can glow, too, and I discuss these in more detail in the next hour, when you'll learn how to build your own glows from scratch.

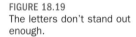

FIGURE 18.19
The letters don't stand out enough.

FIGURE 18.20
The glow helps separate the text
from the background.

Creating Bevel and Emboss Effects

The Bevel and Emboss effects both produce raised type—Bevel produces
sharp edges, giving the type a carved appearance, and Emboss produces
letters that look raised from the surface. Figure 18.21 shows examples of
both. Notice that both effects use carefully placed shadows to simulate a
three-dimensional effect.

FIGURE 18.21
The difference between Bevel and
Emboss is obvious.

You can vary the effect of these styles by changing the blending modes, by varying the opacity, and by switching around highlight and shadow colors. As always, the best way to see what the settings do is to experiment with them.

You can create metallic type in lots of ways using the layer styles, particularly the Bevel and Emboss styles. Choose appropriate metallic colors, such as very pale blues for silver and light yellows, and browns for gold, like the color I used for the embossed type in Figure 18.21. And remember to set the highlight or shadow colors to variations on the original color, not necessarily black or white. Try adding noise and then blurring it for a brushed metal finish. Also check out the Styles panel, which lists a great selection of prepackaged style combinations that you can apply to a layer with a single click.

Warping Text

After seeing the wonders of Photoshop's filter set, it shouldn't surprise you to learn that you can warp type into all kinds of funky shapes. The best part, however, is that it remains editable text the whole time, and you can change shapes as many times as you want. Instead of drawing your own path, the Warp Text dialog enables you to choose from 15 preset shapes. You can also modify each shape to suit your own needs. Figure 18.22 shows the presets available in the Warp Text dialog.

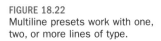

FIGURE 18.22
Multiline presets work with one, two, or more lines of type.

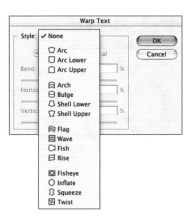

The Warp Text settings, shown in Figure 18.23, can be a little bit tricky at first. Start by clicking Horizontal or Vertical to set the shape's orientation. Then use the sliders to increase or decrease the distance that the shape's curved edges bow in or out. Moving the slider to the right bends words up; to the left (negative numbers) bends them down. Distortion makes the line of type appear to flare out on one end (Horizontal Distortion) or flare from top to bottom (Vertical Distortion).

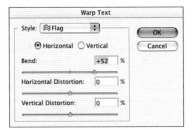

FIGURE 18.23
Move the sliders left or right to change the settings.

In Figure 18.24, I've applied some of the warp styles to various bits of type. The best way to master the Warp Text feature is to play with it. Set a line or two of type and try the different kinds of warp on it. Choose your font carefully, though; you'll get best results with a simpler font, and using all caps often helps to maintain the outlines of the warp shape.

FIGURE 18.24
Can you guess which wave forms I used on each of these words?

Setting Type on a Path

Traditionally, type runs in straight lines, whether it's horizontal or vertical. But in Photoshop, you don't have to stick to straight lines; you can put type on any path, as smooth or as ragged as you care to draw it. Of course, you need to start by drawing a path; review Hour 13, "Using Paths," if you need a reminder of how the Path tools work. Figure 18.25 shows a path I drew.

FIGURE 18.25
You can tweak the curves until the path is as smooth or as wild as you want.

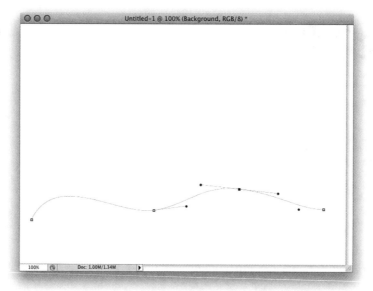

Then switch to the Type tool, choose an alignment setting for your type, and click at the start of the path. You'll see a blinking insertion point oriented relative to the angle of the path at that position. As you type, the baseline of the type automatically aligns to the path, as shown in Figure 18.26.

After you've entered the type, you can switch to the Direct Selection tool to make changes. Drag the direction handles to adjust the path, or click just before the first letter and drag to move the type along the path. After you've set the type, you can go on and do any of the other things we've discussed: add shadows, put in glows, apply filters, or whatever strikes your fancy. Just one word of warning here—make sure your type is legible, even if you have to adjust kerning and tracking at specific points along the path.

FIGURE 18.26
You can still edit this type, unless you rasterize it.

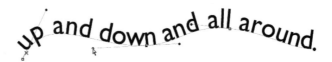

Checking Your Spelling

Photoshop hasn't always had a spell-checker—most other graphics programs haven't. It makes sense for this feature to be there, however; heaven knows we all rely on spell-checkers in our word processors and email programs, so why not Photoshop? Any time you're unsure about the spelling of a word you've typed or pasted, choose Edit, Check Spelling. Photoshop checks the spelling of all the text in the document and, if it finds a potential mistake, offers you possible replacements (see Figure 18.27).

FIGURE 18.27
Photoshop's spell-checker isn't
half bad.

Another word-processing feature that Photoshop has to offer is the capability to find and change words or characters in your poster text. Choose Edit, Find and Replace Text to search for a word, letter, or symbol, and then change it to whatever you specify. Of course, both of these functions work only on editable text; if you rasterize type to apply filters or manipulate it in other ways, it's no longer text as far as Photoshop is concerned.

Summary

You'll never turn to Photoshop for the most sophisticated treatment of type—it lacks the fine control over spacing, character shape, hyphenation, and other aspects of type that you'll find in programs such as Adobe InDesign. On the other hand, Photoshop provides more power than you'll need for most applications of type to images. And when the type is set in the image, you can apply all of Photoshop's myriad filters, blending modes, and special styles to it. You can warp type, distort it, punch it out of a graphic, or make letters out of a picture. So if all you want to do is set type, use a program such as InDesign. If you want to do wacky and wonderful things to type, Photoshop has exactly the tools you need.

Q&A

Q. **What is this baseline thing you keep talking about?**

A. When you write on lined paper, you position the bottom of each letter on the line, right? Some letters have parts that go below that line, as with *p* and *y*, but they all sit on it. That's the baseline. It's the one location that all letters have in common, regardless of height or width, so it's a convenient point from which to measure spacing.

Q. **Pixels, rasterizing, paths, curves—what does all this stuff really mean?**

A. The thing that confuses so many Photoshop users is that the program can actually produce two different kinds of artwork: pixel based and path based. As you know, pixels are tiny squares of color placed in a grid to form an image. Up close, all you see is the squares, but when you step back, you can see the whole picture. Vector artwork, on the other hand, is made up of mathematically defined paths. Remember how you learned to graph a curve based on an equation back in algebra class? Vector artwork looks the same no matter how close in or far away you get; it's always smooth and perfectly formed. That's why Photoshop uses it for type: You can scale type to any size that works with your image, and it will still be shaped correctly, instead of going all jaggy, as pixel-based artwork does when you scale it too much.

Q. **If type is really made out of paths, can I edit the paths to reshape the type?**

A. Absolutely—I thought you'd never ask! With a type layer active, choose Layer, Type, Create Work Path to form a path from the letters. Then you can edit the path any way you want and use it to create selections or fill and stroke it. (Turn back to Hour 13 if you want to review path-editing techniques.) Meanwhile, the original type layer stays put. You can also choose Layer, Type, Convert to Shape to turn the type layer into a shape layer; then you can edit the paths on the shape layer's vector mask to change the letters' shapes. With this option, the original type layer isn't preserved, so you won't be able to edit the text afterward.

Workshop

Quiz

1. **True or False:** Photoshop can set type horizontally or vertically.

2. Photoshop places type on:

    A. The Background layer

    B. Special type layers

    C. Regular layers

    D. Adjustment layers

3. If there's a T in the box on the Layers panel, it means:

    A. You can double-click it to open the Type tool

    B. The layer is a type layer

    C. Layer styles have been applied to the type

    D. Both **A** and **B**

4. **True or False:** There's no way to set small caps in Photoshop.

Answers

1. **True.** For diagonal type, you need to rotate it.

2. **B.** Type layers are editable unless you rasterize them.

3. **D.** And if you see an italic F symbol, that indicates that layer styles have been applied to the layer.

4. **False.** Small caps is one of the options in the Character panel. This style uses regular upper-case letters for capitals and miniature upper-case letters instead of lower-case letters.

Exercises

1. Time to cut back your support for the greeting card industry—you can make your own cards. Choose one of your best photos and turn it into a card by adding "Congratulations," "Happy Birthday," or other appropriate text.

2. With your card image still open, add a drop shadow behind the lettering. Try changing the color of both the type and the shadow so the lettering stands out.

3. Now try using a glow instead of the shadow. Which effect do you like best?

HOUR 19
Taking Advantage of a Few Useful Tricks

So far, we've focused on a very specific topic during each hour. For this hour, however, we take some time to explore a variety of neat things that Photoshop can do, some of which are just for fun and others of which will make you more productive. We look at some cool special effects, explain how to add sticky notes to images, and even show you how to print contact sheets.

Creating Special Effects

You got a taste of some of Photoshop's special effects in the previous hour, when we applied a few different layer styles to type. Now let's unleash the true power of Photoshop as you learn how to create these sorts of effects from scratch. Don't worry, we take it one step at a time.

Glows

A glow is a particularly easy special effect to create. If you break it down, it's basically a drop shadow that isn't offset at all from the original object, and it's usually a color other than black. Building your own glow around an object, as opposed to using Photoshop's Outer Glow layer style, enables you to tweak the glow's shape so that it fills in any gaps or projects farther outward in key spots.

WHAT YOU'LL LEARN IN THIS HOUR:

▶ Creating Special Effects
▶ Making Notes
▶ Printing Contact Sheets

NOTE

Your Mileage May Vary

You'll get very detailed instructions in this hour, with very specific settings for each command or filter. These settings will work with the images shown, but when you create these special effects with your own images, my settings might not always work. Images with different resolutions, sizes, and colors call for different settings. So when you see specifics, feel free to modify them as needed to get even better results with your own artwork.

▼ TRY IT YOURSELF

Create a Custom Glow Around an Object

Let's create a basic glow around an object. I have an object that's practically screaming for a glow—it's the handle from a fabulous Art Deco ashtray I picked up at an antique shop. I've already erased the background; now we just need to jazz it up a bit. You can download this from the book's web page; it's called brassdog.jpg. After the main book page has loaded, click the Downloads link to get to the files. Or, if you prefer, use an image from your own collection. It's helpful if the object that will glow is easy to select.

1. Open an image you want to apply the effect to. Figure 19.1 shows my original photo.

FIGURE 19.1
Here's the original dog, crying out for some bling.

2. First, you need to select the object that will glow—in this case, the dog. Here, it's easiest to select the white background with the Magic Wand and then invert the selection (choose Select, Inverse). Don't forget to make sure that the area inside the curve of the dog's tail is selected, too, before you invert the selection.

3. Copy the selected object and press Command-V (Mac) or Ctrl+V (Windows) to paste it onto a new layer. Now you have two layers: one with the complete original image and one that contains just the selected object.

4. Drag the layer you just created to the New Layer button at the bottom of the Layers panel to duplicate it. Now you have the entire scene as the Background layer and two layers that contain the same cutout object.

5. Click anywhere in the clear area with the Magic Wand, making sure that the Contiguous box in the Options bar isn't checked. Choose Select, Invert to select just the dog (or whatever you are using as a glow object). Expand the selection (choose Select, Modify, Expand) by 50 pixels (or whatever's appropriate for your image). Feather the edges by 20 pixels; this smoothes the selection.

6. Use the Path menu to make a work path around the selection; then edit the path as needed. Eventually, my dog will be standing on something, so the glow shouldn't appear beneath his feet. I edited the path so that it's flush with the bottoms of his paws (see Figure 19.2).

TRY IT YOURSELF ▼

Create a Custom Glow Around an Object

continued

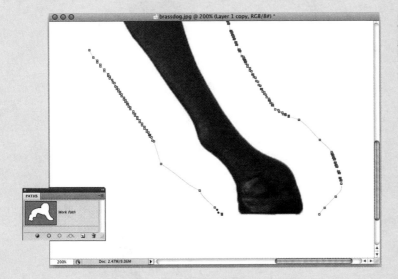

FIGURE 19.2
The path method of creating a glow enables you to customize its shape very precisely.

7. Use the Fill Path command in the Paths panel menu to fill the work path with an appropriate glow color. Then use the Delete Path command to get rid of the path—you don't need it anymore. Now only the color remains on the layer. Figure 19.3 shows this step.

8. Make sure that the glow layer is selected and choose Filter, Blur, Gaussian Blur. This filter will diffuse the glow; I used a setting of around 40 for a very generous glow. (Have I mentioned that subtlety isn't really my thing?)

9. Rearrange the layers so that the glow layer is beneath the object layer. Figure 19.4 shows the final product.

▼ TRY IT YOURSELF

Create a Custom Glow Around an Object

continued

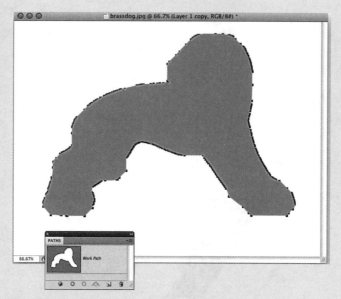

FIGURE 19.3
The filled path follows the dog's contours.

FIGURE 19.4
Is this dog radioactive, or is it just his glowing personality?

Of course, this is Photoshop, so you can accomplish pretty much the same result in several ways. You can skip step 6 and simply fill the feathered selection. Or you can use the Outer Glow layer effect; although it's not as customizable, you can go back and change the settings later, and it's certainly quicker and easier to apply.

In this task, you've only scratched the surface of glow effects, so I encourage you to try all sorts of settings and colors on your own images. You can experiment with the brightness and size of the glow, and be sure to try other Blur filters, such as Motion Blur or Box Blur, for glows that imply movement or dimension. Have fun!

Lighting Effects

Photoshop's **Lighting Effects** filter offers you a whole range of special effects related to how objects are lit. By illuminating objects with different numbers of lights, in varying types and intensities, you can change the entire feel of an image, drawing the viewer's attention exactly where you want it.

TRY IT YOURSELF ▼

Enhance an Object with Lighting Effects

The Lighting Effects filter has a huge dialog with a lot of settings. We try out a few of them in this task.

1. Start with an original image. Perhaps you have an image that's too flat, or maybe it just needs to be more three-dimensional to look more realistic. Figure 19.5, showing a stuffed toy, is such an image. (If you want to follow along, download the image monkey.jpg from the Sams website.)

FIGURE 19.5
Here's the original image, definitely in need of some special lighting.

▼ TRY IT YOURSELF

Enhance an Object with Lighting Effects

continued

2. The first decision to make is whether I want to light the entire scene or just the monkey. Lighting a single object is more dramatic; lighting the whole canvas is more natural. In this case, I'll put a spotlight on the monkey.

3. Choose Filter, Render, Lighting Effects to open the Lighting Effects dialog (see Figure 19.6). From the Style pop-up menu near the top, choose Spotlight. You'll see a preview of your image on the left with the new spotlight effect.

FIGURE 19.6
The Lighting Effects dialog offers a bewildering number of options.

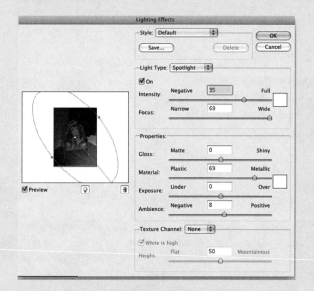

4. Photoshop ships quite a few default settings, but you can view these as starting points for playing around with the various sliders and values. Don't be intimidated by the number of choices here; start by changing one setting all the way up and all the way down, to see what it does. Then move on to the next one.

To change the direction and/or shape of the spotlight, click and drag the handles around the oval in the preview area. You can move it around as much as you want, and you can move the center point to reposition the light. Move the light in your preview area so that the image looks something like what you see in Figure 19.7.

5. Now the unlit parts of the image are a bit too dark. You need to bring up the overall lighting some, so drag the Ambience slider rightward a notch, and change the color of the spotlights to something more interesting than pale yellow.

6. That looks pretty good, but what if you tried something completely different? Figure 19.8 shows the Triple Spotlights preset. You can make each light a different color by clicking it in preview area and then clicking its color swatch box over on the right and choosing something new in the Color Picker.

TRY IT YOURSELF ▼

Enhance an Object with Lighting Effects
continued

FIGURE 19.7
Spotlight on the monkey!

FIGURE 19.8
This is a bit overdone, but it's easy enough to return to the Lighting Effects dialog and back off the settings.

Reflections

If you find yourself bringing various images together in Photoshop to create new scenes, you can't just throw the images together and come out with a realistic result. As you've seen, adding effects such as shadows is essential to create a realistic-looking environment. Creating reflections is another way you can do that.

Add Realistic Reflections to a Surface

FIGURE 19.9
You can easily create a very simple "studio" backdrop.

FIGURE 19.10
Our background is all ready to put something on.

Let's run through an example so that you can add reflections to your repertoire of special effects.

1. We need to start with an object that we want to put in front of a background. I happen to have just such an object, and a simple background is easy to make. First, use the Gradient tool to lay down a very simple oblong gradient from dark to light; mine goes from blue to white. Then add some noise from the Noise filter so that it has a little texture (I used a setting of 8%). We want this to look like a photographer's backdrop, so choose Transform, Perspective to drag the bottom out wide. Figure 19.9 shows this stage.

2. The sides of the backdrop should be vertical at the top, so select the upper area of the backdrop and apply perspective again to straighten the sides. For a final touch, select the gradient area and apply the filter of your choice to give it a realistic surface. I used the Plastic Wrap filter to make the surface look like rippled plastic (see Figure 19.10).

3. Now it's time to set an object in front of this background. (You can download the image I'm using from the book's website. It's called cone.jpg.) I think you'll agree that the effect isn't particularly realistic (see Figure 19.11). It looks as if the cone and background came from two different sources—which they did, of course, but we're trying to fool the viewer here.

4. To start creating a reflection of the cone on the background, first duplicate the cone layer. In the Layers panel, move this new layer below the original cone layer, because the reflection should appear underneath the original object.

5. With the reflection layer active, choose Edit, Transform, Flip Vertical to flip the reflected cone upside down.

6. Now use the Move tool to slide the cone's reflection down into position. You might find that you need to use the Distort or Skew Transform commands to move a reflection into its proper position and shape. The adjacent edges of the two cones should meet precisely, with no backdrop visible between them (see Figure 19.12). The second cone looks like a reflection, right? Well, yes, sort of. It looks like a reflection in a perfectly reflective surface such as a mirror, which this backdrop obviously isn't.

7. To make the reflection truly realistic, some of the backdrop has to show through, just as it does with drop shadows. You can make this happen by adjusting the Opacity slider for the reflection layer until the reflection blends in better with the surface. That makes it a lot more realistic, and if you're satisfied with the reflection as it is now, you're done. I think the reflection still looks too perfect, though.

8. I think my problem is that the reflection is head-on to the viewer; using the Skew command can fix that problem in short order. I also blurred the reflection a bit. Check it out in Figure 19.13.

9. Okay, now our composite image is looking pretty good. The cone image is now interacting with the backdrop image, creating a fairly realistic effect. There's just one more thing bugging me: the vertical portion of the backdrop behind the cone. Shouldn't the cone cast just a bit of a shadow behind itself? Well, we can certainly make that happen. Apply the Drop Shadow layer style to the original cone layer to add this shadow, being sure to adjust the light angle so that the shadow falls on the vertical backdrop, not on the reflection (see Figure 19.14).

TRY IT YOURSELF ▼

Add Realistic Reflections to a Surface
continued

FIGURE 19.11
The cone looks out of place in its new environment.

FIGURE 19.12
The duplicate cone flipped, reshaped, and moved down into its place.

FIGURE 19.13
The lower opacity makes the reflection look much more realistic.

FIGURE 19.14
A touch of shadow on the backdrop behind the cone adds to the illusion of space.

10. Finally, back to the filters. Choosing Filter, Render, Lens Flare lets you put just a little extra light reflection at the bottom of the cone so that there's an obvious reason for the shadow. Figure 19.15 wraps it all up in one.

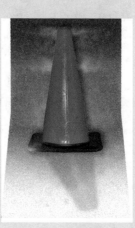

FIGURE 19.15
Now the cone's shadow and reflection look as though they belong there.

Well, I'm satisfied; the final image looks like all of a piece instead of like a cone floating alongside with some random, unrelated pixels. That's what special effects such as reflections can accomplish for you.

Making Notes

If you're in love with sticky notes (and really, how can you not be?), you're going to love Photoshop's Note tool; it's even better than real sticky notes because the notes can never fall off. Switch to the Note tool (it's behind the Eyedropper in the toolbox), and then click the picture anywhere you want to add a note. You can even insert notes outside borders of the picture. Each note is indicated with a sticky-note icon; clicking the icon with any tool displays that note's text in the Notes panel (choose Window, Notes if you don't see it).

Notes are a great feature if you pass pictures back and forth with other members of a workgroup. I also use notes when I first download a bunch of photos from my camera and want to make notes about what to work on when I have time. Figure 19.16 shows a photo that needs a lot of work, with its accompanying notes on what its specific problems are. These will be visible to anyone who views the image in Photoshop.

If a note obscures something you want to see in the image, you can drag the note's icon to another location. To get rid of a note, either drag its icon completely out of the image window or click it and then click the trash button on the Notes panel.

FIGURE 19.16
The pencil icon indicates which note's text is visible in the Notes panel.

Printing Contact Sheets

These days, people are more likely to shoot with digital cameras and print with their own photo printers than take film to the camera shop to get it developed. But one of the services camera shops provide is still quite useful, even when you're working with digital images: producing contact sheets. It shouldn't surprise you to learn that Photoshop can create these for you.

In a traditional darkroom, the first thing you usually do with a roll of film is make a contact sheet so that you can see what you've shot before you spend the time to make larger prints. And this practice still comes in handy with digital photography. For one thing, you don't have to sit in front of your computer to review the photos in a contact sheet, and you can pass the sheet around a room instead of having everyone gather in front of a single monitor.

The first step is to drop the images for the contact sheet into their own folder; if you want, you can even create subfolders inside the main folder. Then choose File, Browse in Bridge to open Bridge.

FIGURE 19.17
In Photoshop CS4, Bridge is in charge of outputting contact sheets.

First, click the Output button at the top of the Bridge window to switch to Output mode. In the left pane, click Folders and choose the folder from which you want to make your contact sheet (see Figure 19.17). Now, in the right pane, click PDF in the Output pane; then choose a template from the pop-up menu. For this purpose, your choices are 4×5 Contact Sheet and 5×8 Contact Sheet. Click the disclosure triangle labeled Document to see the paper size settings. Choose a paper size that your printer can handle. The Low Quality setting is usually good enough to see what's going on in thumbnail images, and using a lower resolution produces a faster-printing document.

Next, view the Layout settings just below the Document area. If you want to change the number of photos displayed on each page of the contact sheet, enter the number of rows and columns you want on each page. Finally, check the boxes labeled Use Auto-Spacing and Rotate for Best Fit to allow Bridge to make the best use of the available space on each page. When you click Refresh Preview at the top of the Output pane, Bridge goes to work all on its own to create a new contact sheet document. When Photoshop has finished its part of the job, you can scroll down to the very bottom of the Output pane and click Save to create a PDF file of this contact sheet, which you can then print just like any other PDF file. Figure 19.18 shows a typical contact sheet, with the pictures arranged neatly in alphabetical order.

FIGURE 19.18
Each photo's filename appears below the thumbnail as a title.

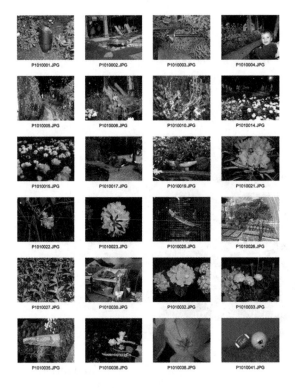

Summary

Learning to get more out of Photoshop isn't really about specific instructions and narrowly defined settings—it's about experimenting with all the features the program has to offer and taking advantage of your new discoveries. As you use Photoshop's features (especially its filters) more and more, you'll develop an endless stream of fun effects and useful techniques. This hour is just a small taste of what's possible.

Q&A

Q. How do I place a reflection on an image of water?

A. You can create a watery reflection in much the same way you put a reflection on the backdrop in this hour, except that you might want to apply the Ripple filter to the reflection layer, as well as blur it.

Q. I'm a teacher; I've taken photos of all the kids in my class, and I want to post them on the bulletin board. Is there an easy way to print the pictures all at the same size, with the kids' names underneath?

A. That's not hard at all. First, make sure that each child's name is the filename for the image of that kid, then put all the files into a single folder. Open Bridge, click the Output button, and click the PDF Output button. Then choose an appropriate contact sheet template; customize the number of columns and rows, if necessary. You can even print only one image per sheet, if you'd like. When the contact sheet document is complete, click Save; then print the resulting PDF file. Ta-da!

Q. Just how did you learn to do all this? It all seems so complicated.

A. I learned the same way you're learning—one step at a time. Each time I wanted to do something that I knew Photoshop could accomplish, I just kept trying things until I got the image to look the way I wanted. I use Photoshop in my work almost every day, and, of course, I learn a lot that way, but I've learned just as much from experimenting with personal projects such as party invitations, joke websites, and photo-related gifts.

Workshop

Quiz

1. How many kinds of preset lighting effects does Photoshop provide?

    A. Three: Spot, Omni, and Directional

    B. Seventeen, including colored spots and multilight patterns

    C. Two: On and Off

2. **True or False:** A glow is a drop shadow that's not offset.

3. How many images can you put on a letter-sized contact sheet?

   A. Up to a dozen

   B. 10

   C. It depends on how small you make them. Photoshop allows you to have up to 100 rows and 100 columns, for a potential total of 10,000 pictures on a single page. However, if the images are any less than a half-inch wide, you might have trouble telling what they are.

Answers

1. B. Take an image with fairly flat lighting and try them all—you'll be amazed by the variation.

2. True. And it's usually in a color other than black.

3. C. I think a reasonable number is 24 to 30 images. Then again, if your eyes are better than mine, more power to you—make those thumbnails as small as you like!

Exercise

Take some time to study reflections. Look at yourself in the door of your microwave. (You might have to polish it first!) Go outside and examine the reflection of trees in water—even in a puddle or a pothole in the street. If you can locate a book of M. C. Escher's drawings and etchings , look in particular for *Three Worlds, Puddle,* and *Rippled Surface*—three well-known nature prints featuring water and reflections. You can also find small images of all three of these works on the National Gallery of Art's website (nga.gov). Imagine what Escher could have done with a copy of Photoshop! If you feel inspired, try creating an Escher-style image showing reflections.

PART VI
Repairing and Enhancing Your Photos

Creating Composite Images

Compositing is often known by other names. You can call it combining pictures, or making a collage, or the art of photomontage. Whatever you call it, however, the goal is the same—to create one image from pieces of other ones—and for several reasons, Photoshop is the ideal program for this kind of work. First, Photoshop offers you all the tools you need to assemble pieces of different pictures. Second, it gives you the capability to place your image components on individual layers so you can manipulate them as much as you want before finalizing the image. Third, its filters, adjustment commands, and styles all enable you to blend pictures, add shadows and reflections, and integrate special effects more easily and effectively than any other graphics program on the market.

You can use the techniques described in this hour, along with all of the ones you've already learned, to produce all sorts of surrealistic images. For many people, this is what Photoshop is all about. For others, compositing is simply a great way to make up for deficiencies in the original picture. Either way, always keep an eye out for good sources of the components you'll assemble to create composite images. These can be photos you've taken yourself, stock photos you've bought online or on a disc, or even photos you've downloaded from other people's websites—*if* you have the photographers' permission to use them.

WHAT YOU'LL LEARN IN THIS HOUR:

▶ Making One Picture from Two (or More)

▶ Tricks to Make Composition Easier

▶ Putting the Pieces Together with Photomerge

Making One Picture from Two (or More)

When I saw a tiny police scooter in New Orleans' French Quarter, I was completely charmed; it's so very different from the police motorcycles we're all used to seeing. So I shot a picture of it. Now, as I look at the image, it seems too static. There needs to be something living in the picture to liven it up. And, in my opinion, almost any photo can be improved with the addition of a greyhound or two. Clearly, the scooter picture needs a greyhound—so let's make that happen. The two images I'll be combining here are both available on the publisher's website: `nolascooter.jpg` (see Figure 20.1) and `oakley.jpg` (see Figure 20.2). Feel free to download them and work along.

FIGURE 20.1
The officer who rides this probably doesn't think of it as cute, but I can't help it—it is!

FIGURE 20.2
This gorgeous lady's name is Oakley.

Select and copy Oakley, the greyhound, and then open the scooter picture and paste her in. Now, the easiest way to select Oakley is to select her white background with the Magic Wand. You'll want to lower the tolerance to about 10 to make sure you don't include any of her lighter-furred areas in the selection. Then invert the selection and feather it slightly, and you're ready to copy. Figure 20.3 shows the image after Oakley has been transported to New Orleans.

FIGURE 20.3
We've got Oakley where we want her, but her size is a bit off—greyhounds are large dogs, but not *that* large.

After we've reduced Oakley to a more realistic size, using Edit, Transform, Scale, she still doesn't look natural, but we can try a few tricks that should help that. First, she needs a shadow. If you look at the scooter, you'll see that its shadow is almost directly under it (I must have taken this picture around lunchtime). So Oakley's shadow needs to match that position, as well as the color. Figure 20.4 shows the image and the Layers panel so you can see the shadow I painted with a big soft brush using a color I picked up with the Eyedropper from the street under the scooter. I put the shadow on its own layer, so it wouldn't cover up any part of Oakley, and I set the layer to 80% Opacity and Overlay blending mode. That ensures that the sidewalk shows through the shadow.

TIP

Controlling Transparency

It's extremely simple to paste one opaque image over another one—just do it. Transparent objects such as shadows are more complicated to work with, which is why Photoshop gives you opacity controls. When you're creating a multilayered picture, as in Figure 20.5, you can control the way the layers blend in two ways. One is by using the Opacity slider in the Layers panel. You can set any degree of opacity, from 100% all the way down to zero, at which point the contents of the layer completely disappear. You can also control how layers combine by using the Blending Mode pop-up menu at the top of the Layers panel. By applying different modes to different layers, you can control the way the colors in each layer overlay what's underneath them.

FIGURE 20.5
The key to realistic composites is matching the lighting.

There's no way to determine which brush and Opacity settings to use, other than trying different ones to see what works best. The only things I could be sure of were the color and position of the shadow, because I could see where the shadows of other objects in the image were falling relative to the objects themselves. Experimenting with the other parameters gives you a chance to play with the shadow, to make it harder or softer, bigger or smaller, until it looks right.

Finally, a Levels adjustment on Oakley's layer and then some burning along her front, along with a slight application of a warming photo filter, helps a lot to match the apparent lighting on the two layers. Figure 20.5 shows the finished photo. Oakley looks ready to hop right on the scooter and zoom off to find some gumbo and pralines.

Creating Realistic Composites

Creating an image that's not meant to be completely realistic is relatively easy. As you've seen so far in this hour, faking realism is a lot harder. The main tasks to consider in making composites are the following:

▶ Isolating the elements on different layers for easier editing

▶ Keeping the edges of pasted elements smooth so that they don't stand out too much against the background

▶ Making sure that the pieces you combine are in proper scale with each other

▶ Matching the lighting and shadows in all the elements of a composite

These become even more important when the elements in a composite don't naturally belong together. When objects seem at home together, viewers are more likely to overlook glitches in lighting or scale. But when you're putting things outside their normal milieu, viewers are already alert to the incongruity and will notice small discrepancies right away.

I'm a summer person; I love lush, green landscapes. One of the shots in my collection is just such a scene (see Figure 20.6). Let's see what happens when we drop the scooter from downtown New Orleans into the middle of that wooded landscape. The scooter will definitely seem out of place, so we'll have to work even harder than usual to make it look as though it's really part of the original photo. This image, woods.jpg, is also available on the publisher's website.

CAUTION

Learning from the Real Expert

As you know, adding shadows, reflections, and other lighting-related special effects can make a big improvement in the final image. Watch out for perspective, too. If it's wrong, you'll know it, even when you can't explain exactly why you're not comfortable with the image. How can you get better at putting these elements together? The key is observation. When you're walking around town or sitting in a well-lit room, notice where the shadows appear and how the light source affects the angle at which they fall from the objects causing them. Watch for reflections, too. When you understand how nature does it, you'll be able to fake it more accurately in your images.

FIGURE 20.6
This is what summer looks like in the woods of New Hampshire.

The first step is to extract the scooter from its background and then to bring it into the new setting. The scooter will probably need some color adjustments, but we'll do those after it's in place. I can do most of the selecting with the Quick Selection tool, but some cutouts will need extra work. For those, I'll switch to Quick Mask mode and use the Brush and Eraser tools to refine the selection. Remember to zoom in when you have a complicated object to trace. As you can see clearly in Figure 20.7, it's much easier to pick up the details when you zoom way in on the object you're tracing.

FIGURE 20.7
I cleaned up the scooter selection in Quick Mask mode.

Now let's put the scooter in its new home. I can either copy and paste or just drag the selection from one image window to the other. Either way, the scooter comes in on a new layer, which is exactly where I want it. In Figure 20.8, I've dropped it into the woods, but it doesn't look really at home yet.

As I analyze what's wrong with this picture, I see several things. First, the scooter is too big; it needs to be scaled down to fit in with the young trees. Second, its angle is all wrong; the back wheel is poised up in the air. Then, of course, the whole thing is floating in front of everything instead of sitting on the ground. And the lighting is wrong; it doesn't look as though it's sitting under the same sun as the rest of the objects in the woods.

Let's tackle the scooter's size and angle first. I like to make quick fixes like this in Free Transform mode. Press Command-T (Mac) or Ctrl+T (Windows), and then click and drag a corner to resize the bike. Remember to press Shift as you drag, to preserve its proportions. Then click and drag anywhere outside the transform box to rotate the scooter to a more reasonable angle. Press Enter on the numeric keypad, or double-click inside the transform box, when you're done. Figure 20.9 shows a close-up of the results of my transformation.

FIGURE 20.8
It's not really comfortable.

FIGURE 20.9
Now the scooter at least looks as though it's on the same planet as the woods.

Now, what can we do to blend the scooter with its environment a bit more? I know—let's park it *behind* that birch log instead of in front of it. Visual tricks like this go a long way toward convincing an onlooker that objects really belong where you've placed them. To reposition the scooter, use the Lasso tool to select the parts of the scooter that are in front of the log; then switch to the Background layer and choose Layer, New, Via Copy. This creates a new layer that contains just enough log to go in front of the scooter, so drag the new layer above the scooter layer. You'll probably need to clean up the log layer a bit along the top of the log; when that's done, the layer should look like Figure 20.10.

FIGURE 20.10
I've hidden the Background layer so you can see the shape of the new log layer.

The final step is to adjust the brightness of the scooter so that its lighting matches the filtered, slightly dim light in the woods. Fortunately, the angle of the light in both images was similar. So all you need to do is switch to the Burn tool and pick a good-sized, soft-edged brush (mine is 150 pixels), and then set the Range to Highlights and the Exposure to 20%. Give the scooter a few swipes—make sure you're on the right layer!— along its front, over the helmet, and on the seat pillar, where the highlights are a bit too bright. *Now* the little police scooter from the Big Easy looks right at home in the Granite State woods (see Figure 20.11).

FIGURE 20.11
Vroom vroom vroom!

Replacing a Background

Many times, the point of creating a composite image is to give something a
different background, as I did by moving the scooter from a New Orleans
street to the New Hampshire woods. Often the hardest part of the job is
separating the object from its original background. The scooter was fairly
easy to select because its shape was well defined against a fairly flat background, without a lot of picky details. Suppose we took something more
difficult and moved it to the same scene. Consider, for instance, the organ
grinder and his instrument pictured in Figure 20.12.

The Magic Wand won't be much help here. I'll begin by tracing loosely
around the organ with the Polygonal Lasso and then inverting so that I can
delete the outer edges of the picture. Figure 20.13 shows the lassoed organ;
Figure 20.14 shows what's left after removing the background.

FIGURE 20.12
This image won't be easy to
extract; there's a lot going on in
the background, and the shape of
the object itself is irregular.

FIGURE 20.13
This rough selection provides a
starting point for my work.

FIGURE 20.14
There's plenty of cleanup work to
be done around the edges.

You can get rid of the remaining edges around the cart in several ways. You
can use the Eraser tool to remove the edges bit by bit. You can remove some
small parts, but not many, by selecting them with the Magic Wand or the
Quick Selection tool. But the easiest way is to use the Background Eraser.
It's behind the regular Eraser in the toolbox, and it's designed specifically
for this kind of work; it erases pixels to transparency as you drag it.

TRY IT YOURSELF ▼

**Use the Background
Eraser Tool**

Pick a photo with a background you'd like to get rid of, and give the
Background Eraser a whirl.

1. In the Layers panel, activate the layer containing the areas you want to
   erase. (It's easier to see what you're doing if you hide the other layers—
   do that in one step by Option-clicking (Mac) or Alt-clicking (Windows) the
   visibility icon for the layer you want to keep visible.)

2. Switch to the Background Eraser tool, located in the same toolbox slot
   as the Eraser tool.

3. Choose an appropriate brush size and shape using the Brush Picker in
   the Tool Options bar.

4. Choose an erasing mode:

   ▶ Discontiguous erases the color you click on anywhere that it appears in the layer.

   ▶ Contiguous erases connected areas that contain the clicked color.

   ▶ Find Edges erases connected areas containing the color you click, while better preserving the sharpness of object edges as it defines them.

   You can switch modes as often as you like; I used a combination of modes to erase the background in this image.

5. Set the Tolerance by entering a value between 1% and 100%, or by dragging the slider. A low Tolerance setting limits erasing to areas that are very similar to the sampled color, while a higher Tolerance value enables the Background Eraser to delete a broader range of colors.

6. To determine how the Background Eraser chooses colors to delete, choose a sampling option by clicking one of the three buttons to the right of the Brush Picker:

   ▶ **Sampling:** Continuous keeps sampling colors continuously as you drag. Use this option if you want to erase adjacent areas that are more than one color.

   ▶ **Sampling:** Once erases only areas containing the color that you click first. Use this option to erase a solid-colored area.

   ▶ **Sampling:** Background Swatch erases only areas that contain the current Background color or a color similar to it that's within the Tolerance range.

7. Check the box labeled Protect Foreground Color to protect areas that match the Foreground color in the toolbox. At this point, it's a good idea to briefly switch to the Eyedropper tool (press I) and click in the image to change the Foreground color to the one you want to protect.

8. Now you're ready to drag the eraser through the area you want to erase. If you've set your Cursors preference to Normal Brush Tip, the Background Eraser tool pointer appears as an outline of your brush, perhaps with a crosshair indicating the tool's hot spot (check the Show Crosshair in Brush Tip box in Cursors Preferences if you want the crosshair). Otherwise, you'll see a block eraser with a pair of scissors on top, just like its icon. Carefully click and drag, or just click, throughout the area you want to delete. This process is easier if you zoom in on the area to be erased, and you may find that you need to keep trying different Tolerance values as you go.

In Figure 20.15, I've erased most of the background. I used both the
Background Eraser, as described, and the Magic Eraser, which determines
where the chosen color ends and erases to the line of color change. (You
choose the color by clicking it with the Magic Eraser.) The organ still needs
a bit of cleaning up with the regular Eraser, though, particularly between
the spokes in the wheels. After that, I'll be able to slide it into position and
rescale it, if necessary (see Figure 20.16).

FIGURE 20.15
The Background Eraser took away
most of the edges; I've added a
white layer below to make it easier
to see what's going on.

FIGURE 20.16
The cart has moved from downtown Philadelphia to the woods.

Tricks to Make Compositing Easier

So far, we've talked about the mechanics of combining multiple image elements into a single composition: selecting objects, positioning them on layers, and adjusting their appearance to make them seem to be parts of a whole. A good chunk of the time you'll spend creating composite images is sheer work, removing backgrounds pixel by pixel and trying to match lighting in different elements. But Photoshop does have a few shortcuts to offer that can speed things up a bit.

Autoaligning and Autoblending Layers

If you're working with an image in pieces—in other words, your images each show part of an element, such as the front of a house—Photoshop's ability to automatically align and blend layers will amaze you. Take a look at Figure 20.17, for example. It shows two separate shots of a baseball field, each of which contains one side of the field. I'd like to put them together into a single image that shows the whole field, and that's exactly what the Auto-Align Layers command can do.

FIGURE 20.17
I want to combine these two images.

The first step is to drag one of the images into the other's window, making it a separate layer in the other image. You don't have to worry about enlarging the canvas to hold it, or lining it up with the other image; Photoshop takes over from here. In the Layers panel, make sure both layers are selected; then choose Edit, Auto-Align Layers. (The command is grayed out unless more than one layer is selected.) Of course, you now have a choice to make; Photoshop can use any of several different methods to align the layers, and you need to pick one (see Figure 20.18). Or, if you're lazy like me, you can just stick with the Auto setting and let Photoshop do the heavy thinking. If your picture is blurry around the edges, check the Vignette Removal box; if the picture was an extreme close-up or was taken with a wide-angle lens, check the Geometric Distortion box to fix any resulting geometric oddities by automatically transforming the image.

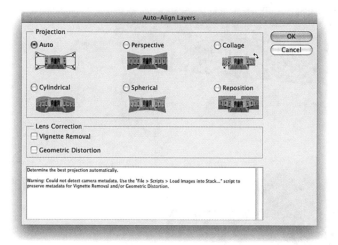

FIGURE 20.18
Photoshop can use any of these methods to put the pieces of my composite together.

Click OK, and in short order you're presented with a revamped image, with an enlarged canvas, if needed, in which the two (or more) layers are aligned perfectly (see Figure 20.19). They're still individual layers, so you can hide and show each one a time or two to see how they fit together.

After that's accomplished, the next job is to get rid of any pesky seams between the two images by blending the layers together. Once again, make sure the layers are selected in the Layers panel and choose Edit, Auto-Blend Layers. Here your choice is between two different Blend Method settings: Panorama and Stack Images. The former works better when there's not much overlap among the layers; use the latter when the images you're blending are just slightly different, as in Figure 20.20. Once again, Photoshop maintains the individual layers, using layer masks to control which layer contributes each part of the image. The result is a seamless image that incorporates the content of both pictures.

FIGURE 20.19
The final image contains the entire field.

FIGURE 20.20
These images were taken from almost the same angle, so the Stack Images option is most appropriate.

Making the Most of Smart Objects

Compositing images involves a lot of transformations; you have to scale objects to fit together, and you might have to adjust perspective or even skew objects so that they work with the rest of the image. Every time you use a Transform command on a layer or selection, Photoshop reshuffles pixels to accommodate its new size and shape. If you do this enough times, you'll end up with a blurry lump of pixels that doesn't look much like the original object at all. Photoshop's Smart Objects feature can prevent that from happening.

When you're working with Smart Objects, Photoshop retains their original size and shape in the back of its mind, so to speak. Any changes you make appear onscreen, but they're not made permanent until you rasterize the Smart Object or save it in a format that forces Photoshop to rasterize it. This means the pixels are reshuffled only once—to put the object into its final form, when you're *sure* of how you want it to be. To make any layer into a Smart Object, just choose Layer, Smart Objects, Convert to Smart Object. After you've made the conversion, you can still move, transform, and apply filters to the layer. Only the Liquify, Lens Blur, and Vanishing Point filters can't be applied to Smart Objects; all other filters turn into smart filters whose settings you can change by double-clicking their entries in the Layers panel (see Figure 20.21).

FIGURE 20.21
As a Smart Object, the scooter can be transformed, filtered, retransformed, and refiltered without damage to the original image element.

TIP

Links in a Chain

Another way to use Smart Objects is to open an image as a Smart Object (choose File, Open As Smart Object). This links the Smart Object to its original file; whenever the original is modified, the same changes appear in your linked version. This is a great trick for logos or other image elements that you drop into lots of other images.

Using Guides

Don't overlook the power of Photoshop's guides and gridlines when you're assembling a composite image. You might think guides are useful only for type-heavy designs—not so! You can use them to line up elements in composites, as well as to make sure that your composition follows the traditional rule of thirds.

Smart guides are particularly useful, since they show up only when you need them. To turn them on, choose View, Show, Smart Guides. That's all there is to it; with smart guides turned on, you'll see a subtle pink guideline any time you move a layer near the edge or center of another layer's content (see Figure 20.22). Let the layer snap to the guide to line up the objects, or ignore it completely—it's up to you.

FIGURE 20.22
Smart guides show up when you
need them and disappear when
you don't.

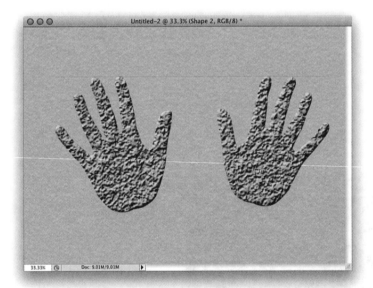

Regular guides are easy to add to your image; just choose View, Show, Rulers, and then click and drag out into the image from either ruler to create a guide parallel to that ruler. Move any existing guide by Command-clicking (Mac) or Ctrl+clicking (Windows) it and dragging it to a new position, or back to the ruler to delete it. For a screenful of guides in a convenient grid, choose View, Show, Grid.

You can also use Photoshop's grid to help you comply with the rule of thirds, a centuries-old composition guideline for artists. The idea is simple: Divide the image into three rows and three columns, and keep strong horizontal or vertical lines near those lines, while placing the objects on which you want viewers to focus at their intersections. To create a rule-of-thirds grid in your images, press Command-K (Mac) or Ctrl+K (Windows) to open Photoshop's preferences, and then click Guides, Grid, and Slices on the left. In the Grid area, set the Gridline Every value to 33.33% and the Subdivisions value to 1. Back in your image, choose View, Show, Grid to see the rule-of-thirds grid (see Figure 20.23).

FIGURE 20.23
Keeping the horizon near the lower gridline prevents it from cutting the image in half.

Putting the Pieces Together with Photomerge

People have been sticking photos together to create wider images—traditionally called panoramas—for close to a hundred years, with varying degrees of success. The theory is simple enough: Take a picture, then take another picture of what's right next to it. Print the two and line 'em up, and you're all set. In life, however, things rarely work out that well. Even a slight difference in angle can make it impossible to match the two images manually, and you also have to deal with subtle differences in lighting and focus. Altogether, it's really rather amazing that panorama artists have done as well as they have over the years. Wikipedia's article on panoramic photography (http://en.wikipedia.org/wiki/Panoramic_photography) features some great examples of early and modern panoramas. These days, thanks to clever software, it's easier than it's ever been to get good results with panoramic photography.

Working with Photomerge

Photomerge automates the process of assembling a panorama. After you've gone out and taken the photos, you plug your camera or memory card into the computer and download the pictures. Then you open Photoshop, bring up Photomerge, and tell it where to find the pictures you want to use. By the way, you'll find the command hidden near the bottom of the File, Automate submenu. Figure 20.24 shows the dialog box. Click Browse and navigate to the folder that contains your individual images, and then choose the pictures you want to use to compose the panorama. If your panorama has some inconsistencies with brightness and contrast, try the Blend Images Together option. It blends together areas of color, while retaining detail. The effect is a softening of these differences, making the panorama seem more like a whole image rather than a collection of images. (It works the same way as the Auto-Blend Layers command.) Finally, choose a Layout option (the thumbnail images show you how each one handles your pictures) and then click OK.

FIGURE 20.24
It's easiest if you drop all the component pictures into a single folder so you don't have to go hunting for them.

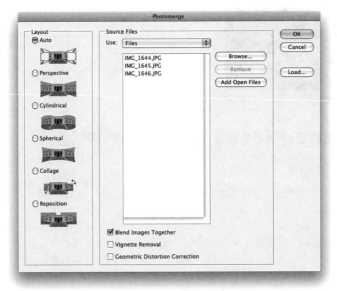

When you click OK, the magic begins. First, Photoshop opens all the photos you specified and creates a new image file in which to assemble them. Then it arranges the images in order, matching the edges wherever they overlap (see Figure 20.25).

FIGURE 20.25
A panorama doesn't have to be a sweeping landscape. You can use any photos of adjacent areas to create your panoramic images.

The Layout options in the Photomerge dialog box affect how Photoshop assembles your panorama. Most of the time, you'll want to choose Auto, which lets Photoshop figure out the best way to put together the component photos. If you choose Perspective, Photoshop adjusts your images to try to compensate for the different angles at which they were taken. Cylindrical adjusts for perspective in a slightly different way that results in a more rectangular final image. Spherical is for images that originally appeared on a spherical surface, and Collage allows Photoshop to apply translation, rotation, or isotropic scaling as needed to match up the pieces of the panorama. Reposition doesn't do any adjustment in size or shape—it just stitches the photos together.

It's still up to you to crop the picture, if you want to. Some photographers argue that the slanting edges and unevenness of the "raw" panorama somehow add to the experience. Others, myself included, prefer to crop. A lot depends on whether, and how, you intend to print the picture.

Considerations When Shooting a Panorama

Here are a few things to keep in mind when you head out to take pictures for a panoramic image:

▶ Be sure you hold the camera steady at one height. Don't take it away from your eye while you're shooting. If you get interrupted in the middle, start over. If possible, use a tripod to keep the camera steady. Remember, digital photos don't waste film, so you can take as many as you have room for on your storage media.

▶ Don't change the focus and zoom levels once you've started shooting.

▶ Don't use a flash, especially an automatic flash, which will throw varying amounts of light as it sees a need. These differences make the exposure all but impossible to correct. If your camera allows, turn off autoexposure and choose a suitable exposure value for the available light; you can try a couple of test shots and preview them on your LCD to check the value.

▶ Use a normal lens, not a wide-angle lens, for best results. Set your zoom lens about halfway between zoom and telephoto, and leave it there. Wide-angle and fisheye lenses distort the focus, which precludes having everything in the same focus. And nothing distorts more than a fisheye lens.

▶ Make sure you have a decent amount of overlap between pictures; around 20% is good. As you pan across the scene, remember what's on the right side of each picture you take and be sure it's included on the left of the next shot.

▶ Take a picture of something clearly different between shooting panorama sequences, to help you keep groups of picture straight.

Summary

In this hour, we looked at the many Photoshop features that make it the best program around for creating composite images: its powerful layer capacities, a wide variety of filters and adjustments, and the capability to control opacity and layer-blending modes. You learned the principles of creating realistic composites, especially that matching both lighting and scale are key steps. We looked at compositing shortcuts, including the clever use of guides, automatic layer alignment and blending, and the use of Smart Objects to avoid resampling elements more than necessary. Finally, we covered the art of panorama photography and saw how Photoshop can make anyone into a panorama artist with a minimum of effort.

Q&A

Q. I tried importing a building into another photo, but it just doesn't look right. Why not?

A. There can be a dozen reasons, but the three most obvious are scale, perspective, and lighting. The new object might be too big or too small for its new location, or its perspective might need to be transformed to match the rest of the image. You might also be trying to match lighting situations that are too disparate; you'll rarely be successful putting a piece of a brightly lit noontime picture into a shadowy late afternoon background. When you choose pictures to combine, try to match both orientation and time of day; matching sizes is nice, but it's also the easiest fix to make in Photoshop.

Q. When I'm creating multilayered images, my files get so big that it takes forever to save or to apply a filter. What should I do?

A. If you find that Photoshop is slowing down because of the size of your files, you can try merging layers when you're done with them; the fewer layers in the image, the smaller the file. Be sure to save frequently, and use the Save a Copy option in the Save As dialog to preserve different stages if you think you might want to go back further than the History panel can take you. Finally, try any of the options in the Edit, Purge submenu to remove copied data or unneeded history states from Photoshop's memory.

Q. When I copy and paste a selection, I often end up with a white halo around the object. How can I get rid of it?

A. Not surprisingly, Photoshop has a command intended to do just that. Activate the layer in the Layers panel and choose Layer, Matting, Defringe. Enter a value in the Width field for the distance from the edge of the object to search for replacement pixels. In most cases, a distance of 1 or 2 pixels is enough, but you'll need to use a higher value if your image is very high-resolution. Click OK, and that white edge is gone.

Workshop

Quiz

1. **True or False:** Any picture you download from the Web can be considered a stock photo.

2. What's the most important thing to master in order to produce good composite images?

    A. Zen

    B. Filters

    C. Layers

3. What's the easiest way to remove a plain background?

    A. Erase it

    B. Select it and delete it

    C. Fill it with clear paint

Answers

1. **False.** Just because an image is posted on the Web doesn't mean that it's free for the taking. Someone took the photograph, and that person usually owns the copyright to it. You should always get permission to use images that you've found on the Web, even on your personal website. On the other hand, if you're just messing around with Photoshop at home and you won't be redistributing the resulting images to anyone, you're probably safe.

2. **C.** Using layers is indispensable when it comes to putting together composite images; they enable you to manipulate individual elements of the image without affecting others.

3. **B.** Of course, you can do this in many ways: You can use the Magic Wand or the Quick Selection tool to select a plain background and then delete it, or you can use the Magic Eraser to delete the whole background with a single click.

Exercise

Pick out two of your own pictures or two stock photos—one a landscape and one a portrait of a person or animal. Remove the background from the portrait subject and transfer the subject in the landscape. Adjust the lighting as needed, and add shadows or reflections to make the person or beastie look as if he or she were actually photographed in that location.

Repairing Black-and-White Photos

The digital camera has taken over for the old-fashioned film camera, that's for sure. Unfortunately, buying a digital camera doesn't automatically turn all your old photos into digital images. So there they sit, in their albums and at the bottom of dresser drawers, just waiting for you to rediscover them and make them part of your new, 21st-century photo collection—the one on your computer. However, many of these photos have sustained some damage during their lifetime on paper. So once you've scanned them, getting them in shape may require you to do some repair work. That's what we talk about in this hour and the next one.

We start by looking at some repair techniques that you can use on black-and-white or color images. In this hour, I show you the basics of retouching; in the next hour, we'll look at a whole range of color-related problems that don't come up with black-and-white pictures, and we'll try out some solutions for them. In both hours, we'll also be looking at ways to "fix" things about an image that aren't technically *wrong,* but that you don't like, such as intrusive extra people in the background of a portrait and power lines that spoil a landscape.

Easy Fixes

Let's start by looking at some of the things you can do to fix an old picture that's faded, yellowed, damaged—or all three. First, we'll examine a couple of my old family photos that need a little bit of touching up. We'll run through the steps required to fix them and the tools you'll need to know how to use along the way. (Remember, you can always flip back to earlier hours in the book to refresh your memory about how these tools and commands work.) Finally, we'll start with an extremely damaged picture and work through repairing it step by step, until it looks like new again.

Some pictures don't need very much work. The photo in Figure 21.1 has discolored over the years, and it was pretty grainy to start with. This photo could also use a little less contrast, and it needs the right half cropped away. The original is sepia tinted, but this picture would probably look just as good or better in grayscale.

FIGURE 21.1
This picture needs relatively minor repairs.

To fix this picture, I first break out the Crop tool to remove the right half (check out that censor's stamp!) and trim the bottom edge a bit. My next step is to choose Image, Adjustments, Black & White and pick a preset (I used the Red Filter) to remove the picture's sepia color and staining; then I set the image's color mode to Grayscale. This takes care of the color issues and also improves the contrast. Next, I use Curves (choose Image, Adjustments, Curves) to tweak the contrast a little more and lighten the image. By using Curves, I can lighten the picture's light and medium gray tones without affecting the dark areas. In Figure 21.2, the very slight curve in the Curves dialog shows exactly how subtle this adjustment is.

In Figure 21.3, you can see the image's improved contrast. Now you can see the difference between the texture of the hat and that of the hair, and the enhanced highlights on the face bring out the facial features. From here, the main concern is smoothing out the picture's overall graininess and its blotchy background.

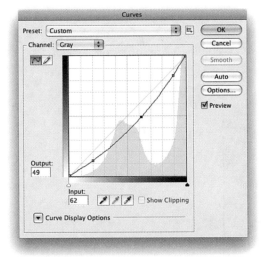

FIGURE 21.2
The curve adjustment is very
slight.

FIGURE 21.3
Better, but not quite there yet

For the clean-up phase of this restoration, I started by applying the
Despeckle filter, followed by a fairly heavy dose of the Dust & Scratches
filter. Then I switched to the History Brush and specified the history state
just before I applied the two filters so that I could paint back in the
detailed, sharp original eyebrows, eyes, and lips. Finally, I decided that

smoothing out the background was more trouble than it's worth, so I selected it with the Quick Selection tool, filled the selection with 30% gray, and applied the Texturizer filter to keep the background from looking too flat. The result, shown in Figure 21.4, is much better.

FIGURE 21.4
Well-preserved photos, regardless of age, can be digitally improved.

CAUTION

To Dust or Not to Dust

Applying the Dust & Scratches filter (choose Filter, Noise, Dust & Scratches) to every scanned photo can be a big mistake because, although it does make dust particles less obvious, it also softens the focus of the picture. If you decide to try it, evaluate the results carefully. Use the Preview check box to toggle back and forth, turning the filter preview on and off until you're certain that it's an improvement. And if you decide that you need it for the majority of the picture, use the History Brush as I did here to restore detail where needed.

Here's another fairly old photo, shot in 1948. This one is in much worse shape. It is both soft and contrasty, and the black tones are bluish. It has sun damage, and it's yellowing around the edges, too. Figure 21.5 shows the untouched photo. Can we rescue it?

We'll start by cropping the image once again, and then we'll remove the color by choosing Image, Adjustments, Black & White. The Yellow Filter preset improves the picture's contrast quite a bit. After the picture has been converted to grayscale, we can switch modes (choose Image, Mode, Grayscale), which, incidentally, reduces the file size quite a bit (see Figure 21.6).

Contrast is still an issue with this picture; I'd like to pull more detail out of the shadows without blowing out the highlights. A quick way to do that is to choose Image, Adjustments, Shadows/Highlights, which enables me to lighten the shadows without lightening areas of the image that are already light enough. Figure 21.7 shows the corrections so far.

FIGURE 21.5
This one needs more serious work.

FIGURE 21.6
Cropping gets rid of some of the problems by removing the affected parts of the picture.

FIGURE 21.7
Shadows/Highlights is the perfect tool to adjust the contrast.

Using the Eyedropper

Now that we can see more of the image's details, it's easier to tell where we need to do some touch-up work. I'm seeing a lot of dust, along with a scratch right down the baby's face. First, I'll try the Dust & Scratches filter (choose

Filter, Noise, Dust & Scratches) to see if it can get rid of some of these flaws without softening the picture; with a Radius setting of 3, it does an acceptable job, so I can move on from there. The scratch is still there, so I'll have to paint over it. That's where the Eyedropper tool enters the picture (no pun intended!).

When you need to paint over part of the image, either to fill in scratches or to remove unwanted lines, spots, or relatives, you can use the Eyedropper tool to choose a color with which to paint. Switch to the Eyedropper and click on any color (or, in this case, any shade of gray) in the image that you want to replicate. That color becomes the Foreground color, which you can apply with any Painting tool. You can also press the Option (Mac) or Alt (Windows) key while you're using a Painting tool to temporarily switch to the Eyedropper so that you can change colors on the fly as you paint. A pop-up menu on the Eyedropper's Options bar gives you the choice of using a single-pixel color sample or of taking an average color from a larger sample, which can range from 3 pixels to 101 pixels square.

With the Eyedropper, Brush, and Smudge tools, we'll repair the damage. All you need to do is to pick up the appropriate background grays from elsewhere in the picture, paint or Clone Stamp the tints in, and then smudge the area a little bit so that it blends with its surroundings. In Figure 21.8, you can see the result of these efforts.

FIGURE 21.8
Compare this to the original image.

When the area to work on is very small, I like to use a very small, very soft brush, and I set it for only 20% pressure so that my brush strokes don't show. When you're making corrections this small, it's much easier to apply them gradually and let the effect build up, rather than trying to do it all in one pass and ending up with an exaggerated effect.

Using the Clone Stamp

The Clone Stamp tool enables you to copy small pieces of a picture to locations elsewhere in the same image. It samples from a chosen point in the image, duplicating the area around that point exactly as if you had made a rubber stamp of it. Figure 21.9 shows the Clone Stamp tool and its Options bar. To use the Clone Stamp, you choose a brush shape, a blending mode, and an opacity level, as you would with any other Painting tool. Then you Option-click (Mac) or Alt-click (Windows) to specify a reference point, after which you start painting. Instead of laying down the Foreground color, you "paint" in a duplicate of the reference point's surroundings, expanding the duplicated portion of the image as you continue to paint. In theory, you could reproduce the entire image if you had enough blank canvas.

If you click off the Aligned box in the Options bar, the stamp behaves somewhat differently. After you specify a reference point and start cloning, the duplicate portion of the image grows only while you press the mouse button. When you release it and press it again, you start creating another duplicate from the same reference point.

FIGURE 21.9
The Clone Stamp tool's icon looks just like a rubber stamp.

To specify a point from which to clone, press Option (Mac) or Alt (Windows) as you click the mouse on the spot you want to copy. Then release the key and start stamping by moving the cursor to a different location and clicking or clicking and dragging. The crosshairs show the spot you're cloning from, and the brush cursor shows where you are stamping (see Figure 21.10). A partially transparent preview of the clone, called an overlay, hovers under your cursor to help you choose exactly the right spot to click.

FIGURE 21.10
The overlay shows you what will appear where you click.

The Clone Source panel (choose Window, Clone Source) enables you to set multiple clone sources (up to five of them!) and switch back and forth among them. To set a new clone source, click one of the buttons at the top of the panel and proceed as you normally would with the Clone Stamp tool. Clicking any of the five buttons when the Clone Stamp tool is active switches you to that clone source.

NOTE

It's All Part of the Pattern

The Pattern Stamp tool, which occupies the same toolbox slot as the Clone Stamp tool, lets you stamp a pattern instead of cloning part of the image. To make your own pattern, use the Rectangular Marquee to select any piece of an image, and choose Edit, Define Pattern. When you use the Pattern Stamp tool, if you choose Aligned, the pattern is tiled as if you started stamping from the upper-left corner of the document, no matter where you drag. If you uncheck the Aligned box, the pattern tiles from wherever you start dragging.

The Clone Source panel also enables you to turn off the overlay cursor, if you find it intrusive, and back on again, as well as change its opacity and blending mode. These changes don't affect the actual cloned pixels—only their preview in the overlay cursor. The X and Y fields in the Offset area allow you to lay down a clone a specified distance away from the cursor, and the Width and Height percentage fields can enlarge or reduce the clone as it's created.

When you use the Clone Stamp tool to retouch a photo, always choose a soft-edged brush in a size just slightly larger than the scratch or blemish you're trying to hide. You'll find that retouching is generally easier if you zoom way in on the image first.

Using the Healing Brush and Patch Tools

From the very beginning, retouching has been one of the major reasons that people cite for buying and learning to use Photoshop. Recognizing this, the folks at Adobe have created some tools specifically designed to touch up your photos: the Healing Brush, the Spot Healing Brush, and the Patch tool.

The Healing Brush, whose icon looks like a Band-Aid, can be applied to any kind of spot that you want to remove, whether it's a part of the original image or not (freckle or dust spot—it's all the same to the Healing Brush). Instantly, the mark is gone, without affecting anything but that spot. Photoshop uses some fairly complicated math to average the texture, lighting, and shading of each group of pixels so that it can locate the ones that are out of the normal range. Those nonconforming pixels represent the offending spot, and they're simply replaced by pixels that match the average tone and texture that Photoshop calculates "should" be there. Of course, you can heal any kind of surface with the Healing Brush, not just skin.

When using the Healing Brush, you Option-click (Alt-click) to choose a source from which to copy pixels. The big difference between the Healing Brush and the Clone Stamp is that the Clone Stamp just copies and pastes pixels from the specified location, whereas the Healing Brush also blends the replacement pixels into the original ones at the new location, making changes much less obvious. In Figure 21.11, I've tried to clean up the zits on the man's cheek and neck with both the Clone Stamp, on the left, and the Healing Brush, on the right. You can judge for yourself which one looks better. The main thing you need to be careful about with the Healing Brush is that if you apply it very close to an area of a contrasting color, it will pick up extra pixels of that color and average them into the correction

as well, making a darker or lighter spot where you applied the correction.
You can mask contrasting areas before you start working with the Healing
Brush, or you can just stick with the good old-fashioned Clone Stamp in
such places.

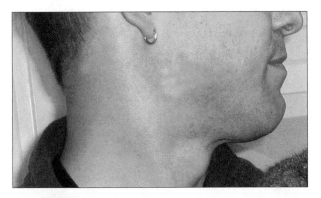

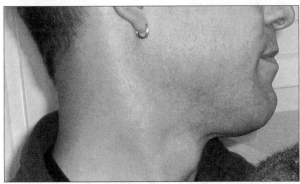

FIGURE 21.11
On the top is the image I cleaned
up with the Clone Stamp. On the
bottom, you see the same skin,
cleaned with the Healing Brush
and the Spot Healing Brush.

The Spot Healing Brush is like a quick-and-dirty version of the Healing
Brush—or maybe that should be quick-and-clean. Instead of defining a
point from which to copy new pixels and then painting, all you do with
the Spot Healing Brush is click on the spot you want to eliminate.
Photoshop looks at the area around the spot, averages the colors it finds,
covers the spot with the average color, and blends the repair with its surroundings—all in about half a second. For slightly larger spots, you can
click and drag, but make sure that the spot you're trying to eliminate is
located in the middle of a relatively uniform area so that the tool doesn't
pull in different-colored pixels from an adjacent area.

For cleaning up larger areas, you can take advantage of the Patch tool. Like the Healing Brush tool, it matches the texture, lighting, and shading of the sampled pixels to those of the surrounding pixels in the new location. It feathers the edges of the patches you place, too, so it blends the new pixels with the old ones. To use the Patch tool, you must first decide whether the piece you select should be the source of your patch or the destination for it, and click the appropriate button on the Options bar. The tool cursor for the Patch Tool is a lasso. In Source mode, select the area you want to replace, then drag the shape you've lassoed over the stuff you want to replace it with, and Photoshop does the rest. In Figure 21.12, you can see how I am using the Patch tool the other way, in Destination mode, to remove the power lines visible against the sky. I've already done a piece on the left, and now I've just dragged the lassoed piece of clean blue sky over the power line on the right side. When I release the mouse button, the patch will fill in the area under the cursor.

FIGURE 21.12
The Patch tool works like the Lasso when you use it to make a patch selection, but you can also use any Selection tool to make the selection. Then click the Patch tool and continue to make the repair.

In the following Try It Yourself section, you'll use the Healing Brush, Spot Healing Brush, and Patch—and probably all the tricks in the book.

Cleaning Up a Picture, Step by Step

As you can see in Figure 21.13, this picture has been folded, faded, and generally beaten up. We'll go through this one step by step so that you can see exactly what happens at each stage. You can download this one from the publisher's web site and follow along. It's called spars.jpg.

FIGURE 21.13
This vintage portrait will take some work before it can be displayed.

TRY IT YOURSELF ▼

Restore a Badly Damaged Photo

To make this picture, or any other, look like new, follow these steps carefully:

1. Crop the image to remove the border, if there is one, and any unnecessary parts of the picture. (Anything you remove won't have to be retouched, so you're saving yourself a lot of work with this step.) Select the Crop tool from the toolbox. Drag it across the picture, holding down the mouse button, and then use the handles on the cropping border to fine-tune the cropping area. When you like the shape of the cropping area, double-click inside it or press Enter on the numeric keypad to crop the image.

2. Choose Image, Adjustments, Black & White and choose an appropriate preset to remove the colored stains and the brown tones; then choose Image, Mode, Grayscale. The Green Filter preset gives me the best contrast for this image, so I chose that and then bumped up the Blues slider to 41%, to avoid making the shadows too dark.

Restore a Badly Damaged Photo

continued

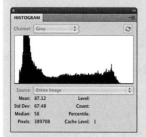

FIGURE 21.14
The histogram shows a lot of dark points and not nearly so many light or medium ones.

3. Open the Histogram panel. Look at the histogram to see what needs to be done to improve the picture's contrast (see Figure 21.14). In this case, both the white and black points need to be reset. To make these changes, you'll need to adjust the levels.

4. Open the Levels dialog box (choose Image, Adjustments, Levels) and adjust the levels by dragging the dark slider to the right until it's under the point where the histogram begins to trend upward. Drag the white slider to the left until it's under the right end of the histogram's graph. Then drag the midpoint slider to the right a bit to lighten the medium tones in the image. Figure 21.15 shows these adjustments.

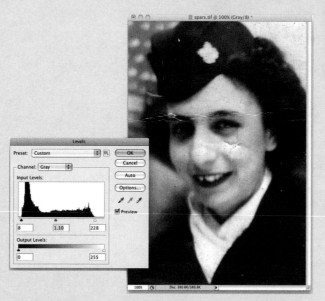

FIGURE 21.15
Adjusting the image's levels improves the contrast.

5. Now we'll try the Dust & Scratches filter (choose Filters, Noise, Dust & Scratches). Because it can blur the image, using this filter is always a roll of the dice. In this case, it seems that the improvement Dust & Scratches makes outweighs the minor damage it also does. In removing the dust, it softens the details just a bit, even at a low setting, but this picture is already pretty soft, so the difference isn't noticeable. (Figure 21.16 shows the filter applied.) Click OK to apply the filter to your own photo, or click Cancel if you don't want to use it.

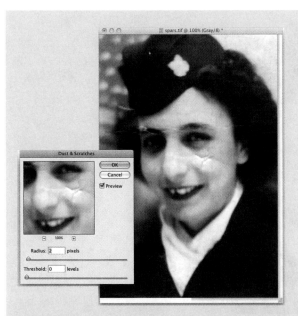

FIGURE 21.16
Removing dust can also remove detail; use the Dust & Scratches filter with caution.

6. Because the Dust & Scratches filter didn't fix all the dust and scratch-
    es in this image, you'll have to remove the rest of the scratches by
    hand. Let's use the Healing Brush to cover them. Switch to the Healing
    Brush and choose Window, Brushes to open the Brushes panel.
    Choose a soft-edged brush. Choose Source: Sampled and make sure
    the Aligned box isn't checked. Remember to set a spot to use as a
    source by pressing Option (Mac) or Alt (Windows) while you click the
    mouse on the spot you want to copy. For small spots located far from
    object edges, try using the Spot Healing Brush with a small, hard-edged
    brush selection. Figure 21.17 shows the partially treated photo.
    Remember to change your source selection as the areas the damage
    runs through change value.

7. Because they cross right through the eyebrow, the best way to remove
    the creases across the face is to use the Brush tool and paint over
    each mark instead of trying to stamp them out. To make the task easi-
    er, enlarge the picture to at least 200%. Switch to the Zoom tool and
    click it in the image window to enlarge the picture, or click and drag a
    marquee around the area you want to focus on to zoom right to that
    location.

▼ TRY IT YOURSELF

Restore a Badly Damaged Photo
continued

FIGURE 21.17
Obviously, I am working in from the right side of the image.

FIGURE 21.18
Be careful not to apply paint too evenly; you don't want the image to lose its surface texture and turn flat.

8. Switch to the Eyedropper tool and click the closest gray adjacent to the scratch. Switching back to the brush, choose a small brush tip and set the Opacity very low so that you can paint over the scratches, changing shades of gray with the Eyedropper as needed. Figure 21.18 shows before and after views of this step.

9. At the same time, you can use a combination of the Spot Healing Brush and the Smudge tool to remove any light spots or small gaps in the image.

10. Next, apply the Dodge and Burn tools as needed to bring out details. Dodging lightens the image, and burning darkens it. Switch to the Dodge tool, choose Shadows in the Range pop-up menu on the Options bar, and set its Exposure value to something low, such as 25%, so that the effect won't be too extreme. Figure 21.19 shows my progress to this point.

11. Now all that's left to do is to select the jacket and try a small amount of Gaussian Blur, or maybe the Surface Blur filter, to smooth out the blotches. Compare Figure 21.20 with the original photo. It's not perfect. It's still a very soft, grainy photo, but it's not folded and mutilated anymore.

FIGURE 21.19
I used the Dodge tool to remove dark shadows under the eyes.

FIGURE 21.20
Now this portrait of Grandma in her World War II Spars uniform is worth framing.

TRY IT YOURSELF ▼

Restore a Badly Damaged Photo
continued

TIP

Toggle Trick

When you're applying filters such as Dust & Scratches, you can instantly switch the filter preview off by clicking in the preview area. When you're pressing the mouse button, the filter effects aren't shown in the preview area. Release the mouse to see the filter previewed again. This technique lets you judge the effect on any particular area of the image.

Applying Tints

Because of photographers' varying preferences for darkroom chemicals, it was common in the early days of photography for pictures to be tinted brown, blue, or silver instead of plain old black-and-white. Sepia toning, which gave a warm reddish-brown color, was very common, and that's the color we tend to associate most with old-time photos.

If you want to restore the original sepia tone to a picture you've been working on, or add a warm brown tint to a photo that didn't start with one, Photoshop gives you several ways to accomplish this. Perhaps the easiest of these is to reset the image's color mode to either CMYK or RGB, depending on whether the finished photo will be viewed onscreen, printed on a desktop printer, or printed commercially, and then use the Hue/Saturation dialog box (choose Image, Adjust, Hue) to add color. After you open the dialog, as shown in Figure 21.21, check both the Colorize and Preview boxes. Then drag the sliders until the image looks the way you want. Don't overlook the Saturation and Lightness sliders; both of these values can make just as much difference in the final effect as the Hue value. Click OK when you're satisfied with the color you've achieved.

FIGURE 21.21
Don't forget to check both Colorize and Preview so you can see what you're doing as you change the settings.

Duotones

A richer color with a wider range of tones can be achieved by using the Duotone color mode, which combines the grayscale image with a colored ink. Duotones are often used in commercial printing to extend the gray range of a photograph because a typical printing press is capable of reproducing only about 50 shades of gray. (Photoshop can generate 256 shades of gray.)

To create a duotone, you need to start with a grayscale image. You don't have to convert it back to RGB or another color mode; just choose Image, Mode, Duotone. In the Duotone Options dialog box, you can also choose to incorporate three or four colors into the image to make it a tritone or a quadtone. Although duotones are usually composed of black plus a single color, as shown in Figure 21.22, there's no reason that you can't use two other colors instead, especially if the end result is to be displayed on a web page or as part of a desktop presentation rather than in printed form.

If you did the last exercise, try applying a duotone to the image. Otherwise, use any photo with a wide range of gray tones. To make a duotone from a grayscale image, follow these steps:

Create a Duotone from a Grayscale Image

1. Choose Image, Mode, Duotone to open the Duotone Options dialog box.

2. Choose Duotone from the Type pop-up menu in the upper-left corner of the dialog to specify that you want to use two ink colors (see Figure 21.22).

3. Choose colors for your duotone by clicking each of the color swatches in turn. Choose black or a dark color for Ink 1 and a lighter color for Ink 2. (Figure 21.22 shows my choices.) You have to use the Adobe Color Picker instead of the system Color Picker so that you can access the Custom colors (that is, colors from ink systems such as Pantone, Focoltone, Toyo, Trumatch, and so on). If you need to switch to the Adobe Color Picker, click Cancel and open the General Preferences dialog by pressing Command-K (Mac) or Ctrl+K (Windows). Set the Color Picker to Adobe and click OK; then start over with step 2.

4. Use the curve proxies within the Duotone Options dialog box to adjust the ink distribution curves for each of your two colors. (They're the small windows with diagonal lines labeled Ink 1 and Ink 2.) If you click one of the small curves, it expands to a full-size curve grid, which works just like the one in the Curves dialog (see Figure 21.23). Click to set points, and then drag them to adjust the curve. You can see the effect of your changes on the image as you work, and you can also monitor the change in how much color is applied to what you're doing using the strip of tone below the curve graph.

▼ TRY IT YOURSELF

Create a Duotone from a Grayscale Image

continued

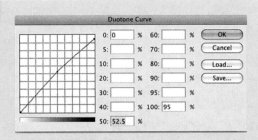

FIGURE 21.23
Here I'm adjusting the curve for Ink 2.

5. Click OK to apply the duotone effect to the image. If you're not satisfied with the result, choose Image, Mode, Duotone again and try a different combination. You don't have to undo the first application; you can change the Duotone mode settings as many times as you want.

TIP

That '50s Look

Using blue as the second color for a duotone, along with black, yields an image that brings to mind the look of an old black-and-white TV set. Using a light-to-medium brown with black, on the other hand gives you a fairly good imitation of old-fashioned sepia-toning, as does a combination of red and green. If you use red and green, though, be sure that you use the same curve settings for both colors; otherwise the image will have unsightly reddish or greenish areas. You may have to convert a duotone image back to RGB or CMYK mode before the image is readable by other applications.

"Hand-Tinted" Photos

Years ago, before color film was readily available and inexpensive enough for the masses to adopt, hand-tinted photos were quite common. These were black-and-white prints painstakingly overpainted with special thinned-out paints to add pale colors to the picture. The Photoshop Brush and its Airbrush option are extraordinarily well suited to re-creating the look of a hand-colored photograph, and with the use of layers, the process is pretty much foolproof.

Start by cleaning up the image that you want to hand-tint, using the techniques you've learned in this hour. Then change the image's color mode to RGB. Make a new layer above the Background layer and set the new layer's opacity to between 10% and 30%. Set the Brush opacity to 80% and paint your tints. Alternatively, leave the layer at 100% opacity, change its blending mode to color, and paint away! You'll see a subtle difference in the effect, and it's easier to get your color everywhere if you're painting at 100% opacity, so you'll probably want to try both methods to see which you prefer.

If you have large, uncomplicated areas to tint, use any of the selection tools, such as the Quick Selection tool, to select the whole area. Choose a Foreground color and choose Edit, Fill; the dialog appears so that you can choose an Opacity percentage and blending mode for the color fill. Set the Opacity to about 25%, and choose Multiply from the Blending Mode pop-up menu. Do *not* check Preserve Transparency; that will prevent your fill from taking effect. In the Use pop-up menu, choose Foreground Color. Then click OK to fill all the selected areas with your chosen color at that opacity and blending mode. If the color isn't intense enough, either choose Edit, Fill and apply the fill again, or undo the Fill operation and redo it with a higher Opacity percentage. If it's too much, undo and try again with a lower Opacity percentage. You can see my finished picture in Figure 21.24.

FIGURE 21.24
Use Fill for large areas; it's faster and smoother than painting.

Vignetting

When you're working with old photos, or with new photos that you want to make look old, *vignetting* is often the trick that makes the difference. It feathers the edges of the image's center, usually in an oval shape, so that the portrait subject comes forward and the background fades to nothing. Here's an easy way to create a vignette.

Draw an elliptical selection marquee around the portrait subject. Choose Select, Modify, Refine Edge and drag the Feather slider until the amount of blur around the edges looks right. Click OK, then invert the selection so that the background is selected. Finally, choose Edit, Fill and set the Use menu to white, Mode to Normal, and Opacity to 100%. Figure 21.25 shows what you see when you click OK.

FIGURE 21.25
A vignetted portrait zeroes right in on the subject.

Summary

In this hour, we looked at several ways that you can repair damaged or otherwise imperfect photographs. If you're working with pictures that are old, cracked, torn, or faded, you can use a variety of Photoshop tools and techniques to cover up the imperfections and restore the image to its original glory. The Eyedropper tool enables you to specify a color or gray tone and apply it with any of the Painting tools. The Clone Stamp puts a perfect copy of selected piece of the picture wherever you want, as much or as little as you need to cover a crack, fill in an empty space, or cover objects that you want to hide. The Healing Brush, Spot Healing Brush, and Patch tools, designed specifically for retouching, can copy the characteristics of a selection and transfer them to another location, maintaining the same lighting, texture, and other aspects of the new location so that the transplanted selection blends in perfectly. To use the Patch tool, you select an area the same way you would with the Lasso tool, whereas the Healing Brush and Spot Healing Brush work like Painting tools, with brush shapes. Tinting old photos to add color can be managed in any of several ways; you can colorize a picture using the Hue/Saturation command or by turning the picture into a duotone, tritone, or quadtone. Hand-tinting can give you a very different "old" look, and vignetting adds to the effect.

Q&A

Q. How can I remove my nasty cousin from a group shot of the family? He's right in front.

A. Perhaps you can find some other face the right size and colors to hide him. (Johnny Depp or Cary Grant, perhaps?) Adjust the size, position, and angle of the new face on a separate layer. Then blur the face you want to hide and use the Layers panel's Opacity slider to bring in the replacement. If you leave the Opacity set at about 80%, the new face should blend right in with the original photo.

Q. I printed some photos on fancy art paper, as you suggested, but my printer jammed up. What did I do wrong?

A. Was the paper specifically designed for use with inkjet printers? If not, you can run into problems when you put it through your printer. There's a huge variety of paper out there made just for inkjet printers, so you're safest sticking with that. If you venture out into unknown territory, be prepared for jams and blurry images. Of course, this isn't to say that experimentation isn't worthwhile—it is!

Q. Okay, I've retouched all the old family photos. What do I do now?

A. The next logical step is to buy a package of photo-quality glossy paper; print lovely, clean new copies of all of your photos; and give them to your entire family as holiday gifts. If you don't have a reasonably good color printer, you can take your photos to a Kinko's or a similar shop and have them printed on a color laser or high-quality inkjet.

Be sure to save the files for future use, too; you might even want to distribute discs containing the files along with the printed images. CDs and DVDs can hold several generations of family photos and can be stored in very little space. One thing you should definitely do is keep a backup copy in a safe place, such as a bank safe-deposit box, so that your precious family history is fire- and flood-proof. You can also put a family album on your web page so that faraway relatives and friends can see how the kids have grown.

Workshop

Quiz

1. Burning is the opposite of:

    A. Covering

    B. Filling

    C. Dodging

2. The Clone Stamp tool places _____ in the image.

    A. Text

    B. A copy of the image area you specify

    C. Random shapes and designs

3. How many colors of ink are used to produce a duotone?

    A. One

    B. One, plus black

    C. Any two, not necessarily including black

4. To remove the sepia toning from an old scanned photo, you can:

    A. Convert the image to grayscale

    B. Adjust the colors using the Variations command to add more cyan

    C. Click the Bleach button in the Options bar

Answers

1. **C.** Dodging lightens the image. Burning darkens it.

2. **B. C** might be fun, though, and you can get partway there if you use the Pattern Stamp tool instead. Try adjusting your brush's Shape Dynamics and Scattering settings to achieve the random placement part, as well.

3. **C.** Although black is most often one of the two colors, it doesn't have to be.

4. **A.** This also helps get rid of colored ink, coffee, or any other light-colored stains you might find on a black-and-white print. It doesn't help much with blood. (That's a joke!)

Exercise

Find a picture that seems in need of retouching, or download an image from this book's page on the Sams website. Clean it up as much as you think is necessary and save a copy of the image with a new name. Then convert the copy to a duotone. Hand-tint the original using transparent tints. The duotone looks something like rotogravure pages from the 1930s, and the hand-colored version looks more like photos or postcards from the '40s or '50s. Try out these techniques with some of your own work or with scanned photos from your family archives.

Repairing Color Photos

Last hour, we worked on some black-and-white pictures that needed help. This hour, we'll do the same with color pictures. In Photoshop, you can adjust the colors to restore a picture that's faded with age or that has too much red, green, or some other color in it. You can compensate for slight-to-moderate underexposure or overexposure. You can take the red out of a person's eyes or the unearthly green out of a cat's eyes. You can even create scenes that never were by adding objects from other images and by modifying what's there. Don't like the blue shirt you were wearing in that photo? No problem—you can make it green, or pink, or whatever other color you like.

Color Retouching

The pictures we retouched in the last hour were old black-and-white photos. In this hour, you'll find that you can use most of the same tricks and techniques in retouching color images. You might even find that color retouching is easier than working in black-and-white because the color tends to help disguise both the image's flaws and your manipulation.

Figure 22.1 is a picture that was taken sometime in the mid-1970s. I don't know what happened to it. Perhaps it was left in the sun—it was taken in south Florida, after all. Maybe it wasn't processed right in the first place. It was way too light to start with, and as you can see by looking at the "green" grass, it's got a decidedly pink tint. Whatever the cause of the picture's problems, I'd like to try fixing them. Feel free to download the picture from the Sams website and work along. It's called swingset.jpg.

WHAT YOU'LL LEARN IN THIS HOUR:

▶ Color Retouching

▶ Editing a Picture's Content

FIGURE 22.1
This picture turned pink over the decades.

▼ TRY IT YOURSELF

Apply a Simple Color Correction to a Photo

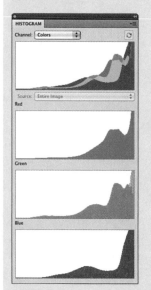

FIGURE 22.2
We need to bring up the mid-tones in all three color channels.

First, look at the Histogram panel, shown in Figure 22.2; I've used the panel menu to switch to All Channels view, turn off Statistics, and show the channels in color. You can immediately see that all three channels don't have much going on at the dark end of the graph; this is confirmed by looking at the composite image, which is obviously overexposed, making it very light. Now, you can also see from the picture that nothing in it, aside from the tire swing, should be particularly dark. But the midtones can definitely use some help.

We could try working with Levels to fix this problem, but Levels won't enable us to darken the blown-out white areas of the image. Curves, however, can do just that (see Figure 22.3), and it can fix the color cast. To adjust the image with the Curves dialog, follow these steps:

1. With the image open, open the Curves dialog (choose Image, Adjustments, Curves).

2. Drag the white point at the top of the curve straight down to darken the image's highlights. Watch the walls of the white houses in the background to gauge the effect of your changes; you don't want to turn them gray, just keep them from being quite so blinding.

3. Next, drag the entire curve's middle downward to darken all the midtones. That improves the picture's contrast quite a bit—now you can see what's happening.

TRY IT YOURSELF ▼

Apply a Simple Color Correction to a Photo
continued

FIGURE 22.3
You can adjust both the channel composite and each of the individual color channels in the Curves dialog.

4. Now choose the color that needs adjusting from the pop-up Channels menu. Choose Red, Green, or Blue if those colors need lessening. If you decide the problem is with cyan, magenta, or yellow, consider the color wheel and choose the complementary color, then increase it. If there's too much yellow, add blue. If there's too much magenta, add green. If there's too much cyan, add red. In this case, we obviously need to increase magenta. But there's no magenta curve, so we'll choose Green instead and increase it.

5. Drag the curve up to increase the amount of the color or down to decrease the amount. Watch the preview as you drag, and click OK when the colors look right (see Figure 22.3).

This photo needs some additional tweaking to increase the saturation now that we've taken out the excess color. It also needs cropping, additional brightness and contrast adjustment, and some spot removal. The final picture, shown in Figure 22.4, is a big improvement.

Fixing Red (and Green) Eye

We've all seen red eye before. It's not a problem in black-and-white photos, but it shows up much more often than most of us would like in color pictures of people and animals taken with a flash camera. It's caused by the flash reflecting off the blood vessels at the back of the eye, which lays an eerie red glow over the pupils of anyone looking straight at the flash. You'll often see a similar phenomenon called **green eye** in photos of animals, which is also caused by the flash reflecting off the back of the eye. You can avoid both green eye and red eye if you make sure that your portrait subject, human or otherwise, isn't looking directly at the flash as you're shooting. Also make sure that there's plenty of light in the room so that the subject's pupils have contracted to as small a size as possible. That's what the preflash feature on many cameras attempts to do, as well—force the pupil to contract before the picture is taken.

You may think red eye is easily fixed these days with a quick application of the Red Eye tool, but this magic solution doesn't work in all cases. For one thing, it doesn't work when the red eye isn't actually red. Figure 22.5 shows a line of hounds suffering from serious green eye. This one was shot in a dim room, and the flash caught all of the dogs staring wide-eyed. If we correct the off-color eyes, it will be an interesting picture. But the Red Eye tool works only with actual red eyes, so we'll have to step in with a manual repair to fix these.

FIGURE 22.5
I don't know how the flash managed to reflect off all the dogs' eyes, considering the different angles of their heads, but we can fix it.

You'll find that this correction is actually quite easy; download `inline.jpg` from the book's website if you want to use the same image I show here. Here's how to do it:

1. Open the image and zoom in on the eyes by clicking the Zoom tool in the image window. I'll start with the dog at the front of the line, a good friend of mine named Gunner.

2. Use the Quick Selection tool to select the parts that need to be corrected, and then choose Select, Refine Edge and adjust as necessary to make sure the entire problem area is included in the selection (see Figure 22.6).

3. Choose the Paint Bucket tool. Set the Foreground color to black or to a dark color from the image—I'm using a chocolate brown because that's the right color for a greyhound's eyes. On the Options bar, set the blending mode to Darken with an Opacity no greater than about 80%. This setting darkens the eye while maintaining the detail; using the Normal blending mode would obscure any highlights Photoshop is able to pull out of the eye.

4. Drop the paint into the selections. If you want to accent the highlights more, use a single-pixel pencil and touch up with white or a light color as needed.

TRY IT YOURSELF ▼

Correct Green Eye

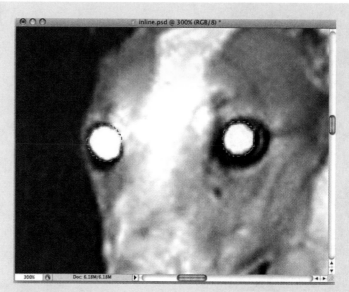

FIGURE 22.6
Gunner's eyes are selected, with the zoom percentage set to 300% so I can see what I'm doing.

5. Press Command-H (Mac) or Ctrl+H (Windows) to hide the selection so that you can evaluate the effect of the change. Figure 22.7 shows how Gunner looks with his eyes brown again.

FIGURE 22.7
The tiny highlights in the pupils are called catchlights. They add a spark of life.

The semi-opaque brown that we poured in effectively darkened the pupils without losing detail. You can use this technique any time you want to change the color drastically in a small area of an image. Be careful not to select any part of the image that you *don't* want to change; to be on the safe side, create a new layer and fill the selection on that layer so that you can clean it up, if needed.

Using the Color Replacement Tool

If the method we just used to fix Gunner's eyes doesn't appeal to you, you'll be glad to know that Photoshop includes a tool created expressly for fixing small spots that need a quick color change. The Color Replacement tool uses the Foreground color selectively to paint over just the color you want to replace. It's quicker than using the previous method, but it might not give as good results with eyes that should be darker (because it doesn't change luminosity), and it can leave a light ring around the edge of the area you're working on. If you find a red (or green, for animals) ring around your corrected eye, you can adjust the Color Replacement tool's tolerance upward so that more of the color will be replaced. Figure 22.8 shows the tool in use, correcting another greyhound's eyes.

FIGURE 22.8
The Color Replacement tool doesn't darken the light spots; it just changes their tint from green to brown. It would work much better on eyes that are supposed to be light in color.

How Much Change Is Okay?

Editing a picture to improve the composition is entirely reasonable, if it's a picture for your own use. Quite different standards apply to photos intended for publication, as the venerable *National Geographic* magazine found out back in 1982. The magazine published an article on Egypt and sent a photographer to get pictures of the country's famous pyramids for a cover photo. After studying the pictures, the art director decided that the composition would be better if he moved one of the pyramids closer to its neighbor. Bad idea! As soon as the issue was published, readers who'd been to Egypt and seen the pyramids at Giza in a distinctly different configuration began calling and writing to the magazine in droves to complain.

The editors apologized for their deceptive image in the following issue, but the incident sparked a raging debate on the nature of authenticity. Now, it seemed, it was impossible to trust that *any* photo in *National Geographic* was genuine. The question has been argued ever since. How much change is okay? How much is too much? Are the rules different for magazines and for newspapers? What about feature articles versus hard news?

It's clear that you can't always believe what you see—that has been the case practically since photography was invented. When we see supermarket tabloids featuring pictures that stretch the bounds of believability, however, we're usually aware that we're not looking at the real thing. Remember the one of the president shaking hands with the space alien? And if a magazine cover model is having a bad hair day or her face breaks out, retouching is considered perfectly reasonable. Where do you draw the line?

My own answer depends on how the picture is to be used. I've created some pretty wacky composite images myself (see Figure 22.9), but reputable newspapers and magazines have strict guidelines about what they'll allow for photo manipulation these days. I think that's a good thing. The general rule tends to be that, if a change affects the content of the photo instead of its appearance, you can't do it. You can lighten a too-dark picture of a politician, but you can't change the soda can in his hand into a beer can (or vice versa).

FIGURE 22.9
Yes, that's a flamingo—it's a long story. I designed this image together with my dad, Richard Binder.

Hany Farid, a computer science professor at Dartmouth College, has put together a great collection of altered photos on his website (www.cs.dartmouth.edu/ farid/research/digitaltampering). It shows the *National Geographic* image and dozens of others, as old as the dawn of photography and as recent as last month, most of them side-by-side with the original, undoctored photos. I highly recommend spending some time checking out Dr. Farid's gallery if you're interested in just how far photo manipulation has come since the early days.

Drag-and-Drop Repairs

Some photos are almost perfect, except for one annoying flaw. Quite frequently, it's power lines running across the sky, and you'll also see litter on the ground in a photo that you never noticed at the time (see Figure 22.10). When the area directly next to the troublesome spot is essentially the same as another part of the image, you can get rid of the clutter by simply lassoing a piece of sky or street or whatever matches and dragging it to cover the offending objects. This technique works well when you have things like power lines or cell phone antennae sticking into the sky, because the uncomplicated background makes it easy to blend the patch with its new location.

Here's a photo of a cathedral in Baltimore, Maryland. I like the picture, but I don't like that streetlight poking the cathedral's spire on the left.

FIGURE 22.10
I could do something with this photo if it weren't for that annoying streetlight.

▼ TRY IT YOURSELF

Retouch a Photo with the Patch Tool

To use the Patch tool to cover up an unsightly object in one of your own photos, follow these steps:

1. Switch to the Patch tool and make sure that the Source button is clicked on the Tool Options bar.

2. Select the area you want to patch over by circling it with the Patch tool. Remember, the Patch tool works just like the Lasso tool for this task.

3. With the selection marquee active, click the selection and drag it to an area of the image that matches the selected area pretty well. (See a close view of this in Figure 22.11.) The match doesn't have to be perfect; Photoshop will blend the patch in with its surroundings.

FIGURE 22.11
Be sure to cover all of the offending object.

4. Repeat as needed to hide any other parts of the picture that you don't want.

Editing a Picture's Content

Having read the sidebar earlier in this hour on altering photos, you now know that the techniques you're learning in this hour should never be used on a news photo. But if you're just playing around for your own amusement, don't worry—the Authenticity Police aren't going to show up on your doorstep.

Replacing Backgrounds

Sometimes you have to remove more than a scratch or a small imperfection from a photo. Sometimes you have to take out a much larger area of the image to save a potentially good picture. Figure 22.12 shows just such a photo. My aunt sent me this in hopes that I could remove the hideously distracting curtain in the background. There's a copy at the book's website, so you can work along. It's called `family.jpg`.

FIGURE 22.12
That curtain needs to come out.

TIP

Another Way to Patch

We just used the Patch tool in Source mode, which works as just described. If you switch to Destination mode, on the other hand, the area you select with the Patch tool becomes the patch, and you drop it over the area to which you drag it, rather than vice versa. Use Destination if the patch itself is the important part of the image. For example, say you want to drop Johnny Depp's face over your cousin's face in a family portrait. First, select Johnny in his image with the Patch tool and then drag him right where you want him in the family image. If your goal is simply to cover up something and you're less concerned with what you cover it *with,* stick with Source mode.

TRY IT YOURSELF ▼

Remove Unwanted Items

The first step in rescuing any photo is to determine whether it needs cropping or color correction. This one is cropped as well as it's going to be—it's a shame that the little girl on the right is cut off—but its colors are very dull. Adjusting using the Variations dialog box lets you add cyan and magenta, and a quick Levels adjustment improves the image's contrast. Now you can move on to a trickier fix.

1. Let's replace the curtain and the wall next to it with a plain-colored background that matches the wall's original color. I'll work on a new layer first and paint the new background color on it. I've used the Eyedropper to pick up the color of the wall at the upper-right corner of the photo and just sprayed it on the new layer over the curtain, not worrying a lot about the edges. Figure 22.13 shows what the image looks like now.

▼ TRY IT YOURSELF

Remove Unwanted Items
continued

FIGURE 22.13
Be sure you catch any cutouts—small background areas surrounded by foreground elements—and paint the new wall color in there, too.

2. Now comes the fun part. You have to swap the position of the two layers, which will temporarily hide the new wall background. Double-click the Background layer, which is the original photo of the five kids. Rename it whatever you want to call it (Layer 0, the default name, is fine in this case). Then, on the Layers panel, drag it above the layer you created in step 1. See Figure 22.14.

FIGURE 22.14
You want the new background layer behind the photo layer.

3. All you have to do now is remove the curtain and wall bit by bit, thus revealing the background you've created. You can do this in a variety of ways: by using the regular Eraser tool (very carefully), by selecting and deleting successive areas of the image, or by using the Background Eraser. I opted to start by simply using the Eraser tool to delete most of the nasty curtain, but the image still needs a lot of work around the edges of the kids' heads with the Background Eraser. See Figure 22.15.

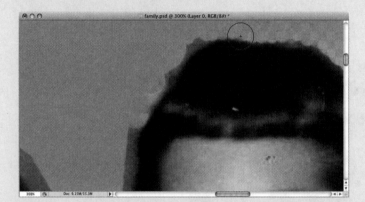

FIGURE 22.15
I'm working zoomed in to 300%.

4. Whew! I've removed the awful curtain and the almost-as-awful wallpaper. Now is a good time to do any last-minute color adjustments. I applied the Despeckle filter to remove the dust from the scanner glass. Finally, because the painted wall looked so flat, I used the Texturizer filter to restore a surface similar to that of the original wallpaper. Figure 22.16 shows the final photo, ready for a frame.

FIGURE 22.16
That looks much better.

Removing Objects

Rats! You thought you had a great shot—and indeed it was, but someone or something crept into the frame that really shouldn't be there. Sometimes you realize it right away, but the moment has passed; other times, you don't notice the trespasser until you offload the pictures from your camera. Well, whoever or whatever it is, you can usually get it out of the picture much more easily with Photoshop than in real life. Figure 22.17 was shot at a children's museum. There's an intrusive unidentified wooden object sticking into the frame from the right, and the boy's shirt is too close in color to the wall; he's not standing out from the background enough.

FIGURE 22.17
Nice shot, but it's got a couple problems we can resolve easily with Photoshop.

I'm going to remove the wooden object and turn the boy's shirt into a nice bright blue, which he says he likes better anyway. The first step is to use the Clone Stamp tool to get rid of that thing on the right. Clicking along the molding closer to the boy, I clone that area right on top of the wood thing, using the overlay to align the molding section perfectly with the molding to the left of it (see Figure 22.18).

FIGURE 22.18
So much for that thing, whatever it was.

This next piece is even easier. Using the Quick Selection tool, I selected the red shirt and then used Hue/Saturation (choose Image, Adjustments, Hue/Saturation) with the Colorize box checked to make it blue. I darkened it a bit and bumped up the Saturation level until I achieved the blue I wanted. All done (see Figure 22.19)!

FIGURE 22.19
Much nicer—the blue shirt doesn't blend in with the red wall.

The fixes required took only a couple minutes, and they definitely improved the picture. This kind of "candid" photo almost always has something in it that you wish wasn't there. Now, thanks to the magic of Photoshop, you can make all of your pictures perfect with just a few minutes of work.

Summary

Color repair isn't terribly different from black-and-white photo repair, except that you need to be more aware of the image's colors and you can make much more use of blending modes. Off-color photos can be fixed with Photoshop's regular color adjustment tools, which we gave a thorough workout in Hour 5, "Adjusting Brightness and Color." Retouching to get rid of obvious flaws and red or green eye is best accomplished with Photoshop's special tools and with the image enlarged so that you can see what you're doing. Use layers to protect the original image while you're working, and merge the changes with the Background layer only when you are completely satisfied with the results.

Q&A

Q. If the picture I need to repair doesn't have enough background to copy, or doesn't have a good background, what should I do?

A. Remember that Photoshop allows you to have more than one file open at a time. You can borrow from another picture and copy the selection onto a new layer in the picture that needs fixing. Scale it so that the texture is in scale with the rest of the scene, and then copy and paste it as many times as you need to. You can also use the Patch, Healing Brush, and Clone Stamp tools with two or more images; your source point doesn't have to be in the same image to which you're cloning the pixels. (However, the two documents do have to be the same color mode and resolution.) If you have a digital camera, you might consider shooting lots of backgrounds—skies, bricks, trees, even street scenes—and keep them in a special folder on your computer. Then when you have a problem photo, you have ready-made scenery to drop the subject into.

Q. What color mode should I be working in: CMYK Color, RGB Color, Indexed Color, Lab Color, or Grayscale?

A. If the image is grayscale, such as a black-and-white photo, and is going to remain grayscale, stay in that mode. Your file will be smaller and all the filters and adjustments will process faster. If the image is intended for the Web or an inkjet printer, on the other hand, stick with RGB. If the image is a color picture that will be sent to a commercial print shop for four-color process printing, convert to CMYK mode, but only after you've done your retouching in RGB mode.

Workshop

Quiz

1. If you want to remove a small blemish in the middle of a flat area such as the sky, which tool should you use?

    A. The Spot Healing Brush

    B. The Patch tool

    C. The Object Replacement tool

2. Originally, hand-tinted photos were colored with:

   A. Natural plant dyes

   B. Chalk

   C. Special paints

3. It's okay to make substantive changes in a photo if

   A. It's intended for publication in *People* magazine.

   B. It's only going in your own photo album.

   C. No one in it is recognizable.

Answers

1. **A**. You can use either A or B, actually, but the quickest fix for this spe-cific problem is offered by the Spot Healing Brush—just one click and it's gone.

2. **C**. They were thinned down so that the details of the photo could show through.

3. **B**. Even if no one in the picture can be recognized, it's still considered unethical to publish an altered image widely without acknowledging that it has been modified.

Exercise

Find some of your own photo portraits that have bad red eye. If they're print-ed photos, scan them into the computer. Then use the tricks you've learned to restore normal eye colors. It's okay to try the Red Eye Removal tool, but if it doesn't work, give the other techniques we've talked about a whirl. Next, find a group photo. Take a look at some modified photos online first to inspire you; then pretend you're a disgruntled political leader and remove one member of the group.

PART VII
Publishing Your Pictures

Printing and Publishing Your Images

By now, I'm sure you've created some artwork that you're pretty proud of. That being the case, you're probably thinking about printing it and maybe even hanging it on the wall. After all, keeping all your pictures hidden in your computer is no fun; you want them out where you can see them, in your home, on your web pages, and enhancing the documents you produce. We'll look at getting images on the Web in the next hour; for now, let's explore the world of printing. Even in this brave new world of the web-enabled camera phone, the inexcusably cool iPod Photo, and other electronic media, printing isn't going away, and it never will. There's an unmistakable appeal to a printed picture that onscreen images just don't have; it seems to be more a part of the real world.

Printing should be easy; just choose File, Print and watch your image emerge on paper, right? Well, sometimes it's not quite that simple. Photoshop offers quite a few variables and decisions to make when you're sending an image to the printer. In this hour, we look at what those options are, from choosing a printer through navigating the series of Print dialogs.

Choosing a Printer

Before you can print anything from Photoshop, you'll (obviously) need to have a printer. If you're shopping for a printer, you've got a lot of choices. There's more than one way to produce color on a page, and, of course, black-and-white prints are always needed. An entire book could be written about all the varieties of printers. In this section, we'll make do with a snapshot of the printing technologies you're most likely to encounter: inkjet printers, laser printers, and dye-sublimation printers.

WHAT YOU'LL LEARN IN THIS HOUR:

- ▶ Choosing a Printer
- ▶ Preparing the Image
- ▶ Printing the Page
- ▶ Picking the Paper
- ▶ Placing Photoshop Images in Other Programs

Inkjet Printers

The most common color printers these days are inkjets, which produce an image by spraying dots of colored ink onto the paper. The quality of their output varies tremendously, ranging from fair to excellent, depending on how much money you want to spend on a printer. Logically enough, a lot depends on the size of the ink dot that a printer applies, but it's also important to know whether a printer uses a four- or six-color process. Basic inkjets use a four-color ink cartridge, with cyan, magenta, yellow, and black inks—the same colors commercial printing presses use. More sophisticated inkjet printers, which these days includes most of what's on the market, use a six-color process that adds two more inks, usually a light magenta and light cyan. With only four colors of ink, the sparsely placed dots in broad light areas, such as sky, can be too obvious. Using lighter versions of those two inks enables the printer to reproduce lighter colors more smoothly. And high-end printers can use up to 12 colors of ink.

NOTE

P.S.

PostScript is a computer language that describes the appearance of a page in perfect detail so that it can be reproduced exactly by a compatible printer. Professional designers and prepress specialists need to worry about PostScript; home users generally don't.

At the inexpensive end of the inkjet spectrum are home and office models, almost all of which can deliver acceptable-quality color printing, such as Hewlett-Packard's DeskJet series, the Canon Pixmas, and Epson's Stylus printers.

Inkjet printers are often not PostScript compatible, which may mean that they can't print PostScript data such as PostScript fonts and EPS-format images. For most Photoshop users, however, this isn't a problem; just stick to OpenType and don't save your images in EPS format.

High-end inkjet printers, like Kodak's Iris models, can cost tens of thousands of dollars; they're usually found at service bureaus or art studios. These printers can produce very large output, measured in feet rather than inches, with remarkable detail and quality. You can have Iris prints made of your images, but they tend to be expensive, so you'll want to save this method for your best work. Prices range from $50 to $100 for a single 16×20 page.

Laser Printers

Unlike inkjet printers, laser printers use toner, just like photocopiers. They fuse a thin layer of fine powder to the paper with heat, producing an image that won't run if it gets wet. Laser printers are much faster than inkjet printers as well, an advantage that's cancelled out for some by their overly bright print colors and glossy surface. If you're not looking for perfectly accurate color, or if you need only black-and-white prints, a laser printer from a well-known company such as Brother and Hewlett-Packard is a good option.

Most laser printers can produce 300 to 600 dots per inch, and some up to 1200 dpi. They're particularly good at printing halftone and grayscale images. Some laser printers can even alter the size of the printed dots to improve print quality. Both black-and-white and color laser printers have dropped precipitously in price in the last few years; you can pick up a black-and-white model for under $100 at CompUSA, and color laser printers start at around $200.

Dye-Sublimation Printers

Dye-sublimation printers are expensive, but in this case, you definitely get what you pay for. If you want true photographic quality in your prints, a dye-sub printer is your best option. Their image quality is superb because they apply dye to the paper by using sublimation instead of by spraying it on. These printers use special ribbons and paper; you can't use ordinary paper with them, and the specially coated paper is expensive. You can often find these printers at a print shop, where you can get a single dye-sub print for a modest fee. If you're satisfied with smaller prints, look into desktop dye-sublimation printers that make 4×6 prints. Several companies make them at reasonable prices, starting at less than $100.

Preparing the Image

If you want to get the best prints, you need to keep your printer in mind throughout the design process. That means using Photoshop's color-management features so that what you see onscreen accurately reflects what you'll get from your printer; otherwise, your color and brightness adjustments won't have the effect you're looking for.

With that in mind, it's important that you configure Photoshop for the monitor and printer you'll be using, before you even consider printing anything important. This is accomplished in Photoshop's Color Settings dialog (choose Edit, Color Settings).

To properly manage the color in your images, Photoshop uses a collection of predefined settings for monitors and printers, and even different combinations of ink and paper. Each setting includes a color profile that describes the characteristics of the device in question and conversion options for modifying colors to match the output profile, which should give you consistent color for a particular kind of printer under typical conditions.

What's Color Management?

Color management is the technology that enables you to move color information from one device (such as a monitor) to another (such as a printer) in a predictable way. Ever heard the term *WYSIWYG* (What You See Is What You Get)? Well, that doesn't happen automatically with color because every single monitor, scanner, and printer "sees" and reproduces color differently, even if only a little bit. So color-management software steps in to translate among all these different devices.

Color management is made possible by International Color Consortium (ICC) device profiles, produced by measuring the color characteristics of each device in accordance with a language agreed upon by the ICC (a group of color-management professionals and vendors). To create an ICC profile for a printer, a special target chart with many small squares of color is printed on the printer being profiled. Then a measuring tool called a **colorimeter** (or, for greater accuracy, a **spectrophotometer**) is placed over each of the color squares to measure how the printer reproduced the target's color. The data goes back to the computer, which compares the printed colors against the theoretically perfect colors of the software target and defines the differences between each pair of colors. These differences are all assembled into an ICC profile for that printer, ink, and paper combination. The profile is actually a set of numbers that tells the computer how to adjust the color information it sends to that particular printer to make the printed colors match as closely as possible the colors in the image file. Scanner profiles are produced by scanning a printed color chart, and monitor profiles are created by displaying the chart onscreen and measuring the color squares with a device similar to the one used to measure the printed chart.

Profiles have to be applied by system-level or application-level software. ColorSync is system-level color-management software developed jointly by Apple and Linotype-Hell, and ICM is a similar program for Windows. ColorSync and ICM include profiles of many kinds of monitors, so you can choose yours or at least one similar to it. They adjust color on the monitor so that printer color space (CMYK) is displayed correctly.

What does all this mean to you? Here are a few suggestions:

▶ Do your work in RGB color. If your system includes ColorSync, be sure that you've set it up to use the correct profile for your monitor. If you don't have the right profile, use the Monitor Calibration Wizard (Windows, free download at www.hex2bit.com) or Display Calibrator Assistant (part of Mac OS X). Consider buying a hardware calibration tool such as the Pantone huey ($70) or the Colorvision Spyder ($60), for truly accurate colors.

▶ If you're printing to a low-end printer with no ICC profile available, don't convert the image to CMYK mode before printing. The printer driver takes care of this, and it makes the translation in the way that works best for your printer.

Figure 23.1 shows the Color Settings dialog. You can find it near the bottom of the Edit menu, or you can press Command-Shift-K (Mac) or Ctrl+Shift+K (Windows) to open it. Be sure to watch the description area at the bottom of the dialog box; it offers you helpful information when you're deciding which settings to use.

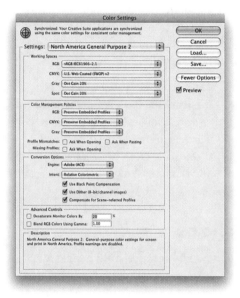

FIGURE 23.1
The default color settings work well for images that may be both printed and displayed on the Web.

FIGURE 23.2
Choose a setting that's appropriate for your work.

As you can see, you need to make several decisions, even without clicking More Options to show the Conversion Options and Advanced Controls settings. First, you need to use the Settings pop-up menu, shown in Figure 23.2, to specify what sort of work you will be doing most of the time and choose an appropriate setting.

If you know that your work will be printed on standard printing presses (not a home inkjet), apply either the North American, European, or Japanese standard prepress defaults, according to where your printing company is. If, on the other hand, most of your work is headed for a website, choose the Web/Internet settings. Monitor Color is the right choice if you're creating presentations that will be shown primarily on your own computer (it disables color management). If you do a lot of different kinds of work, choose one of the General Purpose presets.

Working Spaces

For a nice change, the Working Spaces settings in the Color Settings dialog box are actually *less* complicated than they look. RGB asks for the monitor space you want to work in. Choose sRGB if you plan to share your images mostly onscreen, as web images or via email or slideshows; sRGB is a version of RGB that includes the colors that the standard computer monitor can display. If you will be printing most of your images, on the other hand, stick to Adobe RGB; it includes some printable colors that don't show up in sRGB. In the CMYK field, you need to choose the kind of printer you're using.

Gray is the easiest of all. If you use a Mac, choose Gray Gamma 1.8. If you're running Windows, choose 2.2. These are the basic settings for the method that each system uses to display grayscale images. And Spot refers to pages printed using spot color inks, such as duotones or illustrations done with Pantone colors. The standard setting is Dot Gain 20%, but you need to worry about this only if you're working on designs that use spot colors and will be professionally printed.

Color Management Policies

Color Management Policies refers to how Photoshop should handle files created in another application or in an earlier version of Photoshop. Your choices are as follows: preserve the color-management profiles embedded in the file, convert the image to your working profile, or turn off color management. This last choice lets Photoshop display the file in Active mode, while keeping the embedded profile, until you choose to resave it with color-management information from your own system. You can also have Photoshop warn you when a color-management mismatch occurs as you open a file and ask what to do about it. Figure 23.3 shows a typical warning message.

FIGURE 23.3
This warning popped up because I opened an image created in an older version of Photoshop; the file contained an embedded profile that didn't match my current profile.

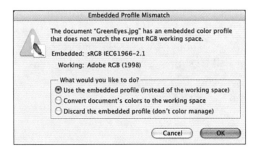

Conversion Options

If you click the More Options button, you'll have additional choices to make. The first of these, in the Conversion Options area, is Engine, which refers to the color conversion engine that Photoshop uses to match colors. Even if you're using a Mac, you should ignore the Apple ColorSync option and choose Adobe (ACE). It's designed specifically to work with Photoshop and the other Adobe graphics applications, and using this option helps keep color consistent across all your Adobe programs. For Intent, unless you need to match another version of the image exactly, I suggest that you use Perceptual, which is usually my choice. This option produces the most pleasing colors instead of the most accurate ones by the numbers. The Perceptual option also allows you to print a wider range of colors than, for example, Absolute Colorimetric. Beneath the Engine and Intent menus, check both Use Black Point Compensation and Use Dither, unless your print shop tells you not to. Again, both of these options generally produce better-looking color.

You can usually ignore the Advanced Controls area. You don't really want to desaturate your monitor or change the color-blending gamma except under rare circumstances, which only an expert user is likely to encounter.

Checking the Gamut

Remember back in Hour 4, "Specifying Color Modes and Color Models," when you learned how to check the gamut of an image to ensure that all the colors it uses are contained in the range of colors that its destination can produce? This is a useful step to take whether an image will be professionally printed, displayed on the Web, or output on a desktop printer, but it's most useful in the latter case. Desktop printers tend to have wildly varying gamuts, so knowing that an image looks good onscreen and prints correctly on Printer A is no guarantee that the image will print correctly on Printer B.

When you've made the appropriate color settings, as explained in the preceding sections, it's a good idea to check the gamut on any image you're about to print. Choose View, Gamut Warning to turn on the out-of-gamut indicator, which takes the form of gray patches in the image window (see Figure 23.4). Now you can use any of the adjustment tools to modify out-of-gamut colors so that they edge back into your printer's gamut. Otherwise, you'll be tossing the dice by letting Photoshop and your printer driver collaborate to convert the colors. Most often, that works fine, but if you want complete control over the color in your printed image, it's best to do this work yourself.

FIGURE 23.4
Gray splotches indicate colors that
can't be reproduced on my printer.

Printing the Page

By now you've probably figured out that printing is a lot more complex
than you ever realized. In addition to the color-management settings we've
just looked at, you'll run into dozens of print settings in various dialogs:
the Page Setup dialog, Photoshop's own Print dialog, and the system print
dialog, which is where you'll find settings specific to your printer. In this
section, we take a look at each of those locations and attempt to make
sense of all the options each one offers.

Page Setup

If you have more than one printer available, be sure that you've made the
one you intend to use active in the Page Setup dialog. You'll find Page
Setup at the bottom of Photoshop's File menu, along with two other print-
related commands: Print, which enables you to make all your print settings , and Print One Copy, which does just that. It immediately sends the
current image to the printer, no questions asked, printing to the selected
printer with whatever settings were used on the last photo. Let's start with
Page Setup; Figure 23.5 shows its dialog.

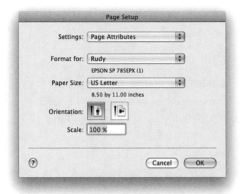

FIGURE 23.5
The Page Setup dialog varies depending on the printer and the system you're using.

Each printer's Page Setup dialog looks a little different (and, of course, Mac and Windows Page Setup dialogs look different), but they provide the same basic functions. (Note that not all options are available in every situation.) A Page Setup dialog generally displays the following information and options:

> **Printer**—The name of the printer always appears somewhere in the dialog. If it's not the one you want to use, you can usually pick a different printer from a pop-up menu.

> **Properties**—On Windows computers, you can click this button to access a dialog where you can change options such as paper size, layout, printer resolution, and halftone settings.

> **Paper Size**—This pop-up menu enables you to specify the size of the paper on which you're printing. You'll generally find a good selection of standard U.S. and European paper sizes, including letter, legal, A4, tabloid, and various envelope sizes.

> **Source**—If your printer has multiple paper trays or gives you a choice of either using the paper tray or feeding one sheet at a time, often you can choose the paper source for the printer to use in Page Setup.

> **Orientation**—This setting determines how the printed image is placed on the page: portrait (the page's height is the larger dimension) or landscape (the page's width is the larger dimension).

> **Scale**—If you want the image to print smaller or larger, adjust this percentage downward or upward, as appropriate.

NOTE

Too Big?

If your image is too big to fit on the specified paper size, you won't find out until later, when you actually click the Print button (we'll get there in the next section). At that point, Photoshop tells you that your picture won't fit and offers two choices: print anyway, resulting in only part of the image being printed, or cancel and adjust the Scale value so that the whole image fits on the page.

The Print Dialog

Now let's take a look at the Print dialog (see Figure 23.6). Back in
Photoshop CS3, Adobe rolled the features that used to live in a special
Print with Preview dialog into the regular Print dialog, so there's a lot
going on here. Notice that you can change printers at the top of the dialog,
and you can also return to the Page Setup dialog by clicking the Page
Setup button.

FIGURE 23.6
Here I'm positioning the photo at
the left side of the page so that I
can later add captions with my
laser printer, which prints black
type more clearly.

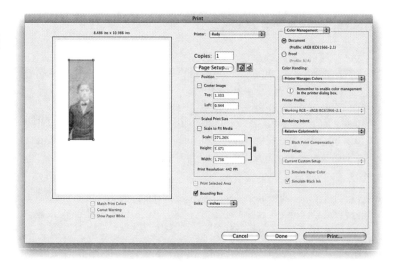

The first thing to do in the Print dialog is choose the printer that you want
to use and set the number of copies you'd like to print. Then things get
more interesting. Next you can choose from the options in the Position
area. If you uncheck the Center Image box, which is turned on by default,
you'll be able to move the picture around on the page by dragging it in the
preview area on the left or by entering different Top and Left position values, placing the picture wherever you want on the printed page. If you
drag a corner of the image preview, you can scale it, just as you would
when using the Free Transform command; the values in the Scaled Print
Size area change accordingly as you drag. You can also resize the image by
typing a number into the Scale percentage field, relative to the original
image size. If you have a photo that's 6 inches wide and you want it to
print 9 inches wide, for example, scale it to 150%. Of course, you can also
change the Scale percentage in the Page Setup dialog.

A pop-up menu at the top of the right side of the Print dialog enables you to choose between Output options and Color Management options. As you change Output settings, you can see your changes in the preview area. In Figure 23.7, I've added corner crop marks, center crop marks, calibration bars, and a label (the filename) to my photo.

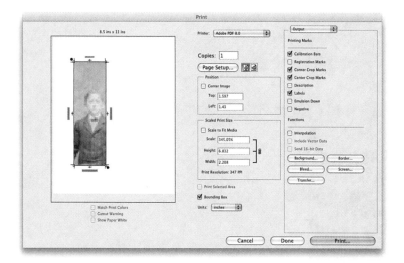

FIGURE 23.7
Output settings include marks that you can add to the printout and printer functions, some of which your printer might not support.

Here are some of the options in the Output section and what they mean:

▶ **Calibration Bars**—Check this box to have Photoshop print calibration and color bars next to your image. A calibration bar is a row of 11 gray squares ranging from 0% (white) to 100% (black) and including every 10% increment in between. A color bar is a row of 11 colors, including the RGB and CMYK colors. These bars can help when you're trying to match a specific printer; this option is available only if you're using a PostScript printer.

▶ **Registration Marks**—Activate this feature to print registration marks at the corners of the image. These marks are primarily used for aligning color separations, so you won't need them if you're printing to a desktop printer.

▶ **Corner Crop Marks**—Corner crop marks appear at each corner of your image, defining where it should be trimmed. They're plain horizontal and vertical lines along which you can line up your straight-edge to cut a straight line along the edge of the picture.

▶ **Center Crop Marks**—These crop marks are centered on each side of the image, defining the sides' center. Figure 23.8 shows the crop marks that were added to the image by the settings shown in Figure 23.7.

FIGURE 23.8
A printout showing various crop
marks, registration marks, and the
filename.

Label

pen box kid.psd @ 33.3% (RGB/8) *

——Corner Crop Marks

——Center Crop Marks

—— Registration Marks

▸ **Description**—When you check this box, any text in the Description
field of the File Info dialog for that file is added to the printed page.
(To add Description info, choose File, File Info and make sure that
Description is selected in the top pop-up menu.) This can be helpful
for providing contact info, copyright data, or other details relevant to
the image.

▸ **Labels**—This check box prints the filename below the picture. And if
you're printing color separations, the name of the appropriate color
channel is also printed on each color plate.

▸ **Emulsion Down**—This setting prints your image as a horizontal mirror image of the original, with everything flipped left to right. Use
this setting when you're printing on T-shirt transfer paper so that the
image faces the right way when it's transferred to the shirt. The setting actually refers to whether a film negative reads forward with the
film's coated side up or down, but you need to worry about that
only if you're producing film color separations to be converted to a
printing plate.

▶ **Negative**—With this option checked, the printer reverses the values of the image. That is, the whites become black, the blacks become white, and everything in between changes accordingly. You end up with a negative image, just like a photographic film negative. As with Emulsion Down, this option is relevant only if you're printing to film for commercial offset printing, because these images usually need to be negatives.

▶ **Background**—If you want to print a background color around your image, click the Background button and Photoshop brings up the standard Color Picker. The color you pick is used only for printing; it doesn't change the actual image file. (If you're printing from Windows, be sure to turn off this feature after you use it. Otherwise, the background will appear around the next picture you print as well.) Be careful about using this feature with an inkjet printer; it uses up quite a lot of ink very quickly!

▶ **Border**—To add a border to your printed image, click the Border button. In the Border dialog, you can set the width of the printed border, which is always black, in inches, millimeters, or points. (As with Background, using this feature doesn't affect the actual image file.)

▶ **Bleed**—**Bleeding** means that part of the image runs right off the edge of the paper, with no empty space between the image and the edge of the page. (This feature won't work on every printer, because some printers can't print to the very edge of a page. Check your printer's manual to find out if your printer can produce bleed prints.)

Click the Bleed button to define how much of the image bleeds off the page in inches, millimeters, or points. Higher values move the crop marks within the boundaries of the image so that less of the image is printed. The maximum bleed value is an eighth of an inch (.125").

▶ **Screen**—The Use Printer's Default Screens box is checked by default, and as long as it's checked, you won't be able to change anything else in the Halftone Screen dialog. Uncheck this option if you want to customize the other halftone options to change the fineness and angle of the grid that determines placement of halftone dots. Most of the time, Photoshop's default settings work fine; this is another setting you need to worry about only if you're outputting an image for commercial printing.

▶ **Transfer**—This dialog allows you to compensate for dot gain, the increase in halftone dot size that takes place when ink spreads out on the paper. Depending on the printer or printing press and the paper being used, a 50% dot, for example, could print as a 58% dot, producing an 8% dot gain. In this case, you can use the Transfer Functions dialog to reduce the size of 50% dots in the printout so that they'll be the right size for 50% dots after the ink spreads out. You can specify up to 13 grayscale values to create a customized transfer function. Transfer functions apply only when you're outputting an image for commercial printing—if you're using a home/office inkjet printer, you needn't worry about dot gain—and they apply only during printing; they don't affect the image itself.

▶ Interpolation—**Interpolation** refers to a printer's capability to resample an image as it prints it. Any PostScript Level 2 (or higher) printer can resample a low-resolution image on the fly to produce a better-quality printout. This feature is valuable only if you're dealing with low-resolution images, and it's available only with PostScript printers.

Figure 23.7 shows the additional options I've selected in the Print dialog box. Figure 23.8 shows the resulting output.

Before you continue, make sure that whatever you want to print is visible in the image window. By default, Photoshop prints all visible layers and channels, but it skips any that you have hidden. If you want to print only certain layers or channels, hide all the other layers or channels before printing.

The Color Management options are fewer and simpler:

▶ **Print**—Choose Document for normal printing; choose Proof if you want to try to match the way your image would look when printed on an output device other than your own (such as a four-color printing press). Either way, Photoshop uses the device profiles specified in the Color Settings dialog box.

▶ **Options**—In the Color Handling pop-up menu, choose whether you want the color managed by Photoshop, by your printer, or not at all. If you choose Photoshop, specify a device profile that matches your printer. Leave the Rendering Intent pop-up menu set on Perceptual for the closest visual match in colors.

Sending the Image to the Printer

Now you're finally getting around to printing the image; there's just one more dialog to get through. Click Print to see yet another Print dialog (see Figure 23.9). The first thing you'll probably notice is that, like the Page Setup dialog, this dialog looks different depending on what printer you have, what platform you're running on, and the color mode of the image. However, you need to supply the same information regardless of the Print dialog's appearance.

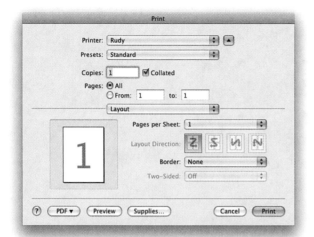

FIGURE 23.9
The ultimate dialog: Print.

Let's look at some of the Print fields and options you might see (you might need to look through multiple panes of the Print dialog to find all these):

▶ **Copies**—Enter the number of copies of the image that you want to print.

▶ **Pages**—You can choose the range of pages in a document to be printed. Of course, this setting is irrelevant in Photoshop because its documents consist of only one page.

▶ **Media Type**—The printer driver needs to know what kind of paper or transparency film you're printing on. This setting determines how much ink the printer applies, because different kinds of paper are more or less absorbent.

▶ **Ink**—You can generally choose Color or Black; black ink and toner cartridges are cheaper than color ones, so it's often a good idea to use just black ink for early drafts.

▶ **Print Quality** (also sometimes called *Mode*)—You can often specify a printer resolution using this pop-up menu, such as 300 or 600 dpi. Some printers use Best, Normal, Econofast, or some variation on this theme, as well as or instead of a specific dpi setting.

▶ **Destination**—You can print to a printer, obviously, but you can also print to a file. This means saving the printed output as a PostScript, EPS, or PDF file (see Figure 23.10). (This option works only if you're using a PostScript-compatible printer or if you're running Mac OS X, which has PDF capability built into the system.)

▸ **Print Selected Area**—When you have an active rectangular selection in your Photoshop image window, you can check this box (labeled **Selection** in Windows) to print just that area. This works only with rectangular selections created with the Marquee tool, and it doesn't work for feathered selections.

▸ **Encoding** (or you might just see a check box for ASCII format)—Here you tell Photoshop which encoding method to use when it sends the image data to a PostScript printer. All PostScript printers understand ASCII, so it's always a safe bet. Binary encoding is more compressed, so it can be faster, but older printers occasionally choke on it. JPEG encoding is even faster, but it results in some loss of data because it's a lossy compression scheme. JPEG encoding works only with PostScript Level 2 printers (or above).

▸ **Print In**—Here you may be able to decide how to print the image: in grayscale, in RGB colors, or in CMYK colors. For some desktop printers, RGB gives better results. (If you have a choice, by all means, try both options and see which looks better to you.)

▸ **Print Separations**—If the image is currently in CMYK or Duotone mode and the composite color channel is active, you might see this option. Checking this box tells Photoshop to print each channel as a separate color plate. A CMYK document would print as four separate pages, one for all the cyan data in the image, one for magenta, one for yellow, and one for black. Each page is labeled with the name of the color it represents.

▶ **Options**—Oddly, Options isn't always one of your options. On a non-PostScript printer, such as the Hewlett-Packard DeskJet series, the Options button is one of your choices in the Print dialog. Options usually lets you make settings such as Intensity, Halftoning, and Color Matching. Leave all three at Auto unless you're printing a photograph. If you are, choose Photographic or a similar setting from the Color Matching menu to get the best color reproduction.

When everything is set to your satisfaction, click Print to send your image to your printer.

Picking the Paper

What you print an image on makes almost as much difference as how you do the printing. You can get various types and weights of paper for all kinds of printers, including special papers both for inkjet printers and for laser printers. If you want your picture to resemble a photograph, consider investing in photo-weight glossy paper. It's a much thicker paper than regular office paper, with a glossy surface that really does help make your inkjet- or laser-printed picture look as though it came out of a real darkroom instead of from a computer. You'll get spectacular color and detail with this kind of paper, too.

You can also get matte coated papers for printing color on inkjet printers. And transparency paper is clear acetate film, specially treated to accept the inks. Use it to make overhead projection slides and overlays.

You can also get art papers for some kinds of inkjet printers. These are heavy rag papers, much like artist's watercolor paper. Find these at www.inkjet-mall.com, among other places. These fine-art papers, including some made from bamboo and others with a wide variety of surface finishes, are ideally suited to printing pictures that you've converted to imitation watercolors, pastel drawings, and so on, because they're the same kind of papers generally used for those techniques. If you do print on a heavy art paper, be sure to feed in one sheet at a time and set the printer for thicker paper (if it has that option).

For some kinds of art projects, printing on canvas or even foil is ideal. You can order treated pieces of thin canvas with a paper backing that go through the printer very well; this stuff will run you about a dollar a letter-sized sheet. There are also foils, fuzzy paper, window cling plastic, and all kind of other materials treated to accept inkjet ink; you'll find a good selection at the

CAUTION

Your Mileage May Vary...

Each printer is slightly different, as are its dialogs. I've covered some of the most common print settings here, but your printer might not have some of these, and it might have settings I haven't mentioned. Be sure to read your printer manual before you start printing; it's your best source for specific printing info.

TIP

Paper Matters

I use inexpensive all-purpose office paper for most of my work. It's fine for printing a quick proof to see how a picture is coming along. For serious proofing, though, you need to use the same paper that you'll use for the final print. Otherwise, you don't know for sure that the combination works. For work that a client will see, I use a coated inkjet paper because the colors are brighter and don't bleed into each other. If I want the picture to look like a darkroom photo, I'll pay the extra money to print it on special glossy paper.

Crafty PC website (www.thecraftypc.com/funpapers.html). You can even buy sheets of rice paper or sugar, as well as edible inks, and put your photos on cakes or cookies. (Check out www.computercakes.com or www.icingimages.com to find these materials.)

Label stocks, of course, come in all kinds of sizes and shapes, and hundreds, if not thousands, of kinds and weights of paper for both inkjet and laser printers. Finally, you can buy iron-on transfer paper (for color laser or inkjet printers), which lets you put your images on T-shirts, aprons, tote bags, or anything else that you can fit under an iron. Be sure that you follow the instructions with the paper, and don't forget to flip your image before you print it so that it reads correctly when it's transferred to its final destination.

Placing Photoshop Images in Other Programs

Printing directly from Photoshop doesn't happen as often as you might think. Most of the time, images created in Photoshop are imported into another application for final placement and output. Most often these are page-layout applications, such as InDesign and QuarkXPress. Photoshop images can even be brought into other image-editing or drawing applications, such as Painter and Illustrator, and printed from there with additions made in the new program, such as type or vector illustrations.

Perhaps you edit a newsletter, or you do Flash movies or PowerPoint presentations. Maybe you've shot a pile of product photos to go into a catalog. The question is, how do you move them from Photoshop into another application? It's not difficult; the other programs do the importing. All you have to do is save your images in a compatible format and put them in a folder that you can easily locate when the time comes.

The main thing you'll need to watch out for when you're printing Photoshop images from other applications is the format in which you save your files. Other than that, any settings related to the image, such as custom colors or halftone screens, are brought with the image automatically. The right format to choose for anything that will end up as printed matter depends on whether the final product is being printed on a Postscript or non-Postscript printer. To print on a Postscript printer, save your image files in PDF, DCS, or EPS format. For non-Postscript printers, use TIFF when you're planning to place the picture in another file.

Using Photoshop with PowerPoint

PowerPoint supports most graphics formats, but GIF (for line art such as logos, charts, and graphs) and JPEG (for photos) are the most compact and best suited for screen display. How you insert the picture depends on whether you're using a preformatted page or making one up as you go along. You can pick out a slide layout for your new slide (see Figure 23.11) and then choose the picture to go into it, as in Figure 23.12.

FIGURE 23.11
The PowerPoint Slide Layout dialog box.

FIGURE 23.12
Locate the picture you want to use and click Insert.

You can also just begin with a blank slide and place your photo on it. To do this, you use the same dialog box as in Figure 23.11.

Using Photoshop with a Word Processor or DTP Program

To insert a picture into a Microsoft Word document, choose Insert, Picture (as shown in Figure 23.13) and navigate to the picture you want to use. It opens in a box that you can move around in your document or resize as needed to fit your layout. The picture has been copied in to the Word document and isn't linked to the original.

FIGURE 23.13
You'll find a similar command in WordPerfect and other word processors.

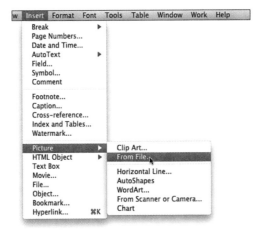

Adding pictures to desktop publishing documents works a little bit differently. Instead of inserting the images in the document you're creating, you add a link to them from the document you assemble in the DTP program. This means that, to keep your pictures where they belong, you can't move or rename any image after it has been placed. If you do, you break the link, which just means that you have to go back and tell your program where the file is now. If I'm creating something like a newsletter or ad that might have several images in it, I keep them all in one folder and make sure that the folder goes to the print shop along with the InDesign or Word files.

Typically, in a desktop publishing program such as Adobe InDesign, the command to insert a picture is Place, and you'll find it on the File menu. Other than that, the procedure is much the same as in a word processor: Navigate to the image you want to use and (in InDesign) click the page to place it. In QuarkXPress, you'll need to draw a box to contain the picture first, but that's the only real difference. When the picture is on the page, you can scale it, move it, give it a border, and wrap type around it.

Summary

Printing Photoshop images isn't difficult; there are just a lot of decisions to make along the way. However, once you get into a routine of printing, you'll find yourself making most of those decisions automatically. During this hour, we discussed those choices, from preparing an image for printing, to setting up the page, and finally setting the printing options. The wonderful thing about printing is that if you don't get a gorgeous printout the first time, you can just change your settings and try again—provided that you have enough paper and ink, of course.

Using Photoshop pictures in other applications is also very simple: Just save them in an appropriate format and then use the other program's method of importing them.

Q&A

Q. So do I need a PostScript printer?

A. If you're just working with Photoshop, no, you don't. PostScript printers are necessary when you work with PostScript fonts and vector EPS images in a desktop publishing program. For anything you plan to print straight from Photoshop, PostScript isn't needed.

Q. If colors aren't accurate on color laser prints, why would I buy a color laser printer?

A. Well, keep in mind that when I say they're not accurate, I mean they're not *perfectly* accurate. For your purposes, a color laser printer might be just right. When you're printer shopping, I recommend going to a computer store with an image or two on disc and asking the salesperson to print your own images so you can see if the output meets your personal standards.

Q. What printer settings should I use for making a proof to check how a design is coming along?

A. The exact settings depend on your printer and how much control its driver gives you over its output. Most printers have a "Quick" or "Econofast" setting that you can use; if not, the most important things you can do to speed up printing are to lower the printer's resolution and print on plain paper.

Workshop

Quiz

1. **True or False:** Dye-sublimation printers need special paper.

2. Registration marks look like:

   A. The letter *R* in a circle

   B. A cross in a circle

   C. Four concentric circles in CMY and K

3. When you print from Photoshop, the print will show

    A. The selected area

    B. Registration and crop marks

    C. The filename

    D. Any of the above, depending on your print settings

Answers

1. **True.** Prices for this kind of paper have come way down in recent years.

2. **B.** These marks make it easy for press people to see when a color is out of register.

3. **D.** Photoshop's print settings are many and varied.

Exercises

1. PaperDirect is a company that sells more different kinds of papers for more purposes than you can possibly imagine. Visit its website (www.paperdirect.com) to see how to get a sample kit of its papers and envelopes. You'll love the preprinted brochures, cards, and other papers that you can customize with your own type and images. Other companies sell this sort of merchandise as well, but I've found that PaperDirect has the best combination of high quality and a good selection.

2. Take a field trip to your local computer store or to a good office supply store (or try a scrapbooking store!) to see what kinds of papers they have for your printer. Also check out art supply stores for unusual papers, such as canvas-textured, silk, and watercolor. Treat yourself to a package or two of high-quality paper and try printing some of your best work. Note how image colors and the overall effect change when you use different papers to print the same picture.

Going Online with Photoshop

Here we are at the end of the book; you've been working with Photoshop for 23 hours now, and we spend this final hour looking at ways to get your images online so you can build a website and share photos with family and friends via email and even your cellphone. First we talk about preparing your images for online use, and then we check out some different ways to get your images out there, both on the Web and on other parts of the Internet.

File Formats and File Size

The first thing you need to learn about preparing web graphics is which file format to use for which kind of image. The two standard choices, GIF (Graphics Interchange Format) and JPEG (Joint Photographic Experts Group), are accompanied by a third format known as PNG (Portable Network Graphics). Though it's still less common than JPEG and GIF, PNG has been out for several years now and is supported by all the major web browsers. Use it if you like it, but be aware that a few folks out there might have older browsers that can't display PNG files.

All web file formats have built-in compression because the Web has limited bandwidth. This means that you have to consider the download speeds to which your site's viewers likely have access. If you want the site to be usable for people who are still using old-style phone modems, you'll want to keep your web page images less than 30KB apiece—a size that a 56K modem can download in a comfortable 6 seconds. This is an area where the preview images in the Save for Web & Devices dialog can be a big help. They let you decide how small you can make a file without sacrificing quality.

NOTE

I Read It on the Interwebs

Most of the images we see on the Internet are displayed on websites—but not all. It might seem like a picky distinction, but the Internet and the Web are not the same thing. Email, online messaging, FTP, Voice over IP—all these are Internet services that have nothing to do with the Web. So you'll want to keep in mind that when I say "the Web," I mean what you see in your Web browser window, and when I'm talking about the whole Internet, the Web, and all that other stuff, too, I'll say so.

That said, most U.S. Internet users do have broadband (high-speed) connections both at home and at work these days. In summer 2007, broadband penetration was up to 83.43% of active Internet users in the United States, according to Nielsen//NetRatings. People who use phone modems and connect to the Internet at 56Kbps or less made up just 16.57% of active Internet users at that time. So file size is much less of a concern than it was in the early days of the World Wide Web, back in the 1990s. It's still true, however, that smaller is faster, and faster is better as far as Internet users are concerned.

JPEG (Joint Photographic Experts Group)

Most of the time, when you see photos on the Web, they're saved in JPEG format. It's the most common format for photos these days, and for good reason. JPEG accommodates 16 million colors, and you can choose precisely how much compression you want to apply to each file. That's especially good because JPEG compression is **lossy**, which means that reducing file size also reduces image quality.

When you're working in Photoshop, choose File, Save for Web & Devices to open the dialog shown in Figure 24.1. I chose JPEG Low from the Preset pop-up menu; I could have chosen GIF or PNG instead. After a short calculation, and because I clicked the 4-Up tab at the top of the dialog, I can see my original image, plus the same image with three different JPEG settings. Photoshop displays the file size and download time for each version of the image.

FIGURE 24.1
You can specify the connection speed that Photoshop uses to calculate the download for each file size.

The original Photoshop file for this image was 1.43MB. As a low-quality JPEG, it's 54.14KB and will take about 2 seconds to download on a 768K DSL connection, which is a pretty common speed in my neighborhood. At high quality, the file size increases to 194.3KB and the download time increases to 3 seconds. Saved in PNG-24 format, PNG's photo-quality flavor with lossless compression, it's a 1.282MB file and loads in about 18 seconds. Is the quality difference worth the download time? The answer to that, in my book, would be a big, fat "No!" My compromise for this image would probably be to use the JPEG Medium preset, which produces an 87.02KB file that still loads in about 2 seconds.

On the other hand, even if I use the high-quality image, I've reduced the file's size from its original 2.25MB to 171KB. That's a tremendous difference with a relatively small loss of quality.

To save your file, click the version you want to save, then click OK. The Save As dialog box opens, enabling you to name your document and save it where you want it.

If you're saving a JPEG file with the File, Save As command, the first thing to remember is this: Don't. Save for Web & Devices gives you much more control over the size and quality of the resulting image. However, if you're in a hurry and are determined to just save and go, choosing JPEG from the Format pop-up menu in the Save As dialog and then clicking Save produces a second dialog, shown in Figure 24.2.

This dialog prompts you for format options:

▶ **Baseline (Standard)**—This is the default option, if you leave the others unchecked. It's a legacy format that was in widespread use only with the earliest web browsers, which couldn't read the Optimized flavor of JPEG.

▶ **Baseline (Optimized)**—This option creates a smaller file by using slightly more efficient compression. Choosing Optimized doesn't reduce the quality of the image, so these days there's no reason not to use it.

▶ **Progressive**—Except for very small JPEGs, this format option is almost a must for web work. Progressive means that web browsers display your file displayed immediately as a low-res preview and then refine the display with subsequent passes, or **scans**, as more file information is downloaded. You can choose the number of scans—three, four, or five—from a pop-up menu. If you choose the Progressive JPEG option, the file automatically is optimized.

FIGURE 24.2
The JPEG Options dialog lets you specify an image quality level and control how the picture is loaded in a web browser.

TIP

See What's Happening

Always keep your web browser open when you're creating web graphics so that you can take a look at them in context. But don't be fooled by how quickly your files open in your own browser. These files are on your hard drive—they're local. When a viewer's browser has to go out on the Web to retrieve the code and images needed to display your pages, the process slows down quite a bit.

TIP

It's Okay to Peek

A good way to choose the file format that's right for an image is to visit websites that have graphics similar to what you want to publish. To find out what file format an image uses, Ctrl-click the image (Mac), or right-click (Windows) the image until a pop-up menu containing a Save command appears. In the Save dialog box, note the image's file extension—.jpg for JPEG, .png for PNG, or .gif for GIF. Click Save to save the file, or click Cancel if you're just looking.

GIF (Graphics Interchange Format)

If you stop and think for a minute, you'll realize that not all web images are photos. Some are clip art, icons, logos, info-graphics (charts and graphs), and the like. For these pictures, GIF is the best format option. Because GIF files are limited to a maximum of 256 colors, they're not as good as JPEG for continuous-tone art (such as photographs), but they're great for line art, logos, and any kind of art with a limited number of colors. Unlike JPEG, GIF also lets you save files with transparent backgrounds, which you'll find quite useful when you're creating buttons and other nonsquare graphics. Furthermore, you can animate a GIF, and that's always fun!

In Figure 24.3, I've created a simple button that I want to save as a GIF file. Notice how much the file shrinks (from 190KB to 1.78KB) when I limit the colors in the GIF. Feel free to try different numbers of colors, dropping lower until you see a difference in the image. The fewer colors the image contains, the smaller its file will be.

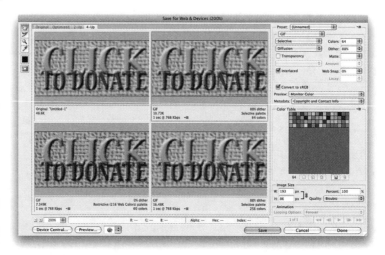

FIGURE 24.3
You can set the number of GIF colors according to what's needed for your image. For this button (shown in the Save for Web & Devices dialog), 128 colors looked slightly better, but I decided that 64 colors would do.

PNG (Portable Network Graphics)

PNG comes in two flavors: 8-bit and 24-bit, which correspond fairly closely to GIF and JPEG. The PNG-8 format uses 8-bit color, which means that each image can contain only 256 colors. Like the GIF format, PNG-8 compresses solid areas of color very well, maintaining sharp detail such as that in line art, logos, or illustrations with type. PNG-8 uses a lossless compression method, which means that no data gets thrown out. However, because PNG-8 files are 8-bit color, using this format for an original 24-bit image— which can contain millions of colors—as a PNG-8 will degrade image quality by reducing the number of colors the picture contains. PNG-8 files use more advanced compression schemes than GIF, so they can be 10% to 30% smaller than GIF files of the same image, depending on the color patterns contained in the image.

As you might guess, PNG-24 file format uses 24-bit color and is suitable for continuous-tone images. Its **lossless** compression scheme means that you never lose image data when you save in this format. However, as a result, PNG-24 files can be much larger than JPEG files of the same image. So when would you use PNG-24 format? Pretty much, it comes into play only when you're working with a photographic image that has variable transparency, meaning that some pixels are partially transparent. This is the kind of transparency you have in an antialiased image on a transparent layer. JPEG can't do multilevel transparency.

Bottom line: If you would consider GIF for an image, consider PNG-8 as well. It might give you a smaller file, and it can do the job just as well. If you'd normally use JPEG, consider PNG-24 if your picture has multilevel transparency. If it's a regular image with no transparency, on the other hand, JPEG will give you a smaller, more efficient file.

Web Tricks

Want to have some fun? Let's look at a few things you can do to your images beyond just sticking them up on a web page. You can use them as page backgrounds, for one thing, or animate them. You can even slice them up into pieces so that they'll load faster and so that each part of the image can function as links to a different destination.

Preparing Backgrounds

Background patterns and images on web pages can really add personality to a website, but they also can make reading the text of the site difficult. To quote legendary web designer David Siegel, "Gift wrap makes poor stationery." That said, however, if you use backgrounds with discretion, they can add considerably to a site's presence. Because HTML includes the capability to tile any image as a background, repeating it as many times as necessary to fill the browser window, your background file can be quite small. You just have to make sure that it doesn't have obvious, abrupt edges (unless that's the look you're going for). In Figure 24.4, I've used Photoshop to create a tile for a web page background, and I'm saving the image as a GIF file using the Save For Web & Devices dialog.

FIGURE 24.4
This tile was created by applying several filters in succession to a plain white background.

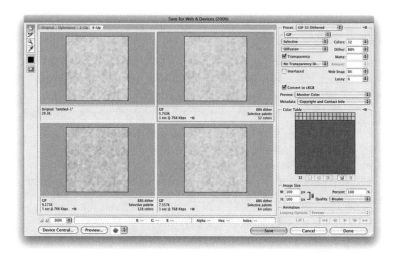

Converting the single tile into a background is easy. You just open a page in your favorite web design program and import the image. Depending on the program, you have to click a check box in the Import dialog box to specify that this image should be used as a background. Some other web design programs have a specific dialog for placing backgrounds. Figure 24.5 shows how to insert a background image tile using PageSpinner's HTML Assistant dialog.

Now all you have to do is be sure that when you upload your page to the Web, the background image is where you said it would be. Figure 24.6 shows the tiled background with some type placed over it.

FIGURE 24.5
In PageSpinner, there are no options for background tiles; all you have to do is specify the location of the image file you want to use as a background.

Here's a trick for adding a stripe down the side of your web page. Make a single tile that's wider than the width of most computer screens (mine is 3,000 pixels wide, just to be on the safe side) by as few pixels high as needed (mine is 20 pixels deep). Place your color and/or texture at the left side of the image, and then save it as a GIF or JPEG and insert it into your page code as a background image. The file will look something like Figure 24.7.

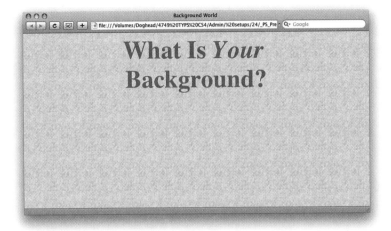

FIGURE 24.6
The background looks even, and
the tiling hardly shows at all.

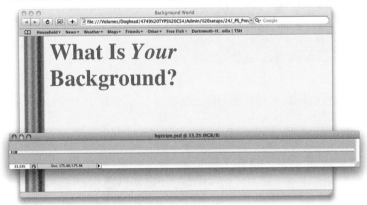

FIGURE 24.7
When you design your HTML page,
make sure you indent the text from
the left margin so that it's not over
the dark stripe.

When you place this file as a background, it tiles vertically but not horizontally: It's already wider than the screen, so there's no room to display
another copy to the right of the first one. You'll end up with a nice stripe,
as wide as you care to make it, in the color and texture of your choice. It
makes a good accent for a plain page.

Building Animations

GIF animations are common on web pages, and they also frequently show
up as chat icons. You can use Photoshop to create your own image and
then make it move. Just don't overdo your use of animated GIFs on your
website; they can get old really fast.

Start by creating a background for your animation. I used the Shape tools
to draw a simple landscape (see Figure 24.8). Any part of the image that

isn't going to move or change in another way can go on the background. Next, create the object that you want to move or reshape. (Let's stick with one animated object for this example.) Again, I pulled out my old standby, the Shape tools, and dropped a flashy red car into my landscape, driving up the hill (see Figure 24.9).

FIGURE 24.8
Doesn't it look as though just about anything could happen here?

FIGURE 24.9
Here's my car, driving onto the scene.

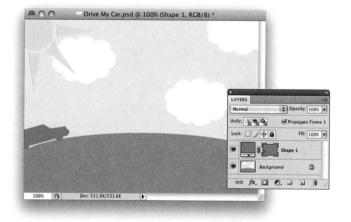

At this point, I needed to begin working with the Animation panel (choose Window, Animation). Photoshop has already created one frame for me, which reflects the current state of the image. Clicking the New Frame button (which looks just like the New Layer button, the New Channel button, and so on) gives me another frame, and then I can configure my image for that frame. How I set up the image for the second frame depends on what I want my animated object to do. I can move it on its layer, alter layer visibility and opacity, change layer blending modes, and add layer styles, all without having to create a new layer. If I want to resize, rotate, repaint, or otherwise modify the animated object, on the other hand, I need to create a copy of it on another layer and modify the copy. That applies in this case because the car needs to rotate slightly to stay parallel with the ground as it moves up and down the hill. So I duplicate the car layer, move the car to the right, and rotate it; that takes care of the second frame (see Figure 24.10).

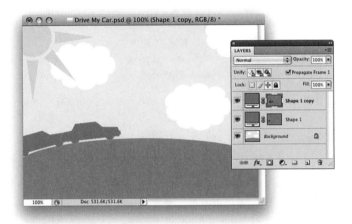

FIGURE 24.10
I've put the second car on another layer so that I can rotate it.

When you've created a frame for every position of your object—my car animation has five frames (see Figure 24.11)—you can go back and assign each frame a frame delay time using the pop-up menu below its thumbnail in the Animation panel. For a very speedy animation, use 0; for my car example, I used a frame delay of .2 seconds. To add "tweened" frames, which contain content from the frames on either side of them at reduced opacity to serve as a transition, Shift-click to select both frames and click the Tween button at the bottom of the Animation panel.

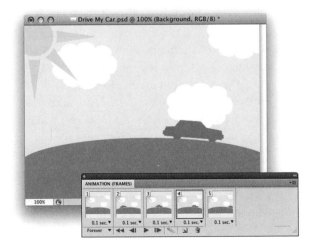

FIGURE 24.11
Here are the five frames in order, with the fourth frame visible in the image window.

Click the Play button at the bottom of the Animation panel to preview your animation. Then, if you're pleased with it, choose File, Save for Web & Devices, and save it as a GIF file. After you've chosen a GIF preset, or created your own combination of settings (number of colors and dithering), the only thing left to do is pick a Looping Option in the Animation area of the dialog at the lower right. Choose Forever if you want the animation to go continuously, or choose Once to make the animation run through its steps once and stop. If you choose Other, you can specify a number of repeats. I don't need very many colors for this particular example, so I can make it a 16-color GIF with no noticeable change from the original.

The file opens in any web browser and plays just as it did in Photoshop.

Creating Slices

Photoshop's **Slice** feature enables you to divide a large graphic into as many smaller images as you like. The whole thing still displays on your web page as a single image, but each slice can have its own color palette, and you can assign a different link destination to each slice to form what's called an **image map**. Meanwhile, the image appears to load faster because each slice is displayed as soon as it's downloaded, so the viewer starts seeing parts of the image almost immediately. The total size of the slices can be smaller than the original image file because you can use different color settings for different parts of the image. For example, an ornate logo on a web banner might need to be saved with 128 colors, while the rest of the image might contain only 2 colors and can be saved with a much smaller palette as a result.

Slices are put back together like puzzle pieces in an HTML table that's part of the document's HTML file. By default, any Photoshop image starts with one slice that comprises the entire picture. You can then create more slices in the image. Photoshop automatically makes additional slices to complete the full HTML table; in other words, you can outline a few puzzle pieces, and Photoshop will create all the other pieces you need to complete the puzzle. Note that you must use Save for Web & Devices and choose HTML and Images when saving a sliced image instead of using Images Only, and you'll need to copy the HTML that Photoshop creates into your web page file.

You create slices by dragging the Slice tool, which looks like a drawing of an X-Acto knife. Choose it from the Photoshop toolbox (it's behind the Crop tool) or press the C key to activate the Crop tool and then press Shift+C to switch to the Slice tool. Drag with the Slice tool to create a selection box across the area you want to slice. If you make a slice across the entire middle of an image, by default, you have defined three slices, including one above and one below where you have sliced. Slices that you create are called **user-slices**, and slices that Photoshop generates are called **auto-slices**. Subslices are created when you overlap two or more user slices. To modify the shape of a slice, switch to the Slice Select tool and drag the corners of its box. Figure 24.12 shows a sliced image in the Save for Web & Devices dialog, where you can assign different settings to each slice.

FIGURE 24.12
The number in the upper-left corner of each section is its slice number. Here I'm assigning a URL to one of the slices so that this portion of the image will link to the page I've specified.

Sharing Your Photos Online

There's no point in taking photos and creating cool images if you don't show them to people, right? And what better way to share photos than the Internet? The Web and all the other components of that vast network we call the Internet provide a fast and easy way to reach millions of people all over the world—or just a few people right in your own neighborhood.

Making a Web Photo Gallery

Want to put your best Photoshop work up on a web page? Sure. But if you just stick all those big images on a single page, it's going to take forever to load, and your viewers might just lose interest and wander off before they've seen everything. There's a better way, and Photoshop's Bridge is your ticket to get there.

Web photo galleries include thumbnail images of each picture you include; then interested viewers can click those thumbnails to see the large versions. Bridge can do all the work of creating these complex structures for you, using a variety of templates and all kinds of customizable settings. Layouts range from a simple page of thumbnails, each of which you can click to open a new window with a full-size view; to table format, again with thumbnails; to scrolling frames; to variations with patterned and colored backgrounds, including the familiar Microsoft navy and gray. You can also choose your own colors for background and type, as well as for links. Last, there is a slide show format that changes images every 10 seconds. Figure 24.13 shows the Web Photo Gallery settings in the Bridge window.

FIGURE 24.13
You can choose photos and then preview the gallery in the same window by clicking the Output Preview tab.

▼ TRY IT YOURSELF

Make a Gallery Page

Let's create a gallery page from your images. Follow these steps:

1. Before you begin, make sure that all the images you want to include are in one folder. Then choose File, Browse in Bridge.

2. Locate your folder of images in Bridge, using the Folders tab at the left side of the Bridge window, and select all the images.

3. Click the Output workspace button at the top of the Bridge window, and then click the Web Gallery button at the top of the Output tab on the right side of the window.

4. Starting at the top of the Output tab, choose a category from the Template pop-up menu and then a particular look from the Style pop-up menu (see Figure 24.14). Then fill out the information in each of these sections:

TRY IT YOURSELF ▼

Make a Gallery Page
continued

FIGURE 24.14
Flash Gallery templates use Flash to animate transitions from each picture to the next.

▶ **Site Info:** Here's where you give the site a title and a subtitle, insert your own name and contact info, and add a copyright notice if you like.

▶ **Color Palette:** If you don't like any of the colors associated with your chosen template, you can change them here.

▶ **Appearance:** These settings affect the gallery's layout. You can have thumbnails in a row at the bottom of the window, in a column on the left, or in a grid on the left, or you can skip the thumbnails altogether and opt for a slideshow presentation in which viewers must proceed through the images in order. Of course, you can also choose the sizes of the thumbnails and of the larger images.

▶ **Create Gallery:** When you're completely happy with the gallery's settings, this is where you go to save it to your hard drive or upload it to your website. You enter all the relevant settings in this pane and then click Save or Upload to create the files that make up the gallery.

▼ TRY IT YOURSELF
Make a Gallery Page
continued

FIGURE 24.15
You can click and scroll around in the Preview tab just like the actual gallery on the Web.

5. To preview the gallery as you change settings, click the Output Preview tab at the top of the window (see Figure 24.15); you might need to drag the divider between this tab and the Content tab, where your pictures are shown, to be able to see the preview. If you change any settings, you can see an up-to-date preview by clicking Refresh Preview at the top of the Output tab. If you're still not quite certain about your settings and you want to see what the gallery looks like in a web browser, click Preview in Browser in the Output tab to open the gallery in your default browser.

6. When you're done changing settings, return to the Create Gallery section of the Output tab and click either Save to Disk or Upload, depending on which you want to do. Photoshop creates the files needed for the gallery, puts them where you've specified, and opens the gallery in your web browser.

Emailing Your Pictures

Sometimes the simplest way to send someone a photo is just to email it, the online equivalent of stuffing a print in an envelope and dropping it in the mail. To add a photo to an email message, use the Add Attachment button or command in your email program and locate the file you want to send. You can't send mail directly from Photoshop. You don't need to save photos for email in any special format, as long as you know that your recipient has software that can open the files you're sending. JPEG is always safe because it will open in any web browser. In any case, make sure that the picture is a reasonable size. You wouldn't want someone to tie up your Internet connection by sending you a huge file, so don't do it to someone else.

One of the most common forms of "malware" today is the Trojan horse. These are files that pretend to be one thing—such as a photo emailed from a friend—and are actually something else, such as a program that will damage files on your computer. Therefore, more computer users are rightfully suspicious of unsolicited downloads. If you want your pictures to be seen and enjoyed, send them only to people you know from email accounts that you're sure are in your recipients' address books, and explain in the body of the message what the image contains. Otherwise, your art might end up in a spam filter.

Creating Images for Phones and More

The Web isn't just for computers anymore. That's right—in case you haven't noticed, people now use all kinds of devices to get online, including their PDAs and cellphones. That's why Photoshop's Save for Web command morphed into Save for Web & Devices back in Photoshop CS3, and it's why Photoshop now includes a special feature called Device Central.

If you're creating artwork to be viewed on a phone or other mobile device, most of your workflow will be the same as ever. Here are the two places where it will change:

- ▶ **Creating a new document**—In the New dialog box (choose File, New), you'll find a new category of image size presets: Mobile & Devices. These presets include common sizes for mobile devices. And if the size you need isn't included, or if you're not sure what size to choose, you can click the Device Central button to look up the right size for the device you're targeting.

- ▶ **Saving the document**—You'll also find a Device Central button in the Save for Web & Devices dialog; here you'll use it to preview your image on a variety of simulated cellphones, complete with a choice of lighting conditions (see Figure 24.16).

FIGURE 24.16
Using the Emulator tab, you can see how your image will appear in all kinds of lighting conditions, even with reflections on the device screen.

Device Central includes a list of available devices in the left column. Double-click the one you want to use to see its specs. If you got here from the New dialog, you'll see a Create button that you can use to create an empty document to the right size. On the other hand, if you started in the Save for Web & Devices dialog, you'll see an Emulator tab that shows your image on the screen of the selected device. You have to admit, this is very cool.

Summary

In this final hour, we looked at putting your work on the Web. We examined what file formats work in today's web browsers and how you can choose the right formats for your own work. You also learned a few tricks that web designers employ to get the most from their images, such as animation, tiling, and slicing.

So what comes next? You've finished your 24th hour, and you know a lot more about Photoshop than you did when you began. That doesn't mean you know it all, but you now have the tools—your imagination, creativity, and a basic understanding of Photoshop. There's still plenty out there to learn; I've been using Photoshop ever since it first came out, and I'm still learning new tricks and techniques all the time. You can spend years with this program and still not try everything it can do. Just don't forget to have fun!

Q&A

Q. Can I mix the kinds of images I use on a web page—some JPEGs, some GIFs, a PNG—or will that cause a big crash?

A. There's no reason whatsoever not to mix image types; web browsers can display different formats side by side with no trouble. So choose the format depending on the image's content. Realistic photos look best as JPEG or PNG files. Graphics with limited color, such as line drawings, are most efficiently stored in GIF format.

Q. How can I use a picture as a page background?

A. For textures and abstract backgrounds, keep the picture small and insert it into the page code as a tiled background. If you keep the edges blurry, they blend smoothly, avoiding hard lines between tiles. You can save your file as either a GIF or a JPEG with any name you like. Your web design program should be able to insert the background tile automatically, but if not, use the HTML tag <body background="*your-filename*.gif"> (or .jpg, if appropriate). If you want to display the entire photo just once, try making the image nearly transparent so that it looks really toned down and use it as a non-tiled background, or *watermark*.

Q. Can I animate photos, or just drawings?

A. You can most definitely create animated photos, which give the effect of very short movies. Just remember that you'll have to save them in GIF format, instead of JPEG, so they might suffer some damage because of the limited number of colors GIF can support. You'll probably find that the effect is least noticeable on very small images, no more than a couple hundred pixels square.

Workshop

Quiz

1. What do you have to do to a native Photoshop format file before you can put it on the Web?

    A. Attach a copyright notice

    B. Save it as a JPEG, GIF, or PNG file

    C. Get a model release on any recognizable people

2. JPEG stands for:

   A. Just Playing Encoding Games

   B. Joint Photographic Experts Group

   C. Justified Photo Element Guidelines

3. What's the most important thing to remember about Photoshop?

   A. Experiment

   B. Experiment

   C. Experiment

Answers

1. B, but **A** and **C** are good ideas, too.

2. B. It's a joint committee formed by members of the International Standards Organization and the International Telecommunications Union.

3. The most important thing is that there's no wrong answer. Keep trying new things, new combinations, and new approaches. Photoshop is a wonderful tool, but without *your* creativity and imagination, it's just software.

Exercise

I have no assignments for you in this last hour—it's time to go forth and create. Most of all, have fun!

Appendixes

Photoshop CS4 Panel Quick Reference

3D Panel

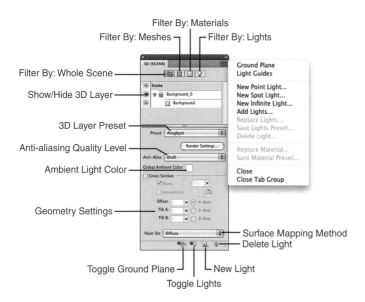

Filter By: Materials

Filter By: Meshes — — Filter By: Lights

Filter By: Whole Scene ——

Show/Hide 3D Layer ——

3D Layer Preset ——

Anti-aliasing Quality Level ——

Ambient Light Color ——

Geometry Settings ——

Toggle Ground Plane — — New Light

Toggle Lights

Surface Mapping Method
Delete Light

Ground Plane
Light Guides

New Point Light...
New Spot Light...
New Infinite Light...
Add Lights...
Replace Lights...
Save Lights Preset...
Delete Light...

Replace Material...
Save Material Preset...

Close
Close Tab Group

Actions Panel

Click to enable/disable step

Click to enable/disable step's dialog box

Click to show settings

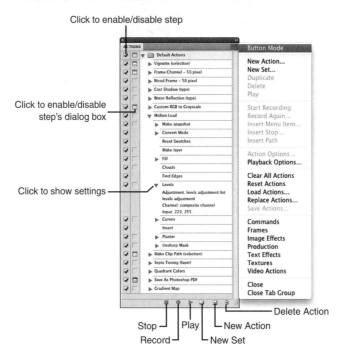

Delete Action

Stop — Play — New Action

Record — New Set

Adjustments Panel

New Adjustment Layer

Click to view adjustment presets

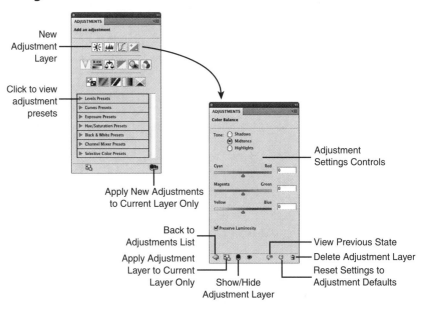

Adjustment Settings Controls

Apply New Adjustments to Current Layer Only

Back to Adjustments List

Apply Adjustment Layer to Current Layer Only

Show/Hide Adjustment Layer

View Previous State

Delete Adjustment Layer

Reset Settings to Adjustment Defaults

New Adjustment Layer

Click to view adjustment presets

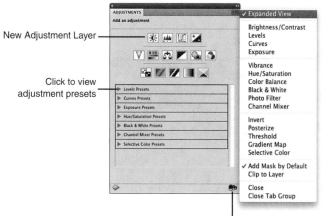

Apply New Adjustments to Current Layer Only

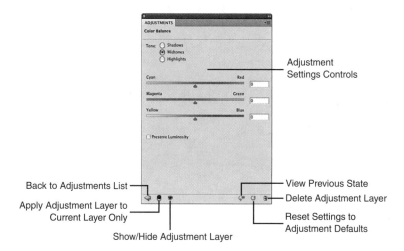

Adjustment Settings Controls

Back to Adjustments List

Apply Adjustment Layer to Current Layer Only

Show/Hide Adjustment Layer

View Previous State

Delete Adjustment Layer

Reset Settings to Adjustment Defaults

Animation Panel

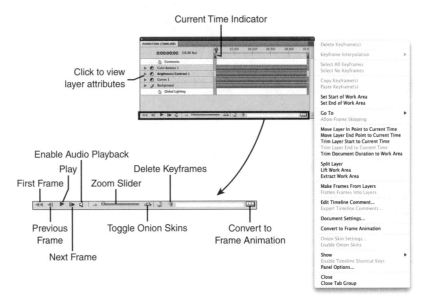

Current Time Indicator

Click to view
layer attributes

Enable Audio Playback
Play
First Frame
Zoom Slider
Delete Keyframes

Previous
Frame
Next Frame
Toggle Onion Skins
Convert to
Frame Animation

Brushes Panel

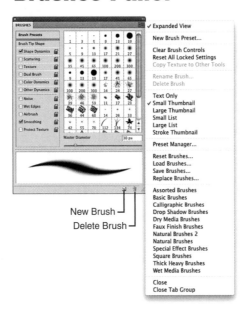

New Brush
Delete Brush

Channels Panel

Channel Keyboard Shortcut

Hide/Show Channel

Load Channel as Selection

Save Selection as Channel

New Channel

Delete Channel

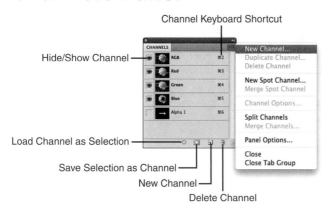

Character Panel

Leading

Style   Horizontal Scale

Font

Point Size

Kerning

Vertical Scale

Baseline Shift

Effects

Language

Tracking

Type Color

Anti-aliasing
Style

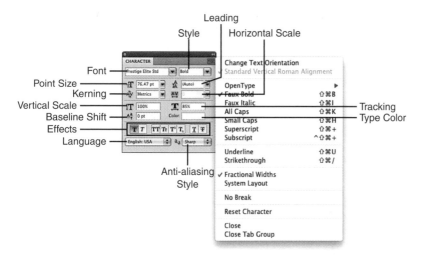

Clone Source Panel

Active Clone Source

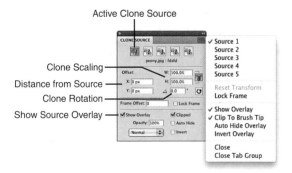

Clone Scaling

Distance from Source

Clone Rotation

Show Source Overlay

Color Panel

Numerical Entry Fields

Color Sliders

Foreground Color

Background Color

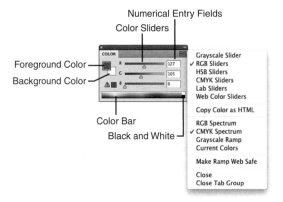

Color Bar

Black and White

Histogram Panel

Color Channel Graphs

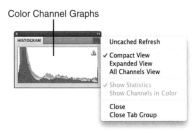

History Panel

History Brush Source

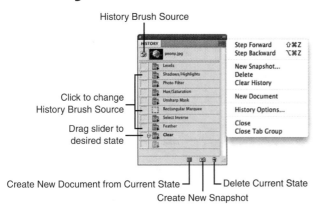

Click to change
History Brush Source

Drag slider to
desired state

Create New Document from Current State

Create New Snapshot

Delete Current State

Info Panel

Second Color Readout

First Color Readout

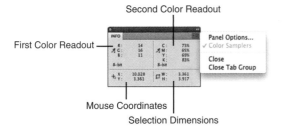

Mouse Coordinates

Selection Dimensions

Layer Comps Panel

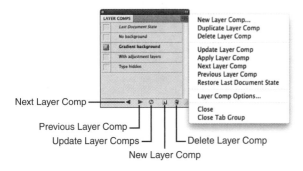

Next Layer Comp

Previous Layer Comp

Update Layer Comps

New Layer Comp

Delete Layer Comp

Layers Panel

Click to Show/Hide Layer

Shape Layer

Type Layer

Adjustment Layer

Layer Group

Active Layer

Link Selected Layers

Add Layer Style

Add Layer Mask

New Adjustment Layer

New Layer Group

New Layer

Delete Layer

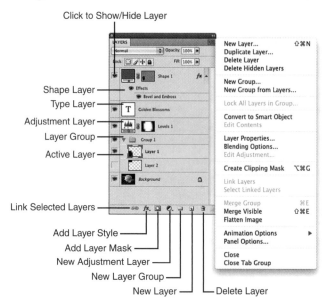

New Layer...   ⇧⌘N
Duplicate Layer...
Delete Layer
Delete Hidden Layers

New Group...
New Group from Layers...

Lock All Layers in Group...

Convert to Smart Object
Edit Contents

Layer Properties...
Blending Options...
Edit Adjustment...

Create Clipping Mask   ⌥⌘G

Link Layers
Select Linked Layers

Merge Group   ⌘E
Merge Visible   ⇧⌘E
Flatten Image

Animation Options   ▶
Panel Options...

Close
Close Tab Group

Masks Panel

Vector Mask

Pixel Mask

Mask Opacity

Mask Edge Feathering

Load Selection from Mask

Apply Mask

Show/Hide Mask Effects

Delete Mask

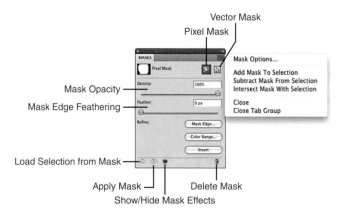

Mask Options...

Add Mask To Selection
Subtract Mask From Selection
Intersect Mask With Selection

Close
Close Tab Group

Measurement Log Panel

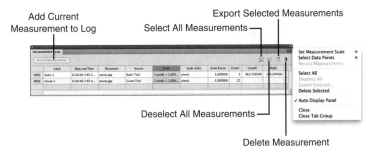

Add Current Measurement to Log

Export Selected Measurements

Select All Measurements

Deselect All Measurements

Delete Measurement

Navigator Panel

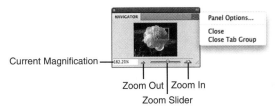

Current Magnification

Zoom Out | Zoom In

Zoom Slider

Notes Panel

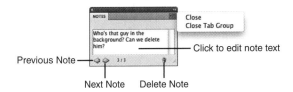

Click to edit note text

Previous Note

Next Note   Delete Note

Paragraph Panel

Alignment Options   Right Indent

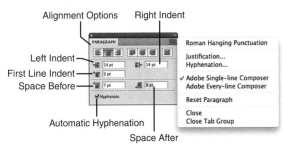

Left Indent

First Line Indent

Space Before

Automatic Hyphenation

Space After

Paths Panel

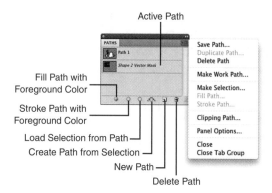

Active Path

Fill Path with
Foreground Color

Stroke Path with
Foreground Color

Load Selection from Path

Create Path from Selection

New Path

Delete Path

Styles Panel

Click to Remove Layer Style

Click to Apply Layer Style

Swatches Panel

Click to Set
Foreground Color

Tool Presets Panel

Show Only Presets
for Current Tool

Delete Tool Preset

New Tool Preset

A Quick Walk on the Extended Side

Photoshop CS4 is a big program—really, really big. It can do a lot of cool things. In fact, it has so many neat tricks that Adobe decided that the best way to wrangle all those features was to release two different versions: Photoshop CS4 Standard and Photoshop CS4 Extended. The Standard program is Photoshop as we know and love it, and that's what we've talked about for the last 24 hours. But there's more to love, and that's what Photoshop Extended is all about. Here's a look at what you'll get if you decide to shell out the extra bucks and go Extended.

Working in 3D and Video

Among its hot new features, Photoshop Extended includes tools targeted at 3D designers and videographers.

In the 3D realm, Photoshop Extended lets you open 3D model files; move, rotate, and scale them; edit their textures; and even paint directly onto them. Three-dimensional objects live on special layers called 3D layers, and you can combine these with regular image layers to give your 3D objects backgrounds. You can even create new 3D layers in Photoshop CS4 Extended, starting from an existing layer, and you can now work with individual objects on a 3D layer.

For video hotshots, the Extended version's Animation panel has a special Timeline mode that offers a visual representation of the time each frame takes up within the video sequence. And once you've created an animation, you can export it directly to AVI, MPEG-4, or Flash Video (FLV) format by choosing File, Export, Render Video. You can also import and export image sequences in Photoshop, BMP, Cineon, JPEG, JPEG 2000, OpenEXR, PNG, Targa, and TIFF formats. And Extended has special video layers and clone options for video frames.

Taking Measurements, Counting Objects, and Analyzing Data

Photoshop's Ruler tool—now renamed the Measure tool—has been around for quite a while, and it enables you to measure distances within an image. But knowing that your cat's eyes are 47 pixels wide in a particular image isn't all that useful in the real world. So Photoshop Extended enables you to attach a real-world scale to measurements within an image. You can use the Set Scale command to tell Photoshop the real-world equivalent of a distance within an image, and Photoshop can then turn around and translate all your measurements within that image into real-world terms.

Extended also features a Count tool: Just click on each object to add to your running tally. Even more useful, Photoshop can store counts and measurements and export that data so that you can use it in spreadsheets. Who would use this feature? Medical researchers might count bacteria on a microscope image, and livestock managers might count cows on a satellite image. The possibilities are … interesting.

Exploring New Frontiers

Speaking of medical researchers, Photoshop Extended supports the DICOM medical imaging format. These are the images you get from a CAT scan, MRI, ultrasound, or x-ray, and often a DICOM file contains multiple images. Photoshop enables you to choose how to view multi-image files: with each image on a separate layer or lined up in a grid format. You can use all Photoshop's tools to enhance and mark up DICOM images.

Many scientists use a program called MATLAB for complicated mathematical computations, many of which involve graphical representations of complex concepts. Photoshop Extended can now make these people's jobs easier by working with MATLAB. Using add-ons that come with Photoshop Extended, MATLAB users can control Photoshop from MATLAB's command-line interface, and they can combine MATLAB's graphics tools with Photoshop's image-processing expertise for a truly powerful package.

INDEX

FREE Online Edition

Your purchase of **Sams Teach Yourself Adobe® Photoshop® CS4 in 24 Hours** includes access to a free online edition for 45 days through the Safari Books Online subscription service. Nearly every Sams book is available online through Safari Books Online, along with more than 5,000 other technical books and videos from publishers such as Addison-Wesley Professional, Cisco Press, Exam Cram, IBM Press, O'Reilly, Prentice Hall, and Que.

SAFARI BOOKS ONLINE allows you to search for a specific answer, cut and paste code, download chapters, and stay current with emerging technologies.

Activate your FREE Online Edition at
www.informit.com/safarifree

> **STEP 1:** Enter the coupon code: JJFWGCB.

> **STEP 2:** New Safari users, complete the brief registration form.
> Safari subscribers, just log in.

If you have difficulty registering on Safari or accessing the online edition, please e-mail customer-service@safaribooksonline.com